CW00401583

Stop the World

'Stop the World, Scotland wants to get on'
– Winnie Ewing's first words to the
crowd outside the count after her
victory in the Hamilton by-election,
2 November 1967

Stop the World

The Autobiography of Winnie Ewing

Winnie Ewing

EDITED BY
Michael Russell

Birlinn

First published in 2004 by
Birlinn Limited
West Newington House
10 Newington Road
Edinburgh EH9 1QS

www.birlinn.co.uk

ISBN 1 84158 239 5

British Library Cataloguing-in-Publication Data
A catalogue record for this book is available from the British Library

Typeset by Hewer Text Ltd, Edinburgh
Printed and bound by MPG Books Limited, Bodmin

*To all pipers everywhere
and for Stewart, who was always there*

Contents

List of Illustrations

Introduction and Acknowledgements

In late 1974, in the midst of British panic about the rise of the SNP, the man I defeated to win the seat of Moray and Nairn – once Secretary of State for Scotland but quickly enobled after I had turfed him out, becoming instantly Lord Campbell of Croy as a sort of reward for failure – wrote a newspaper article under the heading 'Britain must not be Balkanised'. It was full of jibes about a Scottish air force and complacency about the status quo. It stressed the dangers and the risks of independence – even in devolution. But still the fact remained that the SNP was riding high, as he well knew. He simply could not understand it. 'Why is the SNP getting this support?', he agonised at one point and then provided his self-justifying answer in the following sentence, claiming that it was all 'emotional appeal aided by misguided patriotism'.

Well, I have devoted much of my life to the SNP and to the cause of Scottish freedom, and whilst I acknowledge the emotional appeal of my country – who does not? – and whilst I admit to patriotism, there is a lot more to me and to the SNP than that. Our national freedom is about freedom for each one of us – the freedom to fulfil our potential. That is why the idea is so inspiring to so many and why it is vital that it comes to inspire even those who presently reject it.

Scotland is the oldest nation in Europe, rich and full of capable people. Yet we have no say in the world any more – in fact we are spoken for. We have been too long in this condition and the time to end it is now. A fundamental burning passion for freedom and dignity forms the basis of my national crusade to do that job, and that fundamental passion burns in the heart of every member of the SNP, and in many other hearts too.

I will go further. The academic Tom Nairn once wrote that 'Far from being terribly risky, irresponsible and juvenile to move towards getting out of the Union bed, it may be dangerous, even childish, to hang around in it'. A leaflet that I put out during the Hamilton by-election put the matter even more starkly: 'Only a fool likes London rule' said its big banner headline. Since I left the quiet domesticity of my life as a solicitor, wife and mother of three in Glasgow to be thrust into the headlines after winning Hamilton, I have spent every day , and it seems like every hour of every day, arguing that point and trying to persuade Scotland out of such folly, for if we persist with it, we can only grow poorer, less able to succeed, and less confident in ourselves.

It has been a roller-coaster ride. This book inevitably deals with the detail of those years, but sometimes in the detail the overall motivations and excitements can get a little lost. That is particularly true of an autobiography, which is by definition a personal tale and which should include much about the personal experiences of the writer. Indeed for me there is so much to remember and so many people to thank that at times this has seemed more like a frightening feat of memory rather than an exercise in looking forward as well as back. Yet this book is about the future.

In recalling my Hamilton days I may dwell on the minutiae of campaigning, and then on the terrors of Westminster, but I can still feel the thrill of fighting that election and winning it against all the odds, and I want others to feel such thrills too: the thrills that come not only with success but also with battles fought on the basis of principle rather than personal gain.

Not a week went by during my twenty-five years in Europe when I did not feel privileged and enthused by the task of standing up for Scotland, particularly for the Highlands and Islands. And in the Scottish Parliament I was, despite difficulties, always keenly and vitally aware that I was taking part in something that even thirty years before did not seem possible. Everyone has their own specific responses, but the general emotion will be the same for anyone who is determined to make his or her country a better place and to give its people back their self respect and dignity. Having experienced such emotions, I want others to experience them too.

I am telling my story in order to encourage others to keep on with the job of setting Scotland free. There is, after all, so much still to do. Before the

Scotland Act which resulted in our present Parliament there were no less than twenty-four attempts to return some measure of home rule to Scotland. Who now has heard of the 1895 Federated Home Rule Motion, introduced by Sir Henry Dalziel and seconded by Lloyd George? It was passed at Westminster by 126 votes, with only 15 Scottish members voting against, yet it was never implemented or allowed to move forward. Neither was the 1913 Bill, sponsored by Sir W.H. Cowan, nor the 1922 Government of Scotland and Wales Bill, promoted by J.A. Murray MacDonald, nor Russell Johnston's 1967 attempt.

Nonetheless those who believed in Scotland and knew how important change was for each individual Scot kept trying. The terrible events of the late 1970s, when Scotland was betrayed by so many of her elected representatives – some of whom are still active in politics – and cheated out of a Parliament, might have been the end of the matter if there had not been those with courage and determination who would not give up. Some of them were in the SNP and they suffered long difficult years in the wilderness. Others, in civic Scotland, would not be silenced and together they forced the issue back onto the political agenda, despite Margaret Thatcher's hostility to our country and its aspirations and John Major's pathetic lack of imagination. They demanded that Labour honour its promises when a Labour leader – Neil Kinnock – was overwhelmingly hostile to the fate even of his native Wales and they made certain that Tony Blair could not follow his backsliding instincts.

We got a Parliament and made a step in the right direction. But today many remain disappointed. They know Scotland is capable of more, and that disappointment will grow. We have – I say it again – been too long in this condition and only independence will take us out of it.

My Scottish and European political colleague and friend Allan Macartney, in his rectorial address to Aberdeen University in February 1997, quoted from Lord Byron, one of Aberdeen's most famous sons. The words he used are these:

> England, thy beauties are tame and domestic
> To one who has roved o'er the mountains afar:
> Oh! for the crags that are wild and majestic
> The steep frowning glories of dark Lochnagar.

That yearning for Scotland and its beauties was used by Allan to illustrate the need for a similar yearning in Scottish hearts to achieve much more on the world stage. In his address Allan spoke of his vision of 'a new golden age', with Scotland again playing her part in European affairs.

That is no pipe-dream or, to quote Lord Campbell of Croy once more, 'an emotional appeal aided by misguided patriotism'. It is the same spirit that motivated me in every electoral contest, in every fight on behalf of Scottish fishermen or farmers, and in every visit I made throughout the world. It is the spirit that maintained me when I lost Hamilton in 1970, and Moray and Nairn in 1979. It is the spirit that drove me when I sat in the Presiding Officer's chair to formally open the first session of the first Scottish Parliament in three hundred years. And it is the spirit that drives me still as, looking back at my own life, I write this memoir.

We are not outside the world – we are part of it. For three days after the appalling tragedy of September 11 2001 I spent hours trying to phone an American friend who lived near the World Trade Centre. When I finally got through to him he was safe, but many he knew had been killed. Lots of Scottish families had the same experience. Is it not, therefore, obscene that when the Scottish Parliament comes to talk of our response to world terrorism and the way in which we can help to overcome that evil, our present government thinks it desirable to do nothing and instead to allow only Westminster to legislate and Westminster to lead? Such an abdication of responsibility does not just harm Scotland – it harms the world.

It is equally obscene to allow a war to take place in our name in Iraq, or bombing to take place in Kosovo, and to have to endure the involvement of brave young Scottish men and women on the front-line without being able to decide democratically in our own Parliament what our involvement in such conflicts should be. Fourteen years ago, in a European debate on the first Gulf War, I said that Mrs Thatcher's dance to the Bush tune was the dance of hypocrites. Tony Blair's relentless playing of second fiddle to another Bush is equally discordant.

Time after time, on matters great and small, we are still standing on the sidelines, mutely accepting what is decided elsewhere instead of raising our voices and making our own choices. Scotland's much vaunted partnership in the Union is in reality the partnership of Jonah and the whale.

My vision of our partnerships at home and abroad is very different. Since the SNP was founded, we as a party have argued for something different. We see an internationally minded Scotland, sitting where all the other free peoples of the world sit, sharing directly in our responsibility for this fragile planet and those who live on it and participating as of right in the European Union, the United Nations and the Commonwealth. We would give 1 per cent, at least, of our resources to help less developed countries. We would decide which treaties should bind us and which obligations we would willingly enter into. We would not be dealing in the instruments of death, peddling them to whichever dictators suit our purpose. We would be peacemakers, not aggressors. We would welcome those who wish to come here, or who are forced to do so because of persecution in their own lands. We would uphold not just the rule of law, but justice as well.

We would have compassion for those of our own citizens who were less favoured by fate, and less able, and we would create on such foundations a just society, ambitious and enterprising yet also gentle and forgiving. None of our old people would be dying of hypothermia in the most fuel-rich nation in Europe, and none of our young people would be leaving school without hope and without the basics of education. We would see the right to work as being as basic as all other rights and we would nurture our precious cultures – all of them.

That is not just a beautiful dream. It is a possibility, and one whose time must be coming. It needs Scotland to stop wanting London rule, and instead be as free to choose its own destiny as everyone else. Scots need to be made aware that such a desire is perfectly natural. It is the way in which individuals as well as countries make progress. In September 1988, at the height of unrest in the various parts of the former Soviet Union, the Tories in the European Parliament lodged a motion favouring the rights of the Baltic states. The Socialist group, including Scottish Labour members, insisted that it was watered down so that there was no mention of self determination. The Tories of course agreed.

Fifteen years later the Baltic states – independent for well over a decade – are about to become full and free members of the European Union. Those who sought to turn back the human desire for freedom have failed once again.

Many difficulties lie ahead for those countries, as for all others. But at least they are now not only free to dream, but also free to take the responsibility of turning dreams into reality. That is what I want for Scotland and ultimately that is what my life has been all about.

There is not, however, all the time in the world to achieve it. I have a sense of urgency, and so must Scotland. In the answer to a Parliamentary question at Westminster, which I was asked when elected for Hamilton, I was told that the net loss of population from Scotland in the seventeen years from 1951 to 1968 had been 554,000. The total number was even higher. Those figures have increased since then. Yet what is surprising is not the facts – they are inevitable given the present state of Scotland. The surprising thing is that so little is said about them, and even less done. A falling population of this sort can only lead to further national decline. Add to that continued incursions on Scottish institutions, such as the proposal to establish a UK Supreme Court and the theft of Scottish fishing grounds by the Labour Government in 1999 and Scotland runs the risk of having her ability to move forward deliberately undermined forever.

So this book is also a wake-up call. In describing what I have done and not done in my life I hope I shall motivate others to do even more. Above all, those who care for Scotland should be fully aware that despite the setbacks we can make progress and we can achieve our dreams. At the age of seventy-five I am still hungry for new experiences and new opportunities. Being alive demands nothing less.

But I am also grateful to those who have helped me do so much. As far as my long-held ambition to write this book is concerned I am particularly grateful, first of all, to my editor Michael Russell, established author, political colleague and friend, without whose stern imposition of deadlines there would only have been blank pages and good intentions. He ensured that there was an avoidance of repetition, pointed out omissions and gaps to be filled, re-organised as necessary and smoothed the path between myself and my publisher. I also owe that publisher thanks, for Hugh Andrew of Birlinn was enthusiastic about the project from the beginning and tolerated the many delays in getting started. I am also grateful to Clare Netherton, originally from the Isle of Man, who typed the first drafts and who learned to read my handwriting – never an easy task!

Thanks are also due to my Lossiemouth secretary, Marion Hoare, and my Scottish Parliamentary researcher, James MacInnes; to Neil Fergusson, my former European assistant and now a European Parliament official on whose memory and records I have relied for large parts of this book, and to Sam Barber and Jim Eadie, who were dedicated assistants during my time in Europe. I must also thank my European colleagues over more than twenty-five years – those from Ireland, France, Denmark, Greece, Germany, Italy, Portugal, Flanders, Vriesland, Catalonia, the Basque lands, Brittany, Andalucia, Valencia, Galicia, the Canary Islands, Sardinia and Corsica, as well as from the many other places which go to make up the rich tapestry of our continent. The staff of the European parliament and the superb and supportive interpreters also need to be acknowledged with gratitude as do the many helpful staff and friends in the other two Parliaments to which I have been elected.

I am, of course, hugely grateful to my caring family, and on this occasion particularly for our shared reminiscences and for their sensible advice and help at various stages of writing. My sister Jean was invaluable not just for what she recalled but also for her wise counsel, as was my niece Deirdre and all my dear personal friends over many years whose powers of recall were much needed from time to time.

The attention of huge numbers of journalists and others in the media kept me in a state of perpetual alertness over many years, so their contribution needs to be recorded with thanks, but my real heartfelt gratitude must also go to my other family – the members and supporters of the Scottish National Party, without whom much of this would never have happened.

What happens next to Scotland is up them as well as to all those who share a dream of a country worthy of the name. But it is also up to everyone who calls this little place their home.

Winnie Ewing
Miltonduff
January 2004

I

The Tartan Express

I THINK THAT THE loneliest moment of my life was that moment in November 1967 on the Glasgow-bound platform of Euston Station in London when I waved goodbye to the train (called by the media the 'Tartan Express') which was full of all those enthusiastic SNP supporters who had come to see me to the door of the House of Commons and who had come playing music all the way.

After the Hamilton by-election victory earlier that month, the ruthless efficiency of the SNP's magnificent national secretary Rosemary Hall (a direct descendant of Robert the Bruce) had at once put in motion the hire from British Rail of a long train. Bookings were taken for what would be an overnight journey on the night of 16 November 1967 (returning the following night) to see the honourable member for Hamilton safely sworn in at Westminster, two weeks after the by-election itself. The travellers included fiddlers, pipers, accordionists, tin-whistlers and, of course, singers. The only people with sleeping berths were the Ewing family, and we were all there – myself, my husband Stewart, and my children Fergus, Annabelle and Terry, aged at that time, ten, seven and three. I think the children got a good night's sleep but there wasn't much sleep for the rest of us.

The journey was longer than the usual British Rail route. We started from Glasgow Central Station and the Ewing family were escorted there by two Hillman Imps, provided free by the company that manufactured them at Linwood. We were accompanied by my redoubtable Gaelic-speaking nanny Betty Nicholson of Cambustianovaig, Isle of Skye. The take-up of tickets had been so immediate and strong – indeed it was vastly oversubscribed – that my own brother John and his wife Jessie couldn't get on and had to make their own way to London, as did many others: the rest of the trains were also crowded that night.

Central Station was absolutely packed as far as the eye could see. I recognised many faces in the crowd, including Sheriff Lionel Daiches, QC, who often had expressed sympathy with the aspirations of Scotland. I usually joked with him that when I was in power I would appoint him Scottish ambassador to Israel, a job which he would have coveted.

My family and I were much photographed. I was wearing a new black-and-white check coat with long black gloves, had a new hairstyle and was feeling quite elegant. After the children were settled I traversed the train and met the musicians and all the others, including my close friends and supporters, amongst whom was a key advisor during the by-election, Hugh Macdonald, commercial editor of the Outram group of news-papers. When he told his board he was coming to London on the trip he had been instructed to keep a low profile and in no circumstances to have his photograph taken.

The send-off, I was later told, resembled that given to the Red Clydesiders when they went to the House of Commons after the 1922 election. My father had actually been there and had described it to me many times. During that event Jimmy Maxton had climbed onto a luggage wagon and had said, 'Before six months are over we will return with a Scottish Parliament.' Of course, it took a bit longer – in fact seventy-seven years.

The train left, with cheerful scenes of people whose hopes had been newly aroused by what had happened at Hamilton just a couple of weeks before. We stopped at Hamilton itself, where a considerable crowd of supporters were waiting, including the Deans, the Pattersons, the Hills, the McAteers, the Bains and one Oscar Schwiegelhofer, a refugee from Transylvania who had, with all the others, been part of an incredible election team which had put Hamilton on the map.

With another lively (but this time slightly tearful) farewell, the train set off, but not south as yet. We went east because we had to call at Edinburgh where a similar large crowd had gathered. I remember shaking hands with the long time SNP activist Dr Kerr Yuill (afterwards one of my European elections agents) and his wife. The SNP staff (a very small number in those early days) boarded the train and they were ecstatic. Then we started to go towards London, but the halts were not quite over, as Arthur Donaldson, the SNP Chairman, had requested a stop in Newcastle, where a small group of Scots, including Arthur's daughter, were there to cheer us and wave us God-speed.

Amid the mixed emotions of pride and victory and the feeling of gratitude to all who achieved the remarkable result at Hamilton, I myself knew that I was taking part in a moment of history. Yet my strongest emotion was that of fear. How would I stand up to the strains of a political life in the House of Commons? How would my children be affected by the inevitable separation? Would my friends and family stand by me in the hard moments, which were bound to come? Would I – could I – live up to the huge and widespread Scottish aspirations that Hamilton had brought to the surface in Scotland?

I was of course not the first SNP Member of Parliament, though this inaccuracy was reproduced many times by reporters. My sole predecessor was the MP for Motherwell who had taken his seat in 1945, but only for a few months. That young trailblazer was the great and noble Dr Robert McIntyre, my ever-willing mentor and advisor over many years. Sadly, he died shortly before the Scottish Parliament was re-established in 1999. He was, in a very real sense, the father of the party and was held in great esteem in political life, including during his term as Provost of Stirling, as well as in the medical profession. In that profession he was a consultant physician and a pioneer in eliminating the scourge of TB in Scotland.

Eventually the train arrived at Euston and there, too, were vast crowds, complete with several pipers. I was lifted shoulder-high by Angus McGillveray and Hugh McDonald (the man who been told to keep a low profile). The photo of me on the shoulders of Angus and Hugh went right round the world.

We went first to the Rembrandt Hotel, to get ourselves organised. Then it was on to the House of Commons to meet my sponsors, Gwynfor Evans, MP for Carmarthen, and Alistair Mackenzie, MP for Ross and Cromarty. We met in a splendid tearoom. Of course I had met Gwynfor before, at the Plaid Cymru conference in July 1967. I had also shared a platform with him in Aberdeen later in the year, when he had generously given up three days of his time to hold public meetings in Glasgow, Aberdeen and Edinburgh. There was a very sad downside to that Plaid conference, though. At the event I had given a big bowl of white heather to Gwynfor, saying, 'Before the blooms on this heather fade, I'll be sitting beside you in Westminster to speak up for Scotland as you do for Wales.' The presentation was photographed by, of all papers, the *Sunday Post*. At the same time, unknown to me, my father had felt very ill and had signed himself into the Victoria Infirmary where he was diagnosed with pneumonia. By the time I got back to Scotland he was dead. The ward sister in the hospital told me she had shown the photo of me with Gwynfor in the *Sunday Post* to my father in what was probably his last conscious moment. I was always very sad that he never lived to see me take my seat in the House of Commons.

I had never met Alistair Mackenzie before that day. He was a kind man, a complete Gael who spoke English as a second language and a crofter with a gentle disposition who was loved by all who knew him. He was known in the House of Commons as 'Second Week' because he only came to Parliament every second week, using the intervening one to look after his sheep! 'See you second week,' he would always say to me as he left to go home. He too lost his seat in 1970, to the Tories.

After coffee and a somewhat stilted conversation on my part, we were escorted by the Clerk of the House to the Chamber of the Commons and shown where we would stand. Gwynfor Evans was to be on my right and Alistair Mackenzie on my left. We would march forward three steps and bow and then march forward another three steps and bow again. Then I would go to take the oath. This would all be preceded by the Speaker calling out, 'Members wishing to take their seats please approach the bar of the House.' I remember at the time thinking that this all seemed a rather dramatic way of conducting democracy, almost theatrical, but as it was the procedure, I just had to obey it.

Before going into the House to be formally sworn in I collected Stewart, Betty Nicholson and the children. They were escorted to the Speaker's Gallery, which has the best seats in the house, while I was accompanied to the bar of the House with Gwynfor on my right and Alistair on my left, just as had been arranged. The Chamber was packed and all the galleries full. By this stage I was very nervous and keen to get the oath-taking over with. Unfortunately – for me as well as the country – the pound had just been devalued, so instead of the speaker calling out his question, there was a statement followed by what seemed an age of debate. I think we had to stand there for an hour and a half and I was very conscious, as time went on, of the increasing pain from my rather tight new shoes.

From time to time I looked up and smiled at my family, but about half way through I was disconcerted to see that Terry was missing. I later learned he had been restless and a policeman, noticing the problem, had taken him away, in a very kindly fashion, and played football with him in the great Hall of Westminster, where William Wallace had been tried for treason.

Some time later I glanced up at the House of Lords Gallery behind and above me and there was a gentleman waving furiously at me. It was Lord Boyd Orr, ex-Rector of Glasgow University, who was very enthusiastically showing his support for me. He had been an Honorary Vice-President of the Scottish National Party, along with R.B. Cunninghame Graham.

Then, finally, the Speaker called out his question. I moved forward and took the oath. Then I stepped up to shake the Speaker's hand – it was Horace King at that time – and there was a huge noise in the Chamber behind me, which I took to be friendly, although I am not so sure now. Horace King was very kindly, gave me warm words of welcome and said he would make sure I was fairly treated. Someone heckled, 'Give her a kiss', which caused great amusement, though he didn't do it And that was it.

The crowd outside the entrance to the House of Commons was enormous. The Tartan Express people were joined by other Scots, either there for the day or resident in London, and many other simply curious spectators, plus at least two hundred Welshmen. When I was at the Plaid Cymru Conference in Dolgellau in 1967 I had been told by its National Secretary: 'If you win there will be hundreds of Welshmen to see you to the door,' and he had honoured his promise.

We went back to the Rembrandt Hotel where I had two chores: to write my speech for the large evening meeting arranged in a local hall and to write an article on my first day for the *News of the World*. They had offered what at that time seemed the enormous fee of £75, a sum that I was sure that I needed now that I was facing the prospect of a considerable drop in earnings. We had no ghost-writers or spin doctors then – articles had to be written by oneself.

In the evening we made our way to the meeting-room, leaving the children with Betty. There was a pipe band, a huge audience of Scots and Welsh and I don't know who else. Before we started I decided (as usual) to go to the toilet, but I was given complicated directions and found myself lost in a myriad of corridors. I started to panic because I could hear the pipe band and I opened door after door which all seemed to lead nowhere. Eventually I opened yet another door and found I was looking down on the hall below. I was very tempted just to call out 'hullo' and leave, but I felt that wouldn't be dignified and I gradually found my way back to where I should be. I shared the platform with Gwynfor Evans again, and Gordon Wilson. I spoke last, to enormous applause, but I have very little recollection of the content of my speech. I don't think in the atmosphere it would have mattered very much what I said: everyone was too excited to bother about that.

Then, finally, we were off to Euston for tearful goodbyes galore. My last farewell was to George Leslie, who had so nearly won the Glasgow Pollock by-election in the spring of 1967. I said to him, 'George, you stay here and I'll go home.' I didn't feel better when he seemed to shudder at the very idea. As I waved the Tartan Express goodbye, those feelings of pride and dread that I had had the night before came back in waves. Would I be able to do this job? Would I be able to ensure that Scotland and my supporters were not let down?

There were so many supporters. Telegrams had come by the thousands, not just from Scotland but from the Scots diaspora all round the globe. There had been messages from places and people as far away as the Royal Navy Mess in Singapore and from Scots emigrants of long standing in America, Canada and Australia.

My memories of that day in London are still euphoric, but I now know that I had little inkling of the trials and tribulations that awaited me in the chamber of the House of Commons. When I was a solicitor at the Sheriff Court in Glasgow, it was normal to go for coffee or a drink with one's opponents after a trial, no matter the result, and there was a great feeling of camaraderie. I had imagined the Palace of Westminster would be the same, but little did I know that for me it was to become, for the most part, a torture chamber where vicious critics threw endless insults. Nonetheless there were some who were kind, to whom I shall pay tribute in this book. I have always been better at remembering kisses instead of kicks and I have no regrets about any of it.

The family stayed on with me in London before we all returned home for the weekend. On the Friday I called in again at the House of Commons to see where my regular seat would be. Gwynfor Evans was not there for, in his own words, 'I'm off to Wales where the votes are and I'm going to get them.'

I walked in as a rather curious and diffident newcomer, but it was interesting that already the police knew who I was – apparently they do a lot of homework in order to recognise the 650-plus members, and the arrival of a new member after a by-election is always easy for them. My taxi took me to the Members' Entrance, where an elderly man greeted me. He attended to the coats, he said, and was there to take me to see my name tag. To my amazement I already had a beautiful brass name-plate, which read 'Mrs Winifred M. Ewing MA LLB MP Hamilton'. I expressed my astonishment and the old usher replied that all new lady members like to see their name tag first. He then told me a story which made me realise how privileged I was to be here and how exciting it all was. The first ever elected woman to the House of Commons was Countess Markievicz, although she never took her seat, as she was an abstentionist Irish Nationalist. She did however, arrive at the House of Commons one glorious summer day, accompanied by the famous Maud Gonne. She had come only to see her name-plate, and she left straight after, without ever going near her seat in the Chamber.

We went home for the weekend but I returned on Monday as I was very anxious to get my maiden speech over with. On that day there was a debate about young people and their legal entitlements. I made a speech urging that they should vote at eighteen instead of twenty-one and gave all my arguments in favour of this. Even now at well over seventy I believe this was the entirely right topic for my maiden speech. Votes at eighteen have come and now, of course, I and my party support votes at sixteen. That too will come in time.

Back in London there was time to reflect on how I had managed to be elected, against all the odds. Sometimes I asked myself, less positively, how could I account for the fix I was now in? Hamilton was a victory that had dealt a strong blow to the soft underbelly of Labour's supposedly invincible heartland. I remember the Nationalist thinker and wit, Oliver Brown, saying that the Hamilton by-election had sent 'a shiver run along the Scottish Labour backbenches looking for a spine to run up'. The result of the by-election was a tremendous shock to Labour and to the Scottish political establishment, and it brought into being an SNP which would become the major opposition to Labour in Scotland in the closing decades of the twentieth century and into the twenty-first. It also confirmed that the central question of modern Scottish politics would become that of independence, because my victory at Hamilton woke up Scotland and the Scots – worldwide – and made them start to think about their future.

Although the SNP had been doing well in the months up to Hamilton (coming close for example in Glasgow Pollok, which was won by the Tories), an SNP victory was unexpected by the media and politicians alike.

Few remember, however, that this strange and very significant by-election lasted for a full eighteen months, not the few weeks of modern campaigns. It was in June 1966 that we first expected it. At that time, the sitting MP, Tom Fraser (the man responsible for introducing the breath-alyzer, though Barbara Castle took the credit), was appointed the new Chair of the South of Scotland Electricty Board. There was a huge public outcry at this piece of gerrymandering and political nepotism, as he had no knowledge of the power industry and had no substantial record of experience at such a management level. In the end he didn't take up the position and remained meanwhile as MP for Hamilton.

I had been selected in July 1966 after a vetting procedure that was far removed from the present-day rigorous processes. The first time it was considered was, I believe, when Robert McIntyre simply mentioned my name as a possibility. I had spoken for him – in my first political speech – in a by-election campaign in Denny, part of the old Stirling Burghs seat. Then, on a June summer evening in 1966, some young activists came to my door at 52 Queen's Drive, Glasgow and asked if I would go on the short leet for the by-election. I gave these visiting activists from Hamilton a generous dram and said that as I had three young children, I couldn't possibly go to London. That I thought would be the end of it. However, as they were leaving my husband Stewart arrived home. I couldn't resist the slight smug boast that these three young men had asked me to go on the short leet for the Hamilton by-election. Stewart asked in his neutral type of way: 'What answer did you give?' and I replied, 'Of course I said no, I can't go to London and leave my young children.' Stewart said he was not so sure. The young men came back into the house and had another dram and eventually I said yes. Later I remonstrated with Stewart. What on earth would we do if I won? He was more sanguine, pointing out that there were three men on the short list as well, and that therefore I would not be chosen.

That, paradoxically, did it. I was so exasperated by such an expectation that I decided to make my bid in all seriousness. Eventually the candidates – now reduced to two men and myself, though the men had both been candidates before – were invited to make speeches in Hamilton, but then nothing happened for nearly two months. Stewart, the children and I went off on holiday to Minorca with our dear friends Doris and Bobby Littlejohn, both lawyers, and I was much teased – 'Here's to the candidate no-one wanted!', 'Here's to the political career that never got started!' And so on. On returning home at the end of July the mail was overflowing. Stewart, as usual, went straight to the TV to turn on the news while I opened letters. Among them was a letter from the Hamilton constituency: 'We have to inform you that you have been selected as the candidate for the Hamilton by-election.' I let out a cry and at that precise moment Stewart called me to the television, and there was Gwynfor Evans taking his seat as the victor of the Carmarthen by-election on behalf of Plaid Cymru.

The SNP has always loved by-elections, as this was our only chance to get press publicity and to bring the political debate home to Scotland. I was asked to speak in many parts of Scotland for the party, but it became embarrassing to be a by-election candidate with no by-election, as Tom Fraser seemed to have settled down again in his seat.

Gwynfor Evans had won a sensational nationalist by-election victory in 1966 which had caused great interest in Scotland. As part of the start of our campaign for Hamilton he very generously gave us three days in the late summer of 1966, visiting and speaking. I was his fellow speaker in Aberdeen, and of course I went to hear him the night before when he addressed a huge audience in the MacLennan Galleries, Glasgow, as I wanted to get the measure of the man. I remember how he cracked a joke against the Scots. He said, 'It's not that the Welsh are better than anyone else; they're not better, they are just different.' He added, 'Of course it's different with you Scots, you know you're better than everyone else.'

There was a slight hushed pause and then a huge applause. A friend of Scotland like Gwynfor would dare to make a joke against us. I was a great lover of Gwynfor's speeches and his wit. He had the true gift of oratory, combining passion and intellect with humour and style.

As a by-election candidate I continued to travel. I went to speak in Tranent and I went to speak in Stornoway. I was a by-election candidate sitting at the top platform at the conferences of the party and being asked to lots of branches. But I remained a by-election candidate without a by-election. It was all quite embarrassing. Then, in July 1967, when we were on holiday in Jersey, Stewart read in the *Daily Express* that Tom Fraser was to be appointed head of the North of Scotland Hydro Electric Board, and that therefore there would, after all, be a by-election. I rushed to phone party headquarters – 'What shall I do?' They replied, 'Enjoy your holiday, come home and have lots of glossy photographs taken.'

The eighteen-month campaign was supported by thousands of Scots. Every door was knocked at least twice. Helping my agent John McAteer to fight the campaign were Arthur Donaldson, Gordon Wilson, Robert McIntyre, Gordon Murray, Provost Braid of St Monans in Fife and Dr James Lees, as well as many others locally and nationally. In Hamilton Hugh MacDonald was joined by Alex Ewing (not a relation but the art editor of the Outram Group) and the *Express* photographer Jim Hutchinson. Jimmy Logan's father, who was a well-known theatrical producer, also supported me. These were heady days of canvassing, converting and consolidating. But the seat had been fought before, by David Rollo, and so the soil was well tilled. We had tapes to which Sean Connery lent his voice, as he did to our SNP magazine *The Hamilton Herald*. He is no 'Johnny come lately', but nailed his colours to the SNP mast in 1967 and has done so with huge effect ever since.

Many people have asked me over the years if I thought during the Hamilton campaign that I was going to win. I felt I was going to win from the beginning, but it was the motorcade on the Saturday prior to polling day that finally convinced me that it was not a fantasy: that motorcade took an hour to pass by.

For the final eve of poll meeting – still very important in those days – on impulse I had invited Ludovic Kennedy to speak. His presence assisted in ensuring a packed town hall and gave dignity and significance to the event. Subsequently he spoke at a number of other SNP events, including

Burns Suppers, and after Hamilton he wrote some articles about the by-elections, and about his conversion to Scottish nationalism.

The day of poll seemed unreal. Arthur Donaldson and his lovely wife Vi accompanied me by car the whole day. At one stage he said to me 'I have been to many defeats. It is time I saw a victory!' He did. It rained torrentially all day. Perhaps this helped, as disillusioned and disgruntled Labour voters may have stayed at home. The kindly sheriff at the count was a close friend of my brother-in-law, James Forsyth, QC, and he helped to put me at least a little at ease. The atmosphere inside the count was electric but outside it was even more exciting. From the hall I could see vast crowds, all under umbrellas and all, it seemed, waving saltires. When I went out to greet the crowd they were ecstatic and I felt the strongest feeling of euphoria I have ever felt. I was so imbued with confidence that I could have answered questions on any subject and spoken about any matter. Regrettably that was a passing sensation.

Some words that I used that evening to the crowd have stayed with me ever since and have become a sort of motto for our national movement. They are quoted everywhere. During the campaign I had had my picture taken – a famous photo now – sitting on top of the model of the world which is in the David Livingstone Memorial Park in Blantyre. The curator actually got into trouble and almost lost his job because he was a supporter and had allowed me to be photographed there. I must have been thinking about that picture and the globe when I spoke to the crowds outside the hall. Quite unprepared, the words came to me to sum up what we needed to do. 'Stop the world!' I said, 'Scotland wants to get on.' She still does.

Hamilton was a victory for many reasons. I can honestly say, looking back at the campaign, the first of many in my life, that it was ahead of any other in the party's history. Of course we benefited greatly from an influx of hundreds of keen canvassers and helpers, and many of the techniques that we used there for the first time were ones that worked and can still be very powerful, if only the party would use them. Our tapes played in cars stationed all over the constituency, we had a slide-show setting out Scotland's case for independence on a lorry during the campaign, and we had 'room characters' to cheer up the troops and to meet canvassers on their return from knocking doors. We had not only the local stalwarts but also national figures lending advice. We had no shortage of talented speakers from within and outwith the party. Public meetings were well attended in those days and we had meetings everywhere in the constituency. Most of all we had companionship, friendship and a strong common cause. That was shown in the fact that as I fought the seat I had many homes from homes, the main one being that of John and Kate McAteer; but I also had homes in Blantyre, Larkhall, Netherburn and Dalserf. I often look back on those times when I stayed with activists who were also such good friends and gave me some of my most precious memories. The constituency was alive with such people and they had laid the groundwork for success. The Hamilton branch itself was twenty-one years old when I became the candidate in 1966. We also had branches in Blantyre, Larkhall, Netherburn and Dalserf, and Margo MacDonald added to them when she founded a branch in High Blantyre. All the villages contained supporters and they spread the word tirelessly. In Larkhall, for example, one of the main activists in the past had been an old bachelor bank manager called Leishman. So much work had he done, and to such an effect, that when I knocked on almost any door in Larkhall, someone was bound to say, 'Aye, I think Mr Leishman was right all along.'

Larkhall had a most interesting radical history, being very active in the early days of Trade Unionism and the fight for workers' rights. In its history are famous names like Bob Smillie, but just as people like him were about to win concessions from the mine owners and factory owners in flooded waves of Irish immigrants, often starving and willing to work just to eat. Early strikes caused much bitterness, not merely about the manifest injustice of working and living conditions, but also against the Irish, who undercut the striker's efforts. The Orange Order had fertile ground in such a place and in Larkhall some of the railings are still painted red, white and blue. But my message was a unifying one, not the divisive one that other parties had fed on.

Larkhall had, by the time of the by-election, attracted some promising new factories and lots of English couples came to work and to stay. Most eventually identified with the SNP and with me as the candidate, and there was local talk that I got elected in 1967 by dint of the English vote.

By coincidence my second cousin once removed was Willie Woodburn, who was expelled *sine die* from playing for Rangers for bad behaviour, but who, in the end, became a Rangers manager. My maiden name was

Woodburn, and, as most people in Larkhall were fanatical Rangers supporters, this connection was extremely fortunate. Indeed it was almost a political gift from the gods, as was – to balance the ticket – the fact that my agent was a Catholic.

I had wonderful supporters in all parts of Hamilton, including World Boxing Champion Walter McGowan, who had been coached by his ex-boxer father Joe Ganns. Joe took his name from a famous black boxer, as, being a miner in the days before there were miners' baths, he often had a engrained layer of coal dust on his body. Joe was a remarkable man and had a boxing ring and gym in his Burnbank property, where he held a boys' gym club. The police were encouraged to refer boys in trouble to Joe. He was strict and failure to attend meant expulsion. He once said to me with his eyes glistening, 'Give me a vandal and I'll give you an athlete.' Once at a dance in Burnbank Burgh Hall a man the worse for drink wanted me to sing and kept shouting, 'Give us a song, Winnie.' All Joe had to do was take one step in his direction and trouble vanished 'Her job', he said 'is preaching, nae singing.'

Such workers we had! Our patriotic endeavour offered no good jobs, nor any rewards. But people kept at it. Remarkably some – such as Sadie Paterson and her husband –were still there fighting for the cause when my daughter Annabelle contested Hamilton South in the 2000 by-election and so nearly won it.

Of course my agent, John McAteer, a descendant of an Irish rebel, was totally splendid in the job. He was happily married to Kate, a primary school head teacher, and they had four sons. There being council elections every year at that time, almost every twelve months he would be fighting a Hamilton local authority seat. Kate once told me about the embarrassment his election addresses for these contests used to cause her because they started by saying, 'John McAteer is married with one son.' Then a year later it was 'John McAteer is married with two sons' and so on until the last one said, 'John McAteer is married with four sons.' At that stage Kate had had enough. 'John,' she said, 'I don't think you should stand for the Council any more.' Later John became the SNP's National Organiser but, alas, died tragically young of cancer. Kate later married the former SNP National Chairman, Billy Wolfe. My second election agent was Norrie Douglas, who organised our defence of the seat in 1970. He was a successful local fishmonger. He had been in Burma and at the end of the war helped to rescue Japanese-held POWs. I told him my brother had been rescued from an island off Singapore called Blackan Mati. Amazingly Norrie had rescued him.

We fought council elections and had councillors elected. Both during the campaign and when I was the MP I attended every occasion where I was allowed in (some were still reluctant and even fearful to let me in, so powerful was the Labour party and so great was its influence in all community groups). Fêtes, rotary clubs and townswomen's guilds were meat and drink to me and I even went on the early morning miners' buses to Cardowan Colliery and then went down the mine. I was horrified at how hot it was and by the hard, dangerous work these fine men did. Often when I was campaigning, miners would say to me, 'The sooner no man has to go down the mine the better.' At that time many of them were dying of miners' diseases, but the Westminster government was indifferent to their plight. It remains indifferent to the plight of many Scottish working men and women even now.

On the day after the by-election I was on television three times – a new experience for me. One of the interviewers was Magnus Magnusson. I was very nervous, but he was exceptionally kind and told me to enjoy it. I was then taken to do a programme which I was told would be a one-to-one interview with Cliff Michelmore, but when I went to go on – live as it usually was in those days – I found that there was a whole panel of people there to ask me questions. This was in clear breach of the agreement that had been made with the producers of the programme, but nonetheless I had to do it. One of the people who was questioning me, rather harshly, was my friend Mary Gray (the wife of Bill Gray, later Labour Lord Provost of Glasgow), which disappointed me. Another was a man who had married the daughter of the great John MacLean. I managed to make my way through it all and then the BBC asked us upstairs for a drink. I invited absolutely everybody I could find in the studio to come with me, I suppose because I was more than a little peeved at having been lied to by the producers. The BBC, to be fair, rose to the occasion and everyone was well provided for.

The days after the by-election were frantic. The press were everywhere and I found it strange to be in such a media spotlight. As a criminal practitioner one had to avoid the press: if one had a case that had been in the papers it was necessary to slink out of the back door of the court to avoid them. Allowing, or still worse encouraging, a picture would have attracted criticism from the Law Society. But now I was having to live my life in a totally opposite way, because press publicity was, and is, vital for a politician.

After a few days I decided to get away from it all, particularly as I was not due to take my seat until two weeks after the by-election. I went to Orkney and Shetland with my friend Lorna Blackie. I chose the Northern Isles because I felt that if I was going to sit down in London as an MP I wanted to know what it was like to be in the furthest-away places that London ruled. I was given a tremendous welcome in the islands. I spoke at public meetings, one in Orkney and one in Shetland, which were absolutely packed – in fact they had to turn people away. On the platform I expressed my long-held view that Orkney and Shetland should have as much autonomy as they wanted, right up to and including Faroese status, which is only just short of full independence. I genuinely believed in that degree of autonomy for the islands and it remains the position of my party to this day. It was very exciting to see Orkney and Shetland in this way and I fell in love with both, and that feeling has remained strong. I was very fortunate to fight the Orkney and Shetland seat many years later, and then to represent the islands in the European Parliament for twenty-four years.

Memories of my parliamentary years in the House of Commons do not fade and the bitter and sweet moments remain firmly entrenched in my memory. My first Parliament was from November 1967 to the General Election in June 1970, when I lost my seat. Of course I did not know it then, but I was fated to come back before too long.

When I was fighting the Hamilton by-election the SNP leadership urged me to try to come a good second in order to encourage the members. As ever, I overdid it, and as a result my life changed for ever. Hamilton catapulted me into instant fame, not merely in Scotland but across the UK and beyond. Even now I am always recognised in the street wherever I go, although now it is mainly the middle-aged and older people who remember that November night at Hamilton. So much has flowed from it – starting with the Tartan Express and the hard work and difficult times I quickly began to experience as soon as that train left me behind at Euston station.

2

Growing Up in Glasgow

I HAVE CHOSEN TO start telling the story of my life with the events surrounding the Hamilton by-election, which was central to everything that happened thereafter. But of course much happened before. During the by-election reporters would often ask me, 'When did you first become a Scottish Nationalist?' My instant response was that it happened when I heard a band play 'The Road to the Isles' at the age of nine, on a trip 'doon the watter' to Kilchatten Bay in Bute with the Fishmonger's Company of Glasgow. It was a magical Highland summer's day, and I must have got a day off school, because I remember being the only child on the boat. I had never seen such scenery before. Ever since then I have always associated 'The Road to the Isles' with the beauty of the Highlands and the Islands, little dreaming of the huge part these places were to play in my life in later years.

My answer regarding my nationlist origins springs from the bottom of my heart, and it is as relevant today as it was then, but of course when I look back on my childhood and the period when I was growing up, I can also see other influences which dictated what my life's work was going to be and what I would strive for. One of those earliest influences came from a teacher, a Miss Kirkwood, who like many at that time had lost her boyfriend in the trenches during the First World War, and who spent her life looking after her ailing mother. She loved Scottish history, made it come to life and imbued in us a pride in the deeds of Wallace and Bruce. In school, during our music lessons, we heard and sang many Scottish songs which told the story of our past in a way which stays with you for the rest of your life.

I was one of four children. My sister was eight years older than me and my twin brothers were eleven years ahead, so I suppose I was what I remember my mother saying when talking to aunts or friends, an 'after-thought'. At the time I had no idea what the word meant but I had a feeling it was something not quite right! My sister always said I was spoiled, and I probably was, in that all the strictness in which she and my brothers were brought up was somewhat relaxed by the time it came to me. But the youngest was also, to some extent, like being an only child. Because of the age gap I didn't have any connection with my sister's friends, all of whom appeared to me to be exceedingly glamorous, very interesting and completely out of reach. My brothers' friends came around before and during the war and I used to be allowed to go into the front lounge and speak to them for a few minutes. That was a great thrill, though I remember that it did seem to me at the time that they were always talking about the war – both about it coming, and then about the awful events which unfolded when it did.

My sister says that we had a very secure background. Certainly there never seemed to be anything we needed that we couldn't have. We had many books: the complete Dickens, much Walter Scott and many other classics. We also had lots of reference books, so that if I asked my father a question he would say, 'Go and look it up in the encyclopaedia.' In retrospect this, I suspect, was not exactly typical because in most of my friends' houses in the surrounding tenements of the Battlefield/Langside area there were few if any books. The house also had a lot of ornaments in it. Some had been passed down to my parents from other relatives and some my blacksmith grandfather had bought. We had comfortable furniture, nice carpets, and pictures on the walls, including two originals won in the Royal Society of Arts raffle. I suppose I took all these things very much for granted and it was a shock for me to discover, as I grew up, that we were better off than some of my classmates and that, unlike them, we always had enough money for holidays, clothes and treats such as visits to the theatre. I was never aware of any financial troubles at home, although my sister and older brothers remembered harder times. They had gone by the time I was born, although my mother later told me that in her early marriage, when my father started up his business, whatever weekly money she was given by him she made sure lasted not for one, but for two weeks.

Certainly our 'close' was a cut above others that I knew of. My uncle John Woodburn and his wife once took me visiting to relatives who lived in a single-end where they had to share a lavatory on the stairs. We had nothing like that because the tenement we lived in was built from quite posh red sandstone and had a 'wally' close (that is, one that was tiled). We did, however, still have a washhouse in our tenement. My mother had one weekday in the washhouse each week and I used to go with her. I remember well the steam and the back-breaking work that was involved in doing the weekly wash.

We had different clothes for wearing on a Sunday, quite separate from what we wore on a daily basis. My mother used to remark on how stupid it was, as the Sunday clothes never wore out; we just grew out of them. But that pleased one strange regular visitor, the lady we called 'the old clothes wife'. When she came to the door she always had a bundle over her shoulder and she briskly negotiated with my mother the purchase of the clothes we had outgrown. Then she was entertained to tea and home baking.

I remember too a back-court singer who sweetly sang Scots songs such as 'Jessie the Flower of Dunblane'. My mother tossed over the window a coin wrapped in newspaper, but I was not allowed to watch him catch it, as she said it would embarrass the man. I remember seeing the shape of a half-crown and eagerly describing the story to my father. However just as I was about to tell him about the half-crown, my mother's warning glance shut me up. She, I am sure, wanted my father to think that she had only given sixpence or a shilling. I think this was my first introduction into white lies being acceptable, even necessary, in some circumstances.

My early memories of holidays with the whole family were few, as my brothers John and David became motorbike fanatics as soon as they were old enough to drive and went off on their own with their circle of friends, mostly Boys' Brigade members. Therefore, by the time I was at school my holidays were usually taken just with my parents and sometimes with my sister. I recall taking tours to Ayrshire and to Appin, which was of particular interest, as we visited the graves of my Stewart ancestors. My grandmother Jean Stewart was herself born in Appin and when I later read *Kidnapped* I was thrilled to discover that I was undoubtedly related to James Stewart of the Glen. When we went on holiday to St

Andrews I was very keen on watching the outside concerts of 'The Entertainers'. Once I disappeared and my parents and my sister found I had entered a 'go as you please' competition. The winner was decided by audience applause and, wearing a blue dress, I won. The prize was six silver spoons, which became a great treasure of mine and I gained them after singing 'In my Sweet Little Alice Blue Gown'. I believe from that day on I started to nurture theatrical ambitions.

Of course we are shaped by our parents and their own backgrounds, and their parents before them. It is therefore not surprising that I liked performing and I liked music. My father was one of nine children who were brought up in a two-room and kitchen in Dalmarnock Road, in the Bridgeton area of Glasgow. If any of us every defaulted on our manners he used to crack a joke and say, 'Aye, Brigton will oot.' His father had been a highly-paid manual worker who cleaned moving machinery. His oldest sister, Fanny, never married and became like a sister to her own mother, my grandmother, who lived in prefect health and with perfect recall until she was ninety-nine. She was always thin and carried herself like a ramrod and she spoke strong Scots.

All the male Woodburns got a trade and the older ones combined to send the youngest, Willie, to university. My father had to leave school at twelve, yet he had a great reverence for education and continued to go to many classes. He qualified as a turner but finally had to travel to Liverpool to get work. My father was a singer with a perfect baritone who sang all his life. He had hoped for a professional career and whilst in Liverpool he was accepted by the D'Oyly Carte Opera Chorus. Unfortunately he then had his right hand sliced off in a machine at work, and when he turned up to take his place in the chorus they refused to accept a singer with a stump. However, he was awarded £500 – a substantial sum in 1913 – in compensation for his injury, and having been unable to take up a professional singing career he returned to Glasgow and set himself up in business as a paper merchant. On the back of that £500 compensation, and the wise way he used it, his children got a university education. He continued to sing, despite his disappointment at not being able to do it professionally. He sang at functions and parties and for charity. In fact he founded his own charity, The Clarinda Burns Circle, and this raised money for the often forgotten disabled men who lived in a home in

Erskine. After many years of concerts and visits the proceeds of this fund paid for specially adapted buses. Amongst other things, these were used for taking the men out on Saturdays: they would go to a football match, on to dinner at Danny Brown's in St Vincent Street and then to the theatre. In addition there were many other changes at Erskine itself, helped by my father's charity, including a move from sleeping in dormitories to the building of small individual houses.

My father brought me up to love music and song, and I learned hundreds of songs from him, mostly Scots, but also Irish and English ones. When he went to functions he always took his music, as he knew he would be asked to sing. He sang from time to time on the radio, including duets with a soprano called Jannette Schlanders, and he also made a few records. These recordings were claimed by my brother David when my father died, but in his various moves from house to house in Scotland they unfortunately got lost. I would dearly love to have these records again and to hear my father's fine voice.

In addition to singing he poured his energy and considerable intellect into chess and bridge. He was a very keen player all his life and he played both competitively for the Glasgow City team. He had no patience for teaching me chess though he did teach my son Fergus. He also had a strong political conscience and was a member of the ILP. He had been, as I have said, at Central Station to see the Red Clydesiders off to London after the historic 1922 election and he also was there to see off the boys who went to fight in the Spanish Civil War as part of the International Brigade. He took me with him and I remember my mother being some-what annoyed that he had personally paid to kit out for the International Brigade his nephew from Canada, Jim MacDowall, the son of my father's older sister who had been widowed.

On my mother's side my grandfather Anderson was a blacksmith in the Anderston district of Glasgow. His two sons, my uncles James and Frank, followed this trade and indeed they had the last working smiddy in Glasgow. There is still a beautiful wrought-iron gate in Ingram Street which my grandfather made in that same smiddy. My grandfather was widowed when my mother was thirteen and she was taken away from school (although at that time the leaving age was fourteen) to become 'mother' to the two younger children – her sister Mary and her brother

Frank. My mother was thus a housewife, mother and carer from the tender age of thirteen to the end of her life. She clearly was very clever and she loved books and plays, the cinema and the theatre. She was also a very good organiser and it was in her war work that this ability really came to the fore. For over six years she was in charge of distributing servicemen's parcels for Queen's Park Bowling Club and she kept perfect records. From time to time some woman at the club would say, 'My son didn't get his turn of a parcel', but my mother was always able to show that all had been done fairly and accurately.

My parents had very many good friends and amongst them I think particularly fondly of Molly and Eddie Mitchell. They were friends from the bowling green, and they were also theatre lovers and card players. Molly, who was a fine contralto singer, was known as 'the Duchess of Battlefield' because of her glamorous clothes, her well coiffured hair and her overall stylish appearance and stature. She had had a child who died of meningitis and – perhaps as a result – she lavished her love on me and encouraged my mother to buy wonderful clothes for me from a Jewish firm run by a Mrs Etta Camber.

We did much visiting. On Sundays – or at least on every second Sunday – we either received aunts and uncles or we went to their houses. I have to say that the Andersons – my mother's family – seemed to me, as a child, to be much the nicer. Uncle James was married to the very dreamy, posh Aunt Mary, the daughter of a publican from Burnside who extravagantly fed the birds! When we went to her house for tea we felt wicked because we had 'shop-bought' cakes. In all the other houses they were home-made. There was a rather strict rotation system about the quality of food served for these visits, and of course the same was expected when the visits were returned. When it was my mother's turn to provide we always had chicken and roast potatoes or roast beef or steak and kidney pie. A knife-and-fork course was essential, and this was followed by several kinds of jam scones, pancakes, tarts, chocolate cakes and shortbread, as well as other delicacies. Later in the evening we had what we called fruit time, when we were allowed to take whatever fruit was available. Few today will ever experience the standard of such home cooking. My mother was indeed a master chef. Each weekday we had a different soup a different knife-and-fork course and a different dessert, ranging through bread and butter pudding, treacle pudding, upside down apple pudding and tarts of all descriptions.

When I returned from my school round the corner after four o'clock, I would always have awaiting me a treacle scone or a doughnut or a freshly baked pancake to tide me over till my father's arrival home about six. I could smell these delicious appetisers as I came up the steps of our flat. We all took such treats for granted.

Another wonderful thing about my life was swimming. My father believed that we should all be members of a swimming club and be professionally coached. We spent at least two afternoons a week and Saturday morning at the club on the southside of Glasgow, and I was really keen. There were coaches on hand and I not only passed my life-saving certificates but also started to became a competitive swimmer. Swimming has been one of the great joys of my life and part of that joy has been teaching some of my friends how to swim. During the war things like swimming galas were abandoned, and that really upset me. My sister had been a swimming champion and I probably would have been too if the galas and competitions had continued.

In addition to swimming, I played some other sports. I was in the hockey team when I was at secondary school, and although hockey can be a fairly rough game I enjoyed it. I played left wing and often on Saturdays we were up against much better teams such as the Park School and 'Hutchie'. We usually got beaten fairly heavily, but it was a good experience and also helped me to keep fit. I was also in the running team briefly and was the school tennis champion.

These memories of my early childhood come and go. However, I do remember my brother David was very attentive to me and used to take me to the pictures, particularly the ones that no one else wanted to see. Watching *King Kong*, for example, must have been purgatory for him. He was also the one that taught me to walk and taught me to read. There was always a very close affection between the two of us, and we really were a very close-knit family.

It is my memories of the war that come back to me most often. I have frequently tried to tell my own children about my childhood during the war but I have found it very hard to convey completely to them the atmosphere of that time. I was just ten when the war broke out and it coloured all the years as I became a teenager. First of all there was the black-out. There was an absolute need to have your black-out curtains perfect and to nail down every inch. If there was even a chink then there would be a knock on the door from the volunteer wardens. Torches were essential because there were no street lights and the constant fight to keep torches working was my father's Sunday night occupation, as he checked to see if one type of battery would go with this torch or that torch.

In the centre of Glasgow all the lovely advertising lights that I had so enjoyed as a child went out. Glasgow was now in darkness, though in the day time it was brightened up by uniforms from all parts of the Commonwealth including – most memorably – the Australians, with their big hats. There were also the Free French, the Polish Army, soldiers from America and lots of different sailors. The whole town was alive with the war. Although there were no swimming galas, lots of other activities didn't stop. I went to the Brownies with my best friend, Sheila Hunter, who has remained my friend for all of my life and for whom, when she married the cartoonist, Ewen Bain, I was a bridesmaid. There was no fear of crime or abduction or molestation even though it was pitch black. There were very few cars on the road, winter or summer, so when we were old enough to have bikes we would ride about the streets on a summer evening and have them pretty well to ourselves. That was a popular evening pastime, particularly when we became teenagers, and always seemed to end up with all our pals at the local chip shop.

Most people were involved in war work. My father spent two 'all nighters' each week in the Glasgow Lyon Club serving hot meals at the lowest possible prices. My mother, along with her dear friend Molly Mitchell (my second mother), peeled potatoes in the Victoria Infirmary twice a week. At home, of course, we listened to every news bulletin there was, and we followed the war on a kind of chart that my father had put up on the wall. My brother John had been called up to the Militia before the war started. Being twenty-one on 17 August 1939 he was exactly the right age for this early service. His twin brother, David, was already out in Malaya. He had taken a forestry degree and had got a job on a rubber plantation with the Selangore Mati Rubber Company. He lived near a town called Klang and we got regular letters at home describing his life there. He had his own bungalow and he took the odd trip to Singapore and other places on leave.

John also wrote to us from wherever he was posted. Every Sunday during the war, regular as clockwork, my mother wrote to David, to John, to my father's sister, Aunt Meg in Canada, and to her own sister, Aunt Mary, in Birmingham. All letters, apart from the odd one or two to other people, were written on those Sundays, while we all listened to the music of Palm Springs on the radio.

One day a group of Jewish children arrived at my primary school, Battlefield School. They had been saved from the Holocaust, although our headmaster told us all quite openly that tragically their parents had been killed – a fact that we would probably have found out sooner or later, so I suspect he was right to tell us when he did. I was ten at the time and this was a very traumatic thing to hear. The children had been placed in Battlefield School because it was near a large synagogue and they were all housed in a hostel on Sinclair Drive on the south side of Glasgow. It must have been so difficult for them. I don't think we gave them very much quarter in class or the playground, alas, although we did invite them home to our houses to try and alleviate their loneliness, though it probably only made things worse. One by one most of them were claimed by relatives, some of them in America and Canada. But there was a hard core that remained with us right until we finished our schooling at the age of seventeen. Many went on to have fine careers, including one who became a conductor.

One of the major disruptions to city life during the war was the evacuation. My mother and father utterly refused to let me be evacuated, as did the parents of some other children, inlcuding Sheila's. Miss Kirkwood, our marvellous primary teacher, very good-looking and well dressed with great humour, kindliness and brilliance, decided to organise classes for the children who remained in Glasgow. The idea was that the parents of such children would offer the use of a house for a week and the kids would come there instead as the school was closed. There were about twelve of us in total. Miss Kirkwood came regularly and we carried on with our lessons. Some of the children were really much more deprived than I was, and my mother (when it was her turn to host the school) used to lay out annuals for them to read in addition to our school books – and we found that during those weeks many children started to come earlier and earlier. Mother would have a tea-break with Miss Kirkwood in the kitchen, with home-baked cakes, and we would all stay in the big front room reading. I doubt if we as children had any idea of the huge debt we would come to owe to Miss Kirkwood for our early education, particularly during those hard times. I still remain extremely grateful to her.

Even in these early years and even during the war years I can, in memory, detect some Bolshevik tendencies in my behaviour – tendencies that were only to grow as time passed. I have a very vivid memory of feeling that adult rules were often absurd and unreasonable. For example, I had been desperately keen to be able to take my own choice of books out of the excellent local library, a privilege that would become mine when I reached the age of eight. On that date – 10 July 1937 – I rushed to the library, took a book out, took it home and read it within a couple of hours. Then I went back to get another one, to be told I could only borrow a single book each day. Indeed a grim-faced lady with glasses and hair up in a bun spoke to me very severely about the matter. I went home and told my father, who agreed with me, as did my sister, who always took a keen interest in my reading.

Another exploit of being 'agin the government' was shared with my pal Sheila. In the qualifying class we had a teacher who was a terrible bully and who used to ridicule the boys and sometimes make them cry. There was even a boy whose bladder leaked from time to time, and instead of being sympathetic, this teacher shouted and raved at him, which only made his problem worse. Sheila and I decided to teach the bully a lesson. We wrote (in block letters so that we could disguise ourselves) an anonymous letter. We called ourselves 'The Black Arrow' and we told him how cruel he was and how he shouldn't treat people in the way he did. We summoned up all our courage and put the letter in his desk at lunchtime. Heaven alone knows what would have happened to us if we had been caught, but we weren't. It was very exciting after lunch to see him open his desk and read the letter. He then glared up at the boys, clearly never thinking that two girls could be the perpetrators.

My Bolshevism also found its way into the girl guides and the Bible Class. I rather admired girls whose arms were full of Brownie and Guide badges, so I set out to get as many as I could – swimming, diving, life-saving, Morse code, cookery, knitting, sewing, writing and the rest. Each one gave me great satisfaction. However, after I had gained a number of them, the captain told me to stop as my success was, she claimed, discouraging the others. Again I had a sympathetic hearing from my father, who, in any case, did not like the amount of time we spent doing drill. I stopped being a Girl Guide.

My father only went to the Kirk for weddings and funerals, but my mother was keen on us attending Sunday School and, later, Bible Class. I decided that I would stop going after the incident in which I asked our minister, a very learned man called Dr Chisholm, 'How do we know we are right, and not the Catholics or Jews or Buddhists or Hindus?' He refused to answer.

The war was for my mother truly terrible, and she worried constantly about my brother John, who by now was in the tank corps. He rose from the ranks to end up as a warrant officer, based in Alexandria. But she also used to comfort herself that at least she had one son safe in Malaya. Then the Japanese roared down the Malay peninsula. The guns of Singapore were pointing not towards the Japanese, but towards the sea, and the city fell. David had by then joined the Malay Defence Corps and was in the midst of the fighting. Soon he was posted missing and presumed to be a prisoner-of-war. From then on every time the doorbell rang my mother jumped. The tension was intense and it was passed on to me. It was literally never-ending and was made worse the day two police officers came to the door saying that they were there to arrest David. In some way the police had been told that in our home was a young man who wasn't registered in the Forces. They burst into the house and rushed into the bedrooms to search under the beds. My mother stood akimbo in the hall saying, with amazing coolness, 'Yes, have a good look, have a good look.' Then they were told – and were shown proof – that he was in Malaya. They immediately became very apologetic and I think that my mother even gave them tea and scones in the end.

Mother was always visited by pals of John and David when they were on leave, perhaps because the young men had few places to go. Most boys would go to see the parents of their friends when they came home, and in my home they always got tea and scones, and I think a few bob if they needed it. The same thing happened when boys were leaving to go to the war. I remember my brother John's embarkation leave. He went to all the neighbours in our tenement and I think he got something from every one of them. There was always a great nervousness when boys left, as there were huge worries about the dangers of troop-ships and submarines. Yet I suspect we did not fully comprehend the full horror of it all. Life, particularly for a young girl, flowed on.

We went to the cinema a lot. My mother loved the cinema and we made sure we never missed a good film. We were surrounded by cinemas; in fact there were at least eight within walking distance. My mother also went to afternoon matinees at the theatre with Molly Mitchell and in the evenings she would go with my father. Theatre in Glasgow was vibrant during the war, as the London companies would try out their productions in Glasgow first. We had the best you can imagine.

Shortly after my brother David went missing in Malaya my mother was asked – by a lady doctor from Rutherglen, who had been one of the last people to leave Singapore – to be the secretary of the Scottish Japanese Prisoner of War Association. There was a strong feeling that the government seemed to have opted out of giving any practical assistance to the relatives of those who had been taken prisoner in the East and consequently some of those relatives had formed an association which covered the whole of Scotland.

What news there was came usually by postcard, although occasionally a photograph or letter would turn up. All the information that could be gathered from such irregular communication was then circulated by my mother to all the other relatives in the POW Association. By this means some who had been given up for dead were found to be still alive, and this caused enormous happiness. Other relatives found out in which camps their sons or fathers actually were. But our postcard never came – or rather after the fall of Singapore we had only one and it contained no real information. Indeed at one stage during the latter part of the war my father even said that we should perhaps prepare for the worst. We did not know that David was still alive and was in Blackan Mati – then a grim prisoner of war camp, but now a holiday island off Singapore. When I visited it during my years as an MEP I was horrified to discover that it contained not a plaque or reference to its horrific history, a matter I raised with Dr Lee Kuan Yew, the Prime Minister of Singapore, when I met him.

There are a few more pleasant war memories. We had regular visits from a Canadian cousin who was stationed on the Clyde. He was named (after my father) George Woodburn MacDowall and he used to bring other Canadians to see us. My father would take them all out to Danny Brown's Restaurant and then to the theatre. It was wonderful to have such bright company and it made the world seem a little smaller. During the war my father and mother also made annual excursions to Eastcheape in London to meet the managers of the Selangore Mati Rubber Co., for whom David had worked before being captured. I remember one visit when I went with my father. We were solemnly greeted by an elderly director of the company who was distraught at the disappearance of his 'boys'. The feeling in that room of hopelessness remains with me, as well as the feelings of sadness and solidarity with individuals whose fate and future were unknown to us.

This was all a type of education, of course, but my formal education also continued during the war. Yet although I was attending schools in Glasgow there was remarkably little Scottish content in what I was taught at that time. In primary school we got no information about the Scottish Enlightenment, nor about the uprisings of 1715 and 1745. In a city where they could be seen in their numbers each year, there was never any explanation of Orange Walks or the background to sectarianism. We were never told the reasons for Scotland's leading role in the Industrial Revolution nor in the struggle for workers' rights or the franchise. At home, though, my father talked of all these things and he boasted hugely about Scotland's contribution to the world, particularly to the world of ideas. Any Scots culture I acquired was through the songs my father taught me and the visits to the Citizens' Theatre in Glasgow, where we saw the work of Scots playwrights and heard plays in Scots. Yet of Gaelic we learnt little. However, at school there was a Gaelic choir and as I loved singing I volunteered to join it. I was met with a point-blank refusal to admit me because I was deemed not to 'have the Gaelic', although I would have learnt it with enthusiasm. Every time I heard the choir after that I remember feeling like the boy in the story of the Pied Piper who was shut out of the magic land.

Sheila and I scraped into the top class at Queen's Park Secondary School, a matter which was decided by our mathematics marks at Battlefield Primary. We were then immediately surrounded by brilliant mathematics pupils and so we were usually bottom of the secondary class.

This made us feel intellectually inferior, not least because our maths teachers were always obviously critical of our presence in the top set. I was easily bored at secondary school and my mind wandered constantly as I dreamed of other things. Oddly enough, though, I loved homework because the idea of going home to do allotted tasks in my own time, in my own way appealed to me so much. Looking back I think those are the characteristics of a swot.

We had a wonderful teacher at Queen's Park, a Mr Fleisch, who taught French and Spanish. He also held musical appreciation classes after school. There was a group in the fifth and sixth years who went to the Scottish National Orchestra concerts on Saturdays in the old St Andrew's Hall. If Sheila and I did not have a date we used to go and meet up with our other friends such as Gerald Gordon (later Professor of Law at Glasgow University and the author of one of the standard textbooks), Willie Hopper (who became an MEP for a Tory constituency in England, but who lost his seat after a single term), Dorothy Patterson and many others. I was later told that this class was regarded by the school inspectors as the cleverest in Scotland at that time, and we were the first to take the new Higher examinations. Sheila and I always felt inadequate, but learning that, we were quite flattered that we had been able to keep up at all.

But still we were taught no Scottish history. We knew, of course, of Bruce and Wallace and we were all aware at Queen's Park that the local place-names of Battlefield and Langside were redolent of vital moments in the history of our country and of the tragic, romantic life of Mary, Queen of Scots. But of the wars of independence, the founding of the monasteries, Queen Margaret and King David, we were utterly ignorant. The languages of Scotland were also missing but I had heard my grandmother speaking broad Scots so I understood it perfectly well though I didn't let on. The first time I went to a play in Scots – it must have been at the Citizens' – I understood everything and could laugh at all the jokes. However I was mystified to find that some of the other children couldn't understand it at all. That was the first time I got the thrill of realising that I did indeed have more than one language.

One other highlight of these years was my first holiday alone. Sheila and I were allowed to take our bikes on the train and we went all the way to Mull, to Dervaig, where my sister had spent her honeymoon. I looked back at the pages of the visitors' book in the lobby and found the names Jean and James Forsyth with 'Scottish' as their nationality: I was relieved to see that.

My sister got married towards the end of my school years to James Forsyth and I found the whole thing very exciting. The Forsyth family were full of fun and music. My father got on very well with Mr Forsyth, who was a lawyer, and they used to vie with each other in singing. Of course, during the wedding celebrations (before and after) there were lovely meals laid on and I found them very sophisticated. Soon Jean had a child, Deirdre, and I found I liked being an aunt, even though I was still at school.

Jean's husband, Jimmy Forsyth, was a genius. He won first place in the Glasgow Bursary Competition and passed his Highers when he was fourteen years old. However, he was still too young to go university so he was sent to Germany, where he became bilingual. When old enough he came to Glasgow University where he gained first-class honours in maths and natural philosophy. Jean herself got an upper second in economics, and she was taught by Alec Cairncross, author of the standard textbook, *An Introduction to Economics*. He became part of the advisory team to Sir Stafford Cripps when he was the wartime Minister of Aircraft Production. Cairncross took some of his brighter pupils, including my sister Jean, to work for him in London during the war.

When Sheila and I were on Mull we were full of excitement at our freedom. With our bikes, we explored most of the island and then went all the way down to Salen and to Tobermory; we even went on a day trip to Iona. For me it was the first chance to get to grips with places I had long dreamed of and thought of ever since I heard 'The Road to the Isles' on that Clyde steamer. There were other pleasures too. We went to a dance with some of the locals and I found the Highland men very attractive. Years later I met one who remembered dancing with me that night.

Some time later, when I had left school, I went on holiday again with Sheila, this time with her family as well. Her father was an inveterate European traveller, and before the war Sheila and her brother had been taken to many places and had even cruised round the Mediterranean. We went to Westende, near Ostend, and I was so thrilled to hear people speaking French: we were, I knew, actually abroad!

As school came to an end we were all required to fill in forms as to what service we would enter. The war was still going on, though the tide had turned firmly in the Allies' favour. Most of the girls wanted to enter the services that had glamorous uniforms, such as the Wrens and the WRAF, but I filled in the forms for the Land Army, as I never wanted to kill anyone and was sure I never could. I regarded myself as brave even in doing this, as I was terrified of cows and bulls. In the end the Land Army was saved from me, because just after we had made our choices the war finally ended.

On VE Day there was great excitement and George Square was filled with people. My mother wasn't keen that I should go, because, as she pointed out, we couldn't celebrate yet because we didn't know anything about David. We were, of course, still at war with Japan. In the end she relented and I went with my friends to join the crowds, but David was still missing and John was still in the Tank Corps in Egypt.

Over the next year as servicemen returned from the war in Europe the university was flooded with applications from would-be students. Although I applied I didn't get accepted. There was huge competition and I was, in any case, content to go back and do another year at school in order to get some more Highers. Suddenly, however, I was notified that I had a late acceptance, although term had already begun. This was an enormously exciting piece of news, but it was followed shortly by something even more exciting: for just when we had almost given up hope, we were told that David was safe. The news came when I was out of the house at school, just prior to going to the university for the first time. I came round the corner at the end of the day to find what seemed like the whole street dancing, including the many Jewish families who lived nearby. A piper had appeared from somewhere and in the middle of it all was my mother waving a postcard. This was one of the most momentous and moving moments of my whole life. We had had one postcard from David which came at the time of the fall of Singapore and then only one other during the whole three and a half years of his imprisonment. Nonetheless we sent a food parcel every week, costing £5, through the Red Cross, who advised on what should go in it. We later found out that David got only two. Like the other prisoners he knew that the Japanese had taken them, but the fact that they had been sent meant – to all of them – that they had not been forgotten.

David came home on a very slow boat. There was a purpose to this as he needed to build up his strength after a long time of appalling privation. We were only able to communicate with him by short postcards – saying things like 'Jean safe in London, married, John safe in Egypt', but they were enough for him to work out that his twin brother whom he hadn't seen for six and a half years, was going to be nearby as his ship came through the Suez Canal. When he heard this, the captain of the ship immediately agreed to stop and ensure that the Tank Corps knew too. My twin brothers were thus reunited for a short time with much celebration. Thus it was that John was the first to see the damage that imprisonment had done to David. Of course he had yellow features because of anti-malarial drugs. He also couldn't eat and the most he could swallow was a tiny piece of fish. It was only after the atomic bomb had fallen that the Japanese started to dish out any real food, though they withheld the drugs that would have saved lives. Some of the Australian POWs ignored the advice of the senior officer who was in charge of the camp, who happened to be a doctor, and gorged themselves as soon as the food appeared. Many of them died as a result.

When David's boat was due to arrive my mother and father went down to Liverpool to greet him, but I had to stay at home in case by some chance they missed him and he came on to Glasgow alone. He could not be allowed to turn up at an empty house. Sheila stayed in the house with me while we waited. It was quite an exciting tale because my mother and father were standing on a bench with binoculars looking at the hundreds of yellow faces. Yet somehow they kept fixing on one particular face. Then a lady with a loudspeaker who was helping people on board find their relatives, said to that face 'If you are David Woodburn, I'll help you,' and pointed at them. All waved together.

Thus they were duly reunited. Most of the ex-POWs opted to go through all their tests and injections as quickly as possible despite their weakness, and they came back the next day on a train to Glasgow. I always remember the story that when they arrived David was with a friend from Fife who had been in his camp. His friend had expressed the hope that his relatives would not be at the station because if they were 'they would be greeting'. He was right of course: he stepped out of the train and straight into a whole host of greeting relatives, as they all did.

We all got presents from David. Yet some of the few things he had been able to bring back were themselves too far gone to be kept. There was a book that he had had throughout his camp years called *Mathematics for Millions*, and the whole book was covered with tiny handwritten solutions to the mathematical problems. But when he got it out to show it to us it was full of lice and he threw it into the open fire.

I had the joy of taking him into town to spend money. When people saw his yellow face and his Malay Defence Force Uniform they knew that was an ex-POW of the Japanese. Lots came up and spoke to him, because by that time everyone was aware of the terrible suffering that such prisoners had undergone. But David was keen to get on with the rest of his life. He lost no time at all in applying to the Forestry Commission for a job and almost immediately was sent to Argyll, where he temporarily lived in a hotel in Ardrishaig and became the District Officer responsible for the forests of Knapdale, Carradale and Achnaglachcach. It was there he met his lovely Highland wife Sarah McLoughlin, who was matron in charge of the home where the forestry workers lived. I went up to stay with him and met her too, and they were married the following summer with a wonderful Highland wedding in Lochgilphead at which her brothers sang Gaelic songs. I was enchanted by the whole thing, but particularly by David's marriage and his superb and wonderful wife.

War leaves ever-fixed marks and lasting traumas. We all believed that the Second World War would end all wars, so the mood of everyone was unbridled optimism and we were all going to live happily ever after. It was great to see that David and Sarah were taking the chance to do just that.

3

University and After

GOING TO THE 'Uni' after twelve weary years of school discipline in those heady days as the war ended and glad-to-be-alive servicemen poured back from the appalling conflict was an enchanting experience. With my family safely back from the dangerous years each day of peace seemed to bring constant happiness. The war, now safely in the past, appeared almost irrelevant as I eagerly boarded the Number 3 tram to Gilmorehill stop, as the university was always called. The university was the place where petty tyrannies would end and freedom would suddenly begin. I was seventeen and full of optimism, and after doing an MA in history, I wanted to be a history teacher. However I now know that, in hindsight, that 'fresher' state in which I approached my university years in 1946 was only a comparative freedom and a pale shadow of the freedom that students have today. There was a lot of puritanism about, in fact puritanism was the norm. Unwanted pregnancy was viewed by society as disastrous and usually ended careers. Whilst tobacco and alcohol were normal I cannot remember even a whisper about drugs. Romance was certainly in the air, although often the reality proved disappointing. Men far outnumbered women at the university and the ex-servicemen seemed experienced and therefore sophisticated. Mirrors were always surrounded by girls anxious to check their appearance and it was said that for a class at 10, one would have to get to a mirror before 9. Phone calls for female students – always hopefully from men – were continually being paged in the Queen Margaret Union.

The Queen Margaret Union – the Women's Union– was a welcoming place; such excellent new friends; such sessions of talk and gossip; such frankness of subject and expression, such witty and intellectual conversation. Segregation was acceptable and few pined for a mixed Union. I made many new friends, Lorna Blackie and Nancy Anderson in particular.

We sat under a distinguished company of professors. If there was any rowdy heckling, and it did occasionally happen, then it was good-natured and the professorial riposte was usually devastating. I think back on all those lectures with admiration for the erudition and eloquence of our teachers and with affection for the gentle idiosyncrasies of the staff. Yet I found my classes difficult as the gulf between school standard and university standard was at once only too obvious. I suffered from a lack of confidence which was exacerbated by the fact that our classes were full of ex-servicemen. With their background and hard-won knowledge, school kids like me had hard competition, especially in writing essays. Our inexperience always showed. As well as that, I found that self-motivation and self-learning came as a shock. I remember in one of my early lectures stealing a look at neighbouring student's notebook to see what on earth they wrote down, because I had no idea what I was meant to be putting on paper. Study was always left too late, but strangely, when each exam time came round I suddenly found a shaft of light and realised that the subject really was engrossing. The puzzle was: why had I left it all to the last minute? Vows were made to ensure that next time I would undertake consistent work, but I never managed to keep them. Life was too exciting.

The choices for one's social life were legion. I listened to all political parties, but settled for the golden words of 'King' John MacCormick and joined the National Movement, becoming a member of GUSNA, the Glasgow University Student Nationalist Association. Never did that decision cause me a moment's doubt or soul-searching, though I never spoke at debates as I had no school experience of debating and was well aware of the limits of my knowledge. I looked with wonder at those confident enough to debate with vigour: Dick Mabon, who went on to be a Labour MP and minister, and Gerry Fisher, who was of such importance to me when I went to Westminster after Hamilton. I never dreamt that a life of politics lay ahead of me. Famous politicians came to the university to address lunchtime meetings in the Men's Union, and oddly enough there was no shortage of victims for this trial by ordeal, which included heckling and impossible questions. At no time did I ever think I would have to go through this, and worse, myself, when sitting at Westminster.

My political allegiance did, however, cause a rift at home. When I told my father I had joined the SNP he simply said: 'You're a traitor.' My sister had been secretary of the Socialist Club at university and the man she married, Jimmy Forsyth, had been president. They had stayed in the faith, but I had strayed. They all believed passionately in socialism – real socialism, not the New Labour of today. I had chosen something different.

But the story of our different politics – my father's and mine – has a strange and touching ending. When he died I wound up his fairly small estate, small because he had already given us almost everything he had. Amongst his papers I found a Scottish National Party Membership Card signed on 25 July 1967. The party member who had signed it was one Alex Ewing – no relative but the same Alex Ewing who had been art director of the Outram Group and one of my staunchest supports in the Hamilton by-election. That particular 25 July was a fine summer's evening, but 25 July was also my mother's birthday. By this time she had died and my father would have been at home alone. I sought out Alex Ewing one day and asked him if he remembered going round on a July evening in Cathcart, where he was the candidate, enthusiastically selling member-ships? And did he remember an old man with a shock of white hair who almost certainly would have invited him in and given him a large dram? Alex remembered him well, and their conversation. I was able to tell Alex that that man was my father, and that on that day he had less than a fortnight to live. He died on 8 August 1967, only three months before I won Hamilton.

There were other things I did at university which were less controver-sial. I may have been nervous in the debating hall, but in the swimming pool I lacked no confidence and in the first week was recruited to the university team. Swimming freestyle, 50 and 100 yards and backstroke for the team was great fun and a huge honour, and it was also a big part of my social life because we went as a team to Aberdeen, Edinburgh, St Andrews, Belfast and Dublin. In addition, even here, women were out-numbered by men as they had a polo team as well as a swimming team.

I joined the German club and took part in plays in German, and I also acquired lots of new friends, including Nancy Anderson, from Beith, who became the University Beauty Queen on Charities Day. My existing friends were, of course, still around. Sheila Hunter had gone to Glasgow Art School, which was a great bonus as I then had the best of two social worlds – university dances and art school balls. And we were in demand; as the ex-servicemen usually had money to spend and generous dinner invitations came our way. That was a good thing because money was tight for the rest of us. There was an agonising choice for many between smoking and having the money for make-up and nylons. Yet, to be honest, even if the choice was lunch or nylon stockings I chose nylons every time.

I cannot remember ever worrying too much about the future. But others did. Many students lived with worry, about passing exams, and about parental support being withdrawn. Most worried about future security, and there was an almost constant preoccupation with finding a means to earn money as soon as one could. My own father's philosophy was comforting and a good antidote to such concerns. He thought that one went to university not to get a job but to get an education. When I sometimes said to him that I had no idea what I was going to do after university, he would always reply that it didn't matter – for I would be educated. However, it was sometimes harder to live with his other oft-expressed view that we were all privileged, living as we did on the back of the working man: this did gave me a mini guilt complex heightened by the fact that this was a pre-grant era and therefore I was relying on his support.

My first romance was with a medical student who seemed to have a view that being a product of Glasgow High School conferred an invincible aura of supremacy. He was very exciting and good company and over a year of dates and dances passed until I learned that he had virtually arranged to be married – of course to someone else. Indeed he soon married that girl. My first serious romance, however, was with Bernard Heslin, an ex-serviceman also studying medicine. He was talented, had all the social graces, played the piano, sang, acted, was a great mimic, could draw and was a wonderful raconteur. Somehow he seemed always to gather people round him because being around him was always fun. I met him because he was also in the College Pudding Chorus. Sheila and I were members and we toured Glasgow and towns round about by bus, always ending up in a 'Union' ceilidh. There I was fascinated to hear many of the songs my father sang, but just as fascinated to hear Orange songs sung by Catholics and Republican songs by Protestants. It seemed to me that there were far more people who must be Catholic, because those were the songs that people knew and sang with gusto.

On our first date, Benny – as we called him – asked me to marry him. I said that was just ridiculous and laughed it off, but he did mean it. Yet that first date started off a long friendship which ended up in an engagement – and a broken heart. He was indeed what my friend Nancy once described him as – a 'fallen angel'.

Benny had gone off to the war before the legal age of enlistment, but because he was six foot four he got away with it. He started off in the very dangerous minesweepers and then moved to the Fleet Air Arm. Bernard was a Catholic, but he didn't appear to be very attentive to his religious observance. My parents' house (where of course I lived) was open to all at any time. Meals were always on offer and Bernard quickly became a fixture. But it was a long time before I was invited to meet Bernard's widowed mother who was an infant mistress and a very accomplished, good-looking woman. Bernard was her only child. I remember that when I went to meet her I was wearing a new navy taffeta dress with full sleeves. I thought that I had acquitted myself well for the meal was very elegant and the conversation fine. But as time passed I became aware that I was not being invited back, so I asked Bernard if I had offended his mother and was told that as I was not a Catholic she was acting out the correct part of a Catholic mother: she would not invite me back until a year and a day had elapsed, to see if I was serious and if the relationship was serious. In the meantime, however, Bernard's aunts and uncles in Kilsyth (some of whom were miners) were very welcoming and hospitable and they started to refer to the 'year and a day' with great humour.

Such was our developing relationship that eventually I decided to take 'instruction' in the Roman Catholic faith. I had instruction from a Jesuit, Father Battley of Glasgow University, and whilst I found it a most interesting experience, I could make no headway with him nor he with me, so he recommended a lovely Mother Superior of the Helpers of the Holy Souls in Camphill Avenue, Glasgow, the street in which I subsequently came to live. She was an Oxford graduate and a convert, and spending time with her I could almost imagine becoming a Catholic, something that I had been unable to imagine with Fr Battley. We both, I think, enjoyed our meetings, but I was not persuaded or inspired. I think I was an illustration of the fact that, as the Jesuits say, you need to have a child for the first years of his life in order to capture him fully for any faith. My Church of Scotland upbringing had instilled into me the idea that 'every man is the interpreter of his own Bible', and despite my wish to be converted and to join Bernard in his family faith I found I could not do so. But perhaps there were also other reasons that I could not fully commit. I had always associated Catholicism with Ireland, and I have and continue to have a strong love and admiration for that country and its people. In later years I joined Irish MEPs in a European Parliamentary group and greatly enjoyed working with them – many of them became close friends. But the start of my passion for Ireland must have come with the songs, particularly those sung by my father and those I heard in films (usually American) that had Irish themes. Many still spring to mind such as 'The Rose of Tralee', 'The Days of the Kerry Dancing' and 'Oft in the Stilly Night'. When I took up the piano I had books of Irish songs and my father had many gramophone records of John McCormack and others.

Yet Queen's Park Secondary School had, as I recollect, no Catholic pupils at all, and we had no connection with – and had never heard of – Ireland. Schools at that time were firmly segregated and it was only when I went to university that I discovered that instead of there being only a few Catholics in a few schools, they were in fact many of them compared to what seemed only a few in my traditional faith. Prejudice about religion was new to me and I was more than a little shocked to realise the real reason behind the normal question at a law apprenticeship interview, 'What school did you go to?'

I studied both Irish and Scottish History and angrily discovered that there had been genocides that affected both our countries – the Highland Clearances in Scotland and the famines and martyrs in Ireland. Worse for Ireland, the poverty had been endemic and had been exacerbated by political policy and landlordism. I was equally shocked to discover when I first went to Ireland with the university swimming team that such poverty was still very noticeable. Just off the main thoroughfare, O'Connell Street in Dublin, I saw people sleeping on the streets with their emaciated children. Nonetheless – and perhaps when one is young these things register strongly and then are momentarily forgotten – our swimming matches in Belfast and Dublin were merry occasions. Before 'the Troubles' students north and south of the border celebrated and competed together. Belfast had one university – Queen's – but Dublin had two –Trinity College and University College. In Dublin I thought the crowds at the swimming match were generous in shouting for Glasgow to win, until I realised that a victory by an outsider was preferable to a victory by one's bitter opponents. Once again the root of this was religious – Trinity did not admit Catholics.

Perhaps all of this had some effect on my difficulty with the religious instruction. However, the difficulty did not seem insuperable and Bernard and I continued with our engagement. He had a friend whose mother owned a hotel in Dunoon called Hoop House, and in the summer we got digs there free by serving in the hotel. We made friends in Dunoon, including the local blacksmith and his wife, Kathie, who was the daughter of the family that owned the famous Robertson's Shipyards at Sandbank. These were summers of delight and fun. Each evening started about 9 p.m. When we finished our work we went out to the hotels by Loch Eck, the Whistlefield and the Coylet. Although the pubs in those days shut at 9.30, that was only the beginning of the evening, because then the locals moved through into the hotelier's lounge and the ceilidhs began. Bernard also organised for a group of us to go on holiday in Donegal and we toured places of great beauty such as Rossnoulah and Mulluchmore. At night in our modest hotel full of Irish Scots, the singing began. I was particularly fascinated by one of the Irish priests who was on holiday there when he sang the national song, 'The West's Awake'. The words seemed so entirely appropriate, then and now and for Scotland as well as Ireland – 'Alas and long may Erin weep when Connaught lies in slumber deep. / The good creator never planned for slumbering slaves a home so grand.'

When Bernard was in any company everyone enjoyed themselves. To me he was a devoted swain and I was his only girl. Yet it was impossible to ignore the fact that, having had a bad war, he had learned to drink deeply and long. This soon became a problem. He failed medicine and changed to law, but his drinking got worse and worse and eventually I never knew if he would turn up to keep arranged meetings. I began to think the matter was hopeless. One day (I was by this stage working), I returned home to my parents' house and found them waiting to tell me how serious the matter had become. They had discovered that Bernard had opted out of studies completely and had borrowed money from friends and relations. I agreed that I did want out of the engagement and I broke it off, returning my beautiful emerald and diamond engagement ring.

Bernard in time recovered and became very active in Alcoholics Anonymous. He eventually completed a law degree and practised law. He also got married, to Margaret, and we all became good friends. Bernard, Margaret and Stewart and I had many pleasant evenings together.

During the time of breaking my engagement I relied on many kind friends: Sheila and Ewen Bain, Margaret and Alex Cowan, Ena and Jack Millar, Chris and Bill Scott and lots of others, including my brother John, his wife Jessie, my other brother David and his Highland wife, Sarah, and of course my dear sister Jean. Of course word got around that I was free and unattached again and old boyfriends came back onto the scene in significant numbers. But breaking-up with Bernard broke my heart and I decided to be a career woman, for it was a great consolation to find my work so interesting and fulfilling.

My university career had not been entirely plain sailing. I studied hard and got a class prize in history but then I failed the year exam so I could not do honours history and go on to be a teacher. I decided to change course and do a law degree at the same time as my arts degree, and it turned out to be a wise solution, for I loved it. However, it meant completing my MA with one philosophy and one science course, so I took logic, in which I did so well that I almost decided to switch subjects again. Not such a happy experience was had with my chosen science, astronomy, in which I only scraped through due to the kind tutoring of my bother-in-law, Jimmy Forsyth, who had a first-class honours degree in the subject. Even with Jimmy's help I found the whole thing almost impossibly difficult: it seemed to me that I understood the first term's work only in the second term, and the second term's during the third. I never understood the third term's work at all. But Jimmy, who was a genius, was infinitely patient. He would give me an explanation of some part of the course and then hopefully ask, 'Do you understand?'. I would almost always reply, 'No', but nothing daunted him and he would immediately respond with, 'Well, let me try and explain it another way.'

Nonetheless there were compensations even with that subject. The Professor of Astronomy, Professor Smart, was so loved and such a good teacher that students not studying astronomy regularly gate-crashed his class. Regulations of the university decreed that professors should roll-call occasionally, and when Professor Smart did so he always looked puzzled as there were far more people present than those who were listed as his official students. Law lectures were also a delight, particularly those given by Professor Dewar Gibb, who was a great and influential Scottish Nationalist. His political leaning was obvious in his lectures and I of course admired his stance.

Combining an arts degree and a law degree was tough and demanding, but I made it, graduating MA LLB in 1952. Of course to become a solicitor it is necessary to serve a three-year apprenticeship and I had – as was common then – already begun one in 1949, the final year of my arts degree. Time off to study for the necessary university law exams was meant to be built into such apprenticeships, and I was working with the company of Kevin McDowall Kerr through my father's connection with Kevin MacDowall. There I had two good friends who were both called Bill – Bill Hailstone, who was a qualified assistant, and Bill Courtney, who was a fellow apprentice. However we apprentices were suddenly refused the normal week off to study for our exams. Bill Courtney and I took it any way, and were promptly sacked, although technically we could not be dismissed as we were indentured apprentices, not employees, a matter about which the Law Society had to remind our firm. Fortunately, I quickly went on to a new firm, Bannantyne, Kirkwood, France and Co., and the remainder of my apprenticeship with that company was a happy experience. My pay was £1 per week, rising to 30 shillings.

I remember well my first Christmas in my first apprenticeship because of an event that turned out rather better than expected. At Christmas each employee was given an envelope that was meant to enclose a £1 bonus. However, mine only contained ten shillings, which was a great disappointment, as the two Bills and I had intended to pool our money and go to dinner. The plan was further scuppered by being sent by one of the partners to have a deed signed at the Fish Market, just as we were thinking of getting ready to leave the office. I had to do as I was asked and I wearily took the long tram journey to the Fish Market. When I got there the fish merchant who was signing the deed – a Mr Uncles – asked me my name. Learning that I was George Woodburn's daughter he promptly gave me £5 as a Christmas gift and the prospects for an excellent dinner suddenly improved again.

Bannantyne, Kirkwood, France & Co., was a law office straight out of Victorian times. I sat on a high stool and was always called 'Miss Woodburn'. One of the partners was a Mr France, who also sponsored young boys from poor areas of Glasgow to become boxers. Mr France was definitely past his best, however, and some days he used to ask me, 'Miss Woodburn, have I had my lunch today?' He always ate pie and mash standing up in a very old restaurant in Exchange Square called Langs. Another partner, Mr Herbertson, dealt with Sir William Burrell and spent the mornings not meeting clients, but doing the crossword. He was however, very kind and very amusing.

My memories of the years in that company are happy ones and I got an excellent training in trust, executries, wills and conveyancing. I made two very good friendships with two qualified solicitors, Isobel Davidson and Margaret Walker. I have to thank Margaret for my tuition in conveyancing and for my first job as a qualified assistant, but both friendships have survived the years. However, my ambition remained to do court work, and that was not part of the normal activity in Bannantyne, Kirkwood, France & Co., so I knew I would eventually have to seek further experience elsewhere. I carried on for a while with conveyancing though, becoming a qualified assistant in the excellent and happy legal firm of William Murdoch & Son, and taking charge of that subject there. The two partners were Morton Murdoch and Hurll Jackson, both charming and kind. I was their first qualified assistant so I was a sign of their progress as a firm and I remember being asked on my first morning to go to Wolfson's and choose the linoleum for my office. In those days one frequently worked on Saturday mornings, and eventually the two partners would sometimes take the morning off, leaving me in sole charge.

In my time at university and especially in my early years in the legal profession, membership of the SNP invited a lot of ridicule. It was a disadvantage when one looked for an apprenticeship or a job as a qualified assistant, but it didn't seem to worry these two, for which I was very grateful. Thus it was that as I progressed in my legal career I remained a member of the Cathcart Branch of the SNP, attending meetings organised by Unity Miller, the branch secretary, who was later a parliamentary candidate. I also went to SNP functions, and I got a great deal of enjoyment out of meeting other party members, for at that time we seemed rare birds indeed. I did other things for the party too. I was once asked to attend a meeting of the Scottish Trade Union Movement in Glasgow and, as my face would have been unknown, to ask a question about Home Rule. I was called and put my question in the middle of a packed St Andrew's Halls. It caused great embarrassment, which of course was the purpose of it all.

Another thing that came out of my SNP involvement at that time was an invitation by the editor of the *Bulletin*, James Reid, to take on the task of being secretary of the 'Glasgow Buildings Guardian Committee'. This was a group of distinguished Glaswegians trying to stop the destruction of the city's architectural heritage and was chaired by the Principal of the Glasgow School of Art, Percy Bliss. I suppose they thought that a nationalist would obviously be devoted to such a cause, as I was and am still, though so much has been lost in the city.

Those who were in the party worked very hard for the cause. The *Scots Independent*, then and now the only newspaper campaigning for freedom, was delivered house-to-house by a thin fellow called Bob McDougall, who always seemed cold and ill. One winter night, when he came to deliver my copy, I asked him, 'How many more houses do you have to visit?' He told me some preposterous number and I told him that I would do the envelopes, stamp them and post the papers, just to save him the work. In response he looked at me in a rather cunning way and said, 'Just give me the money for the party and I will go on delivering the papers as usual.' Bob McDougall's dedication was not unusual.

Being free and unattached I did other things as well as politics in my spare time. I joined the Juridical Society, a very intellectual legal debating society. I also found out about the Saltire Society and eventually took office in it, meeting the famous Professor Douglas Young, who was an inspiration. I joined the Glasgow Central Soroptimist Club, which met at lunchtime in the Grosvenor Hotel, and I greatly enjoyed meeting professional women in every line of work other than my own. A few of us used to have a pleasant pre-prandial drink from time, including a woman editor of the *Bulletin*, an authoress, the Red Cross Chief of Glasgow and a famous singer. Those were happy days and I became programme convenor of the branch and later its president. I also served on the board of the Queen Margaret Union and was a member of the Glasgow Skiers, going off at weekends whenever there was snow in the mountains. Yet despite all this activity I was still smarting from the end of my engagement to Bernard and still felt unsettled. I began to wonder whether a more dramatic change was needed to snap me out of it.

4

A Husband, a Family and a Career

GIVEN MY STATE of mind at the time, I suppose it was not surprising that I eventually nurtured a desire to change jobs or even towns. I applied for three positions: a legal assistant to McTaggart & Co. in Largs, another legal assistant post for Condie McKenzie and Co. of Perth, and a job as a law lecturer at the Scottish College of Commerce in Glasgow. I was clearly not posh enough for the Perth firm, which was very posh indeed, but I was offered the other two jobs. It was a difficult decision but I felt that I needed a change and I decided to try the new profession of lecturer. I felt it would be an intellectual challenge and it would also keep my mind off my loneliness. In addition I was attracted to the long holidays, which would give me a chance to enjoy European travel, something I wanted to get more experience of.

Law subjects were studied by those seeking to be corporate accountants, to be bankers, to become members of the Chartered Institute of Secretaries, to be teachers of commerce and related subjects and by those who were taking external degrees awarded by London University. Consequently there was a lot of work to be done and I enjoyed it, particularly as it kept me very busy, swotting up new topics and preparing lectures, often late into the night. I have always been happy burning the midnight oil. I also decided to advance my career by studying for the English Bar. This meant removing my name as a member of the Law Society of Scotland, as one could not be registered in two professions. Then I had to be accepted by one of the Inns of Court and I was admitted by Gray's Inn. I got a number of exemptions because of my existing degree and experience, and I set to with a vengeance.

Dining in the Inns of Court at least three times a term was compulsory. Dinner was followed by ceilidhs at which all the legal worthies of the Inn were present. I of course could not resist the singing and soon became much in demand, particularly when introducing the English to the pleasures of Jacobite songs! There were all sorts of people at these dinners and one evening I was astonished to meet an extraordinary character, the Revd John McKechnie, who turned out to be the author of the book, *Gaelic Without Groans*, which he claimed was 'the best seller in the Gaelic field'. As I knew of no other Gaelic books, I was not surprised by this confident assurance.

It was my ambition that with the extra qualification in law which I wanted to gain in England I would then be ready to apply for a lecturer's job in a university law faculty. I also had the same idea of career progress in mind when I first registered to visit the Hague Academy of International Law in 1953. I found excellent digs with a Miss van Droste, a maiden lady of great kindness who told me stories of the impressive daring Dutch Resistance in which her job had been to deliver newspapers. I became thoroughly Dutch, even hiring a bicycle to go everywhere and looking forward to the real Dutch breakfasts – cheese, jams, bread and cookies – that Miss Van Droste made for me every day. She also encouraged me to invite fellow students from the academy to her house, but the first time that I brought a German girl – Gisela Krause– I could see that I had caused an awkward situation. Immediately they started to discuss the war and I had moments of alarm, but eventually they became friends. Gisela was only twenty-two, so she could hardly be held responsible for Hitler or for the occupation, yet such were the sensitivities still that Miss Van Droste said that she had a violent mental reaction whenever she saw a busload of Germans, though, as with Gisela, she did admit this was not the case with individuals.

Every day at the International Academy was a delight. We had a very interesting lecture schedule from world-renowned professors and always had pleasurable days and evenings. Many of us met in a favourite pub and restaurant called 'De Goude Hoft' (The Golden Head). Students were given honorary membership of two exclusive Hague clubs, one overlooking the whole front at Scheveningen. Scheveningen was an interesting place with an interesting name – during the war the Dutch used the name as a test to see if people were German spies, as it was meant to be impossible to pronounce unless one was genuinely Dutch.

I returned to the academy during each of the following two summers. The students were lawyers of all ages from all over the world as well as diplomats from many lands. It was a polyglot gathering and all who took part rejoiced in the company and the experience. Some participants were older than others, and we even had mature serving US judges as fellow learners as well as Japanese, East Germans, Mexicans and Canadians. The academy was one of the great and early international post-war efforts to achieve understanding and co-operation instead of conflict: it was advertised on the notice-boards of law faculties all over the world. And what a wide range of friends I made during those summers in the Hague. One was a Dutch Lawyer, Felice Kalb, who actually spent most of his time as an art dealer. He regularly took me to galleries. On each visit we would look at only a handful of paintings, Felice saying that this was all the mind could absorb at one time. He remained a friend for many years, and when my daughter Anabelle had a scholarship to Amsterdam he gave her excellent hospitality, and he doubtless took her too to look at works of art.

Of course Dr William Howard was unforgettable for a Glasgow University girl. He had earned his doctorate (on the subject of Ethiopia) from a coloured university in the United States, but he was also an arts graduate of Glasgow University. His direct ancestor was the first freed slave in America to get a degree and Glasgow had welcomed him, something his family never forgot. William, his father and his grandfather had all attended Glasgow. Finally I recall a blind girl, Mieps Fonteyn, who had a law degree and spoke at least four languages as well as being a proficient pianist and typist. Her guide dog was called Tostien and regularly lecturers said he was the most intelligent student in the class.

There were also some serious entanglements. I met a very handsome Dutch lawyer called Hans and took such a shine to him that I invited him to Scotland for Christmas and the New Year. Fortunately I quickly found out that we were not at all suited – his view on marriage was that a woman should be in the kitchen and certainly should not follow a career of her own. So it was easy to say to him, 'Tot sienst mijnheer' ('Goodbye, sir'). (It was also easy to say this because the Woodburns did not like him either, not least because he used every towel in the bathroom each time he had a bath.)

At Easter 1954 the Hague students had a reunion which took in Hamburg, Berlin and Bremen. During this time I became friendly with and subsequently very attracted to an ex-Luftwaffe pilot, Albert Schwierman, who was then a lawyer in Hamburg. He was about the same age as my brothers and it was fascinating to hear about the war from his viewpoint. Like my brothers Albert was called up at the very start of the war. He became one of the longest-serving pilots but eventually was badly injured in the leg, ending up in hospital for a year, where he was able to begin to study law. Albert told me that when the war ended every German citizen was made to go and see a film about the extermination of the Jews. Like many others, Albert had thought that this was merely war propaganda, but when it sank in that the Final Solution was indeed something that had happened, he felt a dreadful sense of guilt and horror. I know that I truly could have loved Albert, but I found it impossible even to imagine bringing home a Luftwaffe pilot. I lacked the courage to make a future with him, but the happy memories remain, including that of a ball at the Art Club of Hamburg, overlooking the beautiful Hamburg lake. At the ball I recall asking one of Albert's friends, 'Sind sie ein Künstler?' ('Are you an artist?'), only to have him reply, 'Ich bin ein leben Künstler.' ('I am an artist of life').

Albert organised the whole Easter trip. In Berlin a bus collected us from the airport. We stopped at various hotels as people were allocated accommodation, but Albert seemed to be having problems with the lists. Eventually he said out loud, 'This is terribly difficult. Everyone wants to be in the same hotel as Miss Woodburn.' I blushed. Many years later when I told my husband Stewart about this romance and how I had felt, he urged me to invite Albert to stay with us in Miltonduff. I didn't, but I still have a photograph of him and he was undeniably very attractive.

In Berlin we stayed at the Hotel Geerhus and we were all thrilled to spend an evening with Willy Brandt, who spoke with passion about our duty to build a new Europe. We were also able to travel into East Berlin (this was before the wall was built). When we stood at the Brandenburg Gate, Mieps Fonteyn tried to speak to the Russian guards, but they were not prepared to engage at all and would not answer. From the

Brandenburg Gate all that was visible was a vast area of rubble that stretched as far as the eye could see. Somewhere within it all was the Reichstag. I have never seen anything like it, before or since.

By the time I returned to Holland for the International School in 1955 I could speak fairly fluent Dutch as I had studied it over the winter and discovered that it was very like broad Scots. I was also able to take up old friendships and make new friends and I was beginning to consider doing a one-year degree course in the Hague when, in the autumn of 1955, things changed for ever for I met Stewart Ewing.

After my third visit to the Hague I returned in September 1955 to my lecturing, and my full social life. Shortly after the term began I was hanging up my gown after an evening class in Mr Rae's Room. (Mr Rae was the Head of the Accountancy Department and he encouraged all seven of his staff to use his room as he thought, rightly, that it bound us together as a team.) That particular night there was a stranger there who was also hanging up his gown. He was a new lecturer in accountancy and taxation called Stewart Martin Ewing. Then and there he asked me to go for coffee, but I had a date, so instead he suggested that I met him for coffee the next day. I did, and to my astonishment he took me to an Italian ice-cream shop called The Kensington Ices Palace, not the kind of place I had expected for a first date.

However, we agreed to a further date and this time we went to the Royal Overseas Club, of which he was a member. To my amazement on this, our first evening out, he asked me to marry him, just as Bernard had done on our first real date! I replied as I had replied to Bernard: 'You don't know me!' Yet I was fascinated by Stewart, for he had an amazing positive decisiveness. I soon started to take him very seriously indeed.

Stewart had graduated from Glasgow University with an MA in mathematics and natural philosophy and had then studied to become a chartered accountant. He had put himself through the two courses of study by earning fees from tutoring and by winning his class prizes. This impressed me, for he was obviously someone who would overcome obstacles to achieve what he wanted. I was introduced to Stewart's younger brother Billy and his wife Cathie – school sweethearts – and to his older brother Alex and his lovely French wife Marcelle, and I rapidly felt at home with the Ewings. I also met Stewart's unmarried older sister Margaret, who lived with her father in Dennistoun. Gradually I accepted the inevitable because he was so determined that there was no gainsaying him.

However, when we went to tell Stewart's father we were engaged I was horrified when he demanded angrily, 'What's the hurry?' It was obvious he thought I was pregnant and I was extremely upset, though not as upset as Stewart, who insisted we left immediately, though his poor sister Margaret begged him not to. I was secretly rather proud of Stewart for his reaction, though sad at the sudden nastiness that had spoiled such an important moment.

Admittedly Stewart's father had had a tough life. He was a master plumber with his own business and one of his sons, John, followed in his footsteps. Eventually John emigrated to Australia and ended up as master of works in the Australian Federal Government buildings in Canberra. Stewart's mother, of whom he was very fond, had died just as he finished his MA degree. She had MS and was confined to a wheelchair when Stewart and his brother Billy were young. The stories Stewart told of her made her sound as if she was full of fun and ambition for her six children. All the boys spent Sundays singing in the choir of St Mary's Episcopal Church in Great Western Road. They got breakfast, lunch and tea there, as they were required for all the services. This must have been a great help to a mother in a wheelchair.

My parents were delighted at the prospect of my marriage, though my father could no longer utter his favourite wisecrack, 'This is my beautiful daughter who is on the shelf.' We decided that the wedding should be when college broke up for the summer. I wanted the lot: white dress, bridesmaids, a show of presents and a wedding ceremony in the university chapel. Stewart however had other ideas. He wanted us to get married in the Easter holidays, just as soon as arrangements could be made, and this caused a serious quarrel between us. At the same time Stewart managed to get, through his father's contacts, a flat for us at 33 Camphill Avenue – although it was eighty-eight steps up. It had a wonderful view over Glasgow and at night the city looked like a fairyland. There were two huge front rooms with Rennie Mackintosh wooden fireplaces and there were also two smaller back rooms as well as a bathroom and a kitchen. The quarrel was soon forgotten as I was filled with joy at the prospect of having our own home.

On our wedding day, which was warm and sunny, I wore a beautiful tiered lace dress. We walked across the university after the ceremony to the Queen Margaret Union. The wedding and the aftermath were very jolly and we were surrounded by friends. When Stewart and I departed we took a taxi to our new flat and he carried me over the threshold to the astonishment of the painters and decorators who were working inside.

We had planned an extensive honeymoon which was made possible by the fact that lecturers' salaries were paid in advance for the summer holidays. Suddenly the college decided to change the system and our plans looked impossible. But Bill Gray, a legal friend and later Lord Provost of Glasgow, stepped into the breech and lent us the money. I have always been grateful to him for that kind gesture.

We travelled first to Rome, where we met one of my Hague colleagues, Alberto Fieri, a Roman lawyer. He showed us lots of the city and we also called on another Hague friend, Father Ray Chaput. The college he lived in – the most distinguished and learned in Rome – was beside the Colosseum and we arrived to visit him on Rome's greatest feast day, the feast of St Peter and St Paul. He put us in a small room on our own and each of the many courses in the college's most lavish dinner of the year was served to us separately in what was virtually our own private celebration. We had only a day with Father Ray, but it was full of fascinating sights and stories. Later he came to stay with us in Camphill Avenue and said Mass at the Helpers of the Holy Souls Convent nearby, the place where I had taken my unsuccessful instruction in the Catholic faith.

From Rome we travelled to Florence, where we went to an open-air opera. I particularly remember walking with Stewart on the far side of the Arno and dining in an outdoor restaurant on the hillside, eating pasta and drinking gorgeous red wine. I have always admired the line that goes, 'Give me a beaker of the Deep South with beaded bubbles winking at the brim', and that night it seemed we had such wine. Next we went to Venice and our room was fine – until night-time. We were directly opposite the printing presses of a newspaper that worked through until dawn. The workers merrily waved to us when we looked over in despair – they had a kind of compassion for us, knowing that we had been conned. Nonetheless we walked around that glorious city and visited some of the islands. We went to the Lido by boat and unfortunately I got sunstroke. Everyone on the boat on the way back gave Stewart friendly advice about what he should do for me and he was very kind, giving me lots of lemon juice. Gradually I recovered and I vowed never to allow myself to get sunstroke again; luckily, I never have.

We went on from Venice to Rimini, on the Adriatic coast, where we simply relaxed on the beach for a week. Then it was on to Milan. Switzerland was next, where we visited a small lakeside town called Zug, and we saw rural life as it was at that time. We walked all round Lake Zug before leaving for Heidelberg, where we stayed with another Hague law colleague who was a judge. He and his wife were Jewish and had somehow managed to flee Germany and get to Britain before the war. He worked in the Pioneer Corps and his wife became a German teacher – not an easy job at that time. They returned to Germany after the war and he resumed his position on the bench, but he told us he was not popular in the town as his experiences of the war years were so different from those of his fellow citizens.

On the final leg of our trip we went to the Netherlands and I showed Stewart my old haunts in the Hague. We also visited Amsterdam and Rotterdam. We returned home via England to stay with Nancy and her husband, who was still in the RAF. I remember visiting Oxford and Cambridge, but by that time we were both keen to get back to our lovely new home. My parents had not approved of our lavish holiday and I suspect that others did not either. But I remain eternally grateful that we took this golden opportunity. It was a wonderful start to our marriage and my romantic memories of Rome, of the Vatican, of the Grand Canal and the islands of Venice, of Switzerland and of Germany have stayed with me ever since.

We were abroad again, though, within a year, for at Easter 1957 we went to Paris with my parents. We visited all the sites together, but one day Stewart suggested that we split up and that he and I went off on our own. My father readily agreed and immediately hailed a taxi, telling the driver to go the race course at Longchamps. I suspect he had wanted to go there all along and he came back that evening with considerable winnings, though he had not a word of French! My father had that ability to succeed, by wit and cunning. He demonstrated it again in Paris when, after a visit to Notre Dame, we were looking for a restaurant in which to have lunch. He simply said, 'Let's follow the priests', and we did so, coming in the end to a place in the Rue du Bac which was excellent and which quickly became our favourite spot to eat.

In the summer of 1957 we sailed from Leith to Rotterdam and once more went to the Hague and Amsterdam as well as to Delft and Leiden. Once more I was in touch with old friends. Then Stewart and I went on to Friesland and stayed in a converted boat call The Hotel Schip Alve Meeren (The Ship of Eleven Lakes). We hired a tutor to improve our sailing and we sailed on the lakes of Vriesland, seeing up close the high grasses and the wonderful families of birds which darted between them. But I was beginning to feel less fit than I had been, because I was pregnant, and my first child was due within three months. It was the end of a beautiful first year of marriage. Stewart and I were well suited and we admired each other's achievements. That is always a good foundation for a relationship.

At the very start of our marriage Stewart encouraged me to continue with all my various activities, not least because his time was not his own since he was very preoccupied preparing lectures and doing other things. We worked hard at college during the week, but on Saturdays we usually treated ourselves by going to the Kelvingrove Art Gallery, where we had morning coffee on the balcony adjacent to the tea-room from which we could look up at Glasgow University on the hill. We played tennis at Stewart's club once a week and every week we also went to the Cosmo Cinema, where we saw many famous foreign films. We visited exhibitions and entertained friends. We also saved to buy furniture and each new acquisition was a joy, usually brought from Wolfson's at Charing Cross. We bought our first car, from Stewart's brother, and had another holiday: we went for a week to Montrose, staying in a boarding-house, and every day we toured the surrounding country in our new vehicle.

It was in February 1957 that I discovered I was pregnant. This came as a shock as it was certainly not on our plans to start a family so early. Stewart appeared to be astounded and virtually demanded an explanation! I still admit to being hurt by that, as it was not the story-book romantic development I had envisaged at such a time. Fortunately I was well and not badly affected by the pregnancy. We still went hill-walking a lot and even had weekends in bothies with Bill and Mary Gray. They had no idea I was expecting as I louped over hills and dykes with the best of them.

I decided that I wanted my baby to be born at home. I had heard tales of hospital deliveries which horrified me and which made me determined not to lose control of the matter. I now see that not only was my decision born out of stubbornness, but it was also quite mistaken. I comforted myself at the time with the knowledge that my doctor, Dr Thomson, was very experienced in home births.

On 23 September I went into labour and things quickly started to go very wrong. According to Stewart Dr Thomson turned grey but decided reluctantly to proceed without rushing me to hospital. There was a flu epidemic at the time, so the risks might have been greater. Eventually he had to cut me to get Fergus out, though I remember nothing of that, because I was out for the count with chloroform, which I remember breathing in from a piece of cotton wool. When I came to I had no realisation that I had been in labour, and I thought that the stitches were quite normal. I was lying with my baby son in my arms, which was wonderful, though when Fergus was finally dragged out with forceps he had a slightly dented head. The midwife assured Stewart and me that the effect would fade, which it fortunately did. We had already decided to call our first son Fergus Stewart Ewing. Fergus we chose because it was the name of the first King of Scots, and Stewart because it was both Stewart's mother's surname and my Appin grandmother's name.

One's marriage and first child are momentous events. Life was assuming a very real and earnest face but I was having a very happy time and now had my gorgeous boy as well as a husband to look after. And there was more joy ahead.

I now look back on those years as my 'pre-Hamilton' period, but of course I had no idea that such a life-changing event was looming ahead. I even seemed to accept the fact that I would not be able to continue lecturing, as, typical for the time, it was understood that I would not have a job after becoming pregnant. Indeed I stopped working at the college even before I was required to, because there was an outbreak of measles, which could have been disastrous for my pregnancy. I did however, continue to undertake some extra-mural work, giving a regular series of lectures on famous trials and other subjects, and I also hung up my sign in Camphill

Avenue, very doubtful if any potential clients would climb the eighty-eight steps – but they did and I began to build a legal practice.

So the years passed, and they were happy years – carefree it seems now, and without financial worries. In the Ewing clan boys far outnumber girls; Billy and Cathie had three boys, Alex and Marcelle two boys and – glory be – one girl; and Stewart's brother John in Australia had five boys. I knew that with this genetic inheritance the die was rather strongly loaded against my long-held desire to have a daughter. I even had the name ready – Annabelle – which I chose not only for its lovely sound but also for its Scottish and French historical connection. Mary, Queen of Scots brought an Annabelle with her when she left France to come back home.

In the aristocratic families of Scotland there are many Annabelles, though the spelling has usually been changed to Annabel. But I did not change it for the Annabelle who was born on 20 August 1960, once again at home in 33 Camphill Avenue. This time labour was more painful – I was given less chloroform, I suspect – but it was short, and normal, and I had no stitches. I could have got up and walked immediately after Annabelle was born and I felt so happy to have a daughter at last with dark, curly hair, olive skin and eyes as brown as her father's. As a baby she was as placid as Fergus had been crabbit and she even liked to go to bed and sleep all night. We gave her the middle name Janet after Stewart's mother.

I had been an 'afterthought' and Stewart and I eventually had our own 'afterthought', Terence Colin Woodburn Ewing. Terry, as we called him, was born on 15 June 1964, a joy to all the family, following the death of my mother in April 1964.

My mother developed cancer of the spine and had a very painful and distressing last illness. I used to go and see her in hospital every night and she would plead with me to take her home, though that was completely impossible considering the treatment she was having and the nursing she needed. I would come back in floods of tears and of course I was also pregnant: eventually I was worn out and asked my doctor to give me something to help because I could not sleep at night. He refused, sensibly, saying that nature would take its course. I am now very glad that he was so wise because had he given me something at that time it might have been Thalidomide. My doctor was right. Nature did take its course and after the great distress of my mother's death, Terry's birth was like receiving the gift of a new life for a life that had gone. My father was very pleased to have another child to fuss over and play with. This time I gave birth in St John's Nursing Home, near Charing Cross, rather than at home – I had at least learnt some sense.

Juggling a legal profession with a lot of court cases whilst running a home and looking after three children meant little leisure; but I had devoted help and my legal practice was in my home. On the days that I spent in my office the children could run in and out, though not when I had a client. We had moved to Queen's Drive in 1960, just after Annabelle was born, and this gave the family, and myself, much more space.

We made time to hold children's parties, although I must admit I always found them difficult and a little nerve-racking. I started off with a list of games, only to find after ten minutes or less that they were getting used up fast. There were in the days before bouncy castles and hired magicians – parents had to do the work and try to keep the children entertained.

Stewart and I always tried to keep weekends free from work so that we could take the children on all kinds of excursions. We knew every inch of the Queen's Park and the Rouken Glen and most other such places around the city. We ensured that all three children could swim, and I went swimming with them both to encourage them and to help them appreciate a sport very close to my heart. We even offered them a chance to learn horse-riding, but that was never popular with them. The older two were christened and they attended Sunday school. When it came to Terry I was no longer a regular church-goer and would have felt hypocritical in demanding that he went, so Terry was never christened, a fact that later became of some importance when he married Jacqui, who is a Roman Catholic.

Soon it was time for Fergus to start school at Battlefield Primary, which I had attended too. His birthday was on 23 September and I was anxious that he should not lose an academic year as he might have done had the entry regulations been stuck to rigidly. I had to argue for his admission at the youngest possible age, but I won. As the end of his first term drew near the school told the parents of children in Fergus's class that most of them would have to be held back as they were about to lose a teacher. I appeared to be the only mother prepared to object and I had a considerable battle, but I won again. I knew that if Fergus had had to repeat the baby class he would have been bored. I later had a client whose wife was a teacher at Battlefield, and I was told in confidence that there was much anger expressed by the staff that I alone had thwarted the plan to hold the children back, and that some of them were determined that Fergus would be held back later on, just to spite me. Such petty-mindedness worried me and I began to think that there was a mild vendetta in the school. That was one of the reasons we opted out of state education. We sent Fergus to the private Belmont School on the south side of Glasgow where he was much more challenged academically, but he coped well.

My mother and father lived near us and my mother regularly baby-sat, particularly when I was working in the evenings giving my extra-mural lectures. My father loved playing with the children and taught Fergus to play chess at an early age. All the children adored him and he often sang them to sleep – Annabelle's favourite song was 'Ho-ro My Nut-brown Maiden'. On one occasion when I was putting them to bed and tried to sing it, Annabelle stopped me by saying, 'You can't sing that song, we have to keep it good for grandpa.'

I wish I had kept a diary of all my children's 'bons mots'. I recall sitting in a garden one day during the Hamilton years and Fergus coming over to me to ask, 'Mum are you getting a bit of peace?' He has always shown such great kindness to me, which has lasted a lifetime. One night I was watching with Annabelle the television coverage of a Parliamentary by-election being fought by Dr Robert McIntyre. I had allowed her to stay up because she was interested in politics even at that age. Of course the SNP didn't win, and Annabelle said in an anguished voice: 'Why don't the Scottish vote for the Scottish?'

Stewart and I had a lot of plans for the children and we particularly wanted to ensure that they developed a love of books. This proved not to be difficult as they all quickly became very fond of reading. We also wanted them to get to know their own country: on some weekends we went away to Argyll, to Fife and to Ayrshire. Before Annabelle was born I used to take Fergus touring in the Borders in my open-topped car.

Stewart had always regretted that he could not play any musical instrument, so he was keen that his children should be able to do so. Fergus needed virtually no encouragement, for he quickly asked to learn the piano and made good progress before moving onto the clarinet. When his turn came Terry asked for a fiddle, and whilst he was determined, he was not as good at mastering his instrument. I will always remember the day when I heard nothing but squeaks and discords and asked him what he was doing. He merely said he was 'playing my fiddle walking up and down like Donald Barr' a fine traditional musician and nationalist who very nearly won the Inverness seat in 1974. Terry carried on, though, but he had to give up after he injured his neck at Gordonstoun, as it hurt too much to play. Annabelle took up the cello but, alas, did not persevere.

I continued to be interested in singing and started to take lessons from a fellow Soroptimist, Joan Alexander. I enjoyed the experience but realised that I was what in the Highlands is described as 'ceilidh singer' – best heard in company. None the less I learnt a lot, and in particular much about how to use my voice, and that turned out to be useful later on.

Terry was a bundle of joy, funny, loving and determined. If we had company he never wanted to leave it and he always wanted to clamber into our bed as soon as he was awake. He was a total extrovert and believed the world revolved round him. The same cot had in succession served both Fergus and Annabelle, but it was soon broken by Terry. So lively was he, however, that the replacement did not last any time at all either, and we had to purchase a third one.

It is easier to put pen to paper to describe political turmoils and public events than to tell of a life which flowed on happily and peacefully, interspersed by children, by work, by the odd legal battle and by some fallow but contented years over the kitchen sink. (I did not do too much slaving there or over a hot stove but I did usually make the evening meal which I enjoyed. For the rest I had a lot of help.) Stewart had his own very active life being, by this time, on the board of Strathclyde University. He also was a fitness fanatic and went long-distance running with our dentist, Colin Keith.

As Stewart's subject was taxation, the busiest period of the year was around the time of the budget. Few academics had such a time-sensitive discipline, so Stewart was unusual amongst his colleagues in having to burn the midnight oil so often. But his students found his devotion to his subject very rewarding, and all over Scotland I have met, and continue to meet, ex-pupils of his who always show a huge affection for his memory.

My work prospered too and the Glasgow Bar Association came to play a great part in my daily life. I was the Honorary Secretary and we were crusaders with a cause. That cause included upholding the dignity of court solicitors, ensuring their proper remuneration, establishing a fair legal aid system and securing the appointment of solicitors to the Shrieval Bench. The committee met monthly in my office, and as part of our campaign we often took the Law Society to task, particularly at their AGM when we could muster up to a hundred proxy votes – not a small number by any manner of means. However, we did have 'friends at court' – literally– as some GBA members were also members of the Council of the Law Society. One of our sympathisers on the council was Sir John Boyd. He had once criticised my crisp style of letter-writing to the Law Society's Secretary, R. B. Lawrie, and advised: 'Less of the *fortiter in re* more of the *salvitur in modo.*'

On the night of the GBA dinner dance held to celebrate my victory at Hamilton, I read out a note from Sir John who had been in his last illness during the by-election campaign. Indeed his wife subsequently told me that he had asked her on election night to wake him if I won. Despite his condition he sent me champagne and wrote a note to 'cancel previous instructions'. It said: 'Abandon *salvitur in modo* concentrate on *fortiter in re*'.

As Honorary Secretary of the association I had to arrange many events and functions including study weekends, receptions and dinner dances. They were always impressive events and they attracted a glittering company. An early event which I organised was a wine and sherry reception in the Trades House in Ingram Street in Glasgow. I borrowed manuscripts of interest from the Royal Faculty of Procurators, the Faculty of Advocates, the National Library of Scotland, the Police Museum and the Press in order to add an extra dimension to the evening, which was, I believe, the first ever social gathering where Glasgow court lawyers had the opportunity to mix with sheriffs. One of my favourite exhibits was an editorial from the archives of the *Glasgow Herald*. Published on a quiet Monday in the middle of the nineteenth century it simply said: 'The Princes, Powers and Potentates have behaved well last week and so there is no news.'

The GBA Annual Dinner Dance and cabaret were the social landmarks of the year. I featured on the bill from time to time and my most glorious memory was the dinner dance given in my honour after my victory at Hamilton. Jim Murphy wrote songs which were sung in close harmony. They included one called 'In Good Queen Winnie's Golden Days' and another that went:

> My name is Winnie Ewing
> And I live in slavery
> But I knew what needs doing
> So I joined the SNP
> So I'm off to London in the morn in the morn
> For I'm Scotland's new MP
> And I'm off to heckle Willie Ross
> Till he joins the SNP.

Later, when I had lost Hamilton and was back working in the courts, the same poetic imaginations got to work again, and a new song at the cabaret went:

> Yesterday, life was like a television play
> Now I'm cooking spuds and mince all day
> Why they voted so I don't know, they wouldn't say
> I did nothing wrong but my salary's gone away.

As for politics, I was a Cathcart branch member of the SNP but not very active except with my pocket book. I had no idea what lay ahead and never thought much about a political career: I had a career and it was going well. I did however continue to attend SNP functions and dinners in various places and at these I often heard Robert McIntyre speak, though I was much in awe of him and never approached him. At last I met and spoke to him at a dinner held in Stirling by Bobby and Doris Littlejohn (Bobby was Dr McIntyre's election agent) but I did not know that after that conversation he placed my name on a private list of possible candidates. I might have suspected as much when I was invited to speak in Denny during the General Election in 1966 when he was the candidate. In such campaigns at that time there were usually two public meetings a night, and any invited speaker's job was to keep the audience happy – or at least there – until the candidate arrived. This was my first public political speech and

I was terrified, particularly that I might run out of material. I had secretly decided that if I became desperate I would relapse into a well-rehearsed rant about the iniquities perpetrated by the London government on the Law of Scotland. Fortunately for the lieges of Denny, Dr McIntyre arrived in good time.

During those years, in whatever I did and whatever direction I went in – the Law, societies, the party – Stewart was always urging me on. He was a great encourager. He once said in a remark I quote often, 'I seem to have to push you from behind' and I responded, 'Yes, pushing from the depths of your armchair.' Who knows what would have happened if I hadn't been approached on that summer evening in 1966 by those young men from Hamilton, and if Stewart hadn't encouraged me to think about what I might be able to do if I set my mind to it. Perhaps life would have gone on as it was – and there would have been great pleasure in it. But it was not to be. In November 1967, only eleven short years after marrying Stewart and with three young children at home, I found myself at Westminster and, the Tartan Express having departed, alone and not amongst friends.

5

The Member for Hamilton at Westminster

LOOKING BACK ON my time in the House of Commons as MP for Hamilton I remember a great deal of cruelty and harassment, but there was always a thrill in entering the Commons and a sense of history in the making. I felt hugely privileged to be a part of it all, particularly as it was clearly important to my nation's future.

I had a flavour of what was to come during those years before I even took my seat. Although I won Hamilton on 2 November, I did not take my seat until the 17th, a lapse of a fortnight, which was not uncommon in those days. I had legal work to finish (for I had not really expected to win and had continued to take cases), the rigours of the by-election to recover from and I even took a couple of days away in Orkney and Shetland. There was also the Tartan Express to be arranged. In any case my salary didn't start until I took my oath, so I was certainly not claiming a wage for no work. Nonetheless, during that period, I was attacked even on that score.

But the worst ordeal came at my first Scottish Question Time. I was so worried about taking part in this that I couldn't sleep the night before and I was already waiting outside the door of the chamber when prayers were being said (the same prayer every day, incidentally). Gwynfor Evans had very nobly and kindly agreed to accompany me because he knew from bitter experience what would happen. I was barracked of course, but then Willie Ross, the Secretary of State for Scotland, turned on me when I got my first intervention. With the rudeness and lack of charm for which he was famous he just looked at me and said, 'I thought the Honourable Lady had emigrated.' I was unprepared for such a graceless comment and I was devastated, although since I had appeared in front of some difficult sheriffs in my court days I was able to continue to show a calm and unruffled expression.

However, there was some kindness shown that day too, and from unexpected quarters. After the ordeal I went back to collect my papers from my usual place in the No Lobby. Ted Heath walked by and then stopped. He just said, 'I think Willie Ross was very rude to you, damned rude in fact.'

That first day at Scottish Questions was typical. I was under constant barracking from Scottish Labour benches, but an important plus for me was the scrupulous fairness of the Speaker, Horace King. Sometimes some particularly obnoxious Labour MPs would try and complain about what they thought was favourable treatment being meted out to me, as I was called quite often to speak. Horace King, totally unruffled, would merely say, 'The House knows my attitude is to be fair to minorities.' He also quoted Winston Churchill on at least one occasion, responding to a Labour member with the words, 'A civilisation can be judged by the way it treats minorities.' I certainly was an expert at being in a minority, for there was only me.

Horace King was very hospitable and held regular dinner parties for members and others, to which I was invited from time to time. On one such occasion – it must have been in 1968 when there was a student revolt in France which toppled De Gaulle – Horace said to the company, 'These students do not know what they are fighting for, but at least the SNP know what they fight for. They want to change the constitution but they want to accomplish this by democratic constitutional methods.' It was not an endorsement, but it was a welcome understanding of who we were and what we wanted, and it came from the holder of one of the highest offices in the land. Horace was also very amusing, particularly about the foibles of politics and politicians. At one of his dinner parties he told a funny story about an MP who was desperate to get onto TV but had never been invited. Horace managed to arrange such an invitation from the BBC who rang the member up and said, 'Is payment of £30 okay?' The MP quickly replied, 'Where do I send the cheque?'

Memories of the Hamilton period come into my mind so regularly that I wish I had kept a full diary. So much happened in those first years in the House of Commons and the amusing memories jostle in my mind regularly with much more unpleasant ones. I was interrupted whenever

I spoke, I was regularly insulted and I was even defamed once or twice. Being a lawyer I made sure that I took legal advice when that happened, if only to place on the record the facts, but I never resorted to the courts.

I was even stalked by a Labour MP, though as he is still alive I shall not name him. That memory is not one on which I want to dwell too much in any case, because the whole experience was very frightening. The problem started following a speech I made at the Bannockburn Rally when I said the enemies of Scotland were not the English but 'Scots traitors within the gate'. This infuriated some Labour MPs who took the remark personally, though why they should I don't know, unless they had a guilty conscience. One of them seemed to become unhinged by it. I first noticed the problem in the Select Committee on Scottish Affairs. Wherever I sat this MP sat opposite. If I changed seats, he did so also. Then I noticed that he had started to follow me along corridors, appearing behind me without saying anything. It got so bad that on one occasion I stopped dead in the corridor as an old Tory, Boyd Carpenter, went past and complained to him that this man – pointing behind me – was following me everywhere. He was horrified and told the MP to clear off and not do it again. But later I had to complain again in the library, where he sat staring at me.

Emrys Hughes and Willie Baxter, in whom I confided, told me to complain to the Leader of the House, Fred Peart, as it was becoming very disquieting for me. I spoke to Fred after a vote one night and he was very sympathetic and said he would have a word and make sure it stopped. Fred was also very hospitable and after I had told him about it invited me for a drink in his office behind the Speaker's Chair where he often entertained his staff. I declined as I wanted to go home. Off I set through the dark Chamber and into the Public Lobby to go to the stairs leading to the Members' Entrance, from where I could ring for a taxi. However, as I left the Public Lobby, I saw the door swinging in front of me. I felt afraid but I went on through the door and down the steps, with the sound of my high heels clicking loudly on the stone. As I turned a bend on the stair, there was my stalker right in front of me, looking very sinister indeed. I tried to humour him as I wanted to reach the cloakroom – where there was an attendant–without anything happening. He kept staring and following me, but I made it and breathlessly told the cloakroom attendant what was going on. Then I rushed back up the stairs to Fred Peart's room, which I must have stumbled into, ashen faced. He just looked at me and immediately realised what had happened, saying sympathetically, 'Not again?' The Leader of the House took prompt action and I got a written apology – and, equally importantly, the stalking stopped.

The whole oredeal to which I was subjected wore me down. I completely lost my appetite and went down to eight stones. Even in my wedding photograph – one that shows a very slim-line me – I had been a stone heavier than that. Stewart became quite worried about me and urged me to try and eat something regularly – even if it was only sausage and mash washed down with a glass of champagne (a drink I have always been fond of) I tried to follow his advice, but it was difficult.

I recall on 10 July 1968 – a very lonely birthday for it was my first at Westminster and I felt very distant from my family – eating this unusual fare. Teddy Taylor came past and commented on it. I told him it was my birthday, and to add to my pressures, he wrote a piece in his weekly press column mentioning my curious feast. That of course was a clear breach of privilege, for it had been a private conversation, but he didn't seem to care.

Adding to my problems was the sheer volume of work. I felt, as the sole representative of my party in the House of Commons that I had to be up on everything of importance to Scotland. I never read a book for pleasure during my time as an MP but I did take the opportunity to read about the independence struggles of other nations. I read about Norway and the Netherlands and I read about Israel in a book recommended by Hugh MacDonald, *The Revolt* by Menachem Begin. During the most difficult time at Westminster one phrase from his book jumped out of the page at me. Writing of his attitude towards his country's many foes in its formative days he said, 'When the enemy think there is no retaliation they grow bolder.' I began to mull over that line as I saw my Labour critics getting more and more active in traducing me if I missed even a day or even a single vote, no matter what work I had to do elsewhere and no matter how often they were absent. So I began to plan a retaliation in order to show that I would not just be a victim. I needed to find a chink in their armour, and soon I decided on the one I saw as the 'weakest link' – Norman Buchan.

Norman had opened himself up for the attack by saying in his role as a junior government minister that he would be 'only too happy' to help me with historical research. It was an unpleasant jibe, intended to imply that I was completely wrong about all the issues on which I spoke, particularly about the way in which UK Governments had repeatedly treated Scotland. He repeated the jibe later on in a speech in his constituency. However, I knew that Norman had been the Chairman of the Communist Club when he was at Glasgow University, because my sister was at that time the secretary of the Socialist Club and her fiancé the president. I also knew that he had been a member of CND, but, like many Labour members, had given up on the absolute need for disarmament as soon as he got the prospect of office. His 'history' seemed to be somewhat at odds with his own government's stance and with consistency of principle. So I now had something with which I could fight back. I decided on using the form of an 'open letter' which would spell out some questions for him to answer. I spent a weekend drafting my questions, determined to challenge him and turn the table on him. Oliver Brown helped me with the final polishing of the text, which I sent to the *Daily Express*. The questions did not appear on the day I expected them, nor did they appear the next day. I discovered afterwards that the *Express* had taken legal advice, so concerned were they at the sharpness of my attack. But the next again day they did appear, very prominently, headed 'Challenge'.

My questions were as follows:

1. Is it true that he resigned from the Communist Party because of the Soviet invasion of Hungary? If he did, then he must have acted in support of the principle of the independence of nations. Why does he then deny the same principle in regard to his own country?

2. At one time a prominent member of the CND movement, when did he become convinced of the necessity for nuclear armaments? Was it at the time of his promotion to serve in Government?

3. He says that he is in favour of the right of the Scots to decide their own destiny. How could they, under an omnipotent Parliament controlled by an alien majority?

4. How is it that the Treaty of Utrecht of 1713, which gave Britain the use of Gibraltar, must be maintained in its entirety; whereas the Treaty of Union of six years earlier between England and Scotland could be violated even by his own Government?

5. Why is it that a referendum should be applied to Gibraltar on a matter which is infinitely more complex yet denied to Scotland on the ground that a Scottish referendum would be too complex for the Scots to understand?

Norman was not happy at this approach and he never answered the questions. I did have, and still have, a pang of regret at having indulged in what some might see as a retaliatory bout of character assassination. But I was bitter at what I was having to take and I think it had some effect because the intensity of the attacks on me died down for a while. Perhaps many of my detractors were worried that I was preparing questions for them.

I did feel at times that I was being crucified daily in the Chamber, because I could never experience a period when the attacks and the barbs stopped completely. If for a moment I wasn't on my bench, the shouting would start: 'Where is she?' I was apparently expected to be visible in the Chamber all day long, although few if any other MPs had ever done that. One example which I can remember clearly is of a day on which I was making a speech in the Chamber. I got a card to say that the Glasgow University chaplain who had married Stewart and me was in the gallery but would only be there for a very short time. I went to the Speaker and told him and asked if I might be excused from staying for the speeches immediately after mine, saying however that I would return as quickly as possible. The Speaker was kindness itself and understood that I was not showing any rudeness at all. No sooner had I left the Chamber than I was attacked by the Glasgow Labour member Hugh Brown. He denounced the 'debonair attitude of the Member for Hamilton' who, having just made a speech, had left, freely flounting all rules of politeness and convention.

That sort of thing went on day after day. Yet when I said in a letter to *The Scotsman* – apropos of my supposed absences – that it was a pity that 'many of the members were more often at the bar than the Bar of the House', all hell broke loose. When I arrived back at Westminster on the Monday after the letter had been published the member for another Glasgow seat – Willie Hannan, with whom I had build up a considerable friendship through years of lobbying for the causes of the Glasgow Bar Association – sent me a note to say that he had reported me for breach of privilege. The Speaker ruled that in his opinion a breach might have been committed and consequently the House took the complaint as its first item. I was, as is the practice, invited to speak and then to leave the House. I have the Hansard of the debate in front of me now as I write this. I spoke briefly and apologised. Amongst other things I said this:

> Mr Speaker, if people reading this letter I wrote, and to which reference had been made, read it as impugning the honour of the House of Commons and, in particular, of the Hon. Member for Glasgow, Maryhill (Mr Hannan), I most sincerely regret it because it was not my intention so to do. I may say that the Hon. Member for Maryhill, as an Hon. Member, has lobbied for many years on matters of law reform, and I know him to be a teetotaller. It would be patently absurd for it to be suggested that I would ever impugn his honour in this way – at least, I would hope so.
>
> As I am trying to explain to the House, the motive was self-defence against what seemed to be a double standard in attendance being expected; one for me and one, it seemed, for other Hon. Members. I hasten to assure the House that this was nothing to do with drinking; it was to do with attendance. I wish to explain that so that you will be able to bear it in mind, Mr Speaker, in whatever decision to make.
>
> In the legal profession, to which I belonged before I became a member, this is one of the oldest and most common jokes about being called to the Bar. Lawyers usually take it in jest. If I had stopped to think about it, I would not have put the part in the letter. But I wrote it in the spirit in which I presumed politicians would take it. There was no malice aforethought. I regret very sincerely if I have impugned the honour of the Hon. Member for Maryhill or of the House of Commons.
>
> This letter is one of a chain of many. I would not ask Hon. Members to go back in time to read the whole chain. I felt that I had been the victim of a serious of personal and sometimes vicious attacks. These ranged from implications that I enjoyed free holidays at the taxpayers' expense – including one on a date when I was sitting in the Chamber, when it was then suggested that I was gallivanting in Mull – to being accused of being a well-paid tool of the *Daily Express*, which does not pay me at all.

The Leader of the House then moved that the matter go to committee, but this was opposed by, amongst others, my friend Emrys Hughes. He described the issue as one of 'relative triviality' and he called for tolerance.

But he went on to say something even more important to me and very wise indeed:

> Secondly, and I suggest this is not unimportant, the Hon. Lady is on her own here. She does not have more experienced colleagues to advise and help her about how she should handle a matter of this kind. It is fair to say that she has been the object of a certain campaign of personalised criticism directed against her by certain Hon. Members. [*Hon. Members*: 'Oh.'] Hon. Members, particularly hon. Members from Scotland, can hardly dispute that there has been a personalised tone of attack since she became an Hon. Member. [*Hon. Members*: 'No.'] This is my view. Under the circumstances one would accept that the phrasing of her letter to *The Scotsman* was unwise and indeed perhaps deplorable, but she does not have more experienced colleagues to advise her. We should take that into considera-tion.
>
> Suppose that the Hon. Lady appears at the Bar and says, 'I believe what I said. Do what you damn well like with me.' What will we do then? The House will have elevated the Hon. Lady into a person of supreme national importance. The House will have given the greatest boost to Scottish nationalism that would be possible, and it would probably mean at least 100,000 more votes for Scottish Nationalists.
>
> I ask the House to stop and not go further into this ridiculous business. I am not a Scottish Nationalist. The Hon. Lady has established, I under-stand, about a dozen branches in South Ayrshire, in the hope that I will disappear along with many other Scottish members. I have nothing personally to gain, but I ask the House not to proceed any further with the matter.

Jeremy Thorpe also came in on my side, noting that the House had more important things to do than deal with unwise letters. The Labour member for Govan, John Rankin, moved that the matter be dropped and in the end Willie Hannan withdrew his motion, although I was told – sometimes directly – that many MPs, including Ted Heath, thought my apology inadequate.

While all this was going on I was outside on the terrace on a lovely early summer's day – though not at the bar! As I passed the Members' Lobby on my way out I heard, quietly whispering to me, the friendly voice of one of the Scottish policemen who worked at Westminster; so that only I could hear he said, 'The truth aye hurts!' Emrys came out and joined me on the terrace to tell me what had happened. I had been thinking that I might get three months' suspension, which – in the mood I was in – would have been almost welcome.

The privilege case was much publicised, but even despite Emrys' sensible words, it did not stop the persecution and insults I suffered. Another illustration comes from the adjournment debate I secured in November 1969 on the issue of Scottish statistics. I had worked very hard on this matter and had accumulated a great deal of information which clearly showed that the Government was publishing the wrong figures in deliberately the wrong way in order to try and show that Scotland was a basket case rather than a potentially rich nation. As I read the debate again I realise that it was a precursor to the magnificent work done on the matter of statistics and economics by Alex Salmond, Andrew Wilson and Jim Mather in later years.

The convention is that a member is not normally interrupted during an adjournment debate, but I had not even started speaking when Willie Hamilton shouted out, 'The Hon. Lady is a Tartan Tory.' I was interrupted three more times before I reached the final section of my speech, and then came the most gratuitous intervention of all, from Archie Manuel, the Labour member for Ayrshire Central.

I said in my peroration:

The present Government have produced more statistics than any other but that is the only bouquet that I can throw at the Government Front Bench. I have to throw the bricks because I criticise specifically the basis of the Government's statistics. How can we have economic planning without the basic statistics? To attempt to do so makes no sense to any logical person or politician or economist.

The proposition that the Government are suggesting to the Scottish electors is that they are parasites, when they know that they are paying for everything they get. It is a double insult. It is insulting in itself but it is also insulting –

Mr Manuel: The Hon. Lady is a parasite for drawing her salary and doing nothing.

At this I have to say I lost my temper and I told the Deputy Speaker that I was going to sit down to give the member a chance to apologise, calling his actions 'abusing the time of the House'. I never got an apology but I was allowed to finish my speech before Dick Mabon replied as the Minister of State at the Scottish Office. My sister was in the gallery for the debate and she was horrified at what she saw.

Willie Hamilton was probably the member who was rudest and most offensive. I think I must have been second only to the Queen on his personal hate list. Tam Dalyell, however, ran him a close race in terms of abuse, though, being Tam, he was always a little more gentlemanly. Norman Buchan, Hugh Brown and the aforesaid Archie Manuel were also particularly offensive. Remarks, recorded in Hansard, such as 'The Honourable Lady should be on at the London Palladium', or 'The Honourable Lady should see a psychiatrist' were quite normal. Indeed the Speaker told me in 1970, as the General Election loomed near, that he thought that no one in the history of the House of Commons had been treated the way I had been, day after day and week after week.

Of course the public – and others – noticed all this. How could they fail to when I was under constant attack in letters and articles in the press as well as in the Chamber? It was little wonder that at the end of my time in the House, when the Scottish Lobby gave me an informal lunch, journalists told me that they had watched aghast whilst so many Scottish Labour MPs tried to break my spirit. They were of course afraid of the national movement and the threat it posed to their traditional fiefdoms. They did not want to hear Scotland speaking out, or rather they were the only people they thought had the right to speak for Scotland.

When I ate at the Commons I usually sat on my own in the dining-room at a table for two, beneath the portrait of Benjamin Disraeli. In contrast to most members, the staff were kindness itself and I was usually served by a charming waitress who told me one day that members regularly stole the silver teaspoons, which – like all the cutlery – were embossed with the House of Commons symbol, 'The Traitors' Gate'. In order to have a spoon to use herself she used to take one home each night, though she lived in fear of being found out.

I must admit though that many Liberals were kind to me and often told me I was welcome to join them at one of their tables if they were dining – an invitation I took up from time to time. In addition, despite the attitude of most Scottish Labour MPs, the Tribune Group members from other parts of the UK were kinder and extended me the same welcome. I became friendly with Ann and Russell Kerr, a husband and wife team, and often dined with them.

One evening towards the end of my first period in the House an elderly Tory asked if he could join me at my table. When he had taken his seat, he enquired, 'Whom do you normally dine with?' I replied, gesturing to the painting, 'Benjamin Disraeli.' As we talked about the Labour attacks on me over the preceding few years he commented, 'We Tories didn't attack you.' Perhaps it was unkind of me, but I simply replied by saying, 'No, you just watched.' However, he put my problems in perspective when, towards the end of the meal, he informed me privately that he had just been told that he had only a few months to live. I felt so sad for him that my own worries vanished. That MP was, at that time, in charge of staff relations in the Commons and was due shortly to answer questions in the House, as such MPs had to do from time to time. He asked me to make a favourable comment, if I could. When the time came I rose and asked the Speaker if he could take action about the fact that the 'Complaints Book' – the book in which one was meant to note dissatisfaction with staff in the House – had gone missing. This produced a huge shout of anger from members present, as they thought (and I had wanted them to think) that I had a complaint to make. It got their attention, and then I added that I was sorry that the book was missing because I wanted not to make a complaint, but to note in it my thanks to all the House of Commons staff who in my difficult times had never been anything but unfailingly kind and supportive. It was a genuine sentiment and a comment not only on their humanity but also on that of many of my fellow elected members.

Chief amongst those who were kind and helpful to me in my first years at Westminster was Gwynfor Evans. Indeed I often think that I would not have survived those years had it not been for Gwynfor. Unlike me he wasn't a regular attender in the House. For whatever reasons he didn't suffer the attacks that I got if I even missed a vote. Perhaps it was because there was not such an active press in Wales, but in any case he wasn't a man who would shape his life to the demands of others. When he was present I made a point of being there for Welsh Question Time to give him moral support, and he always did the same for me at Scottish Question Time.

I do, however, remember one occasion when he was cruelly wronged in the House of Commons. There had been some violent activity in Wales – not in any way dangerous to life, simply more of a protest. When Gwynfor got up to speak, one of the nasty English Tories shouted, 'Bring out the bombs!' I immediately rose on a point of order even though Gwynfor tried to pull me down, saying, 'Don't bother, just ignore it.' But I couldn't and *wouldn't* ignore it. I asked the Speaker to rebuke the heckler because it was well known that Gwynfor had been a pacifist during the war.

The Speaker did rebuke the person after my point of order, and when I left the House and was at the taxi rank waiting to go the airport another Tory whom I didn't really know, but who sat behind me on the Opposition Benches, told me that I was quite right to defend my friend. I thought that was really rather nice of him.

Gwynfor's stalwart and magnificent stance always influenced me. I once asked him, 'What should we do if they offer us half a loaf?', meaning a mini-Parliament for Scotland. He said that the SNP would have to vote for it because we could never explain to the people of Scotland why we had turned down any improvement at all in our status. This is an argument I have often used, particularly now that we have a devolved Parliament. It was of particular importance during the Referendum in 1997 when some good nationalists believed that we shouldn't have voted, or that we should have refused what was on offer. Gwynfor's answer completely satisfies me, for although what we have now is only 'half a loaf' and not our heart's desire, it would have been folly to refuse it. And it would also be folly not to attempt to use it in whatever productive and imaginative way we can.

I visited Wales often, not only at Gwynfor's request, but also at others'. I always attacked the Welsh for not having enough women candidates and they got used to that complaint. I remember when I first went to a Plaid Cymru conference I said to the poet Harry Webb, himself a candidate, that I was very struck with the vigour of Plaid Cymru which was full of very articulate young men. Harry replied, 'Yes, that's always been our trouble.'

There was a lot of fun involved in my Welsh connection and I was very proud of it, as I have always regarded Wales as a sister nation with similar aspirations. Their language, of course, is much better nurtured and much more alive than Gaelic, but they have been more militant about it and have also put more resources into it. Yet when I used to say to Gwynfor how much I envied their linguistic heritage, he used to tell me that it was not altogether a blessing. He saw Scotland as a country where support for the SNP could and did come from everywhere and everyone irrespective of language, which was not the case with the nationalists in Wales. He called it 'an inbuilt patriotic response which was not dependent on language'. It was a thought-provoking view.

Another Welshman who was a huge help to me was Emrys Hughes, who became the Father of the House whilst I was there as the member for Hamilton. He represented a Scottish seat – the Labour stronghold of South Ayrshire which Jim Sillars inherited from him. I had been a long-time admirer of his colourful and radical pieces for the paper *The Forward* which my father received by subscription every week. He wrote under some pseudonym which I have now forgotten, but everyone knew his style and tone. I was first introduced to Emrys as I was waiting in trepidation to go into the Chamber for my first Scottish Question Time and I imme-diately told him how I had been inspired by his writing. Emrys looked puzzled, and in his lovely Welsh accent responded by pointing to Gwynfor and saying, 'Funny thing, that's what he said too.' Then he turned to all the waiting Scottish members and intoned loudly, 'Behold, my two illegitimate children!'

Emrys sat in the Chamber in the very front seat in the favoured corner position. He was, of course, a man who always spoke his mind and it became customary for him to give me advice and to counsel me. It became a habit that mid-week we would go together to the tea-room about 5 o'clock. Because he was so popular and so amusing we were often joined by people who liked a bit of banter, and thus it was that, owing to his protection and almost fatherly care, I, a new member with no colleagues to guide me or introduce me, was privileged to have conversations with many of the most interesting and distinguished MPs in the House. Hardly anyone passed Emrys's table without a chat those afternoons, not even a tipsy George Brown, who one day leered at me and said, 'I don't know why you bother with him, Winnie; he can't deliver!' I was angry, but Emrys simply said, 'Forget it, he's drunk as usual.' It took me some time to get accustomed to using first names like this with people I had only seen from afar, or read about in the newspapers. In the Commons first names outside the chamber were de rigeur and eventually I found using them easy.

Emrys was good at tipping me off when opportunities arose for speaking. One day I had my mail in my hand when he found me. There was a morning debate on the floor of the House about removing free school milk from secondary school children and Emrys said, 'Something for you here, I think.' So I went straight in and was called because there weren't many members around. I had had TB and I knew the value of giving children free milk and I wanted to say so.

Emrys was also invaluable in helping me with my speaking style, for of course I had had very little experience. He said to me one day, 'You have a serious fault when speaking in the Chamber. You believe that you are going to persuade your audience. Don't you know that in this place no one ever persuades anyone of anything?'

Emrys' wife was the daughter of Kier Hardie. When she came down to see him they used to sit in the Public Lobby for hours. I once asked them, 'Why are you sitting there?' and he said, 'Well, my wife and I play a game. I know roughly who people are, or I can find out, and my wife likes to guess who they are and what they are doing here.' They were as happy as could be together, playing their little intellectual game – it was a touching sight.

On a Thursday many of of the Scottish MPs travelled by bus to go to the airport for the then evening plane to Glasgow. One evening I was sitting behind Alice Cullen, the 75-year-old member for the Gorbals, and another woman MP. I heard them talking about me. Alice Cullen was saying, 'That one is gey friendly with Emrys Hughes. I see him whistling out of the Chamber at 5 o'clock and off they go together.' I thought this was rather funny and I later told Emrys about it, suggesting that he was losing his reputation by taking me for tea so regularly. 'Lassie, lassie, I lost whatever reputation I had before you were born,' he replied.

When Emrys took very ill I was most concerned and went to see him in hospital in Ayrshire. I was horrified at what I found, for he did not seem to be being treated with the dignity and respect he deserved. When I got back to London I asked to see the Speaker to tell him that I was concerned about Emrys and to ask him to intervene to make sure that he was properly looked after. This was particularly important as by this stage his wife was dead. Horace King immediately undertook to do what he could. Emrys, alas, did not recover and at his funeral Michael Foot gave the oration. I was trembling and Dick Mabon asked it I was all right. I wasn't, because I realised that I had lost not just a very good friend but someone who had become a pillar in my life and one that had held me up amidst a very hostile atmosphere. Michael Foot was right to say of Emrys that he was 'a glass of champagne up on the rest of mankind'.

There were other people whom I came to know and like in the House of Commons, despite the difficulties. Emmanuel Shinwell knew my father, not just because he was a Glasgow businessman, but also from singing. There was some kind of do-it-yourself singing stage near the Trongate, and he reminisced with me about hearing my father there. Very shortly after I was elected for Hamilton he took me for a drink and gave me some advice about speaking in the House which I always followed. He said, 'Speak briefly, make only three points. People here are not intelligent enough to follow more than three points. Then sit down. Let the Speaker believe you when you say you will sit down after a short speech and you will be likely to be called more often.' The advice always worked very well for me.

Late in that Parliament he was given a Press Gallery lunch in recognition of his very long and colourful tenure in the House. This is a rare honour and I was invited to attend by Jack Warden who was the correspondent for *The Glasgow Herald*. When I got there I discovered that not many members had been asked. There was a long line at the door to shake Manny's hand. When he drew level with me, instead of putting my hand out, I said, 'I think I'll just give you a kiss.' But he immediately took three steps back as if horrified, and I was most embarrassed as I thought he didn't want a kiss. But then he said, in front of everyone, 'What good is one kiss to me? It's all or nothing!' Sometime later I was on a Tyne Tees Television programme with Manny and he delighted me and everyone else by telling that story.

There were very few women members in the House in that Parliament, but two of the Tory women were particularly kind to me. I sat on the benches beside one of them – Dame Joan Vickers – who was very elegant and had lightly rinsed blue hair. It was widely rumoured that she had been the mistress of Kemal Atatürk, the founder of modern Turkey, and she certainly had an air of extraordinary beauty and confidence. She used to invite me to parties at her beautiful flat in the West End and she was always very supportive. The other kind Tory was Lady Tweedsmuir, the widow of John Buchan. As soon as I got to Westminster she told me that I should use the Smoking Room as she had done that when she was first there and it had shocked the men. 'There is no place here that should be sacrosanct to males,' she used to say. She and I would sometimes go and have a drink together and she would give me advice. I used to complain that if I was called to speak it was nearly always towards nine o'clock in the evening, but she said that that was the best time because it was the time when the House filled up and, in her words – 'A full House is a fair house. If you have a full House then those people that attack you so much, who are only cowards, won't dare do so under the gaze of all the other members.' Her phrase, 'A full House is a fair House' still rings in my memory.

Alec Douglas Home was also always polite and pleasant. He was a very distinguished member of the House, having been Prime Minister, but he was probably so distinguished that people did not want to bother him by visiting, so I always had far more visitors than he had. In the summer I used to take my visitors down to the terrace to get them a drink and Alec always walked up and down the terrace when he was thinking, or composing a speech. Usually he would sidle over to me and say, 'Oh, you have visitors again Winnie,' and I would ask him if he would like to say hullo to them. Invariably he would say yes and enjoy himself – and my visitors would be very impressed at the chance to meet him.

When I had lost my seat and was back in legal life and living at Queen's Drive, I was watching television one night when Alec was on the news. Terry – who was one of those children who seemed to get himself into all sorts of interesting situations – looked up and said, 'That's a very nice man, he gave me a shilling.' When I was back in the House as the Member for Moray and Nairn, the first time I saw Alec I said to him, 'My son thinks you are a very nice man. You gave him a shilling.' Alec, however, was worried about this: 'I only gave him a shilling?' he asked. Later he came up to me in a very typically Scottish way and returned to the topic. 'I know why I only gave a shilling. It was exactly the price of a coke, so I gave it to him so he could go and buy one. If I had given him any more I would have had to have told his mother.' I laughed out loud, for this was exactly the way my uncles had always treated me when they slipped me a coin or two when I was a child. Alec was one of the nicest men you could meet, probably too gentlemanly for high office even in those days.

There were lots of lesser personalities in the House of Commons, of course. Malcolm K. MacMillan had been the youngest member when he was elected for the Western Isles in 1945, going straight from university into full-time politics. I first became aware of him as a huge tall man, who must have weighed over twenty stones. He was civil, if distant, when we passed each other in the corridors of power. He was very interested in Greece and the restoration of democracy there, and he had other interests too – he owned what was often called a 'Sweetie Shop' in Uddingston. The good folk of the Western Isles thought that his rare presence amongst them was because he was so busy: but in fact when the House of Commons thought he was in the Western Isles, the Western Isles usually thought he was in the House of Commons.

One day as the 1970 election drew near I went up to the Hansard Office to read my speech before publication. This was known as 'correcting' one's speech, as one was allowed to make small alterations, for example to correct grammar. Next to me in the office was Malcolm K., who had just made a speech of record length – over two hours – on the need for a University of the Highlands and Islands. He was just finishing as I entered the Hansard Office and quickly departed. Then the clerk said to me, 'We always know an election is near when we see Mr Macmillan in here.' When Donnie Stewart beat Malcolm in 1970 – our vital but sole victory in that election – he rang me in Queen's Drive after the count. He said in his usual witty style: 'I've toppled him over, the load from the Isles.'

Johnny Dalkeith (later the Duke of Buccleuch) sat in the row in front of me and was always smiling. He was a complete gentleman, and although I did not know him well he always showed me unfailing courtesy, particularly when I was being attacked and insulted by the Labour Party opposite. When I attended my first garden party at Holyrood Palace Johnny appeared wearing the uniform of the Scottish Archers. He asked me, in his stately way, if I would care to converse with the Queen, and of course I readily agreed. In due course Johnny introduced me to the Queen, who was accompanied by Willie Ross, then Secretary of State for Scotland. We had a pleasant chat and the Queen asked me how my three young children reacted to my new life in politics. I replied, 'I like to think the quality of the time I spend with them is more important than the quantity.' She seemed to approve of this sentiment. I then said to her that I was glad to see the Secretary of State beside her because it happened that the day was one when there was Scottish Question Time (which took place only every six weeks) and I observed that I could hardly be attacked for my absence if the Secretary of State was also absent. The Queen's eyes sparkled with interest and, I thought, a little amusement, but Willie Ross looked discomfited. Then the Queen commented that if such was the case then matters seemed to have been rather badly arranged! At this Willie looked even more discomfited. The next day *The Express* carried a photo of the meeting with the headline, 'The Queen Meets Winnie'.

Fitzroy Maclean, then MP for North Ayrshire and Bute also sat in front of me and was endlessly fascinating – a real hero. He seemed pleased that I had been a keen reader of his books, particularly *Eastern Approaches*. Apparently Ian Fleming had modelled James Bond on Fitzroy, though Fitzroy was much more stylish. Years later, when I was the MEP for the Highlands and Islands, I attended the ceremony in which he was given the Freedom of Argyll and I spent a long time with him reminiscing about the old days.

My other connection with Fitzroy was an odd one. I had been active along with my ex-university colleague Leslie Wolfson in trying to help Jews get out of Russian prison camps. There were quite a number of MPs and Members of the House of Lords involved, as well as parliamentary representatives from other European countries. The Jewish Association contacted me through Leslie to ask if I could arrange to meet Fitzroy ahead of a visit he was to make to Russia, where he had once been a diplomat and where he had excellent high-level contacts, as he did in many places. I went with Leslie to Fitzroy's lovely home, Strachur House in Argyll, where he and his wife Veronica (Lord Lovat's sister) also owned an excellent hotel. We gave Fitzroy information about two prisoners and he promised to try to help. Later the two of them were released to Israel via Vienna and Fitzroy I believe was crucial in helping that happen.

Jeremy Thorpe was instantly friendly when I reached Westminster. On virtually my first day he handed me a strange map of the Commons on which there were marked out the sites of the ladies' toilets, which was very useful as they were few and far between. He was always very well dressed and full of fun. In 1975, when I was back as the Member for Moray and Nairn, I was nominated by the Prime Minister to the European Parliament instead of Russell Johnston – a bitter blow to the Liberals. They tried to use every procedure to block the appointment, including keeping the chamber going all night. During that night whenever I passed Jeremy he would say with a grin, 'No hard feelings.' After losing Hamilton he wrote to me to say whenever I was in London I must let him know and we would have dinner. However, I only did so once, and that was after his lovely wife was killed in a motor accident. I went to his beautiful flat near the Commons and met his red-haired son Rufus. Jeremy was devastated by Caroline's death and, referring to his many possessions and his enviable life-style he said to me, 'I would give everything up if I could only have her back.' Like so many of his friends who appreciated his loyalty and charm I was deeply saddened by his subsequent problems.

Those years – 1967 to 1970 – were indeed troubled and busy ones. But they were also absorbing. As I tried to find my feet in the Commons I was confronted with all sorts of issues which, as a one-person party, I had to respond to. Sometimes it was difficult, because I would make a speech without any sure knowledge of what the party was saying at home. But by and large it worked, not least because most of the reporting was about what I was doing and saying at Westminster.

Early on I decided that I must specialise in asking questions so that I would be noticed, and also so that I could find out what was happening because so much was secret then, or not drawn to public attention. Almost without trying I came second in the ranking of numbers of questions asked by MPs – a list that the SNP at Westminster and Holyrood still always tops. In fact Fergus continues to ask more questions in the Scottish Parliament than anyone else – a skill he learnt I suspect from watching me drafting so many. These questions were used mainly to try to extract statistical information about Scotland's economy, industry and public service. I also used questions to highlight issues of importance to Scotland – for example, the desperate need for a minimum wage. When I pressed Barbara Castle on that matter, she said there was doubt as to whether legislation would be the right way to tackle the problem of low pay – a dreadful admission for a Labour minister. I pointed out that we in

Scotland needed legislation as we had some of the most underpaid workers in Europe and I asked why the Labour party had thrown overboard one of its important principles. Somewhat sourly she responded only that she was glad to note my conversion to socialism!

I also used questions to highlight the need to have clarity on whether bills referred to Scots Law. For example, on the bill for the Licensing of Marriages on Unlicensed Premises. I rose to my feet:

> *Mrs Ewing*: On a point of order. I have no opposition to the Bill, sir. It seems to be an excellent one in every respect. But, on a point of clarification, when a private Member introduces a Bill could it not be made clear whether the Bill relates to English or Scots law, because there is no situation under Scots law where the permission of the Archbishop of Canterbury is required to get married?
>
> *Mr Speaker*: Now that the Hon. Member for St Albans (Mr Goodhew) has been given leave to bring in his Bill, it is a matter that the hon. Lady may discuss with him privately – and with the Archbishop of Canterbury, if necessary.

I tried to get a full debate on the situation developing in shipbuilding in Scotland and in particular the crisis that unfolded at Upper Clyde Shipbuilders. More money was urgently needed to keep the yards afloat: I said this in pressing for action:

> The crisis in the shipbuilding industry in the Upper Clyde is affects the livelihood of 14,000 directly and 80,000 families indirectly and the future prosperity of Scotland. The crisis is specific, obviously, in time, manner and place.
>
> We want a solution urgently, because the words 'Clyde-built' are specific and have an important and lasting value in the hearts of men far above the verdict of balance sheets.

I spoke on the Compulsory Registration of Teachers. I was in favour of a register but I was also very sympathetic to teachers who refused to register. Indeed when I was back in legal practice I acted for one teacher all the way to the House of Lords, and I won the case. Teachers who refused to register could be dismissed but those who did refuse were sincere in their belief that they did not need to do so, and should not be forced to.

Having no whips and not being recognised by the Commons as being a 'party', for an official party needs at least two MPs, I got no written notice of business provided in advance to me. I remember during business questions telling the leader of the house, Fred Peart, that

> Although I am just one when I cross the Scottish border, I am, like Cinderella, being magically transformed into a party with all the responsibilities of a party [Laughter]. Some Hon. Members may consider that remark worth sneering at. I am sorry for that because I am describing the real position in which I find myself. I carry the responsibility of representing one-third of the voters of Scotland, as revealed by the last local election results. It is a responsibility which I do my best to discharge, but if I am not to receive notices of business of the House then it is unfair to me and unworthy of the House.

Fred was helpful as ever. He said: 'If I can be Prince Charming, as she says she is Cinderella, I shall do all I can to see that she is well informed.'

There were battles every day. I tried to get a debate on the crisis developing in Criminal Legal Aid but was refused. I raised the issue of English members who attended the Scottish Grand Committee and supported David Steel's request that it should meet in Edinburgh, though eventually I concluded that the committee was ineffective and not much more than a talking shop. I dipped my toe in the emerging oil issues, asking what research was being done into the location and exploitation of oil off the east coast of Scotland. I fought against some of the problems in the Social Work Scotland Bill – in particular on the issue of probation. In education I supported Professor John P. MacIntosh in his powerful plea for egalitarianism and I spoke in the debate on the defence estimates, underlining the need for a nuclear-free Scotland.

I spoke on mining and I spoke on post office services, in the latter debate drawing attention to the situation in Islay and suggesting that the Postmaster General should go to that island and see the real needs of the people and the way they were served by, amongst other people, Ishbel, the woman who ran the telephone exchange. The Postmaster General said he would, though as the Postmaster General at that time was the later infamous John Stonehouse, I suspect that he had other things on his mind!

I suggested if London Transport Debt could be written off so should the Housing Debt in Scotland. I raised the land issue and the way in which land was exploited by landowners with little or no benefit to those who lived on it. And of course I raised constitutional issues, supporting the call for a referendum in Scotland when it was made in 1969 by the Highland Liberal James Davidson.

I even backed a call by one of my arch tormentors to abolish the House of Lords in its present form, arguing that the then proposals for change did not answer the basic problem. On this occasion I was part of the filibuster which destroyed the very flawed proposals from the Wilson government which would have done very little to reform the House of Lords. However, the attitude of Labour remained the same – dismissive and arrogant and reliant only on the rude put-down.

Willie Ross was always graceless in his replies and almost openly offensive. He seemed quite unable to understand the changes that were taking place in Scotland, being prepared only to say 'no' to any new idea and to sneer at any plans for constructive change or national renewal. When a committee was set up to look at the 'regions' of the UK I asked:

> Does the Secretary of State accept that a good beginning point for this Commission is the finishing point of the last Commission – namely, that Scotland is a nation? Is he aware that this house and the United Nations Charter recognise the rights of a nation to self-determination? In the event of the Commission finding against self-government for the next election, will the Secretary of State give an undertaking that he will accept that the verdict of the ballot boxes can overrule that finding?

But Willie of course could not accept something even as simple as this: 'The Hon. Lady has spent a long time proving a point which does not require to be proved – that Scotland is a nation. Scotland as a nation is in a very fruitful partnership, and from my point of view any indication of a change in that will have to be looked at very carefully indeed.'

In addition to my work on Scottish issues – which was constant – I was also keen that the Scottish perspective was put on international matters. There were many to comment on, for example, the invasion of Czechoslovakia by the Russian army and the emerging horrors of the Biafran war. There were important lessons for Scotland in both these tragedies. On Czechoslovakia I said in the Chamber:

> Like Czechoslovakia, Scotland had no wish to be dominated by any other

nation. I believe that Czechoslovakia wishes to control its own affairs in its own way.

I hope that when Scotland takes its place in the United Nations, as I hope it will, it will be able to welcome Czechoslovakia, not as a satellite country but as a self-governing one, choosing its own ideology, in its own way and under its own control. Conversely, if Czechoslovakia gets there before Scotland, I trust that it will welcome us.

The issue of arms for Nigeria gave rise to one of the most passionate controversies during my Hamilton period at Westminster. Uganda and Canada had suggested in the UN a universal ban on the supply of arms, as Nigeria was in the midst of a brutal civil war. I spoke in both debates on the issue – on 12 December 1968 and on 10 July 1969 – and I was lobbied by many churchmen and others in Scotland. They were campaigning for a complete arms embargo and were much in support of what I said and argued at this time. I had discussed the situation with two fellow women MPs – Ann Kerr (Labour) and Joan Vickers (Tory) – and initially we proposed to form an all-woman delegation to meet both sides in the conflict on the ground. My party hugely opposed such a move – Gordon Wilson told me he thought I would be shot, which he said sinisterly would solve a problem for the British Government as well. Stewart was equally and adamantly opposed, so eventually I had to withdraw from participation. Ann Kerr however, pressed ahead on her own, earning my undying respect.

On 12 December 1968 I said this in the Chamber:

I have taken every opportunity to speak to those who have lived in both parts of Nigeria. Former divisional officers in my constituency have told me how much there is to be said for both sides. There are few facts which I have gleaned from the evidence available to me which are an encouragement to believe that the two sides would come together if they were no longer the pawns of the big powers which are supplying arms to both sides.

Perhaps one of the really encouraging things is the meeting at Aburi, at which both sides were prepared, I understand, to consider confederation on a loose basis and entered into an agreement to consider plebiscites for the minorities. Since this had happened after the massacres, is that not the most encouraging thing for us to remember when we wonder whether the two sides can ever get together?

The other argument is that if we did not supply arms, others would. But others have already stopped. Which is more likely – that the other suppliers, Russia and France, will stop supplying arms if we stop or if we continue? If one of the big suppliers stopped, would not the others be glad of the excuse to do the same? Is that not more likely than the strange logic of the argument that, by supplying arms, we are helping anyone to do anything?

The Federal Government rely on British arms, small-arms ammunition and military vehicles for ground fighting. The soldiers naturally have to be trained in the use of these arms and, if we stopped the supply, would there not have to be a delay – before they learned the new techniques of arms supplied by other countries? Would not that be a good moment for the parties to come together?

I also suggest that we should make a declaration that we shall not supply arms, and we should appeal to the other powers to take the same attitude. We should remind Russia that she once fulfilled a magnificent function as arbiter in a dispute between India and Pakistan, a dispute which at one time was thought to be impossible of solution. Could not we similarly appeal to France? This declaration must be made. Whatever these countries do, we should not have blood on our hands.

I submit that the supply of arms if wrong in itself; it is immoral. One cannot supply arms with the one hand and aid with the other.

History and the citizens of this country will judge us unless we do all that we can right now to stop the supply of arms.

James Griffiths, the minister replying to the debate, had stayed in our house in Glasgow when my father was active in the ILP. His speech was one of the most moving I have ever heard, and it was no doubt made more so by the fact that he was, as we knew, terminally ill at the time.

In the second debate on 10 July I condemned the quick kill theory. A local paper in Nigeria, *The Daily Times*, which was an organ of the Federal Government had said this: 'Chief Awolowo declared yesterday that he was totally opposed to relief materials being sent to the Nigerian rebels. "All is fair in war and starvation is one of the weapons of war".'

I quoted it and went on:

I come to the question of relief. I do not wish to exacerbate the situation and we all hope that the two sides will come to the conference table sooner or later. However, the blame seems to be cast in one direction. I am not casting blame. I do not believe that we should talk about 'General Gowon and his gang' any more than we should talk, as one Hon. Gentleman did, of 'Colonel Ojukwu and his gang'. These are not becoming expressions to be used by people who are obviously sincere.

Willie Hamilton claimed that if we were to stop supplying arms now it would be interpreted as support for Biafra. I would propose to look at this more logically than the Hon. Member. If we stopped supplying arms, it might be taken to mean that the Government had recognised that it might be morally wrong to supply them.

After the war ended with huge loss of life there was a total exclusion of the press and countless public executions. This was a very sorry chapter and Britain came out of it with no credit at all.

Voting in the commons was done by filing through lobbies – the 'Yes' lobby or the 'No' lobby, a great difference to the speed and comfort of electronic voting in both the European Parliament and in the Scots Parliament. Nonetheless it had its compensations, particularly the opportunity to talk to other members as we filed through.

When I was MP for Hamilton I always knew exactly what I was voting for because every one of my votes was scrutinised by my opponents and in the press. This was in stark contrast to the voting habits of most MPs who just obeyed their party whips and thus often had no idea what the issue before them was. As time went on some started to consult me because they knew that I would know what the vote was really about and I was often accosted in the lobby. When I eventually cottoned on to the fact that I was being used as an unpaid advisor to half of Scotland's – and Britain's – MPs I started to refuse to explain, telling them to ask their own whips. I remember one evening in particular studying the legislation in front of us which was full of double negatives, and I must have hesitated for a moment before going into the 'No' lobby. A very charming Scottish Tory MP, Sir John Gilmour, came up and took my arm saying, 'That's right, my dear, come along in with the nicer chaps.'

One other thing I regularly noticed in the voting lobbies, and which I have never forgotten, was that Labour MPs were on average one foot shorter than Tory ones. Doubtless the latter enjoyed much more of the roast beef of old England, but behind this strange and seemingly amusing fact there was an eloquent statement about the effects of a difference, often a great difference, in standards of living on young people as they grow up.

As a result of my victory in Hamilton, the government set up a Select Committee on Scottish Affairs, so that they could be seen to be doing something. I was appointed as a member. Our first subject was the economy and finance and I felt that being on the committee looking into such a thing was a bit like sitting a degree exam every week. However, I had tremendous help from Professor David Simpson. He used to call on me every Sunday at home in Glasgow and we would go through the material for the coming week. The meetings were held in public, in various towns and cities throughout Scotland and they were, such was the interest at the time, usually well attended. At the end of our deliberations I felt that I had to lodge a Minority Report and this was virtually written by Professor Simpson.

It was the essential support that I received from David Simpson that led to one of the very rare fallings-out I had with a member of the Commons staff, though happily it was short-lived. Because I had so many visitors I had to deal a lot with the Sergeant-at-Arms who was the normal source of tickets, but on one occasion I needed to be absolutely certain that David Simpson would get in to listen to the Budget, as I knew I would require a detailed briefing as soon as it was over. Television, radio and the press would be pressing me quickly as I was the only nationalist. David had very kindly agreed to come down at his expense, so when it appeared that there was a difficulty about getting him in I went to see the Speaker to explain the problem and he ensured that I got the ticket I needed.

The next day was Budget Day and I was talking, for some reason now forgotten, to Teddy Taylor, the Tory member for Cathcart at that time and actually my own MP, because my home in Queen's Drive was then in the Cathcart constituency. Suddenly the Sergeant-at-Arms barged into our conversation and his face, usually pretty red, was now purple with anger. He tried to interrupt us but I asked him to wait. Teddy was quite amused and said that I must have done something very wrong to offend the Sergeant, Sandy Gordon-Lennox, who was a retired Rear-Admiral and used to getting his own way.

As soon as I had finished talking to Teddy, the Sergeant tackled me. He never spoke in sentences, so he simply blurted out, in a very disagreeable and loud voice, 'Bit hasty . . . above my head . . . Speaker.' I was not prepared to take this. I told him again that I had had a very important need for a ticket and that as he could not guarantee me one I had gone to the Speaker, quite properly. I could not have risked David Simpson paying his fare and then not being there. However, the Sergeant was not finished. Eventually I lost my temper with him and drawing myself up to my full height said to him, 'How dare you speak to me like this. I am a Member of Parliament, and you are nothing but the best paid janitor in Britain.'

At that he nearly exploded with rage and stormed off. However, strangely, from then on we became the best of friends and I was later told that he had taken to dining out on the story of how he had been told that he was nothing but the best paid janitor in Britain. When I returned to the Commons as the Member for Moray and Nairn he took to inviting me to have strawberries and cream on the terrace with him, and I was much teased by my fellow MPs that he was becoming my boyfriend. He also later told me that when he heard that I was to be the candidate in Moray and Nairn he sought out Gordon Campbell, the sitting member and the Secretary of State for Scotland, to tell him, in that inimitable style of his, 'Means business . . . Hard campaigner . . . After your seat . . . Look out.' But, he said, Gordon Campbell didn't listen.

MPs could walk along and watch the Lords' debates at any time but we had to stand at the Bar of the House of Lords and I once sat down in my ignorance of the rule, only to be ticked off. I found the debates in the Lords to be very interesting and the style of many of the speakers was eloquent. The Lords keep their own order and speak according to their own lists. Few MPs seemed then (and I presume now as well) to take this fine opportunity to hear high quality debate. Many members of the Lords used to comment to me on my regular attendance.

Some members of the Lords also befriended me. The first to do so was Lord Saltoun, who had a castle in Banffshire. He claimed that he, not the Duke of Hamilton, was the senior peer in Scotland. He used to come through to invite me to lunch, saying of the Commons: 'This is no place for a lady.' He gave me a tour of the lobbies in the House of Lords which, unlike the Commons, are not 'Yes' or 'No' but 'Content' and 'Not Content', and we went into the Lord's Library where, in a glass case, is the actual Treaty of Union. He had it unlocked so that I could hold it in my hands, but I think the Librarian suffered a moment's anxiety as I held it. The menus in the Lord's Dining Room were also different and a cut above the Commons – I had never eaten pigeon pie in puff pastry before!

Passing the Book of Remembrance of relatives of members of the Lords killed in the war, Lord Saltoun told me that every day he wrote to any remaining member whose son's page was on view: the pages were turned daily. It seemed to me such a caring and respectful gesture from a truly feeling man.

Such kindness was the hallmark of a number of friends I made in the Lords. Johnny Bannerman was given a life peerage after a distinguished career, during which he had tried to win a Commons seat. He was generous and supportive at all times but alas he did not have long enough to make his mark in the Lords. On the way to his funeral my taxi driver said that 'Johnny Bannerman had Scotland written on his heart', and that was true. The funeral was a very moving affair and I was honoured to be asked to sit with the family, whom I had visited when Johnny asked me to his home in Balmaha. A Gaelic choir sung in what was almost an unearthly fashion and everyone was hugely touched as well as quite desolate to be losing such a wonderful individual. Johnny's daughter-in-law, Chrissie, eventually became an SNP candidate and one of our leading Gaelic members.

Another Lord who came to call on me one day was Lord Fenner Brockway. He came to the Commons Lobby and asked for me to come out. When I did he enquired if I was George Woodburn's daughter, and when I said I was he turned to the policeman on duty, and said, 'She once sat on my knee. Do you think she is any the worse for it?' The policeman of course replied immediately, 'Oh no, my Lord, she's certainly none the worse for that!' Fenner then told me that my father had put him up in our home when he had spoken in Glasgow.

These were very busy days and I was also inundated with visitors from all over Scotland, particularly in the summer. It sometime seemed to me as if the whole of Scotland was coming to see me and I became an expert at finding tickets for visitors. The usual request was to the Serjeant-at-Arms – my old adversary – but a request in advance wasn't enough to satisfy the demand, as I already knew. In special cases, such as Prime Minister's Question Time, the highlight of the week, one could ask the Speaker, and once when I was doing so he gave me a tip. He told me to phone the Prime Minister's wife, Mary, because the wife of the PM was always a regular attendee and often had spare seats. I wondered if I could really do that, but he urged me to try, and from then on one of my sources for tickets was Mary Wilson, with whom I became on friendly, if only nodding, terms.

In those years, unlike today, there were only a small number of members who were regulars at Prime Minister's Question Time, though the public always wanted to see it and the galleries were crowded. There were a few of us who always tried to get in, and in order to increase my chance I used to take the question paper and frame anticipated answers, and therefore supplementaries, to all the earliest question in the hope that if I constantly stood up I would be called. There was a kind of recognised quota for questions and if you were a regular attendee you had a greater chance of getting in because the Speaker – and the traditions of the House – are always rather fair in that respect. On one occasion there was a question by Mr Rankin, the Member for Govan, who was a Home Ruler of the old Labour school. He was a kindly man and his question was about Home Rule for Scotland. I had prepared several possible supplementaries, but one by one the Speaker called member after member until I thought the chance was over and all my possible questions had been used up. But then I was called and, in desperation, asked the Prime Minster to explain why he had abandoned the policy as laid down by Home Rulers like the Revd James Barr, who had introduced Bills year after year, as well as Kier Hardie, James Maxton, Tom Johnston and others. The Prime Minister looked up at me, said something which produced a roar and closed his briefing book. I was seated beside Sir Robin Turton, who was at that point the Father of the House. I think he was quite embarrassed that I had chosen to sit next to him, but I had only done so because that was where Gwynfor Evans sat, and in the midst of the tumult I turned to him and asked, 'What are they shouting about? What is happening?' He replied that he would explain to me later, but that the Prime Minister had just paid me a great compliment.

I had no idea what he was talking about and it was only later that I discovered that his answer to me was as follows: 'The Honourable Lady has asked me such a difficult question I will have to do some historical research.' In other words, he couldn't answer and his civil servants hadn't prepared him for it, a fact he had the honesty to admit. For ever after I had a great affection for Harold Wilson, and he always showed his generous nature to me. He had every reason not to be so kind to me. I was bitterly resented by Scottish Labour members because at Hamilton I had over-turned a Labour majority of over 16,000.

One of the reasons for my victory was that the by-election occurred mid-term, and governments always have a tough job mid-term. Through-out Scotland, and particularly in the Hamilton constituency, miners and their families were very angry with the way that they had been treated. During that period miners' widows were being asked to sign a paper to allow the exhumation of their dead husbands so that the Coal Board could prove that they had not died of diseases brought on by the hazards of their occupation. Doctors, the Coal Board thought, had been too generous in putting the cause of death on certificates as 'occupational illness' and were trying to get causes of death rewritten so that their obligations to widows were fewer. Despite these difficulties for his Government and the way my victory had pointed them up, Harold Wilson never seemed to hold my success against me, unlike many of his more junior Labour colleagues. And he was always very civilised if I met him at events or even shared a platform with him, as I did at the celebrations of fifty years of votes for women.

I felt very fortunate to be in the Commons for that anniversary. I was asked to speak at the huge rally because I was the youngest as well as the newest woman member. The great thing at that time was not just to celebrate but to continue to make progress. The meeting was packed with women who had been suffragettes and over the balcony they hung their old banners. I was very, very thrilled by this. They sang the great suffragette hymn, 'The March of the Women', with enormous gusto. I looked around at these brave women and my heart really burst with pride to think of what they had accomplished.

Afterwards there was a reception and I met some of these distinguished ladies, many of whom had been jailed for their beliefs. Those who had been imprisoned wore a little golden representation of a creature that looked like a caterpillar, which differed according to the jail they had been in. I asked one what hers meant and she replied, 'Oh, that means I was in Wormwood Scrubs.' So I went on, 'What did you do?' and she told me that she had shouted out 'Votes for Women' at the Lord Mayor's banquet. Another saintly-looking lady, who was wearing a different badge, had thrown a brick through the window of the Home Office. I was extremely honoured to be in their company.

There were lots of other invitations to attend things in London. Alastair Stewart, London editor of *The Scotsman*, invited me to lunch at the Caledonian Club shortly after I had been elected. Only men could join, though women guests could be invited to lunch. In 1970 he asked me back, and when I was once again signing the visitor's book I idly glanced back to see exactly when I had last been there. It was in November 1967, but I was horrified to see, scrawled across the page in black ink by my name the words 'Not acceptable'. Alastair was horrified too and complained to the committee who were not only embarrassed but quite rightly worried about the defamatory implications of such words, left in the book for all to see. I quickly got an apology in writing, but they also asked if there was anything else they could do? I had noticed that Alastair had been drinking his beer out of a silver tankard belonging to the club, bearing the inscription 'Scotland Forever'. He had told me that there were only a few left, but I asked for one, and I got one. It was a sort of trophy of war!

Another such 'trophy of war' is my London bobby's hat. One Christmas I came into Westminster wearing a silver fox fur hat and a young policemen, as a joke, changed his hat for mine. I liked the feel of his and it fitted me very snugly so I said that it was a fair exchange and that his wife could keep the silver fox and I would keep his helmet! He looked a bit worried, but agreed, but then another MP told me that the young policeman might get into serious trouble for losing his regulation wear. With his hat still on my head I went to see the Head of the House of Commons police and explained. I was allowed to keep the hat and told, 'We always lose one or two to the members at Christmas.' Now I wear it every Ne'erday at the Lossiemouth Golf Club ceilidh.

Some of the things I had to go to were not so straightforward. The great Scots boxer Ken Buchanan was to feature in a boxing match in London and I was asked to speak as a guest of honour. I did not have the wit to insist a car be sent for me (though Gerald Nabarro always advised me to 'Make sure they send a taxi' whenever I said I was doing something) and when I arrived in a new Roman-style white draped dress in the rain the doorman would not let me in. He said very snootily that the event was only for men. My hairstyle and dress were getting progressively ruined but he would not budge until one of my hosts, thinking I was late, came out and rescued me. Ken had asked me to shout out, 'Come on Ken' when he was fighting, and although such behaviour was not allowed, I did it just for him. Fortunately my friendship with Walter McGowan had equipped me with some boxing knowledge and I could follow what was happening.

There was another problem with being met and welcomed, this time at the Caledonian Club's St Andrew's Night Dinner. I had been asked to speak, but when I arrived at the venue there was no one to tell me where to go and what to do. I found it very strange – it was as if they felt they had had to ask me, but that they didn't really want me there. Eventually, after about ten minutes I made it known that if no one came to greet me and to take me to where I was to sit I would just go home. That brought some attention. Most of those in charge seemed to me to be not very interested in Scotland or its future – they were just quite happy to wear their kilts and turn up and have a good evening in a sentimental, nostalgic sort of way. I was irritated by quite a few things that happened that night, so when it came to my speech I said that unless they were on my side, wanting a dignified and free Scotland, then for all their kilts and tartan, they would just end up like dinosaurs, stranded on the shores of time.

These remarks were reported in the London press and they didn't go down too well in some quarters. But at least a nationalist had spoken there from the heart and after the dinner two very strongly supporting couples came back to my flat and made the evening end well.

I was elected Scotswoman of the Year and the dinner was held in London – I felt hugely honoured and was delighted when the Gaelic singer who was to perform turned out to be someone I had heard in Tobermory. That night we ended up singing a duet – 'The Crookit Bawbie'.

There were also Burns suppers galore every year in London. I recall on the night of the prestigious London Burns Club Dinner bumping into Alec Douglas Home. As he was on his way to address a different Burns supper we had a drink and exchanged useful stories. As we were parting he said, almost wistfully, 'I am a Scottish Nationalist in my heart you know, Winnie, but not in my head.' It being Burns night, I quickly replied, 'Alec, you know what Burns would have said to you. It is in his epistle to his brother poet, Davie: "The heirt's Aye, The pairt Aye, That maks us richt or wrang".' He smiled.

I also spoke at one of Foyle's famous literary luncheons. The book being launched was David Frost's *To England with Love*, and in my speech I said I was the most appropriate speaker possible as I had been sent to England with the love of most of Scotland. The audience was very amused at my description of my Commons experience as a party of one, in particular the tale of a kindly old Tory MP from the shires who asked me 'Have you settled down yet?' to which I replied, 'I didn't come here to settle down; I came to settle up.'

Busy as I was – and under constant scrutiny – I also had to find time to travel because I was constantly being asked to do so. One of the happiest and most important trips was the one I made to Ireland. My knowledge of Ireland was drawn from the songs my father sang and this had inspired me to read Irish history. I was full of admiration that Ireland had managed to win free at least most of its territory. I was also aware of the strange history of the settlements imposed on Northern Ireland to undermine the Catholic population. I knew about the history of the walls of Derry and I knew that many of those settled and given land in Northern Ireland were actually Scots. I was also aware that in the struggles for independence which had gone on for hundreds of years, many of these patriots were actually, like the martyr Patrick Pearse, Protestants. My first visit to Ireland was as a member of the Glasgow University swimming team, and whilst I have recounted that story already, I have not said that during my trip I went to the National Gallery to see the portrait of one of my heroes, W.B. Yeats. I always felt liberated in the free state of Ireland.

In 1969 I was invited to appear on the Late, Late Show, which was an enormously popular television programme in Ireland. When I got to the hotel prior to the programme I decided that I should also try and see the President, Éamon De Valera, who was also a hero of mine. I went to the hotel reception desk and said that I would like to ring the President. They behaved as if I was slightly mad, but once they discovered I was a Scottish MP they took me a bit more seriously and they managed to find the phone number of one De Valera's sons, a doctor. He was utterly charming and asked why on earth I had not let them know I was coming. He said that his father was not very well but that he would ask him to phone me if he could.

The hotel receptionist by this time was agog but I went back to my room, and shortly afterwards the phone rang. It was the President's wife and she asked me to go and get a taxi immediately and ask it to take me to the Áras an Uachtaráin (the President's residence), where I would be met at the door. I was so excited that I said to her that I found the whole thing extraordinary, like a fairy tale coming true. I did not know that Mrs De Valera actually wrote fairy tales, but all she responded was, 'In Ireland we specialise in making fairy tales come true'.

When I got to Áras an Uachtaráin I was greeted by a green uniformed soldier and shown into a magnificent stateroom. Then into the room came President De Valera himself. I hadn't realised how blind he was, but he knew where all the furniture was situated and he walked directly across to me. He was a very tall, very proud-looking man. He took my arm and guided me through to his study, where he sat down. His first words to me were, 'Now I am rather blind and I can't see you very well. However, from what I've been told I'm sure that's a great pity.' Charm oozed from his every pore and he carried on with a simple, delightful conversation. He told me that when he became very short-sighted he stopped making public speeches because he could no longer see the faces of his audience.

We had a very long conversation. A photographer appeared and I was photographed with him beside the portrait of Patrick Pearse. I hesitated at first when he asked if I had any objection to being photographed, as it occurred to me that maybe he thought I had told the press. I had told no one and I hastened to assure him of that, but he said, no, it was he who had summoned the photographer. 'I want a photograph with you,' he said. I have that photograph still and it is one of my prized possessions.

Eventually I had to leave to go to the television studio. On the programme was also a Breton nationalist whom later, when I was an MEP, I had to help get out of a Breton jail. He was called Jan Fuere and at that time he had taken refuge in Ireland. Before I was due on I waited to be told what the format of the programme was, something that always happened in Scotland and England. The production assistant kept re-assuring me, but then suddenly a door opened and we were shown on to the set. I immediately realised that we were on live and that I had been given no chance to prepare myself or to get an idea of what the programme would be like. It was soon obvious that the whole thing was a set-up. There were people planted in the audience with questions to make me look foolish, and although I tried to grin and bear it for a while, eventually I simply said that I hadn't come all the way to Ireland in order to keep quiet, so I intended to make the short speech I had prepared. And I made it plain to the host, Gay Byrne, that if I wasn't allowed to do so, I would just walk off.

At the end of the programme there was a drinks reception. Lots of Scots in Dublin had heard I would be there and had turned up to the studio where they joined the crew and guests. Fortified by their presence I expressed my anger to the producer about how I had been misled and told him that I didn't think they had acted fairly. He was not very apologetic but said he was sorry I thought I had wasted my time coming across. 'Oh no,' I said, 'I didn't waste my time coming to Ireland because I've had a very pleasant afternoon with President De Valera,' at which point his face fell a mile. It turned out that De Valera was a sort of honorary president of the broadcasting corporation, RTE.

The next day I went to the airport to catch my plane to Glasgow, which was due to leave about mid morning. No sooner had I got there than I heard a message on the tannoy system, 'Would Mrs Winifred Ewing please pick up the nearest green telephone?' I did so and immediately I was told to wait until I had been met at the phone by two soldiers, who arrived very promptly. I was shown to a private room where there was a phone call waiting for me. It was President De Valera himself. He told me that he didn't want me to leave Ireland thinking that the television programme was typical of the way that the people of Ireland regarded me. 'I was very angry about the way you were treated and I have made a complaint about it,' he said. I was astounded that the President of Ireland had bothered to have me found at an airport in order to apologise about the actions of a fairly irrelevant and very rude political commentator. I still think of it and of his huge kindness and greatness.

A very different but equally remarkable man was Compton McKenzie. I first met him at the annual show of the Royal Scottish Academy when he was ninety. We sat together for a while and he said to me, 'I have long believed I would never live to see a Scottish Parliament but, looking at you, madam, I pledge myself I will live to put both my feet inside it.' Alas, he didn't.

Compton never managed to come to see me at Westminster, but so many others did. On the first occasion when I had a party of visitors arrive for a tour of the Commons a friendly policemen, seeing my inexperience, advised me to follow any group escorted by Jimmy Dempsey, the Labour MP for Airdrie and Coatbridge. Jimmy always welcomed any addition to his group as he was an expert guide and had a wonderful fund of stories, many of which, in time, I borrowed.

Visitors dropped by the Commons for all sorts of reasons, but one of the most memorable and touching of them was our only SNP councillor in Aberdeen at that time, a true merchant of that city, well-built with a fine shock of white curly hair and known as 'Curly' MacDonald. One dark and cold winter evening a green card was handed to me bearing his name. I was delighted to welcome him and I asked what had brought him to London at that particular time. He replied in a way that surprised but delighted me. He said, 'I feel so alone in the town council as a member of a party of one, holding the balance of power. Every vote is a subject of dispute and argument. Suddenly I thought of you all alone too and on impulse I just decided to come to see you.'

They came of all ages and all types. Charlotte, Lt. Col. Muriel Gibson's mother, came to stay with me and accompanied me to many events, including my address to the Royal Society of Physicians. I recall phoning to ask if I could bring a young friend – Charlotte was over eighty but she was always a great success at social events. I had a lovely flat in Weymouth Street and put up a lot of visitors there over the years. A young Margo Macdonald often came to stay and enjoyed coming with me to a Press Lobby lunch amongst many other events. She was always very political and desperate to be involved. A regular visitor was Jock Hay, the Chief of Clan Hay, who lived in Dalgety Castle. He had shepherded people to the poll in Hamilton in the pouring rain, driving his battered Landrover. He stood 6ft 7in tall and always wore a very disreputable kilt, though he spoke very loudly in a cut-glass Old Etonian accent. The word 'eccentric' was made to describe him. I used to ask him if he would like to listen to a debate, but he would always reply, 'No thanks, I only came for a drink.' The House of Commons measures were small, so the first time I ordered him a double. But then I looked at it and at Jock and decided to order a quadruple instead. He took it in one slug and the barman was very impressed.

James Lees, a very distinguished and long committed Nationalist, came on a lovely summer's day and heard me speak. Then I entertained him on the terrace. He paid a memorable compliment to my work and expressed concern at my plight and for my health. Gravely he said that, despite it all, the hand of God was upon us. Other senior Nationalist figures came, including Billy Wolfe, who was assiduous in advising and supporting me and in offering comforting reassurance when I needed it! Billy Wolfe is a remarkable Nationalist and I was glad to have his help, though our relationship was at times somewhat uneasy. He was, for example, a strong opponent of private education and when I sent Fergus to Loretto he wrote me a most critical letter which moved me to tears. I phoned Dr McIntyre who was comforting as ever, saying that 'This can be a terrible party which takes everything and gives nothing'. A strong cultural Nationalist, he realised that culture alone would not propel Scotland to independence, and being a 'joiner' of things – he was active in the Scout Movement and the Saltire Society – he joined the SNP in 1959 and became Parliamentary candidate for West Lothian, which he almost won on a number of occasions. His election address in his first context is worth quoting, for it sums up a philosophy of Nationalism that I subscribe to. In it he said:

> The reasons why William Wolfe wants self-government for Scotland are quite unexceptionable. He wants self-government because only with it will he see the sort of Scotland he wants. Which is one 'where the population will be able to stay and work in Scotland if it wants to and a Scotland which is more democratic'. This is not a criticism of the Scot, though. 'The outlook of the Scot is naturally a democratic one – self-government is more the key to unlock the secret recesses of the people's democratic outlook.' And the sort of Scotland that William Wolfe wants is one to which no one could have any objection. No dear old Lallans, no kilted soldiers at the Border, no retreat from the twentieth-century world. William Wolfe's political criterion is a simple easily remembered one. What is good for Scotland is a good yardstick to go by.

Very welcome too were the actors and artists with Scotland at heart. Sean Connery came, as did Johnnie Beattie and his wife several times. Chic Murray, Albert Finney and Iain Robertson, the fine Scottish actor and his lovely wife Gudrun Ure, were also my guests, amongst many others.

Afterwards Albert Finney, who had sat in on a debate in which I had spoken, remarked that my job was similar to his, but that I had the disadvantage of having to write my own scripts! Iain and Gudrun lived in London and gave me a standing invitation when the house rose after 10.30 p.m., which when I took it up was always fun.

The Gaelic community in London was particulary welcoming and it included a very young Anne Lorne Gillies and William Kerroher, who worked for the Foreign Office but who had been editor of the *Stornoway Gazette*, leaving the job of being a leader writer on the *Glasgow Herald* to do so. He had a Gaelic-speaking grandfather and that inspired him to master the language, which he did superbly, going on to be a very distinguished Gaelic radio broadcaster. I also received a regular stream of supportive visits from friends from the Glasgow Bar Association: John Boyle, Brian Hughes and many others including the redoubtable Keith Bovey.

Well do I remember a Monday when Keith dropped in. I was due to give an address to the Monday Club, of all things – for it is the really right-wing political association in the Palace of Westminster. After that (I do not recall what I said) he came on with me to the Connolly Association in the constituency of my good friend Lena Jaeger, where I was also due to speak. I shared a platform with Lena, Claud Cockburn (a descendent of the famous Edinburgh judge, Lord Cockburn – and at that time the editor of a famous political magazine *The Week*). Completing this line-up was the legendary Irish nationalist firebrand and beauty, celebrated by Yeats, Maud Gonne, who was at least ninety, and who, when her turn came to speak, threw away the microphone. 'Do I need this?' she shouted in her ringing voice, and they all roared at the back, 'No!'

Keith, a lawyer and a nationalist of great intellect, passionately interested in everyday life, absolutely loved the contrast between the two meetings. After the second we all repaired to a fine London hostelry. At one point I asked Maude Gonne, 'What was it like to be in jail?' She put her arm round me and said, 'My dear, you won't find it too bad.' She had obviously taken one look at me and decided that was where I was destined to go, with a kind of nationalist inevitability. I asked Maud about Countess Markievitz, the first elected woman MP (although she never took her seat). She related to me the wonderful story of how she and the countess had rolled up to the Members' Entrance, just in order to see her brass name-plate, the story I had been told by the House of Commons cloak-room attendant on my very first day.

After this splendid evening I saw Keith off at Euston on the sleeper. I was worried about the effect my enforced absences at Westminster were having on my family – incredible as it seems now, as a working mother in the public eye I regularly received anonymous letters from women attacking me for child neglect – for I asked him as an old dear friend whom I could trust to tell truth if he thought my children were suffering because of the present situation. I was taken aback by the vehemence of his response: 'Never – ever – say that to anyone.' I suddenly realised that some mutual friend at home must be criticising me on this front, and although I begged him to tell me who it was, he would not.

Perhaps his silence was best. I was always worried about the children. Fergus was bullied at school and after a lot of thought Stewart and I decided to take him away from his current school and send him to a boarding school. We had no knowledge of boarding schools as we had never thought of the possibility before so I wrote to all the Scottish boarding schools asking them if they could meet two conditions which were, as far as I was concerned, non-negotiable. There had to be no compulsory membership of a military corps of any kind and there must be no beating of boys by boys. Only two schools claimed to be able to fit these requirements – one was Loretto and the other was Gordonstoun, where my younger son eventually went, not least because it was only three miles from my wee cottage in Lossiemouth.

We applied to Loretto to find out if there were any musical scholarships, which there were. Even better, Fergus was successful in wining one and this helped with the payment of the fees. It turned out to be a suitable school for Fergus because he was very academic and he could work on his own: he didn't need to be hounded to work. He was also always very musical and the school allowed him to try a number of different instruments. He learnt to play the organ and, to some extent at least, the saxophone, and he achieved Grade Eight in both the piano and clarinet. For these reasons Loretto was the right place and I was glad that we had made the change.

The relentless pressure of publicity, though, and the attacks, were really pretty terrible at this time. It affected everything, and at times I felt that we lived in a glass bowl. Years later I used to often ask the children anxiously whether they had suffered and whether these years affected them adversely. They all replied that it was the only life they knew. They had no other experience with which to compare it, and I like to think they had a certain degree of pride in what I was doing, and quite a lot of interest too.

Of course there were compensations. I remember Fergus telling me that on one occasion at Loretto he was day-dreaming in a poetry class. He could hear that there was some very broad Scots poem being read and the teacher, realising that he was paying no attention and hoping to catch him out, said, 'Ewing will know who wrote that.' Fergus, put on the spot, didn't think it was Burns, so made a wild guess and said, 'Hugh MacDairmid.' The teacher was absolutely astonished, and replied, 'I suppose you'll know Hugh McDiarmid.' 'Yes,' came the reply, 'He's a friend of my mother's.'

My most important visitors were Stewart and the children. They came in the first year for the whole of July and Stewart's first visit was to Hamley's Toy Shop, where he kitted out Terry in a London policeman's outfit, complete with rubber baton. He had the freedom of the Palace and the policemen pretended he was one of them and gave him tasks. On one occasion they told him that the Strangers' Bar on the terrace was for members only, with an absolute maximum of three guests each. Accordingly he stationed himself at the door of the bar and would demand of each and every person who tried to enter, 'Are you a member?' and then rigorously count the guests. Gwyneth Dunwoody, who was always a good friend to me, joyously recounted the tale of being one of Terry's victims. Terry's uniform made him bold and invulnerable, for he was looked after by the real policemen. In his wanderings he once invaded the office of Harold Wilson. Wilson's PPS (Private Parliamentary Secretary) was an elderly Welsh MP heavy of build and fierce of manner. Stewart, Annabelle and Fergus and I were on the terrace when this MP – breathless and hassled – came rushing out carrying a large camera, 'Where is the small policeman?' he demanded of us 'Harold wants his photo.' We owned up and Terry was found and sent to the Prime Minister. Unfortunately Terry only remembers Harold as 'a boring old man at a desk'!

My life at Westminster for those years was incredibly full and rich, though also at times incredibly hard. But of course it was only one part of my life: for there was the Hamilton part that was equally important, and the part that demanded my presence in almost every area of Scotland.

6

The Member for Hamilton in Scotland

WHEREAS IN THE Commons during the Hamilton years I some-times felt like a pariah, in Scotland I was a VIP and I confess to having enjoyed it. The joys and the good wishes and the love made up to some extent for the rough side I was suffering south of the border. There were friends and smiling faces all around, and if snide remarks were being made, even in my own party, then I rarely if ever heard them. The most important support I had was that of friends. Hugh MacDonald, a nationalist of long standing and huge influence in the party, and his wife Agnes had a ceilidh house in Busby called Garaidh Gualach, and every Saturday any visitor was given a superb welcome. There was plenty of food and drink and an equal abundance of singing and poetry. I found it a huge help to know that on Saturday evenings, no matter what had happened during the week, I could go there and be amongst friends in absolute security. However, it was not Stewart's choice of scene so I went on my own quite often. There were many other such friends who gave so much to help me: in particular I remember that every New Year's Day George and Louise Leslie held open house in their top flat in Pollokshaws, the place where I also first heard 'Flower of Scotland', sung to me one year when I arrived by the whole company!

Then there were the great days of the annual celebrations of the Battle of Bannockburn and of Wallace Day at Elderslie. These are, alas, much shrunk in importance and turnout now but in the 1960s and '70s everybody went and they became huge commemorations. After the Bannockburn march and rally there was always a ceilidh at Robert McIntyre's house in Stirling.

At Bannockburn I made speeches year after year until eventually I had problems finding themes that I hadn't used before. One year at Elderslie I spoke about a film that had just come out – *Zulu* – and used the poignant words that the scriptwriters put into the mouth of a young Welsh soldier. Watching the hoards of Zulu warriors coming towards the fort he turned to an old recruit and asked, 'Why does it have to be us?' The answer of course was, 'Because we're here, lad, because we're here.' With a burning sense of impatience I asked why so few of our fellow Scots fought Scotland's cause and I called on all Scots to realise that such a fight was necessary 'Because we're here'.

Life as the MP for Hamilton was divided into two compartments – life at Westminster during the week and life in Scotland at weekends. So compartmentalised did I feel I had to keep them that I rarely phoned Stewart from London. I could not bear to hear of any additional worries or problems to add to the ones I was experiencing, and it was sometimes upsetting for him. I usually arrived back from London on Thursday, and I tried to make that night a family night. Sometimes on Thursday evenings Terry was allowed to wait up for my return, and more than once he said, 'Where you been and why you went?' I felt so guilty and neglectful. Friday was given over to constituency work and mounds of paper as well as visits and surgeries. Yet at the weekends I also had to continue to try and help my legal practice, for I had employees and I was determined to keep something running to get back to if I needed it.

When I was elected I had been invited to write a weekly article by both the *Scottish Daily Express* and the *Scottish Daily Record*. I couldn't decide which to favour, so I took the party's advice and Arthur Donaldson strongly urged the *Record*, as it was a Labour paper and we had to get Labour votes. I accepted that advice and took the *Record*'s offer, which was for six months, later extended to a year. I was a lawyer, not a journalist and certainly not a tabloid journalist. I couldn't write in the style they needed so Michael Grieve, a nationalist and one-time office-bearer of the party who was a *Record* journalist came to my home on Sunday evenings to help. I always had a draft ready and he brought to it some more ideas and the proper style. It would have been impossible without him.

Sometimes Michael brought his father with him and that was thrilling, for his father was Hugh MacDiarmid. I was delighted that the children had the chance to meet such an immensely distinguished and important Scottish writer. The first time, when Michael and I had finished working, we returned to the sitting-room to find to my amazement this famous poet with three children either on his knee or draped around his seat. I said to him I was very surprised at the sight, because he had a reputation for being crusty and difficult to get on with, yet there were my children hanging not just on his very word, but actually on him. He simply said, with a smile, 'Children are much more interesting than adults!'

For my constituency work I was tremendously fortunate in having one of my dearest friends from school days, Margaret Cowan, working as my parliamentary assistant. When I returned home at weekends there was Margaret's envelope ready for me with a list of engagements on the outside and inside the papers that detailed all the facts and background to the things I had to do. Margaret always bolstered up my confidence and helped me to keep going: she accompanied me to everything. Whilst I was the MP for Hamilton she was my essential bridge to constituents and activists alike and she became loved and respected by all, applying her great reserves of skill, tact, diplomacy and caring concern whenever they were necessary. In one of life's full circles, her daughter Dawn, who is my much loved god-daughter, now performs the same function for my own daughter in her work as MP for Perth.

I held regular surgeries throughout the constituency from Blantyre to Larkhall and Margaret had a superb record of every date, every meeting and every constituent. The main problem in all this was that so many issues related to housing, which was entirely a local authority matter. When I raised issues with the totally Labour dominated and controlled council – which was very anti-SNP – I was never accorded the normal assistance and courtesy that a Member of Parliament has a right to expect; no doubt this was deliberate so that my constituents would come to believe that I, being a nationalist, was unable to help them. But being a lawyer was useful and I was able to assist many people. Margaret and I always tried our best.

Margaret's husband, Alex Cowan, was a former professional footballer. He helped too and took over the polling-day organisation for the 1970 election, performing a splendid job. It was largely due to his expertise that the results were so good, even though I lost.

Between my victory in November 1967 and the defeat of 1970 I knocked on thousands of doors, visited anyone who asked to see me, and some who didn't, and generally tried to make myself well known and indispensable. Part of the that task was to be seen to be keen to host visits to the House of Commons when constituents or constituency groups were coming to London. On one occasion a group from the School for the Deaf in Hamilton paid a visit. They toured the Houses of Parliament and their greatest fascination was to find loudspeakers on the back of all the members' benches. As I took them round the House, Enoch Powell passed. The teacher who both 'signed' and spoke clearly enough for lip-readers said, 'That's Enoch Powell. What is he famous for?' One girl who had never heard a sound in her life at once replied, 'He does not like black people.' Years later when I was an MSP, I was asked to address the Deaf Association. I told this story only to find that the very teacher who had signed the words was in the audience that day!

Despite the support of groups such as this, the animosity of the council towards me and their desire to stymie me at every turn became more and more obvious to my constituents and to others. I was at first invited to events by the council, as MPs are, because the Provost was a lovely independent man, a chemist in the town, called Robertson. Unfortunately he was defeated at the next set of elections, partly because of SNP intervention in his seat, and from then on I received no invitations and no co-operation, in fact quite the reverse.

The most notorious example concerned the opening of the new Marks and Spencer's store in Hamilton. I was invited of course by Marks and Spencer itself but when I got there Marcus Seif, the legendary Chairman of the firm, told me that the new Provost had responded to his invitation by personally informing Marcus that if I was going, he wasn't, and neither would any other councillor. Marcus Seif had simply told him, 'Well, she is coming; so if you don't want to come, Mrs Ewing will open Marks and Spencer's in Hamilton.' Of course they came.

I did go to many non-council functions in Hamilton, of course. In addition to the fêtes and galas I addressed rotary clubs and townswomen's guilds and I went to the Saints and Sinners Races at Hamilton racecourse, which I enjoyed very much. I went with David Hill, a teacher who was a party supporter and who always enjoyed a flutter. I opted to be a Sinner of course, as did most people, and I wore the red carnation. I also had a good regular association with the local press and The *Hamilton Advertiser* was always very reasonable towards me. I was also invited to attend other special events, such as a huge dinner held in Hamilton to welcome Round Table members from many other areas. I was at the top table between my long-time supporter, the World Boxing Champion Walter McGowan and my predecessor as MP, the warm hearted and always courteous Tom Fraser, who had become Chair of the North of Scotland Hydro Board. He never bore me any animosity at all, though Labour had partially blamed him for what had happened at the Hamilton by-election.

Tom told me a fascinating story about the opening of the Hamilton Museum the day after my Hamilton victory. Complacently expecting just another Labour win, they had already invited my Labour opponent Alex Wilson, a trade union official, to perform the opening ceremony. Tom said that the whole thing was like a funeral.

At the Round Table event I had chosen to wear a silver sheath dress. I was the only woman present and I entered to wolf whistles from a company neither terribly youthful nor terribly sober! I immediately realised that the speech I had prepared was going to be of no use, so I scrapped it and spoke impromptu. I started off by expressing my delight in having so many men all to myself and followed that up by remarking that the last time I had seen Walter McGowan he had been in bed. This provoked great hilarity, even though it had, of course, been when I visited him in hospital!

There were others who were supportive and I found friends aplenty amongst the Showmen's Guild. The Scottish Showmen, who have a long history, jealously guarded their separate status and were therefore very sympathetic to Scotland's cause. Each year they held a lavish lunch in London at which speeches were made extolling their Scottishness. It was a lunch to which I was always invited and always loved to go. One famous member of the guild was a Mr Cadona, whose family still run the rides at many of Scotlands 'shows' during the summer. I made an annual visit to the circus and shows at the Kelvin Hall in Glasgow to meet this supporter who was the chief showman. He once took Terry onto the scenic railway with him. The whole hall stopped and stared because they had never seen Mr Cadona go on one of his own rides, but Terry was unfazed – he loved it so much that when it stopped he merely asked Mr Cadona, 'Can we go on that again please?'

Despite the fact that there was so much to do in London and in Hamilton, I also had a duty to build support for the party throughout the country and it was a duty I welcomed, though the touring I had to undertake was very tiring. I spoke at countless Burns suppers, including that arranged annually by the Greenock Burns Club, which claims to be the mother Burns club for the whole world. I seemed never to be off television or the radio and in 1968 I took part in a debate at Christmas time on a television programme called 'The Year of the SNP', which truly reflected the progress which we had begun to make, including at local government level. I was invited to address the various Scottish universities, and whilst they were always challenging engagements, the real ordeal was speaking at my own Alma Mater. As a student I had often seen how speakers could be treated and I was very nervous.

The meeting was in the Men's Union and the gallery was full. Beforehand I was taken for a meal (I think it was a sort of fish-and-chip tea) and I noticed that my hosts from the Glasgow University Student Nationalist Association (GUSNA) could hardly eat their food because of their trepidation about what might follow. However, as I recalled once seeing Jo Grimond lowered on a trap-door just by the microphones, I too was fearful. When the meeting started I carefully removed the microphones from beside this same trap-door, and got great applause immediately – obviously the audience saw that I knew the ropes.

I started my speech by saying that after I won Hamilton (great cheers and loud screams), there was a cartoon in the *Hamilton Advertiser* of George Brown with his arm around me. Before I could say any more someone shouted from the back: 'What was in his hand?' and that set the place in uproar! I managed to control the situation, however, and ended I think unscathed, or relatively unscathed. I was very relieved when I got to the end of my speech and received lots of applause, but then spoilt it by going around to the side door of the stage and forgetting there were steps and almost no rail. I stepped straight off, fortunately into the arms of a GUSNA member.

Strathclyde university was also quite tough, as there was a wide range of very difficult questions. In St Andrews it was much more genteel. In addition to the Scottish universities I also was invited to debate at both Oxford and Cambridge. In Cambridge I was with Gwynfor Evans, as he had studied there, and my debating partner at Oxford was Professor Neil MacCormick, the son of (King) John MacCormick. At Oxford I was also allotted a student, who was Jo Grimond's son, Johnny. The resolution was that 'This house believes that Scotland should take its place between Saudi Arabia and Senegal in the United Nations'. There was an open vote at the end and we won, to polite cheering. At Cambridge, however, one speaker opposing me mentioned the word 'fascist' in connection with my politics. I immediately sent him a note across the chamber, saying that if he did not withdraw the word, I would leave. The whole thing was being televised and that would have caused huge ructions. I have never tolerated being described with such a term, particularly given my experiences during the war and the suffering of my family, and I abhor those who descend to such levels. The speaker in the chair at the debate insisted that the word was withdrawn, and it was. I stayed and finished the debate.

The highlights of my speaking travels, however, were the comprehensive tours of all parts of Scotland, which were arranged by the SNP national secretary Rosemary Hall and by my assistant Margaret Cowan so that they could dovetail with constituency and Westminster work. In those days my accommodation while on tour was in the homes of SNP activists and I tried to take my children on a kind of rota system. Fergus went to Inverness, Ross and Cromarty and Caithness and Sutherland, Annabelle came to the Borders and Terry went with me to Perth and Angus. My memory of those tours is vivid, not least because they were such a mixture of experiences – nervousness on account of the many speeches I had to make, delight at the warmth shown to me and fascination at the things I saw and did. The strain of the tours was great and they took a lot out of me. I had no help in writing speeches, no researchers and no publicity officers. It was all down to me, so there was always a new task every moment, whether it be another speech to be drafted, or local articles to be written, let alone keeping up with questions to be framed for the Commons and constituency correspondence. There were not enough hours in the day.

The tours had a number of purposes, but the most important was to create interest in the party and to stimulate political activity. In some places we were able to form constituency associations or branches on the back of very well-attended meetings. In Inverness hundreds of people had to be turned away and the Town Officer asked me to address an overflow outside the hall, because the fire regulations meant that they could not let them in. In Selkirk Annabelle and I stayed with Walter Elliot and his family and we attended the Selkirk Common Riding on foot. I shall never forget being told to meet a very tall SNP lady councillor at a central spot, only to be whisked off by her into the front line of a whole town that was dancing and singing. We all proceeded to the Square where the flag ceremony took place and the town organisations awaited the arrival of the riders from their tour of the Marches. I spoke with the Provost who was not riding that year and, almost in jest, made a bet with him that next year we should both ride or one would pay the other £10.

After the day's events there was a wonderful ball at which many Border songs were sung, songs such as 'When the Beacons Are Lit on the Border', 'Up with the Soutars of Selkirk' and 'The Soft Rolling Tongue of the Borders'.

On the day itself I went to visit patients at the local hospital. I was bedecked with coloured ribbons from the Border lads and I met an old man who looked gravely ill who asked if I had been at the Riding. I said I had, and he said that he had been there too. Clearly I showed my surprise, for he explained by saying, 'I just closed my eyes and I was there.'

The people of the Borders are proud of their history. Referring to their reputation as strong and determined my host Walter Elliott said to me in his own rolling Border tongue, 'Never you forget Winnie, we are the men who kept the Border.' I confess a shiver ran up my spine as he said it. We went on to Galashiels and in an old folks' home I expressed a desire that the lady residents sing to me. They sang 'The Braw, Braw Lads of Gala Water' very sweetly and I still thrill at the memory of their voices.

The following year I went back to Selkirk and I rode that time. Hamish Hastie, a local vet and our SNP candidate, provided horses for Stewart and myself. Stewart lost his specs near the beginning, but he bravely rode on even though he could see nothing. I fell off my horse at one stage and Hamish had to exchange his for mine. Thus it was that I went out on a white horse and came back on a black one, with my sweater bearing the tell-tale marks of a fall. While I was out I met up with a kindly local farmer who could see that I was distinctly nervous. He told me to follow him because he knew a short-cut round the hill where, as he put it, 'dozens always fall off'. This was cheating but he also told me that his ambition was for me to arrive back before David Steel. To facilitate this, as we approached the town he gave my horse a huge whack on the rump and it took off at great speed, with me hanging on for dear life. However I did beat David Steel and, better still, when we met up with the Provost he had to give me £10. He had as his excuse the fact that his son was the 'Border Lad' that year and he had told his father that he was too nervous about coping with his duties to have to worry about his old father on horseback as well.

In Tain the local headline was, 'Who rang the bell in Tain?' It seems it had only been rung in recent years for Winston Churchill and Ted Heath, but they also rang it for me. Ever since I have had a warm spot for Tain and have revisited the town many times, particularly when I was MEP for the Highlands. In Wick I was formally received by Provost Mowat, duly wearing his chain of office, and the baillies of the town were also 'chained'. Provost Mowat, who was a superb civic leader, subsequently became a very good friend despite a somewhat rocky start to our relationship. He asked Fergus that night, 'Would you like some day to be the Prime Minister for Scotland?' Fergus replied, 'Oh no, I would have to work far too hard,' and then, as people laughed, added, 'but I wouldn't mind too much being a provost!' to even greater hilarity.

It was in Wick I tried to persuade Donald Barr, a music teacher, to be SNP candidate. Donald was reluctant at the time but subsequently did become our standard-bearer in Caithness and Sutherland, commenting afterwards, 'That's what comes of talking to strange women in bars late at night!' Later he stepped in at very short notice to the SNP parliamentary candidacy in Inverness after the original choice had withdrawn. Despite having only a three-week campaign he came within a whisker of winning.

The tours went on. Terry was with me in Angus and Tayside and he had the great thrill of being driven round the towns in a police car. It was wonderful to meet so many supporters in those areas which were becoming very supportive of the SNP, as they are still. However, there was a dreadful moment during that tour as well. My sister phoned to tell me that her husband, Jimmy, was in hospital with hepatitis and had been given seven days to live. I thought I was hearing her wrongly and said, 'You mean seven years surely?' 'No,' said Jean, 'Seven days,' and the prediction was all too true.

Like many lawyers Jimmy didn't have a mortgage protection policy, but thought he was financially secure after he became a sheriff. However his shrival pension agreement required him to be on the bench for five years before it took effect. He died after four years and eleven months in office and the Treasury, to its eternal shame, refused to pay out, saying that if they did it would 'open the floodgates', although to my certain knowledge there was only one similar case. Everyone thought Jean was comfortably off as a sheriff's widow, but in fact she had to sell the family home in Bothwell and move into a much smaller flat in Glasgow.

Jean's biggest financial asset was Jimmy's law library, which had been built up over two generations. This would have fetched a considerable sum if sold, but when the van came to take the library away for auction she decided that she could not part with it and instead resolved to use it to study law herself. At the age of fifty-one she was called to the Bar.

There was meeting after meeting and I simply had no time to prepare scripts. I had to be alert and aware during the entire evening and be able to think on my feet, for Labour and the other parties constantly ensured that there were hostile questions and hecklers. In Ayr Town Hall Jim Sillars, who had written, 'Don't Butcher Scotland's Future', in which he described my tours as 'ego trips', asked a knocking question. I replied, 'When the questioner has seen as much of Scotland as I have and done as much for Scotland as I have then I will answer his questions.'

The formal tours were one thing; the casual opportunities were another, and these seemed to arise wherever I went. For example in 1970 we went *en famille* to Skye for a few days. We stayed with Colina and Ian Willoughby, who were both members of the Skye Mountain Rescue team and I also had to hold a number of public meetings. At one an old man asked me, 'What would you do if the Queen became a Catholic?' I said, 'Nothing!'

Whilst on Skye we were all invited to lunch at the house of Dame Flora Macleod. The setting was magnificent and the table was loaded with lace and silver. In the middle of lunch Terry spilled his milk all over the place but I must admit that Dame Flora didn't bat an eyelid!

It was very important for us to get away as a family. Among of the happiest occasions were the three weeks we spent in Islay. We took Stewart's sister Margaret with us and the weather was magnificent. There were some wonderful ceilidhs and lovely days on the beach and the whole holiday was a great relaxation, although I remember in the bar of the White Hart Hotel in Port Ellen being asked, 'How long are you staying?' and when I said 'Three weeks', an old local gentleman replying, 'We can only stand the pace for two.'

Part of the reason for ensuring that we spent time together as a family was my guilt about the children. But I also had a wider feeling of inadequacy about my political life because it seemed that I had to do almost very job myself, from being constituency member to being sole representative of my party in Parliament and sole spokesperson on every subject. I was always seeking advice and getting it from such wonderful figures as Robert McIntyre, Jimmy Halliday, Arthur Donaldson, Gordon Wilson and Professor David Simpson. Nonetheless the greatest burden remained on my shoulders all the time and it was good to shrug it off, if only temporarily.

Stewart had always been good at ensuring that I did get away, and the holidays that he arranged were culturally challenging, but always interesting. Some months prior to the Hamilton by-election we had been to Russia, visiting Moscow, Leningrad and Tblisi. Tourism to Russia was a new phenomenon and the communist government was not entirely comfortable with the idea. Nor had the country yet begun to realise that it would have to cater for people with different expectations, but nevertheless the tour was fascinating. The difficulties were apparent from our first hours in Moscow. We arrived at the Hotel October, and wanted a meal. We quickly found a restaurant which we assumed was part of the hotel and we had borscht followed by beef and potatoes. However, when we stated our room number in order to settle the bill complete chaos broke out. This was not part of the hotel, we had no Russian money and we shouldn't have been there anyway. However a harassed hotel manager was summoned and sorted things out. The hotel routine was inflexible. On the first evening we were told we had to report for a meal at six, but when we got there the food was cold and the tables covered in dirty dishes. In addition our guide – a formidable blonde goddess – gave Stewart and me a terrible row for escaping from her earlier in the day.

We did see the magnificent sites of Moscow, including Lenin's tomb. When we arrived we were ushered to the front of the queue and we had to apologise to the Russians behind us who had been waiting patiently for hours. I will never forget their kindly looks, which implied that it was not our fault, but simply how their society worked. We also went to the Bolshoi, where you could buy Georgian champagne by the glass during the interval and where the front rows were occupied by a host of very youthful-looking Chinese soldiers, male and female. You could also get champagne with your coffee at the main Moscow railway station while watching a carnival of travellers from all over the vast country, many in colourful local dress. I was particularly thrilled to hear announcements for trains to places like Vladivostok, the other side of the world as far as I was concerned.

Leningrad was positively light-hearted in comparison to Moscow. However, once more Stewart and I escaped and went to museums on our own, which again greatly displeased our guide. On our own one evening we tried to ask the name of a good restaurant from passers-by, and although we tried to speak in English, French and German no one could understand us, or claimed not to. Eventually we resorted to sign language and one citizen indicated we were to follow him, though he would not walk with us. He led us to a Ukrainian restaurant where we had a splendid evening.

Tblisi, our last port of call, was also gorgeous and we had a formal visit to a large school where the teachers were very old but spoke the most charming English to us. In Tblisi I developed severe tummy problems and could not eat. One evening I had to stay in my room, gnawing the odd piece of dry toast, but Stewart went down to the bar to have a drink with a Welsh army major. I could see them from the balcony of our room in what had been a five-star establishment and, glancing out, I noticed that they had been joined by three other people whom I did not recognise. Stewart then appeared and told me to come at once, for they had met three local teachers and they were going to the major's room, one floor above ours, to talk and have a dram. I couldn't resist this, but it meant running the gauntlet of the large Russian women stationed on every floor whose job was not just to note the comings and goings of the guests, but positively to discourage them.

How effective these women were was quickly borne out. As I approached the major's room I heard a commotion and saw the teachers being marched away by three men in long leather coats. Apparently they had only just entered the room when the door was virtually broken off its hinges by the men, who were KGB officers, and although the teachers protested, and asked the KGB to tell the visitors why they were being arrested, they were quickly forced out. Apparently they had all fought in the International Brigade in Spain. Next day Stewart and I went to the police station to complain, but we were very much discouraged from taking the matter any further and our guide was furious with us.

The most memorable period of getting away from it all came in the autumn of 1969. I knew that with an election likely at some stage in the next year or so, Stewart and I should try and spend some time together without the pressures of politics or family life, so we booked a package deal to Israel, arriving at Lod airport on 23 September, Fergus's birthday. On our arrival a loud announcement boomed out asking Winnie Ewing to report to the airport reception desk. I was worried in case it was bad news, but we were met by a staff member from the British Embassy who told us that the Israeli Government had invited us to be their guests for the first week of our two-week break. We accepted with alacrity and there followed one of the most spectacular and significant weeks of our lives. Our Israeli guide was a Colonel Barak who asked me, 'What would you like to see?' I simply said, 'Everything.'

I had long been interested in Israel and in the Jewish religion. The tenement in which I was brought up was situated near a synagogue, a lovely sandstone building which was a great mystery to us all. Many Jewish families lived in our road and in the surrounding area because the houses were near the synagogue and on the Sabbath Jews must walk to worship. Some of these families were very strict in their observance and that meant they could not do so much as put a match to their household fires on the Sabbath. But others could do it for them and I was recruited for the task by a neighbouring family called Grossman. I became what is called a 'Sabbos goya' and in return for my service I always received a silver shilling, which was wealth indeed. As time went on I would be given food too – cookies which were delicious and so different from my mother's recipes.

During the war years all our Jewish neighbours were sympathetic and supportive to my mother as time passed and we had no knowledge of what had happened to my brother David. Their sympathy was borne out of hard and bitter experiences which they had suffered, and continued to suffer.

In addition to these formative experiences I had, as a child brought up in the Church of Scotland, some knowledge of the Old Testament, and of course that gave me a good grounding in the geography of the Holy Land. Our experiences of Israel over the next seven days were dazzling. To our amazement we travelled everywhere in the Prime Minister's limousine. Our host would point to a village: 'That's where John the Baptist was born', and I would exclaim, 'Stop the car!' Then it was Siloam's Pool and I said again, 'Stop the car!'

Colonel Barak's youthfulness surprised me and as we got to know him I expressed my surprise that he had gained such a high military rank at such an early age. He explained that the Israeli Army preferred to have younger men in charge of fighting because they would be more eager and more determined. Much was at stake for them, every day.

The programme for our visit was presented to us in book form and was very thorough, verging on the exhausting. On a single day, for example, we visited not only the Holocaust Memorial but also the Hebrew University and the Ministry of Foreign Affairs. We also visited Bethlehem and Nazareth, both of which seemed real yet unreal: it was amazing to be standing in places whose sacred names echoed so resonantly down the centuries. We saw the site of Massada, and the magnificent Knesset, Israel's Parliament, where the windows of the synagogue were by Marc Chagall. When the Six-day War took place the Israelis were terrified lest any damage occur to those windows, but when Chagall heard he simply said, 'Forget the windows and win the war.' In the windows biblical figures are represented by sympathetic animals. Our guide to the Knesset had sparkling eyes and in the synagogue showed us where women prayed. She said, 'That spot is where Golda Meir prays – when she prays. But I can tell you she certainly did during the Six-day War!'

I wanted to meet Menachem Begin, who later became Prime Minister, and whose words had inspired me at the time of my persecution in the House of Commons. When I asked, we were told that he would be delighted to take us to lunch in the Knesset. We were joined at the table by an Arab MP and I told Menachem about how his phrase 'When the enemy think there is no retaliation they grow bolder' had made me think about how to fight back at Westminster.

The hospitality was warm and magnificent. One memorable Friday I had the thrill of a swim in the Sea of Galilee, where I was surrounded by golden fishes. Later we also bathed in the Dead Sea. We had a Sabbath dinner in a kibbutz. We saw the mix of old and new Jerusalem and the part of it where totally Orthodox Jews lived as if time for them had stopped millennia ago. We were invited to many homes, including that of judge Elas Kteily and that of advocate Moskau Landan so we could talk about the law and the differences and similarities between Scotland and Israel. We also made a visit to the artist colony of Tsfat, where we were given drawings of Yemeni Jews. These Jews, of ancient lineage, had been airlifted from Yemen by the Israeli Government at a time of great crisis for them. They were also brilliant silversmiths.

We visited Haifa where we learnt the quaint saying 'In Jerusalem you pray, in Tel Aviv you play, but in Haifa you stay'. In Haifa there is the main shrine of the Bahai religion and as I had met many Bahais in Scotland I took a particular interest in it. At a second kibbutz my coffee was served by David Ben-Gurion, a tremendous honour and thrill. Like many of the distinguished Israelis we met he asked about Scotland and appeared to be sympathetic.

One of the most noticeable things about Israel was the sight of the army everywhere, with beautiful girl soldiers taking their place to defend their country alongside the men. Conscription applied to all men up to the age of forty-nine and to all women, except mothers, up to thirty-five. All entered it willingly.

The teaching of Hebrew was also impressive. Immigrants started with an *ulpan*, or immersion course, which taught them a hundred words very quickly and then another hundred, and so on. I thought that Scotland could learn a lot from their methods, particularly with regard to the Gaelic language.

When we said goodbye to our host I was in tears, as he had become a marvellous and attentive friend. He was a fiercely patriotic man who explained everything with wit and verve. I so clearly recall him telling us that the Israeli national fruit, called the *zabra*, is like the young Israelis themselves: prickly on the outside and sweet on the inside.

At the end of this remarkable week we dined with the British Ambassador John Barnes and I was introduced by his wife as an MP from England. I had to contradict Mrs Barnes, which she did not like: senior diplomatic wives do not care to be told that they have said something wrong. The final week we spent in Caesarea as joyful and privileged tourists. We could visit Tel Aviv and go for a walk to the beach at Caesarea and we loved the freedom and sunshine. At the beach our heads, like everyone else's, were always turned down towards the sand in the hope of finding some of the remarkable things that sometimes turn up from the past. Stewart and I did manage to find something, a precious piece of Venetian glass.

During our trip I remembered about an ILP candidate whom my father had supported in the Glasgow Cathcart by-election and whom I thought had emigrated to Israel to work for the government. He was called Nathan Jackson and when I enquired I discovered that he was in the Israeli Diplomatic Service. He had been Ambassador to Norway but was back living in Israel. Stewart and I had a wonderful evening of reminiscence with him and his wife and it brought out the Glasgow in him. When we expressed our surprise at having had Golda Meir's car for our entire tour Jackson replied, 'She wis nae need'n it that week.' Apparently she had been in America and there were only a few cars in their Government car pool. Nathan had taken the Jewish name of Jakov and was a wise and thoughtful man. He observed to me that night that the Arab attitude to the problems of the Middle East was to ignore events prior to 1967. 'It is like trying to explain Northern Ireland', he said 'as if its generations of problems started only three months ago.'

I learnt a great deal on that trip, and when I returned to Westminster for what turned out to be my last session for a while, I felt sadder but wiser about the problems of the world, and particularly the problems of the Middle East. On St Andrew's Day, just a couple of months later, I attended a special service in the Scots Kirk in Fleet Street. The preacher was the Moderator and his text was 'Let us give thanks to the Lord that there are those who know what to do in the state of Israel'. The text sent shivers down my spine.

I did not travel overseas as much as I would have liked during my Hamilton years – I was just too busy for that – but I did meet many interesting visitors from abroad, most of whom were fascinated by what was happening in Scotland. Lee Kuan Yew, the Prime Minister of Singapore, asked to meet me when he was in London and I had lunch with him. During it he expressed his support for the aspiration of those Scots who wanted to be free. Some of those visitors also had strong Scottish connections, such as the lady minister from Blantyre in Malawi. She came to the Blantyre in my constituency and had her photograph taken outside the SNP rooms.

Inevitably all this work took its toll. During one of the Hamilton years I was determined to attend the Queen's Speech because I was hopeful of some progress on issues in Scotland. I should not have gone because I had caught a shivery cold during a wet visit to a factory in Hamilton and I was feeling very ill. As I stood waiting to listen to the speech I fell into conversation with Lord Rutland, who asked me how many Lords were my supporters. Feeling very woozy I said about five. He then said, 'Ah, but are these five the hard core of nationalism or the soft core of patriotism?' At this point I fainted and poor Lord Rutland had to carry me out of the Chamber. This was the first and only time I have ever fainted although I discovered later I was not alone at that moment – Lord Montgomery had also keeled over! I, however, had contracted pneumonia and had to go to hospital. I got back to Glasgow and Stewart took me to the Bon Secours, where I spent ten days recovering.

I think that my period as the MP for Hamilton was the busiest of my life. It certainly changed things utterly for me, and instead of having a pleasant, ordered existence as a mother, wife, lawyer and occasional political activist, I became, almost overnight, a full-time politician, constantly in the public eye and with a reputation in Scotland which was at times difficult to live with and live up to. But I still had to be a mother and wife and even think about the future and earning a living if politics went wrong.

As the General Election loomed in 1970 I got even busier. We had a tremendous team in Hamilton and whilst I was concerned at the level of attack on me by Labour I went into the election determined to try and hold my seat. But it was not to be. We fought hard. My opponent was Alex Wilson, who had lost to me in 1967, and he got huge help from the Labour party in Scotland and throughout the UK. I was not assisted by a comment in the *Glasgow Herald* on the Monday before polling day, speculating that I would come third, despite my efforts. In the end I got 35 per cent of the vote – 35 per cent more than in the previous General Election, when we did not even stand in the seat. That was 10 per cent down on the by-election, and Labour were just 10 per cent up. Labour's 52 per cent of the vote was 20 per cent down on their 1966 result. In raw figures I retained almost 17,000 of the 18,000 votes I had taken in the by-election. Of course the General Election poll was much higher, with Labour dragging out everyone they could and letting it be known that they would remember any of their own who dared to vote for the SNP.

It was, no matter the figures, a bitter blow. As the night went on it seemed as if we would once again go back to having no voice at Westminster. But then something wonderful happened. I was at home with Douglas Henderson, Billy Wolfe and Gordon Wilson waiting in suspense for a phone call from the Western Isles, the last seat to declare, as they had a cold count the day after polling day, rather than a count on the day itself. Eventually Donnie rang. He had won and was going to Westminster to carry on where I had left off. In my excitement I phoned Gwynfor: 'We've won a seat,' I said. Gwynfor sounded mildly irritated. He thought it was a council seat. When he found that it wasn't, his irritation vanished.

7

After Defeat – New Opportunities

I N THE FRANTIC DAYS and years after the Hamilton by election I had no real leisure. My nerves uses to cry out for time for myself and I used to dream of reading books for pleasure and going to see theatre and opera. I often longed to meet up with friends whom I rarely saw and to relax at dinner parties which had nothing to do with politics. But one should be careful, I have learnt, of what one wishes for. When reality sank in I suddenly found myself with lots of time to do what I wanted and yet I felt only boredom – boredom beyond belief.

I was shattered, first of all at losing, but then also shattered by this new feeling, for I could not remember ever having been bored in my life before. In effect what had actually happened was that all the longings, desires and dreams that I had worked on during the Hamilton days had come to a crashing halt and I was suffering real ennui. I could not be bothered to read or visit people, or even sometimes to talk, and I became terrified that this state of mind would last for ever.

I believe I was graceful in defeat. That is the least one can do to ensure self-respect and respect from others, but there was a sense of having failed Scotland, the cause and all the activists. Many in Hamilton thought I should not have toured so extensively, but on my defeat the press did concede the high and constant level of my work as a constituency MP. However, from the first day after the election I had one fixed idea about politics, and that was never to return to the House of Commons. I was grateful to Arthur Donaldson when he said in his speech introducing my address to the SNP Conference in 1970 that 'If she never does another thing, she has done enough'. It was how I felt about politics at that stage.

However, one thing which did begin to absorb my waking hours – and which started to give me sleepless nights as well – was finance. In 1970 MPs got no pay for the three or four week election period, so those who lost seats found themselves already out of pocket. There was also no resettlement grant or termination package as there is now, yet one continued to have staff who needed, at the very least, a period in which to be paid off. In addition I already had an overdraft secured on our property – our home and our office – a double flat, five rooms up and five down, with two bathrooms. I must also admit that our lifestyle had become fairly lavish. In this time of worry, as in all times of financial concern, Stewart was of little help, because he was always optimistic and also genuinely believed that money would turn up from somewhere. This was his belief all his life, and it was always in contrast to my natural tendency on the matter. I have to admit that he was usually the one who was right.

My legal practice had been nobly carried on by my trusty assistant, Mrs Sibbald, greatly aided by legal friends such as Keith Bovey and Doris Littlejohn. However, inevitably it had greatly diminished as clients do not like solicitors who are regularly absent. My bank manager phoned interminably even when I pointed out that harassing phone calls were upsetting and did not encourage me to solve the problem – they simply made me spend more time worrying. The persecution continued, however, until I vowed, that when I paid off my overdraft I would change bank. Things got so bad that I used to lie in bed at night racking my brains to think of someone who could give me an interest-free loan to tide me over. It was at that moment that the ever loyal and supportive Glasgow Bar Association came into its own. I was asked to resume the post of Honorary Secretary. In addition, some of the most distinguished criminal court practitioners came to my aid when clients had a conflict of interest, therefore needing separate court representation. They started to pass these clients on to me and I found myself quite quickly rocketed to the High Court with many fascinating cases. I instructed a number of advocates: Charlie McArthur, Donald Robertson, David Smith, John Smith (later the leader of the Labour Party) and a young James Douglas Hamilton, whom I was to get to know better through politics both at Westminster and in the Scottish

Parliament, and who never tired of telling people that I had given him his first case.

I began to have considerable success and this led to me being sought out by accused facing trials. I also resumed my two weeks a year acting as a duty solicitor for any person in custody, a system I greatly approved of. The Glasgow Bar Association's campaign for criminal legal aid – a campaign fought with many others – had succeeded, so some money began to flow in. I also cajoled the Civil Legal Aid office to send me as many cases as possible. Many women facing a divorce wanted a woman solicitor, and this helped. Some supportive colleagues also passed on to me cases they did not want, and despite the inconvenience of some of them they were welcome. I well remember a very early rise on a winter's morning to catch a ferry to Rothesay to act in an affiliation and aliment case, thinking my new life lacked some of the glamour of the old!

Knowing I was back, clients passed word of mouth, as did family and friends, old contacts from the Soroptimists and The Saltire Society, and of course from the SNP. Slowly my wakeful nights and the harassment of my bank manger became a thing of the past.

Clients who came to see me at 52 Queen's Drive could have no doubt, even if they had not heard of me, of my political affiliations. I had a large SNP poster in the hall which showed Robert the Bruce pointing a finger and saying, 'I'm in, why not you?' I was often asked if this propaganda did not alienate potential business and I always told the story of a very posh elderly lady who had come in to make her will. She was just the type who might have objected, but when I went to collect her for the appointment she pointed to it, smiled and said, 'I like that.'

One of my most colourful clients was the poet and playwright Dominic Behan, the brother of Brendan. He asked me to find him a house and gave me specifications so I should be able to select the right one. I liked him a lot but I had to abandon any attempt at public socialising with him after a lunch in Rogano's when he insisted in bursting into loud song – the songs being ones such as 'Up the Bold IRA' and 'Come Out Ye Black and Tans!', as well as his own famous composition, 'The Patriot Game'.

One consolation of my defeat was that it gave me time to enjoy being with the children again. By this time Fergus was thirteen, Annabelle ten and Terry six. Fergus was already away from home at Loretto and we used to pay him a monthly visit, often taking him out for a slap-up lunch at my favourite restaurant in Edinburgh, Prestonfield House. Soon I began to find great pleasure again in my family, my home and my work. I even had time to go to a Scotland versus England match at Hampden. I hadn't intended to, go but as the fans passed along Queen's Drive I stood on the steps wearing a long kilt waving the Saltire to the enthusiasm of the Scotland supporters. One group asked if I was going to the match but I explained I had no ticket. They all started 'tutt-tutting' and talking amongst themselves. Soon one was produced and I was asked for £5. On the spur of the moment I bought it and then Stewart appeared and another ticket was made available and purchased. It was Glasgow spontaneity at its best.

Of course I was still deeply involved in politics; how could I not be? The Bannockburn Rally took place hard on the heels of the General Election and I spoke to a warm welcome. I wore a photo of Donnie Stewart on my lapel, and as Donnie's result had been the last in the whole UK to be announced, there were some at the rally who did not yet know that he had won. When I started to speak and paid tribute to Donnie first of all, there was a huge cheer. The SNP National Executive appointed me as the liaison for our new member, so I regularly visited London. I had the use of my old flat despite the fact that it had been taken over by Lorna Blackie. I was not totally cut off, therefore, from Westminster and what was happening there.

Donnie, who was from Lewis of course, had been in the Navy during the war and had risen to be a director of McKenzie's Harris Tweed Mill, subsequently becoming Provost of Stornoway. He was hugely popular in the Western Isles and became just as popular throughout Scotland and at Westminster. He had enormous charm and enormous recall – he never forgot anything or anybody. He was largely self-educated and read voraciously. He was a fountain of knowledge and could quote aptly for any occasion. He was blessed in his wife Chrissie, who was a Gaelic speaker. Donnie also had a great deal of Gaelic but he was not as fluent in the language and he always deferred to Chrissie's superiority. Chrissie accompanied Donnie to London each week and they had a pleasant flat which they made very homely. She came a lot to the Commons and used the Visitors' Sitting Room a great deal, so consequently she came to know the families of many MPs and became friendly with them. She was acceptable everywhere, and later on, when we had eleven SNP MPs we used to call Chrissie our 'secret weapon'.

I enjoyed going to London occasionally and I was happy that the SNP continued to make demands upon me, as long as those demands did not include returning to Westminster. But as the months passed I began to have pressure put on me to stand once more for Parliament when the opportunity arose. Hamilton, of course, wanted me back to fight the seat again and it was thought by many that such a return would be my obvious choice. But I remained unconvinced, so once more I sought advice from the wise heads in the party. The consensus from Billy Wolfe, Arthur Donaldson and Robert McIntyre was that I should not go back to Hamilton as I might continue to feel some bitterness about my defeat and such bitterness might show. It was wise advice but I agreed to go to a meeting in Hamilton to discuss the matter. Before I left Queen's Drive to go the meeting Stewart made me promise that I would not let my heart be swayed by the emotion of the evening and that whatever happened I would not accept the invitation that night, but would continue to think about it.

However, the decision was easier to make than I thought. When I got to the Larkhall Rooms I saw, addressing the meeting as a potential candidate, one Stephen Maxwell, who had attacked me during my time as MP over and over again. This crystallised my thoughts wonderfully. I would not come back to Hamilton and I would not seek to return to Parliament. I believed again that my first thoughts about all this had been right. Thus it was that I told the party that I would do anything they wanted: I would go anywhere to speak, I would attend by-elections and canvas, but I would not go back to the Palace of Westminster. And that, I thought, was that, for I was gaining fulfilment from my work, which was profitable again at last, and I had time to do the things I wanted.

The bulk of my time was now taken up by work and family. It was very convenient having my legal office in my home and this enabled me to be with the children a lot. My sister-in-law Marcelle taught French at Langside College and she dropped off her son Mark each weekday at Queen's Drive. The two little boys (Terry and Mark) were looked after by my housekeeper, Mary Morrison, a fine experience for both, and they were always there for me to spend a moment with them when I could.

Stewart, by now an academic with tenure at Strathclyde University, was also at home a lot. He would work on papers whilst I burned the midnight oil preparing deeds, drawing up questions for trial cross-examinations and trying to draft jury speeches. Some evenings I would go with Margaret Cowan to the Citizens' Theatre whilst days were spent visiting Edinburgh for court cases, consultation with advocates and seeing Lorna and others.

Back as Honorary Secretary of the Bar Association I once again took up the job of arranging events and entertainments, and the task of making the annual dinner and cabaret more special each year. I also enjoyed working with the wide range of people involved in the GBA. For example, Ross Harper, who was my Tory opponent in Hamilton in 1970, was also one of the presidents of the association during my time as Honorary Secretary. He had an enormously large practice and it seemed as if he deliberately chose people from other parties to add a balance to it. Jim Murphy, Ross's partner, was on the SNP candidates' list, Donald Dewar once worked there, as did Terry Grieve, then a Liberal but now Labour. Robert Brown, the Glasgow Liberal MSP, was also in the firm.

One famous case in which I was involved was that of three men who were accused of holding up a hotel with a sawn-off shotgun. The advocate I had chosen was Charlie McArthur. At the time the law had a 110-day rule which required trials of accused in custody to be over within that period. If they were not concluded in this time the accused went free. Normally calculations taking into account the amount of time the accused had already spent in custody were made and the Procurator Fiscal gave priority to cases in which time was an issue. However, in this particular case the three solicitors and three advocates realised that on the first day of the trial (a Monday) the 110 days were almost up. They would conclude on the Wednesday. Somebody had blundered. And this posed an acute ethical question for all of us – where did our duty lie?

We held a hurried meeting in a room hired in the North British Hotel in George Square. After much thought we all agreed that our duty was to our clients, but that we could say nothing at that time to them or anyone else. On the Wednesday we thought that the case would carry on to midnight if necessary, which the court has power to do, so that the 110-day rule would not be violated. But Wednesday came and went as any normal court day without a word being said by us or by the Procurator Fiscal.

First thing on Thursday morning Charles McArthur, acting for the first accused (my client), asked that the jury be withdrawn. Charlie then moved that the accused be free to leave the dock in view of the expiry of the 110 days. The judge did the same calculation as we had done and realised we were right. He recalled the jury, dismissed them, and told the astonished accused that they were free to go. The trial was at an end. As we all returned to the robing room we met the policeman in charge of the case and he was apoplectic with rage. This was a historic moment and much was written about it, some of it critical, but the legal profession, and its most senior members, concurred that we had acted entirely properly. The Law was more important than individuals. Subsequently the rule was changed so that the trial must merely start within 110 days.

In addition to work I started to take proper holidays again. It was sometimes difficult for Stewart and I to get away. He was on a number of important university committees and he had a lot of private clients as well. Lorna and I often went off together as we got on so well and we had some wonderful trips.

My favourite holiday – though not one free from complications – was a Swan's Archaeological cruise to islands of the Mediterranean. We were to visit Crete, Cyprus and the Greek islands, but when we arrived in Athens to embark the Swan official asked us to hand over our passports for the duration of the trip. Lorna refused point blank and I supported her all the way. Swan's became difficult and even made a threat to leave Athens without us, repaying our money but abandoning us stranded in Greece. We decided to go to the UK embassy for advice and they wrote a letter to Swan's saying they had advised us to keep our passports. Swan's did not give up however – on the first morning out of port an official again tried to separate us from our passports, but we again refused.

One of the guest lecturers on the cruise was Bishop Robert Runcie, later Archbishop of Canterbury. He had his concert pianist wife with him and we all quickly became good friends. His tasks included conducting a short evening service and giving lectures on the Bible, and particularly on Paul's journeys. I had never warmed to Paul in the New Testament but Robert Runcie spoke of him as if he had known him personally. A trip to Tyre had to be cancelled due to trouble ashore but Swan's miraculously found two large buses and took us instead to Antioch, where Paul had preached. The joy of seeing so many wonderful archaeological treasures and sites will stay with me for ever. It brought to life those words from Keats: 'Much have I travelled in the realms of gold, / and many goodly states and kingdoms seen.'

Most passengers were elderly, yet they willingly climbed up steep and jagged mountains to see the ruins and the views. They were indefatigable. On one occasion, however, when we were expected to climb a virtually perpendicular slope Lorna and I decided to seek out a local hostelry instead and asked a passing Greek man for directions. Mr Angelopoulos took an arm of each of us and led us gravely into a magnificent pub whilst our fellow passengers watched in astonishment. The pub itself was at the top of a mountain, and had a view to die for. Appropriately it was called 'Arcadia'.

The cruise was hugely enjoyable but for me it was also hugely significant. One of the reasons I had come away was to consider an invitation I had had to stand for Parliament again, this time in Moray and Nairn, a constituency with which I had developed a special relationship. Ever since my first SNP conference I had always fallen in with their delegation and spent time with them. I had also been to the constituency on many occasions, to speak first for Arthur Donaldson when he was the candidate, and then for Tom Howe. It was about the only constituency that would make me even think about reconsidering my decision not to return to Westminster.

I don't know if Dr McIntyre was heavily involved at first, for he respected my decision not to stand again, but later at his house I found myself on the sofa between Hamish Watt, candidate for Banffshire, and Douglas Henderson, candidate for East Aberdeenshire. Dr Mac drew a chair up to face me and they explained a plan they had called 'The North-east Clean-up'. It involved me standing in Moray and Nairn to draw the fire of the big Tory guns from London, leaving Hamish and Douglas free rein to win the two neighbouring seats. The sitting MP for Moray and Nairn was Gordon Campbell, the Secretary of State for Scotland, and the Tories would not let him lose, even though it meant drawing resources from other seats. Obviously I was not expected to win, but I could not help thinking that as I had won a Labour seat, why not try to win a Tory one too? Facing, and possibly beating, a member of the cabinet would add icing to the cake. I did not commit myself at that meeting, but I went on the Mediterranean cruise actively considering the invitation and wondering what to do. After three years' absence I must admit that part of me wanted to get back, though part of me still dreaded the idea.

I had two experiences on that trip which helped to make up my mind. In Knossos we visited the magical remnants of an ancient and fascinating civilisation. Amongst the ruins there is a stone cabinet where the Delphic Sybil was consulted – not about personal problems, but about matters of state. I entered the cabinet and immediately heard a female voice saying to me, 'The Scottish voices are calling.' It was clear as day and I came out white-faced. Lorna knew from my appearance that something was wrong. I had never had – and have never had since – an experience remotely like it. I couldn't decide if it was real or self-induced. I still can't.

Then, on our last night on board Lorna and I went to one of Robert Runcie's services. We had avoided them up until then but felt that we should show willing at least once. Runcie preached a brief sermon and his text was 'He who once puts his hand to the plough and turns back will never enter the kingdom of Heaven'. Lorna nudged me as he said it and it did indeed seem a sign which might help me make up my mind. At the end of the service I said to him, 'You have a terrible gift – the gift of tongues.' He replied, 'So do you.' And that confirmed my feeling.

When I returned from the 'realms of gold' I had made up my mind. I went up to Moray and told the constituency I would accept the nomination, but only if it was unanimous. They readily agreed and I was selected without any dissenters.

Now I started back in politics in earnest. I went up to the constituency every two weeks for a long weekend, staying with supporters. Whilst I enjoyed my stays in the houses of the Howes, the Bichans, the Davidsons, the Munros and the Coulters I began to be aware that I desperately wanted my own house in the area, so that I could be more flexible and more firmly rooted. My search was advised by Hugh Coulter and whilst I dearly loved a quaint cottage in the lovely village of Dyke, Hugh was very strong in his view that I needed the votes of the fisherfolk and that therefore I should live in Lossiemouth. He admitted though, that there was a risk in this because the fisherfolk might reject an incomer. Fortunately I fell in love with Lossiemouth, and, although I was a stranger, they took me in. Who would not fall in love with Lossie, for it is flanked east and west by beaches with the mouth of the river Lossie meeting the east beach? It had two harbours full of fishing boats, some wonderfully attractive old houses and also wide streets and a lovely golf course.

I found and was able to purchase a small stone house on the square. It was firmly attached to its next-door neighbour in which there lived an elderly lady called Mrs Reid who had been a fisher girl, following the fleet round Scotland and England. She was fascinating to talk to and I loved to hear stories of her life and of her travelling from Orkney to the Western Isles and to Great Yarmouth, to name but a few of the many places she had worked in. I paid about £9,000 for the house and it was only then that I told Stewart. He was astonished, if not horrified, but in October 1973, as I began to move some furniture up from Queen's Drive, he came to see it. It had a front lounge with a small room off, which was big enough for my couch/bed and a large fitted wardrobe. This also led to a kitchen and pantry; upstairs there was a bedroom and bathroom. Once the carpets were down and some bits of furniture in, it was very pretty. As a huge bonus the house also had a walled garden with two sheds. This was typical of fishing houses: one was for the garden and the other for the hooks and tackle. I had one shed removed and then I had the garden paved and planted with flowers, trees and bushes. It was my first proper garden, done to my plans, and I loved it.

The first time Stewart visited he decided to go for a walk to see what the place was like. He went down to the left and came to a raging sea; so he went down to the right and again was faced by the sea. When he returned he asked, 'Is Lossiemouth an island?' He did, however, approve my purchase and he always enjoyed Lossie, which at that time had a fine variety of small shops. He was also totally supportive of my fight in Moray and Nairn and the time it took up. Perforce I spent a lot of time alone in my wee house as the months went on. Two women came to my door at my first New Year. One of them was Betty Gault and the other Sheila Campbell. We all became great friends and through them I made many others.

I decided I would like to call my house after the oldest boat in the local fleet. This turned out to be *The Goodwill* and it, by coincidence, had the youngest skipper, Billy Campbell, whose wife was the Sheila who had first-footed me. Billy and his crew agreed that I could use the name, but I began to have worries about the superstitious aspect of it all. Suppose I failed to win – would they feel that this could damage them in some way? Nobly they scoffed at the idea and I proudly named my house 'Goodwill'. When Stewart and I later set up home in Miltonduff we took the name with us. I could never have thought of a better and more significant name: boats called *The Goodwill* always had two clasped hands painted on the side, a fine and confident symbol.

That house in Lossie remains very special to me. I occasionally write poetry and the house inspired me to do so. This is what I wrote about it:

> My 'Goodwill' house now silently awaits
> Return of life, and then at once relates
> To me and my kind friends who seek to be
> In her safe keeping and serenity
>
> Is my retreat a mix of stone and brick
> Is its warm air of welcome some quaint trick
> Of painted rooms and pictures on the wall
> Secluded patio flowers, trees and that is all?

There are more verses, but the last one is the one that means most to me:

> The voice of logic in my head says no
> These are just things and neither ebb or flow
> But when into my door I place my key
> A sense of love and warmth reach out to me.

I still retain the fondest memories of those days in the first 'Goodwill'. My friends do too.

Of course a number of famous people came from Lossie, chief amongst whom was Ramsay MacDonald. Betty Gault had aunts in the seatown where the houses were end-on to the prevailing winds, for protection against the sea and storms. Two of these aunts had been maids at 10 Downing Street when Ramsay MacDonald was Prime Minister. Ramsay – loyally and sensibly – always brought maids to London from his home town. One of these ladies told me that his instruction was never to let the window cleaner inside in case of theft. At that time window cleaners wore top hats and when she saw a man in Ramsay's study wearing a top hat she attacked him with her broom saying, 'Get out, get out.' Alas, it turned out to be not a window cleaner but the Queen's Surgeon, there to attend to the Prime Minister, as he was ill!

Sheila Campbell's sister Catherine, whose father was a friend of Ramsay's, told me that the people of Lossie had an open invitation from him when he was Prime Minister to visit 10 Downing Street on a Sunday. They were always told not only to go, but to come in by the front door. I eventually asked both Grampian TV and the BBC to come to Lossie to tape the wealth of stories about this former Prime Minister, most of which were known only by old people who would not be around for ever.

Ramsay loved walking and on his weekends in Lossie (a train brought him all the way in those days) he found doing thirty miles not excessive. One day he passed an old school pal sitting on a bench with a walking stick. Ramsay said sympathetically to him, 'Taken you in the legs has it?', but the old man replied, with true Lossie wit, 'Your case is waur. It's taken you in the head.' Another Ramsay story was of the occasion he went to Sweden to an international pacifist conference. The boat from Aberdeen was delayed, and to pass the time Ramsay walked about thirty miles for relaxation. He was being followed by two MI5 agents and they were completely exhausted by the experience. At night they comforted themselves with the thought that at least he wouldn't do that again the following day. But the boat was further delayed, and he did.

Ramsay's daughter Ishbel kept 10 Downing Street for her father when he was Prime Minister. She eventually married a local chemist in Lossiemouth called Peterkin and I became friendly with her, accepting her invitation to tea. She told me of her life in 10 Downing Street, acting as hostess even though she was still a teenager. She described it as being terribly lonely and she maintained she used to look out of the window wistfully wondering what it would be like to lead a normal life like those outside. She quickly had to become expert on what foreign dignitaries and diplomats liked to eat and to anticipate any of their foibles.

Another supporter and friend was Lydia King, who was head teacher of the local primary school. She had a host of Lossie tales to tell, including her experience of being stirred by hearing Wendy Wood address the lieges by loudspeaker in Lossie Square, just outside my house.

I had to learn a great deal very quickly in Moray and Narin. At my first public meeting as candidate in Hopeman I had noted a well-tweeded farmer and said to my self inwardly, 'That will be the Tory.' Then there came in a somewhat noisy fellow whom I took to be a Labourite. But both were loyal SNP members and the former finished the meeting by giving me a sack of potatoes. Sheila Coulter and I put these to good use and started to hold 'stovie' parties. Bettie Rennie was the expert stovie maker and Sheila made and brought enticing cakes and sweets. We invited Lossie shopkeepers, Moray teachers and numerous other people and always we had music. Many supporters old and new came along, including Major Harry Lawrie and his wife Irene, who worked as administrator of the Fisheries Office in Lossie. She was very eloquent and witty and had been a West End actress. Harry had a fine bass voice and sang songs like 'Drake is in His Hammock'. There were others too – the MacPherson family for example. Duncan MacPherson was an art teacher who sang and played the guitar, and his wife Patsy was the daughter of a strong SNP supporter in Rothes who was also a potato merchant. So the potatoes continued to be given.

Campaigning went on in earnest. I went to games and gala days and scores of functions. I met teachers, fishermen, farmers – all sorts and occupations. I went to factories and businesses and it was a great advantage that I was known already after Hamilton and that I had spent time locally. It was also an advantage that I had already chosen to buy a house there. The children came up for all their holidays and they loved the beaches. They played and we all integrated ourselves into a beautiful, historic constituency.

One of my first tasks was to learn the history, not just of my wee town, but of the whole of Moray and of Nairn. The partnership between the two councils was a harmonious one and when Nairn was later transferred into the Inverness East, Nairn and Lochaber seat the people of Nairn were resentful and felt like 'tail-end charlies', never fully included.

I found that the first clear contrast with life in the central belt was that passers-by always said 'good morning', or at least smiled. It was a friendly and egalitarian place, much to my taste. One story that proves the point is that of a previous Tory candidate who told a packed Lossie Town Hall that his party was 'born to rule'. This produced much ridicule and the candidate, a little discomfited, dug himself ever deeper by asserting that 'one wouldn't see the doctor going about with the dustman'. That produced further gales of laughter which intensified when two men sitting next to each other in the front row got up. The first, addressing the audience, pointed to himself and said, 'Doctor'. The second did the same, only he said, 'Dustman.' And the whole town knew that that is precisely who they were.

As I studied the history of Moray I began to understand the enormous pride that the men and women of that county have. Moray was a wealthy land and the Bishop of Moray was almost like a king in his splendid Castle of Spynie. Kingston, on the Spey, was a great port trading with the Hanseatic League. It was also a shipbuilding centre and logs were floated down the Spey to make fine ships. The cathedral at Elgin was dedicated in 1224 by Bishop David of the De Morvain family. They lived during the stirring times of the Wars of Independence and jealously supported the rights of Scotland and Robert the Bruce in his struggle to free his country from English supremacy. De Morvain compared this task to the Crusades, seeing it as equivalent to expelling the Saracens from the Holy Land. Edward I of England got a Spanish cardinal to excommunicate him. His wealth enabled troops to be sent from Moray to the Border and when Bruce won Scotland he was offered every title in the land. He took only one, that of 'The Earl of Elgin', in gratitude to the fighting men of Moray.

The Wolf of Badenoch, Alexander Stewart, Earl of Buchan, was the second son of King Robert II and held sway over the dense forests to the south of Elgin. He exacted money from the Bishop of Moray, amongst others, to keep him in splendour and isolation. He got his nickname 'The Wolf of Badenoch' from his reputation for savagery. In 1390 with his 'wylde wykkyd heland men', as they were called, he swooped down from his stronghold in Lochindorb and burned the town of Forres. A month later, on the town's feast day, he burned Elgin, including the Church of St Giles, the eighteen Manses of Canton and the 'Nobel Church' (the cathedral) and all its charters and valuables. The Wolf was already excommunicated, so no human authority, not even that of the Pope, could harm him. After the burning the Bishop, a man called Bur appealed to the King for money to restore the cathedral, claiming it was 'the special ornament of this country, the glory of the kingdom, the delight of strangers and the praise of visitors'. Alas, we are still left with a ruin – a splendid one, but a ruin nonetheless.

Religion has played a strong part in this area's past. The Reformation brought its share of violence and the despoiling of paintings and statues for which the local ancient churches were famous, but Catholics residing near Elgin used to worship in secret long after that time – certainly until 1714. The last public Catholic mass solemnised within the cathedral was surprisingly late, in fact in 1594. It was attended by the Earl of Huntly and Errol, who must still have been a practising Catholic. A Jesuit priest called Gordon urged the local Catholic notables to remain in Scotland despite the problems, but many of them later emigrated to Catholic Poland where their descendants live to this day.

As 1973 drew to a close, party activity was increasing all over Scotland. There were by-elections in November and Gordon Wilson came very close to winning in Dundee East. That same night Margo MacDonald won Glasgow Govan in truly sensational style and joined Donnie in the House of Commons – the first time we had ever had two MPs there together. Margo's relationship with the SNP since then has been a chequered and troubled one, but it was the SNP that made her a household name, and to many 'The Blonde Bombshell'. I campaigned in Govan during that by-election and saw quite clearly that the people of the constituency were able to contrast the emerging oil wealth of Scotland with the terrible housing and social conditions which they were being forced to tolerate. Others made the connection too, and Margo attracted many supporters from outside the SNP, like Dr Craig Rankin, the son of the Labour MP John Rankin; James Anderson, former Labour Chief Magistrate of Glasgow, and Sam MacQuatrie, the former Chair of East Kilbride Labour Party. Margo was a very attractive candidate, popular with the people and the press and also with other politicians. Unfortunately the seat that she fought was in its last incarnation. The Boundaries Commission report had recommended huge changes and those came into effect in time for the February 1974 General Election. It was essentially a different seat and with less than three months to dig in, Margo had an impossible challenge. She could not hold it, but that did not diminish either her original victory or the huge blow that Labour in Scotland had taken at a vital time.

In Moray we stepped up our efforts. In 1970 Tom Howe had got almost 8,000 votes with the slogan, 'Howe, the Man for Moray'. His strong result indicated to me that a victory might just be possible with the right type of campaign. Tom was local, was a councillor, and worked as the manager of the Crown Fisheries at the mouth of the River Spey. His job meant that he had to get written permission from his employers to stand for Parliament in 1970. The sitting MP, Gordon Campbell, became Secretary of State for Scotland after the 1970 election, and therefore technically his employer. In an act of spite Tom was then summarily sacked. Tom sued and won in what was a disgraceful episode of vindictiveness by a large party that had come to take its place in society for granted. Fortunately he was an expert gardener, often acting as judge at flower shows and was able to start up a successful market garden.

It was agreed that John Bichan, a farmer, whose land lay beside Kinloss airbase, would be my agent. His wife Francis came from Findhorn and her father's name is on the Findhorn war memorial. Johnnie was a treasure and did such a good job that we won. The team was experienced and organised and the literature splendid. We did attract press comment of course (one of my favourite articles was by a journalist called Campbell who wrote an article about his Tory namesake with the headline 'A Campbell Who May be Going'), but the Tories appeared blissfully unaware of a serious challenge. We toured and visited every kind of event and every village and town. We wrote specialist pamphlets for teachers, nurses, factory workers, fishermen.

Through my friends I met many others who volunteered to help. John Smart, an ex-National Secretary of the party stayed with his wife Fiona in Lossiemouth and in time Fiona became my parliamentary secretary, for she was super efficient. John's contribution to the campaign was very significant. He sent very clever letters to the local press which began to hit home. One local Tory said to me one day, 'That fellow Smart is too bloody smart.' Clearly this meant he was getting his message across.

The campaign was hard and serious. When the actual election was announced in early 1974 we started to hold meetings everywhere, large or small and we always had packed halls. I recall most of them, but in particular one held on a Saturday afternoon in Elgin Town Hall. A young man got up and said that he was English and serving in the RAF. What would happen to him if the SNP won? I was wary of such questions, which were usually planted by the Tories, so I started by merely correcting him: 'When we win,' I said. But then I got bolder as he seemed to be genuine. I carried on: 'We will pass a law. Those we have caught and we like we will keep. For example, you will not be free to go back to England again.' There was a pause then a gale of laughter and the young man gave me the thumbs up.

On election day we found that many Tory activists had not been solemnly sworn under the Act, a process that was essential to allow them into polling places during election hours. We were ruthless in ensuring that only those who had the necessary permission were allowed to fulfil their duties at the poll. I later discovered that the Tory agent, who was a paid official, hard-working and always very charming to me, had got the blame for this gaffe and for the damage it did to their polling day organisation. It was not all her fault. The true blame should have gone to the candidate and those around him because they had always taken the votes for granted. When they started to wake up on the Saturday before polling day it was too late. Gordon Campbell appeared in Lossie that day wearing his blue rosette and with others around him dressed the same. No one had seen them like that before, and it was noted.

On election night we all gathered in my wee house on the square in Lossiemouth and heard of marvellous SNP victories: Gordon Wilson, Hamish Watt, Douglas Henderson, George Reid, Ian McCormack – five in all. Donnie Stewart's count, like mine, was the following day, but I was sure he would hold. Already we had done better than we had ever done before and now there would be not one SNP member holding the fort, but many tackling the real job of gaining Scotland's freedom. I hoped I would be one of them.

Stewart had not been present in Moray for much of the campaign, for he was also fighting a seat – that of Glasgow Central. He did so well in that unpromising territory that he even saved his deposit, and after his count he high-tailed it up the road to be with me for my count the next day. Moray was still a constituency that believed in the 'cold count' rather than the hotter tension of the overnight reckoning-up of the ballots.

When my result came, it was spectacular. I had overturned a Tory majority of 6,000 and now had an SNP majority of almost 2,000. I had also beaten the Secretary of State for Scotland. At the count Gordon Campbell was reluctant to shake my hand. He made an incredibly embarrassing speech about my victory being a blow to the disabled in society (he had a disability himself), making the point that I was able to rush about while he couldn't. It was a mean-spirited performance that bordered on the offensive. Stewart, who regularly bought tapes of programmes, wanted a copy of it and wrote off for one but the speech was never repeated and we were told that the film of it had been 'accidentally destroyed'.

After the elation of the day we all went through to Aberdeen, where a celebration had been arranged at the Amatola Hotel. The 'North-east Clean-up' had succeeded beyond our wildest dreams and there were three North-east SNP MPs able to speak that night of their gratitude to the election workers and the voters, and to look forward to an unprecedented number of SNP MPs at Westminster. Surely this was the start of Scotland regaining her freedom?

It was a remarkable feeling I had as the evening wound down. Less than four years after the bitterness of losing Hamilton, and vowing that I was done with Westminster, I had won once more and was on my way back. And this time I was not going alone.

8

The Member for Moray and Nairn

IN EBRUARY 1974 the SNP had seven MPs elected to the House of Commons – by far the largest total in our history. It was great to be one of them.

Before we went to take our seats we met in the Caledonian Hotel in Edinburgh to choose office-bearers for the group, to allocate portfolios and to discuss our parliamentary tactics. Hamish Watt, the member for Banffshire, had indicated to me that he would like to be the leader of the group, but Donnie Stewart, who had now served four years in the Commons (the longest any SNP MP had been there) and who had been re-elected (another first), was the clear choice and it was unanimous. Gordon Wilson, now the member for Dundee East, proposed me as Deputy Leader, but I declined as I believed Gordon himself was more suitable, particularly as he had been an outstanding National Secretary of the party in recent years. I was right because he and Donnie made an excellent team. In any case I was so happy to have become the MP for Moray and Nairn that I wanted to ensure that I kept my seat. That would take much hard work and much travelling.

Accordingly I did not clamour for any particular portfolio; in fact I was the height of reason itself when the discussion took place. Douglas Henderson, the Member for East Aberdeenshire, was appointed our whip because he had the necessary fighting edge and biting wit to survive in even the toughest political maelstrom. Hamish, who had been a successful farmer, got the agricultural portfolio. Douglas, with huge fishing interests in his area, was a natural to speak for us on the important issue of fisheries.

Iain MacCormick, the Member for Argyll, had been the senior maths teacher at Oban High School until his election, so he was asked to take on education as well as rural affairs, transport, local government and Highland issues. Gordon Wilson, who had masterminded the most successful campaign in the SNP's history, agreed to lead on energy, industry and finance. George Reid, the member for Stirlingshire East and Clackmannan, was asked to look after housing, health and social services, but he also took on the formidable task of defending Scotland in the constitutional debates which were soon to come fast and furious. He was also subsequently appointed to be a member of the Council of Europe. I mopped up the remaining portfolios, taking on law, defence (for I had two RAF bases in my constituency) foreign affairs and Europe. Strangely enough there were no volunteers to take on the European issue at all, which was surprising, and which quickly became significant. All of us agreed to speak on other subjects as and when debates took place, according to whatever the group agreed. Thus readied for the fray the so-called 'Magnificent Seven' went off to London to fight for Scotland, but when I got there I had something special I needed to do for Moray and Nairn first.

In January 1974, just weeks before the election, I had been given a piece of the 'clavie'. The clavie is a barrel, strongly tarred and carefully prepared, which is set on fire at the old new year (twelve days after our modern new year) in the little fishing town of Burghead. Burghead is an ancient place which can boast not only prehistoric cave paintings but also strong Roman connections, and the burning of the clavie is one of the most ancient fire rituals in Scotland. Once alight the clavie is carried on the backs of the clavie men' – from the same families for centuries past – round the town. A strut is removed for each VIP in the town and placed on their doorstep, and then what remains of the clavie is placed on a venerable plinth and more fuel poured onto it. At that moment people rush to grab a piece, some burning their hands in their enthusiasm, because to possess a piece of the clavie is meant to bring good luck for the rest of the year.

I had been introduced to Burghead by a local publican, Denis Scaithe, who was a prominent SNP supporter. He also introduced me to many local people, including one locally called 'Tolmey' but whose real name was Ptolemy and who claimed to be descended from the Roman map maker! The clavie rite is for Burghead folk, not for tourists, and I was therefore very touched and honoured to be given a piece of that year's clavie, and told that it would help me win the election. But I got it only on condition that I carried it in my hand on the floor of the House of Commons when I took my oath. I kept my promise and, clad in a pink silk coat, I intoned the well-known words holding in my left hand what must have appeared to everyone else to be simply a blackened stake of wood! Astonishingly no one commented at all, nor asked what on earth I was doing. I continue to get a piece of the clavie each year and now I need it because I believe strongly in its power and in the tradition behind it.

Overall my second term as a Westminster MP was in total contrast to my first. The personalised cruel attacks and the continuous heckling that I had suffered from so greatly between 1967 and 1970 came almost completely to an end. Of course there was still overwhelming opposition to us politically and resentment at Scotland and its demands, but I was no longer on my own and our group was too clever, too tough and too good on its feet to be targeted maliciously. Those who tried to attack came off worst. In addition, the government was short of votes and needed all the support it could get, so it had an interest in reining in the worst offenders. There was even a Government whip, Walter Harrison, who was allocated the special duty of liaising with us, Plaid Cymru and the Ulster Unionists in the hope of ensuring our support from time to time. He endeared himself to the SNP because he had patience, tact and understanding, a far cry from the qualities shown to me by Labour just a few years earlier.

The biggest and most welcome change for me was the ability to meet with colleagues and to consult with them. Sometimes one even came upon a fellow SNP member by accident in the endless corridors, a huge joy when I considered how I longed for a friendly face previously.

The SNP group met regularly and we decided policy and strategy by majority vote. On the whole it was done without rancour and with a great rapport between us all, no matter our views on individual issues. If attacks were made on any of us individually, or on the group collectively, we were well able to defy the rude and intemperate. We were happy in each other's company and we admired the skills of the other members. As the only woman in the group I enjoyed myself even more than the rest.

We were also all very busy as we knew that we had to be hard-working and devoted constituency MPs if we were to keep hold of the progress we had made. We held surgeries throughout our large constituencies, and in Moray my little house in the square in Lossiemouth became a sort of headquarters for my work. We also travelled the length and breadth of the country, speaking at SNP meetings and encouraging candidates. The party continued to gain strength and influence and it all seemed to be happening so quickly.

The first time that a delegate to the annual SNP Conference rose to speak and was introduced as 'Councillor' there was rapturous applause. Now we had lots of them in every part of the land, and provosts too. Labour had its urban heartlands and the Tories used to have their rural areas, but the SNP was popping up everywhere, in every nook and cranny of the nation, north, south, east and west.

Following on the pattern I had set, and Donnie had continued, we all used to attend Prime Minister's Question Time every Tuesday and Thursday from 3.15 to 3.30. However Scottish Question Time, our real opportunity to press the Government, was still held only once every six weeks and the Scottish Grand Committee turned out to be a talking-shop. All Scottish MPs were in membership, along with some very reluctant English MPs drafted in to make up the numbers, but it did nothing and achieved nothing.

I was appointed to the Select Committee on Violence in Marriage which was often called the 'Battered Wives' Committee'. We took much evidence from women in terrible circumstances but virtually none from men, who I knew from my legal career, also suffered in this way. The chairman of the committee was Willie Hamilton, my bête noire during the Hamilton years. During the hearings he was politeness and consideration itself, even when I wrote a minority report pointing out the differences that arose in the matter because of Scots law. In fact he even thanked me for my effort in doing so, but as soon as the committee had finished its work he returned to type and became boorish and rude.

Given the political circumstances of the time, the narrow government majority and the clear changes taking place north of the border (of which our group was a constant and visible sign), Scotland was frequently on the agenda of the House of Commons. This annoyed many non-Scottish members who were very intolerant, none more so than Tory back benchers from the shires. Every time a Scottish issue was raised they would start to jeer and shout. 'Too much time on Scotland' was their constant baying refrain, but we always replied, 'Just get rid of us then!' They had no answer to that. If we had not already realised how hard our task was going to be in winning power for Scotland, then such behaviour whenever discussed would have soon woken us up to the fact. But we did realise very quickly what we were up against and it was regularly confirmed to us, most dramatically of all on the occasion that the Queen spoke to both Houses of Parliament in 1977 (I think it was for the twenty-fifth anniversary of her accession). At this stage the time being spent on the Scotland Bill in the House of Commons was at its height.

All was going well until at a certain point the Queen looked up and, looking straight at her mother as if it had been pre-arranged, said, 'I cannot forget I was crowned Queen of the United Kingdom.' It was a clear and obvious political rebuke to the SNP and to the hundreds of thousands of Scots who supported the party. It was clearly the wrong thing for her to have said, whether the remark was advised by Government or personally motivated.

There is a clear distinction between the Union of the Crowns and the Union of the Parliaments and the SNP had no plans to dissolve the Union of the Crowns. At the end of the speech Donnie and I went out together into the Great Hall of Westminster, where William Wallace had been tried and sentenced. The press were all around and eager for a quote from the SNP Group Leader. He was clear and calm. He merely said that if he ever had to make the choice (and he hoped he never would) between the Queen and the freedom of Scotland, he would choose the freedom of his country. And as usual he finished by saying, 'Thank you for listening, gentlemen.'

Resentment at our presence took other strange forms as well. To be entitled to a seat in the Chamber (there are only enough seats for two-thirds of the members) one has to go in for prayers at the start of the day at 2.30, get a prayer card and insert it in a holder in the seat you intend to occupy. On our first day in the Commons I got all seven SNP MPs to prayers and got them prayer cards. We sat as a group, as I had intended, above the Liberals, but this was deeply offensive to one member in particular who had obviously decided that she wanted to sit there. She had not put in a prayer card but she had left her handbag, which we pushed along the bench. Then she arrived back – the formidable figure of

Elaine Kellet Bowman. She protested loudly and then plumped herself straight down onto Douglas Henderson's knee. She was no lightweight so Iain MacCormick edged his knee over to try and help a clearly suffering Douglas. To great guffaws throughout the Chamber she remained in this uncomfortable position for over an hour. I kept asking Douglas, 'Is your knee sore?' and eventually he had to reply, though gritted teeth, 'It's a lot worse than that!' Elaine eventually gave way, but she continued to try and sit in the middle of the SNP bench whenever she got the chance, which did not please the Speaker, who liked MPs to sit in the same seat all the time in party groups so that he could more easily allocate fair speaking time to them. Elaine was eccentric and could be difficult but she was hard-working, as I discovered later when she was in the European Parliament with me.

The Commons staff were very different and seemed to like our group more than most. The Serjeant-at-Arms, Rear Admiral Sir Sandy Gordon-Lennox (whom I had previously called the 'best paid janitor in Britain') was still in his post and he was very keen on my company for the odd drink or afternoon break, which we spent eating strawberries and cream on the sunlit terrace by the river. He owned an estate in the north-west of Sutherland and invited Stewart and me to stay but the party's attitude to 'lairds' made accepting the invitation unwise!

This was not the only invitation I got from the landed gentry. After the election I was invited by virtually all such individuals in the constituency to visit them. I sent them each the same letter to say that I couldn't fit in such an engagement at that time, but if they wrote again in a few months I would be sure to arrange something. Of course, not all of them repeated the invitation but some did, such as Lord Cawdor, who was extremely charming, and Lady Houldsworth of Dallas, who was welcoming and interesting. The Lord Lieutenant, Sir Iain Tennant, who was related to the Queen, was unfailingly courteous and helpful. His wife, Lady Margaret, had been a Moray councillor until she became too deaf to continue with the job.

Whereas in Hamilton I was rarely invited to any official event, in Moray I was invited to all of them. I paid frequent visits to the RAF bases and attended local functions and formal occasions. The council was helpful and made sure I was included in everything it was doing. Most local societies wanted to be in touch with me and in Lossiemouth particularly there wasn't a lifeboat day, a raft race or any other sort of happening that didn't check to see if I could come. In Moray and Nairn I was always opening things, giving prizes and presenting trophies. It was enjoyable to be a member of such a diverse and active community.

One event that I particularly enjoyed was the annual dinner of the Incorporated Trades of Elgin. They had been established by a charter granted by Alexander II in 1234 and the members of the six crafts – Hammermen, Glovers, Factors, Soutars, Weavers and Squarewrights – got together to form their Trades Guild which had the right of political representation on the Town Council until the First Reform Act of 1832. Of course the trades had much changed but the guild was strong and committed to the town and its history made fascinating telling. Apparently bribery to secure election with the support of the guild was not uncommon, and in the seventeenth century one candidate, Lord Fife, presented the Deacon of the Wrights with a psalter which contained not 300 pages (as it should have had) but 300 pound notes.

Despite such pleasant events, the sheer volume and scope of constituency work was frightening, but I remembered well how it had been the same in Hamilton and I got used to it. Issues were constantly arising, but in Moray and Nairn it was easier to get things done because I was no longer regarded as a temporary freak, but as the local member who was building local connections and who lived locally. Of course I had to blow my own trumpet, as all MPs do, and when I look at a typical week's press release for the local media I realise that today it would be spun even more determinedly. But I got coverage and was seen to be doing the job.

In the last week of June in 1974, for example, only four months after having been elected, I note that I told the press that I had met in London with the director of Ladbrokes, who were involved in a proposed leisure development in Lossiemouth. Amongst the matters discussed were possible locations for the development and arrangements for sewerage. I had also been at the annual lunch of the British Trawlermen's Federation at which I spoke about the need to stop the worst aspects of EEC regulation of fisheries – something that I was involved with for the next three decades.

In the House of Commons that same week the SNP group was trying to force another election, using Labour's delay at implementing the

Kilbrandon recommendations on devolution as our reason. I got in at Prime Minister's Questions to attack Harold Wilson on the issue of EEC regulations for whisky (our membership of the EEC was new and very unpopular in my constituency), pointing out that the water directives made our peaty rivers and springs 'impure'. Harold had to respond by admitting that many of Europe's rules were fatuous, including that which demanded that no brand, even quality ones, could be more than 70 per cent proof!

I was back on the EEC theme on the Friday, when I spoke at Willie MacRae's adoption meeting in Ross and Cromarty, pointing out that in energy – a key issue for Scotland as the largest oil producer in the European Union – the EEC wanted to control the rate of exploitation and the selling policies of oil producers. That meant that Europe would control the oil. I had already raised this matter in the Commons and been given a flat denial that this would happen by the Chancellor, Jim Callaghan, but many were not convinced. I made it to Dingwall and Alness for Willie's meetings by the skin of my teeth, for fog had stopped my plane landing at Kinloss.

My press release went on to note that I had been writing questions to the Secretary of State about rents in Findhorn and that I spoke at Bannockburn (where there was a crowd of over 10,000) on behalf of the Parliamentary group. I called the present generation of Scots a 'privileged generation' because I confidently expected it to be instrumental in bringing back a Parliament to Scotland. I think I would have wept had I known that it was to take another twenty-five years!

I finished the week doing Desert Island Discs for Radio 4, but the only records that I can now recall choosing were Kathleen Ferrier singing 'Blow the Wind Southerly' and Hugh MacDiarmid reading one of his poems.

There were always other matters of concern to attend to. In the first few months after the election I returned to the issue of the Scottish economy, on which I had secured a debate in 1969, and which I took as the topic for my maiden speech on the 1 April 1974. I started that speech with a reference to how things had changed very greatly, for me and for Scotland, in the years between winning Hamilton and returning as the Member for Moray and Nairn. I quote the Hansard report directly:

> This is the second time I have made a maiden speech, with a long gap between them. It is pleasant to be back again, particularly in view of one of

the outstanding contrasts which Hon. Members will have noticed. I was not even a party when I was here before. According to Mr Crossman, then the Leader of the House, there had to be two to be a party, so I did not qualify for a desk or a filing cabinet, and only the kindness of a Labour MP secured me a locker. Times have changed; I now have six colleagues. This is a pleasant contrast.

Another contrast is that I now represent a very different kind of constituency. Before, I represented an industrial constituency and I now represent the fair land of Moray and Nairn. I, too, will boast about the weather in my constituency, as did the Hon. Member for Eastbourne [Mr Gow]. Hon. Members may be sceptical, but I can tell them that we have the highest rate of sunshine in Scotland. We have very fair towns and a mediaeval cathedral city, as well as the best farming land in Britain and mine is the second most afforested constituency in the United Kingdom. I recommend all Hon. Members to visit it for their summer holidays.

I hope that the House will forgive me if I get on to the subject of Scotland as quickly as possible. The third contrast is that when I was last advancing my case for self-government for my country, the argument always was, 'Scotland is too poor; you need us.' Now, the argument is turned on its head. This is the most striking contrast of the lot. It is now said, 'Scotland is too rich; we need you.'

The period from February to October 1974 was very strange. It became obvious early on that the Parliament was not likely to last very long, so each of us not only needed to dig in locally but also master our briefs in the House of Commons in record time. I had a great deal of reading to do on Europe and on defence and foreign affairs, and I became an ardent reader of the *The Economist*, *The Times* and other serious papers and periodicals. Stewart was an enormous help as he always read about ten daily newspapers and everything else he could lay his hands on, and he remembered most of what he read. The legal portfolio was, in comparison, quite easy, as having just been working as an active and busy practitioner, my legal knowledge was up to date.

When a debate was due on one of my subjects I felt as if I were sitting a university degree exam all over again, for I was pitted against real experts on the issues. The group was always great in these circumstances, crowding round in support, and Donnie was the best leader it was possible to imagine – supportive and, because of his very fine reputation in the House, always listened to.

The European issue was dominant at that time, and I began to be glad that I had taken it on. Our policy was 'No voice, no entry', just like the position of the American states in their rebellion against their colonial masters. Nonetheless we wanted to find out what Europe thought of us and what our prospects might be if we were not hanging onto England's coat tails, so I visited Europe with Gwynfor Evans to work out the lie of the land. We met with Nicholas Soames, our first European commissioner and the son-in-law of Winston Churchill. He wanted the UK Parliament to take up the available seats in the unelected European Parliament in which all members were nominated representatives of their own state Parliament and chosen by their government. We were interested in the idea but made no commitment to it, believing that we would not be selected. We also believed then, as we do now, in the primacy of elections as the means of choosing representatives. Soames, however, emphasised that there would a welcome for our parties and clearly he was a very keen European, not hamstrung by the 'little Englander' mentality of so many. Later on I went back on another visit on behalf of the SNP, this time accompanied by George Leslie and Douglas Crawford. We were entertained by the British Ambassador to the Common Market, Sir Richard Majoribanks, who once again was keen to stress that our party would be very welcome in the European institutions.

Stewart did a great deal behind the scenes, and not just the reading. He was a very committed activist by this time and made audio tapes which were used by canvassers during election campaigns. He was a strong enthusiast for campaigning with a high visual profile and he also believed in writing directly to as many people as he could, as well as to the press. One of the many VIPs he wrote to, setting out the party's case, was Sir Hugh Fraser, who owned the Outram Group, Fraser's Stores and much much more.

One day I answered the phone in my Queen's Drive office to be told I was speaking to Sir Hugh Fraser, who wanted to join the SNP. I confess I said I thought someone was playing a joke, so he asked me to put the phone down and to phone the Outram Group and ask for him. I did so and he confirmed his intention, asking for an early meeting with Robert McIntyre and myself.

It turned out that some years previously Dr Mac had been invited to talk to some business men, including Sir Hugh. After that he had started seriously to consider supporting the SNP and had finally reached a decision after seeing the results of the February 1974 election. We all met in Outram's boardroom and I was photographed giving Sir Hugh his SNP membership card. He then immediately set to work, providing generous financial assistance which helped the SNP to establish our new offices in Manor Place in Edinburgh. He went further and on 15 June 1974 held a lunch in Glasgow for 150 businessmen and other key figures in order to seek further backing for the party. Many well-known individuals from commerce, finance, the trade unions and other areas of public life accepted invitations to attend and our MPs were present to speak and to answer questions. It was the first time that an audience of that calibre and size had turned out for the SNP and it was most impressive.

Afterwards Sir Hugh was quoted in the press as saying that he had joined the SNP because he was convinced that

> if we all put our backs to it and roll up our sleeves we will be able to show the rest of the European countries that we are as good as any of them. The SNP movement is simply the means whereby the self-expression and self-fulfilment of a great country can be attained without malice to others. Today, as never before, the growth opportunities and industrial development potential of Scotland are opening up an entirely new vista. In these circumstances, who better to shape and preserve the true interests of Scotland than the Scots themselves?

This was a most useful and important endorsement at a crucial time and it added to the momentum that was being built up between the February and the October elections.

The Government's principal problem in Scotland was its failure to do anything about Scottish devolution. The Kilbrandon Report had clearly indicated that progress was needed, but the new government elected in February 1974 simply sat on the issue.

If Labour was to go to the country, we all knew that their failure to take constitutional change forward would be an issue on which the SNP must campaign and on which it would do well. Thus, as another election was being talked about within weeks of the first one, it was a time of anticipation and rapid building rather than settling in for the long haul.

As summer approached, pressure for an election grew too and, although Stewart had arranged a splendid Russian holiday for us for the summer of 1974, I felt that I could not go, so he went alone to Samarkand and Tashkent and all those fabulous-sounding, magical places. We did however, manage to have time with the children away from home, in Carloway in Lewis. Despite our efforts, and the enormous influence of Donald Stewart the local MP, we totally failed to find a house for rent or a self-catering opportunity. Eventually we booked into the Doune Braes Hotel. On our first evening we wanted to take the children to a nearby beach, but when we emerged from the main door of the hotel we found ourselves in a scene resembling a traffic jam in the middle of London. Cars at all angles occupied every inch of the car park and all the surrounding verges. We could not get our car out to go anywhere and appeals to the owner of the hotel were totally in vain as he was fully engaged serving crowds of thirsty local customers in a bar that looked like a Wild West saloon. Pints and whiskies were even being slid along the counter to customers at the far end. The cause of all this was the severe local restrictions on licensing which had coincided that night with a warm evening and lots of people desperate for refreshment after a day at the peats. Thereafter we were careful to park outside the car park.

There was a fête in Carloway during the first week of our holiday, and despite being on holiday I was asked to open it, and felt I couldn't refuse. I decided to try and do so in Gaelic so after dinner the night before I enlisted the help of the hotel maids to help me write my speech. One was from Skye and one was from Lewis; both were native Gaelic speakers but they had very different accents. My attempts at pronunciation were treated with gales of laughter but somehow I managed to get together what I wanted to say. When I opened the fête and, to the astonishment of all, spoke only in Gaelic, I was even better received than usual. After the opening I mingled with the ladies of the fête committee and told them about the great difficulty we had had in trying to rent a house for a fortnight. The reply was illuminating: 'Mrs Ewing, we will never develop the tourist trade in Lewis until we get rid of all our friends and relations.'

No sooner had summer come to an end but the election was called. I was twice-blessed in my loyal band of activists and in the fact that Johnnie

Bichan agreed to be my agent for a second time. Everyone set to work with a will and it was a hard-fought campaign, as the Tories desperately wanted the seat back. Gordon Campbell had gone to the House of Lords and my Tory opponent was an advocate, Alex Pollock. For the first time the Liberals put up a candidate in the person of Keith Schellenberg, a millionaire with a colourful background who went to on earn notoriety as the owner and landlord of the island of Eigg. His intervention drew votes away from both the Conservatives and me, and the Liberal intervention in other seats in Scotland, for example in Lanark, made the difference between us winning and Labour or the Tories hanging on.

However, I still expected to win, and at the count Alex Pollock quickly conceded the election. The SNP samplers had, with their usual considerable accuracy, estimated my majority at 1,367, on a lower poll than in February. The Tory counters must have come to the same conclusion about the margin of victory for their party to concede so quickly, and the press had also heard that the figure was 1,367. However, when the sheriff read out the result he said I had won by only 367 votes. When I heard the majority I had an awful moment of panic, as it was 1,500 votes less than in February. I had thought that the majority might go down, given the lower poll, but this was a much bigger drop than we had believed possible. I am still not sure what happened that night. Could a box of 1,000 votes have been left behind a curtain, deliberately or accidentally? The official majority remains at 367, but I have my doubts.

During the campaign the press had started to predict that the SNP might win up to fifteen seats. In fact we got eleven, but we were in second place, often a very good second place, in another forty-two seats. Later on Michael Foot said to me, 'It's not the eleven of you who terrify me; it's your forty-two seconds,' and certainly our close pressure on all parties in Scotland was a big factor in events as they subsequently transpired.

Our group of seven had now become eleven, often referred to by the press as 'The First Eleven'. Douglas Crawford had won Perth, Andrew Welsh had won Angus South, Margaret Bain (later Ewing) had won East Dunbartonshire and George Thompson had been returned in Galloway.

Margaret had had to suffer three recounts before emerging with a majority of twenty-two, but George had the narrower win, a mere difference of seventeen votes. When they met up in the Caledonian Hotel in Edinburgh for our first group meeting after the election Margaret said to George, 'Well, we made it – just!' to which George replied, 'What do you mean? You have a huge majority.'

That first group meeting was even more exciting than the one we had held only eight months before, because now we were absolutely certain we were on the way to freedom. To have gone from one MP, elected at a by-election in 1967, to eleven only seven years later was progress beyond our wildest dreams, and a sure sign, we thought, of even better things to come. With more members we could spread out the portfolios. Douglas Crawford took the finance brief, for which he was perfectly suited, as he had been an economic journalist and had been employed by the Scottish Council for Development and Industry. He knew how to deal with the complexities of finance bills and was already able to draft the difficult but vital amendments. In addition he took very seriously the need to court the Scottish business scene and was always ready to entertain key financial and commercial figures to lunch or dinner.

George Thompson took on the forestry portfolio as Galloway was the most afforested part of Scotland (though Moray and Nairn was in second place on that score). George had been a principal teacher before his election and Margaret Bain had also been pursuing a successful career in education, so the two of them could also talk on education and other social matters. I carried on with the law, with defence and also, because no one else wanted it, with Europe. I was glad to do so, because I had been working very hard to master that brief and was beginning to develop a range of knowledge about European affairs, and to be enthusiastic about what was possible for Scotland if we were ever able to negotiate our own terms of entry.

Andrew Welsh became our housing spokesperson but he soon developed an expertise across the whole local government area. I had been on the interviewing panel when Andrew was first passed as a candidate, and when he was asked what seat he would like to try for he replied that he would go anywhere in Scotland, and he meant it. At his interview for the Angus South seat he wanted to ask a few questions, as he was originally from Paisley and did not know the east of Scotland very well. 'So how many branches do you have?' he asked. 'Seventeen' was the answer. And how much money for the election?' 'Thousands.' After all the struggles in other constituencies Andrew thought he had found himself in heaven and after his election he completely identified with the seat, so much so that we used to call him an 'Angus nationalist'. Andrew suited his constituency ideally, and they him, and he went on to mastermind the capture of the council of which he became Provost during his time out of Westminster after 1979. That we have retained power in that area for so long is a huge tribute to Andrew's organisational abilities and his skill in building a winning team. He is not only a safe pair of hands but also a stalwart friend in times of need.

The London *Times* said we were the most talented group ever to be in the Commons and we revelled in that distinction. We attended each others' maiden speeches and all of them were notable. Indeed Douglas Crawford, who had been at Cambridge and was a devoted Anglophile, positively seduced the Chamber by saying, 'On independence England will lose a surly lodger and acquire a sympathetic neighbour.' George Thompson was different, but no less memorable. When going in to hear him, Douglas Crawford said to me in jest, 'Shall we warn the House of Commons about George or shall we just let them find out for themselves?' The point of this remark was the contrasts that George presented. His broad Galloway accent would be dismissed by the majority of very southern English members, but then they would discover, as we knew, that this masked a brilliant mind and a razor-sharp wit. George had been a 'stickit' Roman Catholic priest who had got to his final year at the Scots College in Rome and spoke Greek, Italian, French and German. Now he learned an extra language each year just for fun! George did not disappoint us or the Chamber. He quickly became such a renowned and popular speaker that when his name went up on the board many MPs came in simply for the pleasure of listening to him.

Margaret Bain, as she was then, was also outstanding. In fact Donald Stewart always described her as the 'star' of our little group, saying that she had 'the wisest head, the best idea of SNP strategy and the most persuasive style of speaking'. Margaret was the youngest MP in the Commons at that time and wore, as was then fashionable, the shortest of short skirts, for which she got to be known as 'Legs' Bain. As the only other woman in the group she quickly became my best friend in the Chamber and out of it. Yet little did I dream that she would end up not just an abiding and dear companion but also as my daughter-in-law. It is not often that someone so close to the mother marries the son.

The election had made debate on the constitution a certainty, but the downside of that was that our group became virtual prisoners in the Palace of Westminster. We could not risk departing lest a vote was held to catch us out, and our whip had to work hard to secure a temporary lull and a period when it was guaranteed that there would be no division. At those times we were like children getting out of school and we rushed off to find a suitable restaurant where we could relax.

The core group of diners were George Thomson, Iain MacCormick, Douglas Crawford, Andrew Welsh, Margaret Bain and myself, but others joined us as they could. George Reid, sociable as he always was, spent much of his time studying and writing, for the constitutional brief was central to our concerns and vast in scope. Donnie Stewart came occasionally but he was much in demand by members of all parties in the House of Commons.

Donnie not only commanded virtually universal respect but he was also extremely well read and seemed to have total recall – he could summon up at any time the right quotation from poets, playwrights and all manner of writers, thinkers and politicians from many countries and could recall an apt joke for every occasion. He was soon made a Privy Councillor and when he retired in 1987 he was offered a seat in the House of Lords, but he turned it down flat. I must say that I disagreed with his decision. The SNP does not want to be at Westminster, but whilst we are there we have to make use of every opportunity to make the nationalist case and to have our voice heard in the decision-making process. The hereditary principle is deeply objectionable, but we are not abstentionists and we should be present and vocal whenever we can. The party has only debated the issue of the Lords once in recent years and I found myself on the losing side. I continue to think, however, that we are missing an opportunity to further our cause.

The group continued to hold regular and detailed meetings but afterwards we usually took our staff for a drink, to the Kremlin Bar on the Terrace. Donnie made it a strict rule from the beginning that none of us drank alone, fearing that if we did so then we could be misquoted or compromised by those who wanted us to fail.

Robert Maxwell, already notorious and very wealthy, had been the MP for Buckingham from 1964 to 1970 and had been put in charge of the catering committee at the House of Commons. His first action – to replace all the linen napkins with paper ones – was a classic business cost-saving measure, but it was met with furious protests and soon abandoned. He then decided to sell off the large stock of champagne held in the House of Commons cellars as he claimed it was 'going off', – something that apparently happens to champagne after fifteen years, though I have never put that to the test. The result was that the best champagne was reduced to £3.50 a bottle, a fact that was not advertised amongst the members. It was the staff who knew and they kept the information to themselves, although they used to tell members they liked. Many of the waiters were Catalonian and strong nationalists, so we were always in their good books and we were quickly let in on the secret. Despite the passage of time bottles were still available to those in the know, and at that price a bottle to share was cheaper than a round of drinks, so the SNP quickly became known as the 'champagne party', though whether the term was one of contempt or envy I never discovered.

The period from October 1974 to the General Election in May 1979 seemed to pass in a rush. Of course, as I shall recount later, I became an appointed member of the European Parliament in 1975 and that task took up vast portions of my time and much of my attention. My perspective on what was happening became much more European, although we rushed backwards and forwards to London all the time, and backwards and forwards to Scotland too.

Of course family life went on as well. One tradition that restarted was visits from Stewart and the children each July, which always kicked off with a trip to Hamley's and took in jaunts in and around London. My former flat now belonged to Lorna Blackie, but she generously gave me the use of it whenever I wanted it and the family stayed there. Terry was at school in Glasgow when I was elected but we soon decided that for as long as I was the member for Moray and Nairn he should go to Gordonstoun, as the school was only three miles from Lossiemouth. In good weather he would cycle over to my house and on winter days I would sometimes send a taxi and he would bring a group of his friends, many of whom were from overseas. During Terry's time there I was invited, as the local MP, to undertake a question and answer session at the school. One boy asked what would happen after independence if one owned a house in Scotland

and a house in England. Would one be Scottish or English? I told him that he would just have to choose. The questioner was none other than Prince Andrew!

One of the reasons for Terry going to Gordonstoun was that I could see much more of him than I had ever managed to see of Fergus when he was at Loretto, and I was glad of that. But the whole family came to my little house in Lossie a great deal over the years and they were able to accompany me to many events as well as spending much time on lovely Lossie beach. This all worked much better than it had when I was the MP for Hamilton.

Constituency work, the Commons, Europe and family all curtailed my other travel, but I did go to Dublin in 1975 for the funeral of Eamon De Valera. When I heard that he had died I knew that I must go and pay my respects, not just because of the tremendous meeting I had had with him but because he had been one of my great heroes. The only way I could manage the trip was to hire a small plane at my expense, and this I did. It stood at Dublin Airport alongside the US presidential plane and the one that had brought Princess Grace of Monaco. The British political representation was poor – in addition to myself I saw only Ted Short, Leader of the House, and Jeremy Thorpe.

It seemed as if there were millions of mourners there – in fact it seemed as if the whole country was in mourning. There was no music, just the slow beat of drums, and I was honoured to be part of it, to be a friend of Ireland and a friend of the great man they were burying.

However, reality returned more quickly than I would have liked. I had to fly back the same day to a meeting in Scotland at which I discovered that I was the subject of some criticism within the SNP for having attended the event. Nonetheless I did not regret going for a moment and I do not regret it now.

Perhaps some of the criticism was because of a slowly-building frustration in the SNP in Scotland, and at Westminster, about the issue of constitutional change. The key and central concern for all of us was that of a Parliament for Scotland, and all the main parties had stood in the October 1974 election committed to the establishment of such a Parliament. But election promises were one thing; delivering those promises was quite another.

Labour introduced a devolution bill, but it soon ran into enormous opposition from various quarters, most especially from Labour MPs from the north of England, who were opposed to privileges being granted to Scotland that they would not get. Labour itself was very split on the issue, with the emergence of a small group of Scottish Labour MPs who were very worried about the sincerity and commitment of the Government. After the failure of the first bill and a set of new proposals, this impasse led one of them, Jim Sillars, to leave the party and start his own Scottish Labour Party.

The SNP had problems too. Gwynfor Evans once told me he thought the SNP Group was misguided in not holding the reins of the party back home, and although at the time I thought such a view was too centrist, I now see that he was right. We were all as dedicated and hard-working as we could be, but we trusted those back home too much and we discounted the jealousy the unelected can feel towards the elected. Such a fracture in the essential unity we needed was a fatal blow for the struggle.

Our liaison with the party National Executive, and thus with the party back home, was Margo MacDonald, who was by then the Deputy Leader of the SNP. She would visit often, and as time went on these visits became more and more difficult. She would often stay with me, but she was always very keen to find out where 'Jim' [Sillars] was and if we could see him or dine with him. Of course I was not to know then what would transpire, but the signs were already there of a growing affection between them.

One of our problems was political naivety, both in Scotland and at Westminster. We simply did not realise until it was too late that on the matter of devolution, let alone independence, we were and are up against an unscrupulous enemy, for all the unionist parties have no compunction about indulging in dirty tricks. Even Jo Grimond, such a gentleman at times, let us down when he sought a special deal for Orkney and Shetland and fuelled the fire of those who wanted to exploit the fact that the islands had a natural distrust of the Central Belt.

Successes in local government made by the SNP in 1977 were, unfortunately, followed by internal squabbles and by a failure to deliver what had been promised. The crucial Garscadden by-election was a difficult contest, made more difficult because of the way in which the excellent candidate, my old friend Keith Bovey, was traduced by the press and misrepresented by those who knew what a formidable foe he would be if elected to Westminster. Donnie Stewart, in particular, couldn't believe what was happening, for we all knew that Keith had been in the army during the war and had been much respected there as everywhere else. Yet he was vilified for his moderate and responsible stance on weapons of mass destruction.

As the Labour government dragged out the devolution issue and failed to deal with it effectively, there was a growing weariness in Scotland with the whole process. It was reflected in our group at Westminster, as night after night the SNP group would troop through the voting lobbies becoming more and more disenchanted with the matter and the way in which it was being handled. Donnie did a superb job in keeping our morale up, but it was soul destroying to see the great opportunity for change being gerrymandered in this way. George Reid in particular suffered terribly as promise after promise was broken as he spent those years devotedly as our principal constitutional spokesman

One night after a particularly terrible House of Commons defeat on the Scotland Bill Donnie ordered the other ten of us to sit on the bench and stay where we were. He then, in an almost deserted House of Commons, went onto the Liberal bench in front of us and told us this story:

> John Wayne was having a whisky in a saloon. When he was finished he went out and found that his horse was gone. He went back in, ordered another whisky and told the assembled company that he was going to finish his drink and if his horse was not returned by then, then what would happen might well be what happened in Denver, Colorado that very night one year before. That struck fear into all who heard it, and when he had finished and went out the horse was back where it, should have been.
>
> He mounted up and as he prepared to ride off a man ran out of the saloon and said fearfully to him, 'Mr Wayne, we are sorry about that. But what did happen in Denver, Colorado this very night one year ago?' John Wayne just looked at him and said, 'Well, of course, I had to f——g-well walk home'.

The whole group dissolved in laughter and we were still laughing as we left the Chamber. Those who had defeated us were astonished, but the image it gave – as Donnie knew – was the right one. We were not going to be ground down and we were not going to despair.

Yet if ever there was a time for despair it was as the second bill approached its conclusion and we found ourselves trapped by the appalling prospect of a false and fiddled referendum. There had only been one referendum before this, the European one of 1975 in which campaign the SNP had opposed membership, and that had been decided on the fair basis of a simple majority of votes cast. Even Margaret Thatcher had been on record saying that in a democracy 'one vote will do'. Throughout 1977, 1978 and in the early part of 1979 a huge number of myths began to be perpetrated by those who opposed any change. Cost was always given as an excuse for inaction, although we worked out that the cost of running the new Parliament would be less than the cost of running the military bands in the British Army. Enoch Powell took up the argument by saying that even the smallest change would put Scotland on the slippery slope to independence, a slogan that attracted – from the other side of the political spectrum – Tam Dalyell and the many virulent Labour anti-devolutionists.

Despite the recommendations of Lord Kilbrandon and their endorsement by all the major parties (and Kilbrandon had pointed out that an Assembly was likely to be a civilised Parliament given Scotland's record and our desire for change), both principle and the detail were undermined again and again by those who claimed to want something better but actually wanted nothing at all. The infamous Tory 'Declaration of Perth' was the worst example of this deceit, for once the Tories had power, the whole issue was relegated from their thinking, as they always intended.

The power of institutional inertia was much to the fore, too. The Secretary of State for Scotland had in his favour no fewer than 4,819 posts – quangoes and similar bodies – and civil servants and backward-looking politicians did not want to give up even a fragment of such undemocratic power. They were quite prepared to deceive and ignore the wave of decentralisation which was sweeping across Europe and putting at least a little power into the hands of the Basques, the Catalans and many others. They were also prepared to ignore their own history. Keir Hardie fought his first election, the Mid Lanark by-election, on a platform that included Home Rule for Scotland. The Red Clydesiders were passionately committed to Home Rule and saw its achievement as a way of changing Scotland for the better for working people. Clement Attlee was at one time the chairman of the London Scottish Home Rule Association and the ILP (Independent Labour Party), and later the Labour Party embraced the policy of 'dominion status', which was the status of Canada.

It was only on entering office after the Second World War that Labour relegated constitutional change to the back-burner. This was largely because it became obvious that Labour needed the votes of Scotland and Wales in order to run the UK and to have any chance of defeating the Conservatives. So Scotland became valuable in the Westminster power struggle and Scotland's desire for self-government was sacrificed by Labour at Westminster in its own interests.

Nonetheless that desire did not go away, despite common myth. In 1950 two million Scots signed the covenant organised by Dr John MacCormick (known as 'King' John), father of both Iain MacCormick, MP for Argyll and of Professor Neil MacCormick, later an SNP MEP. That covenant demanded a Scottish Parliament. Westminster responded to the demand by reiterating the view that it could only be made through the ballot box, which meant the parliamentary ballot box. Yet how could it be made in that way when none of the main parties was prepared to offer it? The covenant signatures were sent back to Scotland, and London proceeded to ignore the very existence of a desire for change. Their view seemed to be if it wasn't talked about at Westminster, then it didn't matter and wouldn't happen.

But the issue continued to exist. I had been particularly impressed by the covenant and what it meant to Scotland, and when I was the MP for Hamilton I advertised to find out the whereabouts of the original documents, as no one seemed to know what had happened to them. A builder in Rutherglen contacted me, for he had had them in his yard for years, a place selected by the late Dr MacCormick as one which would provide secure storage out of the ken of Westminster and safe from those who would regard them as two million rebukes to their own complacency. My agent in Hamilton, John McAteer, there and then hired a lorry so that we could take them immediately to the National Library in Edinburgh. I still have a photo of myself delivering them there.

Now at the end of the 1970s the desire for change that the covenant represented had resurfaced. But Westminster was still determined to have none of it, so it cooked up the biggest political swindle of the century.

All previous elections in the UK had been fought (and continue to be fought) on the principle that a simple majority of seats is sufficient to form a government. The Tory Government in 1970 was elected by only 33 per cent of the UK electorate and the two Labour governments of 1974 were elected by a mere 29 per cent. Nonetheless they won and entered office.

In the only previous UK referendum, no special provision was made by Parliament for interpreting the result other than accepting the majority decision, and this was also true of the referendum on the border question in Ireland. But the 40 per cent rule which was applied to the Scottish referendum was without precedent and without principle, as it meant that if the 40 per cent hurdle was not cleared, the matter of devolution would be decided by a vote in the Commons. It was naked politics designed to thwart change.

The 40 per cent amendment was introduced by George Cunninghame, the MP for Islington, who had been at school in Scotland but who had spent his career working for the diplomatic service and the Labour party. On the face of it it appeared simple and reasonable, for all it required was that 40 per cent of the electorate must approve the measure before it could be automatically implemented. However, the implications of the 40 per cent rule quickly became clear to most Scottish MPs. The vote would be held on an electoral register which would be at least, in some parts of Scotland, 20 per cent inaccurate given the fact that it was not completely up-to-date. Normally the dead and those who have moved home are not counted in any election, but under the 40 per cent rule they would all automatically be included as 'No' voters; so would the sick and those who chose to stay at home.

But there are other problems with a fixed tariff. Twenty-eight thousand students were registered then, both at home and at their place of study. A 'Yes' vote in one place would be cancelled by the implicit 'No' vote in the other. This ludicrous situation was exemplified by the case of George Reid, whose house had two doors on different streets and who, by an error, was registered to vote at both addresses. His front-door vote would be cancelled by not appearing to cast his back-door vote! But if he voted twice he would be breaking the law.

The arithmetic of the 40 per cent rule clinched the matter. If, for whatever reason of weather or difficulty, only 40 per cent of the Scottish electorate voted in the referendum, every one of them would have to vote

'Yes' in order for it to succeed. Even on a reasonable turnout of 70 per cent, 58 per cent would have to vote 'Yes' in order to win. That is not democracy, that is gerrymandering.

There was furious opposition in Scotland. Sheriff Peter Thomson, who was sacked from the bench for his constant public support for a plebiscite of the people of Scotland, toured the streets of our cities with a sandwich board which read 'If you do not vote/You are voting no/To Scots having control/Of Scottish affairs', and that about summed up the matter. Even so the amendment was passed, largely by the votes of English MPs.

Of course we were heartbroken at first, but we knew that we had to keep fighting. So we redoubled our efforts. But even then Westminster had not finished its deceit. Although during the referendum on membership of the EEC a leaflet had been sent to every household, the Government refused to do the same for this referendum, despite it being Government policy to introduce devolution. The Government also refused to lay down even the mildest ground rules for the campaign or to make any public money available to campaigning organisations to offset the massive funds supplied anonymously to the 'No' campaigns, although such funds had been available during the EEC referendum. And to round off the insults the Government connived to blacking-out party political broadcasts on TV which might have compensated in a small way for the lack of official information.

Nonetheless we all campaigned. I spent days and days persuading, arguing and campaigning in the run-up to 1 March 1979. So did all my colleagues, but we were pitted against those who were, to quote Margaret Bain, 'a motley collection of sinister influences'. Big Business was helping – and helping with stacks of cash – people such as the Labour Old Etonian Tam Dalyell and the young and viciously anti-SNP journalist Brian Wilson, who had been an SNP member himself only a few years before. The Marxist-dominated 'Labour Says No' campaign was happy to appear on platforms with the increasingly right-wing Teddy Taylor and his ilk. To add to the mix, Scottish entertainers like the Alexander Brothers and Kenneth McKellar were unwisely inveigled into supporting those people who wanted Scotland to remain powerless and voiceless. Government ministers who should have been out in front arguing for their proposals were mostly invisible.

Much of the press supported with various degrees of enthusiasm a 'Yes' vote – but some were vitriolically opposed, such as the *Daily Express*, which on the day of the vote published a terrifying set of predictions about what would happen if Scotland chose to change. These included the closure of Linwood and of the Scottish steel industry and a disastrous drop in our exports. Those things happened, but they happened because we didn't change.

When I look back on it I am surprised that such a weight of opposition did not have more effect. Yet despite the obstacles and one of the roughest winters for years, the people of Scotland voted 'Yes' by a clear margin of 4 per cent. And they voted in greater numbers than they did at the EEC referendum. But of course the result was not represented that way either in Scotland or in London. The proposition was deemed to have failed, due to the notorious 40 per cent rule, yet by all the criteria of democracy hitherto applied in the United Kingdom, the Scottish electorate had returned an indisputable 'Yes' on 1 March to a Scottish Assembly as proposed in the Scotland Act. One million two hundred and thirty thousand nine hundred and thirty-seven Scots said 'Yes'. Those voters represented 51.6 per cent of all those voting. Only by overturning every precedent and making a mockery of the basic principle of democracy, that the majority vote defines the will of the people, did Westminster refuse to set up a Scottish Assembly.

After the referendum it was inevitable that Labour would soon have to go to the country. The 'Winter of Discontent' had made the government one of the most unpopular of all time, but if James Callaghan had sought an election in October 1978 he might have hung on. Now it was just a matter of time, and the vote of no confidence brought to an end a Government which was already finished. Nonetheless it is interesting to note, in the light of repeated jibes from Labour about the SNP's role in this matter, that Jim Callaghan himself in his memoirs blames the English North-east Labour MPs for making his Government collapse, not the Nationalists. We wanted to ensure that constitutional change was not dead and that the process could continue. That was our aim from start to finish, for that was what we were elected to do.

There was still the faintest glimmer of hope in that regard. The referendum amendment meant that the question of the implementation of the Scotland Bill would now have to return to the Commons, where the Government could seek to get it passed. However, the SNP National Council had been understandably incensed by the referendum debacle, the 40 per cent rule and by the Government's careless and incompetent approach to the whole question of Scottish self-rule. They insisted that the SNP Group at Westminster table a motion of no confidence and only the magnificent eloquence of George Thompson managed to get us thirty days' grace.

We continued to try to salvage something, but alas a government in its death throes which had almost gone full term was incapable of either restoring faith in its intentions or keeping faith with the people of Scotland. It did nothing and it became clear that it had no intention of trying to help – its North-east of England members saw to that, as did its anti-devolution Scottish representatives. Eventually, it was obvious that it was going to collapse but the knife-edge electoral arithmetic which had been so important over the past four years was still a factor. Frank Maguire, the Independent Republican member for Fermanagh and South Tyrone, was the swing vote and he had usually supported the Government, in exchange (it was said) for the release of a couple of prisoners from Longkesh each time he turned up in the voting lobby. This time he was persuaded by Gerry Fitt to attend the vital session, but it turned out that he had only come, as he put it, to 'abstain in person'. The Government fell.

The election of May 1979 was hard-fought again, and once more my opponent was Alex Pollock. I had an increasing sense of confidence during the campaign because it seemed to me that despite the difficulties of the SNP I had, like many of my colleagues, gained strong local support for local reasons during the past five years. I went to the count believing that I had probably won, perhaps with an increased majority. It was thus the strangest political experience of my life to find myself quite clearly winning every town and village with more votes than in 1974, only to be astonished by the late appearance of a huge number of postal votes from the RAF bases. Normally RAF service personnel did not vote in the constituency, though they had the right to do so, and wives only voted if they had the necessary residence qualification. This time something or someone had motivated or cajoled them to turn out and to defeat what was the clear will of the local community. Everyone at the count, even non-

SNP members, were horrified by this development because it would not be good for local relations or local democracy. Indeed the law was changed afterwards to allow service personnel to vote only at their normal home addresses and not where they were temporarily resident.

The figures spoke for themselves. I lost by only 420 votes, having gained over a thousand more than in October 1974. Both the Liberal and Labour votes were up, with the Liberals now in third place. Once gain the Liberals had been the spoilers, allowing the RAF votes to swing the result. I felt dazed as my defeat sank in, for only a few moments earlier my victory seemed assured. Of course I had to speak from the platform and I said that I feared for my country without Scottish voices to defend it, for by then I had heard of some of the other defeats of fellow SNP MPs. It was a dismal night. I hope I was as gracious in defeat as I was determined to be, not least because no one looked more surprised to win than Alex Pollock.

The family had all returned to Glasgow, but my brother David came back with me to my house on the square. We had not been back for long when the police called to ask if I intended to go anywhere as they anticipated possible trouble in Lossiemouth. People had heard that it was the RAF who had stopped the candidate they wanted being elected, and although the police had made a mild request to the RAF that their servicemen should stay on the base, many poured into the Lossie bars, almost gloating. There were quite a few fights that night, but no arrests, and I felt desperately sad at this turn of events. David and I sat in the gloom in 'Goodwill' as we heard the wail of police sirens outside.

Then suddenly the phone rang. A voice said, 'This is Andrew.' I said, 'Andrew who?' and he replied, 'Prince Andrew. I am sorry to tell you that your son Terry has been in an accident and has been taken to Dr Gray's hospital in Elgin with a neck injury.' All political thoughts disappeared at once as I imagined my lovely son becoming a paraplegic. I dropped the phone and David drove me into Elgin in record time. On arrival we saw a grey-faced and unconscious Terry on a stretcher being wheeled into the operating theatre. I was devastated and unable to think of anything else. My heart was in my mouth as we waited in the hospital for news. Eventually a doctor emerged to tell me that although Terry had an injury to two of his neck vertebrae it was not grave, and that he would recover in time. Only then did I feel that I could phone Stewart, who, unusually, completely lost his cool and announced that he was on his way up by car.

Terry was taken to the school infirmary after his initial treatment, and he found himself the only patient there. David and I followed on and when we arrived at the school we were met by the headmaster, the housemaster and a rather nervous-looking Prince Andrew. We went in to see Terry, who refused to explain precisely what had happened. His reluctance did not change in the weeks, months and years afterwards. When Stewart got there he wanted to remove Terry from the school immediately, but Terry opposed this and would not budge.

Prince Andrew was the head of Terry's house, but unusually the housemaster and deputy housemaster had been out, so Andrew was actually in charge of sixty teenage boys when the incident – whatever it was – happened. It was the day of the annual 'Old Boys' versus the Gordonstoun first XI cricket match, where custom dictated that the 'Old Boys' supplied generous amounts of spirits for the post-match celebrations.

Whatever happened, I suspect that Andrew and the others (for the Palace had been quickly informed) were fearful of headlines like 'Winnie's Son Breaks Neck – Prince Andrew in Charge'. I suspect they were almost as relieved as I was that Terry's injury was less serious than at first appeared. I cannot imagine that it was not in some way connected to what was happening only a few miles away at an election count, though Terry continues to reassure me that it wasn't.

9

The Unelected Parliament

THE TWO GENERAL ELECTIONS of 1974 had been fought against a backdrop of continued Scottish unease about the European Economic Community, as it was called then. Strange as it may seem now, at that time the Tories were generally in favour of Europe and Labour was generally against. Heath had secured accession but Wilson promised that he would renegotiate the terms if he was elected. In early 1975, after two Labour election victories, Wilson announced that he had achieved what he thought was necessary and that the promised referendum on continued membership would take place in June. The SNP campaigned against membership, not because we were implacably opposed to the EEC but because we felt it was essential that Scottish membership was undertaken on Scottish terms. Our fishing and other vital industries would be affected and we needed special consideration of such matters.

The referendum took place on 5 June 1975 and in the UK as a whole the vote in favour was 67.2 per cent to 32.8 per cent on a 64.5 per cent turnout. However, it was much closer in Scotland when the Western Isles and Shetland voted against; the only places to do so. As they were likely to be hardest hit, this was not surprising, but it was an indication of how many in Scotland worried about the future as part of a formalised Europe.

Membership of the EEC gave a country the right to nominate members to the then unelected and much weaker European Parliament. The four largest nations – Britain, Italy, Germany and France – had thirty-six seats each and the smaller countries were represented pro rata, though even tiny Luxembourg had six, for an area with half the population of Edinburgh.

The thirty-six British seats had not been fully taken up prior to the referendum as Labour refused to take part. The Tories sent eighteen members and the Liberals two but Harold Wilson resolved to change that by allocating the seats more fairly. The Tory seats were reduced to sixteen drawn from the Commons and the Lords, and Labour took eighteen, with a similar mix from the two chambers. The Liberals were offered only one seat. Greatly to our surprise, the Prime Minister asked to see Donnie and offered the SNP the remaining place. But there was a sting in the tail – Donnie met the Prime Minister at 4 p.m. in 10 Downing St, but Wilson demanded an answer by 6 p.m. or he would give the place to the Ulster Unionists. He was keen to get the vote through that night.

A hurried group-meeting was called and we discussed the matter and then voted on it. Gordon Wilson nominated George Reid, who had served in the Council of Europe, but I was also nominated and I took the view that I was entitled to the seat as I had worked hard on the European portfolio when no one else had wanted to. I had taken it on twice and had begun to make an effective contribution, and I didn't think it fair that it should be removed from me when suddenly there was the prospect of speaking out in another Parliament as well. That argument seemed to work and I won the vote very comfortably. My name went forward before 6 p.m.

The Liberals were of course furious. The two representatives they had selected on the assumption that they would get two places were Sir Gladwyn Jebb, now in the Lords, who had been the first Director General of the United Nations and also UK Ambassador to Washington, and Russell Johnston, the MP for Inverness. These two had been the nominees for the last year and had been working hard. With only one place it was a difficult situation, but the Liberal leadership decided to keep Gladwyn Jebb in place for another year to let him finish a book he was writing on European defence. Understandably Russell was bitterly disappointed, for he was a keen European. But the Liberals were not going to rest until they had made everyone realise how angry they were. They used what seemed like endless procedural devices to keep the House debating through most of the night.

The reason the matter had to be concluded so quickly was that those nominated were due to attend the European Parliament the very next day (10 July), which was also my birthday. I had a weary sense of unreality (I had, after all, been up all night) as I was waved off by Andrew Welsh and Iain MacCormick. The meeting was in the old Parliament in Luxembourg so I booked in to the Holiday Inn and set off for the building quite unaware of where it was and what I was expected to do. I had known about my appointment for less than 24 hours, and yet there I was.

There was no settling-in time at all. As I climbed up the staircase in the hallway of the building my arm was grasped by an Irishman whom I did not know, but who turned out to be the Director General, in charge of visitors who came in their thousands. Without even an introduction he said to me, 'Please come and address a visitors' group from Tipperary – they are waiting for you.' I had not yet found my seat or even the Chamber, but I was expected to start addressing visitors – moreover, ones that had come a long way from Tipperary!

Once I had finished with the Irish I needed to find somewhere to sit in the Chamber, for I was back to being a group of one. I knew that there had been an independent member called Lord O'Hagan, so I decided to sit in O'Hagan's seat. Interestingly enough he sat behind the British Labour members at the back on the left side, which is where I also wanted to be. But it was not where Willie Hamilton wanted me to be. My old adversaries, Hamilton and Dalyell, were amongst the Labour contingent and Willie complained that he had to keep looking round behind him to see what I was doing and how I was voting. So he, or someone on his behalf, formally complained to the Parliament's authorities and asked for me to be moved. This was done without me being consulted at all. When I heard about this I rushed to the office of Hans Nord, who was then Secretary General. He was a Dutchman, so in my best Dutch I complained about his staff moving the seat of a Member of Parliament without telling that member first. Wearily he called for his advisers and 'het Plan' – the Plan – and then spread out the seating arrangements before us and asked where I would like to be.

I told him that I wanted to sit at the back where I could see everything that was going on and that I wanted to sit on the left. So he provided a seat in the back row immediately to the left of the dividing middle corridor. This satisfied me, not least because it was the best seat in the house, and there were no further complaints (at that stage) from Willie Hamilton. My seat also marked me out as an independent member and not a member of any of the political groups.

The UK delegation, who were all members of either the House of Commons or the House of Lords, tended to stay together in the same hotel. At first this was the Holiday Inn, but then we would stay at various places as rooms became available. Accommodation was stretched in both Luxembourg and Strasbourg, but I got into the way of making sure that I had a reservation and then dropping my luggage at the hotel on my way to the Parliament from the airport. On one occasion, however, the plane was severely delayed and I had to go straight to the Parliament. When, much later, I got to the hotel, they had given away my reservation and there was no room for me. A taxi driver took me to four or five other hotels, but they were all full. Eventually I told the taxi to take me to the British Consulate and the consul answered the door in his dressing-gown. I asked him for a telephone directory and a phone so that I could find a hotel in which to rest my very weary head, but he surprised me by saying, 'Oh no, Winnie, you had better just stay here for the night.' So I did and was served breakfast in bed in the consulate, something not many taxpayers have experienced. I then teased him as I was saying my thanks on leaving by telling him that he had an excellent hotel and that I intended to recommend it to my thirty-five other UK colleagues!

All the travelling was very wearing and sometimes we had to do it a couple of times a week; it was not unusual to be called back to the House of Commons to vote and then have to go straight back again to Europe. On such occasions we travelled in a special aeroplane which the ex-Foreign Minister, Patrick Gordon Walker, always referred to as the plane 'of elastic bands and Sellotape'.

I remember once, wearily, trying to impress on the Government Chief Whip, Michael Cox, that there was no point in my coming back because I was going to be paired. But he had other ideas and kept insisting that there was an inflexible rule that if we were needed, we must return So I did, as usual, arriving back at the Commons just in time to go into the lobby for the ten o'clock vote.

In addition to the formal work there were many grand social events and receptions, the most glittering of which were given by the cities of Luxembourg and Strasbourg, which alternated their role of hosting the Parliament. Events were hosted by a variety of bodies (for example those supporting direct elections to the Parliament, a cause I believed in) as well as by the member states, and I seemed to be invited to most of them. This may have been because I spoke good German and good Dutch, but it could not account for my constant presence at the frequent Irish parties. On one occasion at which not just the Irish MEPs were present but also all the Irish working in the Community, I found myself the only non-Irish person present and was very touched when the Irish Prime Minister, Jack Lynch, said in his speech, 'There is a young woman here who is striving for her country to get the rights that we in Ireland have so long fought for.' This remark was followed by loud applause.

The Irish soon became very supportive of me. There was, unfortunately, precious little support of other kinds, for poor as our allowance was at Westminster, there was absolutely none in Europe. I had no staff, and nobody to undertake even the most basic research; all the preparation for questions and speeches had to be done on my own. I quickly found that in some ways making speeches in the European Parliament was more difficult than speaking at Westminster, for it was necessary to know about the relevant issue, not just in relation to Scotland or the UK as a whole; it was also necessary to know about the issue in its European and often global contexts as well. Although preparation was more difficult, the atmosphere when one was speaking was much more friendly. Rudeness to speakers was frowned upon and heckling was not possible due to the process of simultaneous translation. In any case it seemed to me that the tradition in Europe was to behave a great deal better than was normal in the circus that was the House of Commons. Perhaps that is because most such Parliaments sit in a hemicycle, in contrast to the face-to-face confrontational seating of the Commons. In addition, there were few stultifying rules of procedure and our method of working was constantly evolving. It was easy to be called to speak (unlike at Westminster) and sometimes a member could even speak twice in one debate.

I quickly found myself very much at home in the European Parliament, as I had never done at Westminster, and I received a tremendous welcome from across the House, particularly from the Irish and Dutch members, with whom I already had so much in common. Some of the high officials of this new institution had been senior clerks in the House of Commons and they were also very welcoming. David Millar (who was later a Liberal candidate) and John Taylor became particularly good friends in Europe, although when I first saw John in Luxembourg I did not know who he was and he had to remind me. He had been a senior clerk at the Speaker's Table and I had spoken to him about parliamentary questions on innumerable occasions, but on those occasions he had worn a wig.

The British Civil Service laid on cars for the leaders of delegations – the Tories had one, as did John Prescott, who was in charge of the Labour contingent. A third one was put at the disposal of Gladwyn Jebb, the Liberal member, and myself, which was somewhat ironic as he had been used to such treatment as an ambassador and I had never had experience of such perks myself. Having the car was very useful, especially when one wanted to take a friend out to lunch. The Civil Service would not hear of me refusing it or making my own arrangements, even for such events.

Gladwyn and I eventually became the best of friends, for he was rather lonely in Europe. He did not fraternise at all with the Labour members, although some of them had had equally distinguished careers, such as Lord Bruce of Donnington and Lord Alnwick, who had been a tabloid editor. Gladwyn must have been almost eighty but he was still very tall and handsome, with a shock of white hair. As I was invited out all the time, I took to asking if I could bring Gladwyn, who otherwise would have been on his own. His conversation was quite unique, for he had been through so much and taken part in so much. He would frequently bring conversation to an abrupt end with a remark like, 'I warned Winston of that at Yalta,' which was quite impossible to follow.

Gladwyn and I had something else in common too. We were both the object of animosity and attacks by Willie Hamilton. I was well aware why Willie disliked me, but he seemed to have an equal dislike for Gladwyn, apparently because he was unelected, though it shouldn't have escaped his notice that his Labour colleagues who were peers were in exactly the same situation. Gladwyn's wife, who was equally striking and very accomplished, was very annoyed at this persecution and on one occasion when she came to visit she asked me to point Willie Hamilton out to her. I did so and then she very deliberately walked across the café where we were sitting, making straight for Willie. This caused much interest and many people were straining their ears to hear what she was about to say to him. She was icily polite but she certainly discomfited him. Smiling, she said ever so gently: 'I'm worried about you Mr Hamilton, because you are so full of bile that in the end you will destroy your health.' And then she turned and walked away.

However, Willie Hamilton, along with Tam Dalyell, had a shock in store. Each time I made a speech in the European Parliament one of them would speak after me and ridicule what I had said. I tried to speak later and later in debates to forestall this pantomime, but the flexible rules meant that it was easy for them to make their comments, no matter when I spoke. This went on for over a year and was the subject of increasing comment, for it was very alien to the style of the Chamber.

One day the President of the Parliament, the French Socialist M. Spenale, asked me to call on him in his office. M. Spenale was a most genial man who looked like the French actor Jean Gabin and I could not imagine why he wanted to see me – perhaps I had unknowingly done something terribly wrong. When I got there he had an interpreter present, for he had little English and my French was poor. He was very friendly and told me, to my absolute amazement, that he had telephoned the Speaker of the House of Commons to tell him of his strong objection to the way in which I was being treated by Willie and Tam. He went on to say that he had told the Speaker that in his opinion the two of them were not fit to represent their country and Parliament in Europe, and that if their behaviour did not change then they should be withdrawn.

That day we all had to return to London for a vote at 10 p.m. and on arrival at the House of Commons I received a note saying that the Speaker wanted to see me. Douglas Henderson came with me and we were very pleased to notice on the mantelpiece a picture of the eleven SNP members. When I asked him about it he said that he took care of all the members, and why shouldn't he have a picture of some of them in his study? He then went on to give me his account of the phone call from President Spenale. Afterwards he had spoken to the Prime Minister, who had now warned the two MPs that if they did not behave themselves they would indeed be recalled. I was impressed by and grateful to a President and a Speaker who did indeed take care of their members.

Europe put a new perspective on all my work, and especially that which I was doing as the constituency member for Moray and Nairn, a place I had grown to love very greatly. But Moray and Nairn, far as it might seem from the centre of Europe, had strong European links itself and none stronger than those forged by the twinning of Lossiemouth with Hersbruck in Germany. Straight from my first week in the European Parliament I travelled by train to Hersbruck for yet another twinning event. The twinning had started in 1971 and the partnership was created not by local government officers but by two Hersbruck girls, Evie and Hannelore. They had chosen Lossiemouth and had made the first contacts. The links had quickly grown so strong that I recall hearing at my first twinning reception in 1973 one of the local men introducing two girls with the words, 'This is my daughter, and this is my German daughter.'

When I later chaired the European Parliament's Culture Committee in the elected parliament, town-twinning became one of my responsibilities, and by then I knew at first hand how beneficial it was and how it helped Europeans to get together and learn about each other. As the years passed I held parties for the Hersbruck and Lossiemouth contingents, though having eventually moved to a larger house in Miltonduff I was able to use the conservatory and a hired marquee to accommodate the throngs. Sam Rennie would be the chief organiser, the Moray Brass Band would attend to delight the company, and Dick Freeman and Milly Herd would provide further magnificent music. We would always sing Scots and German songs and we would end with assurances of further meetings and further friendships.

One of the key issues on which understanding of Scotland in Europe rests is fishing. It is vastly more important to Scotland than it is to England, but that fact has been ignored by successive British governments, which have regularly used our fishing interests as bargaining chips in order to secure other objectives.

Over the years delegations of fishermen came regularly to lobby the European Parliament despite feeling increasingly betrayed by the way they were treated. This was summed up early on when I first introduced the then President of the Scottish Fishermen's Federation, Gilbert Buchan, to President Simonet, and he said in response to M. Simonet's mention of 'negotiations', 'But what are you negotiating with – our fish?'

One of the many fisheries debates was to take place on a Thursday, which coincided with England playing in Strasbourg, for what I think was a European Cup match. Scotland was playing somewhere else, but the fishermen were in Strasbourg, lobbying as ever. However, John Prescott, who led the Labour delegation, wanted to attend the match and asked me if I would object to him getting the debate deferred until the following day. As a sop he promised to get the Scottish fishermen tickets for the England game. I would not even discuss it with him; one can imagine the press headlines: 'Fishermen Defer Debate on Their Future to Attend an England Football Game!' It was an absurd suggestion.

Most of the Strasbourg restaurants had closed for the evening, fearful of the damage that might be caused by English fans, for their reputation had preceded them. However, as a regular I gained admittance to one of my favourite eating places and took some of the fishermen to dine with me. At the next table there were a group of Irish Fianna Fáil MEPs who joined in what became a celebration, for one of the fishermen went off regularly to phone home to ask how the Scottish team was faring. It won, and England lost. After dinner we went to meet a British MEP, Lord Murray of Gravesend, who had invited some of the fishermen to meet members of the English team at the Holiday Inn. The fishermen fortified themselves with 'carry-oots' and the English team was very friendly and gracious, signing autographs and generally belying the reputation their fans had gained them. The evening was going very well when it was spoiled by the arrival of John Prescott. He was in a belligerent mood and spoke to me in terms that could only be described as rude and aggressive. However, he shortly disappeared, and one of the fishermen told me that they had 'spoken to him', whatever that meant, as they had all taken offence at his attitude towards me. The 'talking to' seemed to have worked, in fact better than might have been imagined, for he did not appear for the flight back to London the next day, and for some considerable time afterwards he avoided speaking to me, even if we passed in the corridor. However, one day some months later he approached me and, without even referring to the incident, asked me to come and meet his mother, who was visiting and who had asked to speak to me. That was a rapprochement of sorts.

I was involved in a very different rapprochement in the run-up to another fisheries debate. As I was sitting in the Chamber writing my speech, I was approached by the Irish EEC Commissioner, Ray Burke, who asked me if I could spare him half an hour. I declined because I was busy, but he told me that the fisheries discussion would not begin for some time yet. As he seemed so determined, I went with him, and he took me to one of the committee rooms where a reception was being held. There was a row of grim looking men standing on one side and another row of slightly less grim looking men on the other. Commissioner Burke told me quietly that one lot were 'Orange men from the north' and the other lot were 'Fianna Fáil men from the south', and that somebody needed to mix them up or they would stand like this all night. Would I mind trying to do it? It seemed a tall order but I agreed to have a go. As I walked across the room I thought of the Scottish dance 'Strip the Willow', so I took one man by the hand and led him over to the first man on the other side and said, 'You talk to him.' And then I did the same for each 'couple' until they were all in conversation. Then I took a drink from Commissioner Burke and by the time I left for the fisheries debate laughter and jokes were ringing out, into the corridor. He said to me afterwards, 'Only a Scotswoman could have done that to Irishmen!'

Would that the real problems of Ireland were so easy to solve! I have a very vivid memory of an incident that proves this point, although it took place in the first elected Parliament and not in the un-elected one. I recount it here not only because it fits so well, but also because it became one of my most abiding memories of the European Parliament.

One Thursday I was in the coffee room when I was asked to met a group of Irish priests and nuns. They had with them wives and mothers of prisoners at Longkesh Prison in Northern Ireland and they had a petition which they wanted to present to the Parliament which demanded the right to visit and the right to correspond with their men folk, in other words basic human rights. There was no Irish member presently available to present the petition to the President of the Parliament, Madame Simone Veil, and although I felt a momentary reluctance to be drawn so directly into the issue I immediately thought of the Biblical quotation, 'I was in prison, and you visited me'. The wives and mothers asked me directly to present the petition, which by rule had to be handed over personally by a member to the President, who was obliged not to comment on it. The procedure was meant both to ensure that daft petitions were not entertained, as no member would seek an urgent meeting with the President on a frivolous matter, and that Parliament was also protected, as there would be no instant response.

I explained how awkward it would be for me to undertake this task, being both a Scottish member and a Nationalist, for the press would be merciless. Surely there was an Irish member who would help? But there was not, for even those who were there had made themselves scarce. I wondered if one of the other Nationalists might do it, maybe one of the Flemish Nationalist members, but by then most members had gone home. I told the group that I would think about the matter over lunch when I intended both to take advice and also to wrestle with my own conscience. I phoned the party in Scotland was told that on no account was I to agree to present the petition – Gordon Wilson was particularly insistent. Yet I could not leave the wives and mothers without help. How, I asked, could I live with myself if I supported human rights yet refused to help those who asked me to secure such rights? So I went back to the group, who were still having a sandwich, and told them I would lodge the petition. I then rang Madame Veil's office and was given an immediate appointment.

I took the petition into Madame Veil's office with some trepidation, but although her English was as poor as my French she had dispensed with interpreters so I had to explain in my halting French about the petition and about the women of Longkesh. Madame Vail took the petition and asked: 'Où est l'Irlande aujourd'hui?' I said, 'L'Irlande n'est pas ici aujourd'hui.' 'Mais', responded Madame Veil, 'L'Ecosse est ici aujourd'hui,' and she looked at me very carefully.

The rules of procedure meant that this should have been the end of the matter – indeed Madame Veil had already said more than she usually did in such circumstances. But she asked me to sit down and then she rolled up her sleeve. 'I shouldn't say this,' she began 'but I want you to give a message to these women. I too know what it is like to be in prison,' and with this remark she indicated the tattoo on her arm, which marked her as a former inmate of a Nazi concentration camp. I was very moved by her remark and I went back and told the women about it. They were moved too, and overjoyed to have had so humane a response. However, I was immediately surrounded by the press who had found out about the story. Did I support the IRA?, I was asked. Was the SNP sympathetic to terrorism in Northern Ireland? And so on. I responded as calmly as I could that I did not support and never had supported violence of any kind but that I supported human rights and this was an issue of human rights. I saw no point in hiding what had happened, so I gave out copies of the petition and reconciled myself to ghastly headlines and the fury of my party at home.

However, just as I was leaving the Parliament I was approached by a young man of the utmost politeness who introduced himself as the Deputy British Consul in Strasbourg. He asked if it was true that I had lodged a petition supporting the IRA, and I had to go through it all again. I even gave him a copy and he thanked me profusely for it.

I got home late that night and prepared myself for the next day, though I did think it strange that the phone was not ringing. It was still not ringing the next morning and there was nothing, nothing at all, about the petition in the papers. The British Government, I later discovered, had served a 'D' notice, making it illegal to report the whole matter as it was regarded as being of national security. Much as I hated such secrecy, I was more than a little relieved.

One paper, I discovered, had published. The *Press and Journal* had already printed and distributed its first edition for the West Highlands before the 'D' notice was served. That paper was of course a crucial one in my future Highland constituency, though no one who read it ever mentioned the matter to me. Others did, however. Many of the visiting groups from Ireland would seek me out. My hand would be shaken and people would look me firmly in the eyes and say, 'Thank you for what you did for the women of Longkesh.'

As time went on I developed more and more connections with the Irish delegation. Senator Yeats was a Vice President of the Parliament and a son of the poet W. B. Yeats. He told me many stories about growing up with his father. He was a very scholarly man as well as a great friend to Scotland. However, I disagreed with his view that the elected parliament would result in a loss of European idealism and would, in time, turn out to be a backward step. Like many, I believed that we needed an elected parliament as quickly as possible so that the emerging European Community would develop a strong democratic base. I still believe I was right, even though some of that European idealism has gone and we have certainly lost much of the vision and passion for Europe that was present in the first unelected European parliament. The change perhaps is most noticeable in the UK where the Tories, even the Tory peers, were fiercely

pro-European at that time and the Labour members split between enthusiasm and hostility. Now Labour is more or less reconciled to Europe,
though without the imaginative engagement that it needs. The Tories,
meanwhile, have drifted off into the wilder shores of Euro-scepticism.

Some Irish members had political problems but, like us, they faced up to
them while enjoying themselves. Jim Gibbons had been a Fianna Fáil
Government minister but had lost that when he became a defendant in the
famous arms trial, alongside Charlie Haughey and Neil Blaney, who was
also in Europe but who had left his party in disgust although he kept on
winning seats in the Dail. Jim was well versed in Scottish history and
Scottish literature, and as a consequence had a huge fund of Scottish
songs. We found ourselves one evening sitting on bar stools in the Holiday
Inn in Luxembourg when the Eurovision Song Contest was on, and
somehow we got ourselves involved in a very different type of singing
competition. Our version required one of us to start a Scottish song and
the other to sing the next verse, and so on. It was neck-and-neck for a long
while, but then I (for some unknown reason) got the verses of 'The Rowan
Tree' mixed up and Jim was declared the winner of the stake, which was a
ten-pound Scottish note and a ten punt note from Ireland. There were a
number of journalists present, who went on to write about the *real*
European Song Contest in the bar, as well as the Eurovision one somewhere else in the tiny principality that night.

To socialise well it was important to be friendly with the Irish. They
always found (as they still always do) a watering-hole with a fluid
approach to opening hours where there was no objection to singing.
The bar they frequented in Strasbourg became the haunt of many of us
and it was a place where, if one arrived very late, one simply 'banged the
bell' and if one's face found favour, the door was opened. Indeed the Irish
came to call it 'Bang the Bells' and few of us ever knew its real name.

Many a ceilidh was had in those years, both in Luxembourg and in
Strasbourg. It may have been the enervating nature of constant travelling,
but most of us in all the delegations were keen to relax of an evening into
the wee small hours. But it was the Irish who led the way, with the UK
delegation (usually the Labour ones) meekly following, except in singing,
as the English members always seemed to get stuck after a few hideous
measures of 'On Ilkley Moor Baht 'at'! That is perhaps unkind, for their

were UK members who were good company and even supportive. I was a member of the Legal Affairs Committee, which was chaired by an English MP who was excellent and fair. He was a barrister and appreciated my grasp of the European legal scene, I having studied both Scots law and at the Hague.

On one occasion the Legal Affairs Committee decided to meet in Rome and we stayed at the Grand Hotel. I was interested in furthering my knowledge of Italian law and legal practice and I contacted a member of the Glasgow Bar Association, Osvaldo Franchi, who had an Italian legal qualification. He put me in touch with a Roman lawyer who appeared on our second night and swept up the staircase of the Grand Hotel to take me to dinner and then on to a night club. A group of us decided to go and one of them asked us to wait in the foyer for five minutes while he phoned a restaurant. My Italian escort, who seemed as if he had been drawn from a Mozart opera, responded to this in ringing tones with the words 'Starò qui come l'agnellino', which means, 'I will stand here like a little lamb.' The rest were dumbfounded. Worse was to come. On being escorted back to my hotel my Roman lawyer wanted a drink, but I was told that I could only order from my room. With some misgivings I took him upstairs (he was very insistent) and ordered drinks. However while we were waiting for them to arrive, I was subjected to a strongly amorous advance.

I asked him hurriedly, 'La buona conversazione non è abbastanza?' ('Is good conversation not enough?') 'Si, si,' came the reply. But there was a sting in the tail, for he added, 'La buona conversazione è abbastanza ma l'amore è un altra cosa' ('Good conversation is enough but love is another thing'). Fortunately our drinks arrived, and he had to make do with conversation. But over the years he would sometimes phone me in Glasgow.

Fortunately all this happened away from the prying eyes of journalists. The press who covered Europe were usually attentive and interested but such interest could quickly turn into a double-edged sword. When Fergus left Loretto I suggested he come to work for me in the European Parliament as I dearly needed help. I got him fixed up with digs in the home of a Parliamentary official and his French, which was good, got better and better. He was a great help to me in framing questions and doing research, but the *News of the World* decided that there was some-

thing wrong with a son helping his mother in this way, and so a knocking
story duly appeared on its front page.

One of the reasons I had been so keen to get help was that being an
independent without a group was very hard. Not only was there a
complete absence of formal support, but some things in the Parliament,
mostly motions and amendments, needed more than one signature, and
this meant that I had to scrabble around to get them lodged. I was urged
from the beginning to join the Technical Group, which contained a
Flemish National Party member, but I was also wooed by the large
Christian Democrat Group which had people in it from every member
state except the UK. The Irish Fine Gael party was a member and a Dr
MacAlonad came to London to meet the SNP Westminster group and to
put the case for us joining his group. In the end it was decided that the
Christian Democrats were not for us – they were too right-wing, a fact
which was borne out when the UK Tories resolved to join them, as
eventually did the Spanish, who had been pro-Franco.

Of course I did have support from my colleagues at Westminster, and
even though there were at that time no allowances for MPs to visit the
European institutions, they did try to come and see me when they could.
George Reid, our constitutional spokesman in the Commons, came on a
formal visit, and given his good relations with the press as a former press
man he commanded considerable attention. One of the Scottish papers ran
a headline the following day which asked, 'When Will the Nine Become
Ten?' and our serious intentions about Europe, and our positive enthusiasm about it, were beginning to mark us out in Europe as well as at home.

Europe between 1975 and 1979 was a fast-changing place. Not only
was the UK struggling with its new-found engagement having, in Adlai
Stevenson's famous words, 'lost an empire but not yet found a role'.
Germany was emerging as the economic power-house on a continent
which still resented its presence and in which the mental and physical scars
of two world wars remained real. Portugal and Spain emerged from
dictatorship, with Franco still in power when I went to Luxembourg, but
dying in the November of that year. Fascism in Spain kept the memory of
the International Brigade very much alive. One of my Canadian cousins,
Jim MacDowall, had enlisted in the brigade, and I remember seeing him
off at the Central Station in Glasgow. Spain remained a presence in my life

and I read much about it. When I became a member of the unelected
Parliament I became aware that two of my thirty-five UK colleagues had
also been in the International Brigade, one of whom was Lord Bruce of
Donnington and the other a north of England Labour MP, a Mr Evans.
One day I asked Mr Evans if by any chance he knew my cousin Jim
MacDowall, and he replied with enthusiasm, 'Of course, he was in my
platoon.'

He told me that a third MEP, Lord Rory St Oswald, had also fought in
the Spanish Civil War but on the Franco side, and that the three of them
had planned to have dinner soon to talk over past events and different
experiences. I begged a place at the table and all of them were happy to
have me there. It was a fascinating evening, and as everyone expected
Franco to die soon there was much speculation about what would happen.
Rory thought that the King should be invited back at once, a remark which
was very prescient. Rory, who lost both feet in Spain and who had
what he jokingly referred to as 'tin feet', had been given an estate in that
country by Franco as a reward for his services.

Many MEPs were interested in Spain and in helping the country to
move to democracy, and delegations from various group visited to
establish political contacts as soon as it was possible for them to do so.
I had been to Spain twice before, the first time on a package deal with a
friend from college, Ina Miller. We went to San Antonio de Calonge near
Palomar in Catalonia. When I tried out my school-room Spanish on the
children on the beach they looked blank and their mother explained to me
that they spoke only Catalan. However, the police – who were heavily
laden with all sorts of fearsome looking equipment, so much so that one of
them told me he must look like a *burro* or donkey – were only too delighted
to converse with tourists. Yet I discovered that they spoke no Catalan at
all. Soon the penny dropped – all the police in Catalonia were brought in
from other parts of Spain. Local police could not be trusted, or so the
Franco regime thought.

One day two beggars came to our hotel and the proprietor shooed them
away angrily. I was a little shocked, but he explained with some pride to
me that they must be Spanish, as Catalans, no matter what, do not beg.
Indeed the people seemed to be very dignified and very hard-working
despite the terrible time they had had under Franco.

My other visit to Spain had been in 1958 with Stewart. We noticed immediately that when a priest passed by, most people crossed the road because the Church had taken the side of Franco and a huge suspicion of the Church had grown up as a result. We went to Madrid and then on to Toledo, where we wanted to buy train tickets for Cordoba. We queued for ages until the ticket office suddenly shut, without apology and without us having got tickets. Stewart sought out the stationmaster and remonstrated with him, but he was quite complacent about it: he could not know, he said, how many tickets he could sell until the train left Madrid and would therefore not be allowed to sell any until then. Nothing could be done without central instruction and permission. Eventually he sold us our first-class tickets, but when we boarded we found in the first-class compartments only a solitary and very posh-looking Spaniard. People were not encouraged to travel and every difficulty was put in their way to stop them, as we had discovered. The solitary Spaniard was at first rather disconcerted at having company but he soon began to take a keen interest in us. Few tourists tried to travel on their own without a prearranged package (it was also discouraged), but he gave us very good advice about where to stay in Cordoba as well as in Seville and Malaga, where we were going on to. He also told us what to see, where to hear real gypsy flamenco and the best places in which to eat. He was absolutely right about all of it and when we returned home I wrote an article about our holiday, with the help of Lorna Blackie, who also arranged to have it published.

Most of my European colleagues were aghast that I had been on holiday to Fascist Spain, but I was glad that I had seen for myself the reality of a country under dictatorship and I learnt much from it. I had also been to a dinner at the Spanish Embassy in London some months before Franco died, due to my membership of an organisation devoted to the establishment of democracy throughout the world, which embraced Israelis and Arabs, people from the Baltic States and Yugoslavia, as well as Russians and many others, including Spaniards. I found it interesting and valuable to hear all opinions and to try and influence them where possible.

Few UK MPs would accept an invitation from the Spanish Embassy at that time and fewer still attended the dinner. In addition those who came had to run the gauntlet of angry crowds outside. At the dinner I found myself seated next to the ambassador, Señor de Fraga, a fervent supporter of the Caudillo. I was wearing a long, slinky, emerald green dress and he greeted me with the words, 'Ah, the green of Galicia', which was his home province.

The Spanish Embassy was splendidly appointed, heavily panelled and hung with famous paintings by the great Spanish masters. After dinner I was shown into a smaller, but equally magnificently decorated room where Señor de Fraga introduced me to a number of very young, serious-looking members of the diplomatic staff. My presence and my nationalist politics made me a curiosity and I was immediately asked my opinion of the various regional cultures of Spain and in particular my views on the Basque and Catalan questions. I had of course visited Catalonia, which surprised them, as did the fact that I had danced the Sardana, the Catalan national dance, and learnt something at first hand of Catalan nationalism. I pointed out that if you tried to stem the tide of a nation's culture, prohibited their flags and outlawed their language, then you should not be surprised if there was trouble. These things, I said, were necessary to a nation's dignity and to the ability of people to live constructively in their land. I argued that self-determination was a vital and treasured aspect of democracy and that it could not be safely denied. I was listened to with respect and without hostility and I was pleased that as democracy was built in Spain the nations and parliaments of the Basques and the Catalans were in time allowed to flourish again.

Of course Spain eventually joined the European Union in 1986, during my second term as an MEP, and I believe that Europe was influential in helping that country to emerge from its period of self-imposed political exile. Indeed to a great extent that is the European ideal – the ideal of free peoples and free democracies helping each other to grow and prosper. Born as it was out of the horrors of the Second World War, the noble purpose of the European Union, as it is now called, is one that should bring only benefit. Despite the many fears of Scots – some of which have turned out to be well-founded, such as those of our fishing communities – Europe must encapsulate a vision of a better continent and a better world. Such a vision was always made real to me when I passed a particular button on the wall of the first Parliament building in Luxembourg. Pressing that button caused Beethoven's 'Ode to Joy', the European anthem, to ring out through the corridors of the old building. These may not have yet been corridors of power, but they were corridors worth walking in pursuit of something even more important: national and international solidarity and communication.

I had understood that issue very clearly in my time in the unelected Parliament and the way in which it could help my country of Scotland to be free again. I was keen to continue as a member to try and help bring such progress about but I thought that such a role would be taken on, as it had been in the first four years, jointly with that of representing Moray and Nairn in the Westminster Parliament. That was not to be. Yet when I left Europe for the last time as an unelected member I felt certain that I was not going away for long. And so it was, for within a month of losing my seat in the House of Commons I had fought, and won, the first direct election for Europe and become the Member for the Highlands and Islands, the largest constituency in Europe.

10

The Member for the Highlands and Islands: Amongst French and Irish Friends

M Y DEFEAT IN Moray and Nairn was a terrible blow which was made much worse by the loss of all but two of our eleven seats. The bright hopes of 1974 seemed to have vanished completely, along with the prospect of bringing back power to Scotland. But fortunately for me there was little time for all this to sink in because the European election date had already been set and I was due to contest the Highlands and Islands within little more than a month. So it was back out onto the stump almost immediately.

I had one new advantage, though it was one I did not want to have. As I had lost my Westminster seat I could not be attacked for seeking the dual mandate – for wanting two jobs – and such attacks had been increasing as the elections drew closer. But Russell Johnston had retained his Inverness constituency, and he was now vulnerable on that score. Even some of his own people openly attacked him for it, saying that whenever you wanted him, the answer was, 'Russell's in Brussels'.

Soon I was pounding the plain paving stones of Elgin again, a sight which must have bewildered the lieges, who thought that I had lost and was gone for ever. Yet here I was, assailing their ears with my loudspeaker. Campaigning one day Stewart jokingly remarked, 'They thought they had got rid of you, but here you are back again.' And so I was, large as life and twice as loud, and that was immensely therapeutic.

Hard as it was for SNP activists to pick themselves up and start again, that is something our party is always good at doing, for our cause inspires us to overcome ever the bitterest of defeats. A headline in the *Scots Independent* said it all: 'And on to Europe . . .!' So Stewart and I toured the vast area and discovered something that we already knew – that there were many, many passionate and articulate supporters of the SNP north of the Highland Line, supporters such as Sandy Lindsay in Aviemore who led us through that town carrying a huge saltire. Their appetite for the fray was undiminished despite the difficult and disappointing times.

Although there was much help to be had from our supporters, as usual the BBC and the press were distinctly unhelpful. It seemed to be a foregone conclusion, according to them, that Russell would win, and the BBC went further, actually formally awarding victory in the Highlands and Islands to the Liberals on the weekend after the vote, although the count was not due to take place until Monday.

That count was, in itself, an electrifying experience. The votes, once counted, were placed in shoe-boxes which each held 1,000 papers. We could all see the boxes from where we were allowed to stand and it became obvious after a while that the boxes on the table allocated to Russell Johnston were piling up faster than mine. I went round the SNP supporters telling them not to believe that I had lost and to keep up their sampling. As a seasoned veteran of counts I knew that that the candidate and agent were entitled to be convinced that everything was proceeding fairly, so I went forward to check the shoe-boxes because it seemed to me that there was something not quite right. The returning officer tried to remonstrate with me but I pointed out that I had a right to do so, as for instance it could be that a box for Johnston was full of Ewing votes!

The boxes were piled up on the tables but as soon as I counted the base of the pile on my table and compared it to Russell's I realised what was happening. My base consisted of eight boxes, but Russell's was seven – so his pile just looked bigger than mine. I actually had more boxes than he had. I asked the returning officer why there was this discrepancy, which could only mislead those who were not allowed close to the tables. He would only say that my table was bigger than the other tables, though it didn't look like it. He would do nothing to correct the false impression, but I was able to return to the SNP supporters and tell them not to worry; we were winning, though it didn't appear so.

Michael Joughin, my Tory opponent, had also noticed that something was odd but he had been able to spot the difference himself from behind the ropes that separated off the actual counting area. It was greatly to his credit and the honourable nature of his candidacy that he came over to me immediately he had noticed the problem, both to tell me and to reassure me that he thought I was sure to win. And win I did – though only by just over 3,000 votes, spread over eight constituencies. It was narrow but it was enough, and it defied the predictions of the BBC and others. Russell was as devastated as I had been a month before, but he was gracious in defeat. My supporters and family, though, were ecstatic, as were SNP activists throughout Scotland.

Many people were genuinely surprised that I had won, but I think the reasons for my victory are quite clear. Firstly, I used the slogan 'Winnie Works', and it chimed with the reputation I had gained at Westminster over the years and in Europe. I also published a newspaper for the election which not only had myself on the front surrounded by the crew of *The Goodwill* fishing boat at a time when there was much concern about the impact of Europe on the fishing industry, but which also illustrated the disparity between the number of speeches I had made and questions I had asked in Europe compared to Russell's. I had made sixty speeches to his thirty-nine, asked 109 oral questions to his thirty-four and lodged ninety-four written questions to his twenty-five.

My election victory was also helped by the large amount of EEC funding which was beginning to flow to the Highlands and Islands. Scotland, after much debate and after much SNP pressure, was awarded almost one third of the £68 million that came to the UK from the Regional Development Fund in Europe and people knew that without the SNP this just would not have happened. The £21,200,000 awarded covered long-needed improvements to harbours, roads, sewerage and water infrastructure and many other vital services. The Highlands and Islands were tired of always being last in line and they knew they needed to keep up the pressure.

Of course the upbeat and energetic nature of my campaign was also a reason for my success. Ewen Bain contributed a cartoon that was much talked about and Stewart was a tireless organiser and mastermind, with many ideas for creating and maintaining a high visual profile. They nearly always worked.

After the election the first serious question to be addressed was membership of a group. This was now essential and whilst I had been already invited to join the Technical Group, which included various regionalists and nationalists, a much more intriguing invitation quickly arrived. I was asked if I would go to Dublin to meet the Tainiste (Deputy Prime Minister). Ireland then had a Fianna Fáil government and when I went to Dublin I was very well received. The Tainiste had asked me to come and see him in order to invite the SNP to join the European Progressive Democrat group, which included Fianna Fáil and the French Gaullist Party called the RPR which was also in government in France at the time. The Tainiste had the authority to offer me a Vice Presidency of the group, should I accept.

I was very attracted to the offer but I could not agree there and then – I naturally had to consult my party and I told the Tainiste that I would need to do so. The party was aware of the possibility of my joining the Technical Group but a number of wise voices, particularly Gordon Wilson, were quick to see the advantages of being in a group with two governing parties. Gordon called it 'joining the successful nationalists'. Stewart posed another important question: 'Joining which group would annoy the UK Government the most?' Of that, of course, there was no doubt

I felt a little guilty at not going along with some of the other nationalists in Europe, such as the Bretons, who had lit beacons when I won Hamilton but who were passionately anti-Gaullist because of the persecution they had experienced from the French State. But there was no doubt what the sensible and mature political choice was, for me as well as for Scotland, and I informed the Tainiste that my party would be pleased to join the European Progressive Democrats. Immediately I had done so, flowers started to arrive: from the Taoiseach in Ireland (then Charlie Haughey) from Jacques Chirac, the former Prime Minister of France, from De Malene, the Chair of the group and the Deputy Mayor of Paris, and from many others. These were charming gestures from my new friends and they foreshadowed a number of happy years.

In the European Parliament the minimum number of members needed to form a group was twenty-one and our new EPD group easily overcame this hurdle as there were fifteen French, seven Irish, a Dane and myself. The French had devised a new electoral system for Europe, called the Guillotine, under which MEPs retired after six months in favour of the next one on their list. The first tranche of Gaullists elected included three ex-Prime Ministers but they all seemed genuinely to welcome the prospect of such a rotation. However, there were downsides, not least the quick exit of the experienced and those who were just beginning to gain valuable experience. I certainly found that having had four years as an unelected member was a huge benefit and gave me a flying start, but even so I was still learning much in this new institution which was itself only beginning to develop.

I found immediately that I had a strong rapport with the French members of the group, and they with me. We were, in a sense, old allies from an old alliance and of course at one time Scots and French enjoyed joint citizenship. Now in the modern world we were finding ways to rekindle that relationship. In addition they played very fair – my conditions for joining the group were honoured in full and I had full freedom to vote as I wished on matters of conscience and on all Scottish issues. I was appointed to the Fisheries Committee and to the Development Committee, which led to membership of the Lomé Convention which I immediately saw as a great opportunity to put Scotland's case around the world, and to impress upon Heads of State, Foreign Ministers and others the fact that Scotland not only existed, but was getting stronger and more interested in the world again. I was also able to go to the Legal Affairs Committee as a Substitute Member.

I had greatly enjoyed my days as an unelected member of the European Parliament, but my first period as the elected member for the Highlands and Islands of Scotland was even better. I had a sense of wonder each day when I entered the hemicycle which was like a huge and very colourful film set brimming with positive atmosphere. This was a forum full of enthusiastic Europeans, gathered as 518 proponents of the best type of co-operation, chosen by the people themselves to chart and travel on a new European journey. We clearly all intended to travel hopefully, and none more than myself, for I had great hopes for my country in this gathering too.

At first some of the Labour and Tory members found it difficult to adjust, particularly those who had been at Westminster. The back-biting of the Commons had no place here and when anyone indulged in it (and I showed quickly that I disapproved of such behaviour even if it came from Scots) then the proponents found themselves quickly criticised and told, sometimes directly, to 'take their petty insults back to London'. Good arguments were listened to from any corner of the Chamber and, unlike Emrys Hughes' criticism of the Commons, it was possible here to persuade one's audience. What was even more remarkable – and I felt this so strongly as a child of the war – was that here the antagonists of a fearful conflict that had not yet been over for four decades were able and willing to sit together in political groups and to work together for a common benefit. I was particularly thrilled to see Willy Brandt take his seat, for I had heard him in Berlin in the early 1950s. Here he was again, building with his own hands his dream of peace.

Our first task in the new Parliament was to elect our President. Madame Simone Veil was chosen, not least because of her record in defending the oppressed of the world and her strong advocacy of women's rights. She was also symbolic of the past and how it could be overcome, having been in a Nazi concentration camp.

The opening speech of this first elected Parliament was given by the oldest member, the great French film-maker Louise Weiss, who was also a member of my group. It was a fine speech, but then she was a fine speaker, and brilliant into the bargain. She spoke exquisite English and had studied in Oxford. In contrast, when Louise heard me speak French (for our French staff were always trying to encourage me), she said, kindly but firmly, 'Winnie, please do not speak French to me. I am over eighty and I cannot stand it!'

The sheer variety of members was fascinating. My group sat in a triangular arrangement, covering both sides of a corridor. I was on the outside edge of the triangle and found myself sitting beside a German ex-general. Next to him sat Otto von Habsburg, descendant of the last Emperor of Austria–Hungary and, by dint of that, a direct descendant of the Holy Roman Emperors. One affectionate European Parliament story about him went the rounds when Austria played Hungary in the European Championship. Otto was meant to have said, 'Yes, but who are they playing?'

Otto spoke seventeen languages in all and his English was absolutely perfect, so he hardly ever used the headphones to access translation. He remained a member all the time I was there and when a party was held for the twenty-first anniversary of my election he made a speech in which he said, 'Winnie Ewing is a person who gets things done,' which for him was the supreme accolade.

Otto's family history gave him a huge sense of responsibility about Europe and his own children had continued with that positive engagement. Although he was a German MEP his son became an Austrian one and his daughter, who lived in Sweden, had ambitions to serve that country in the same capacity. He was well-versed in everything to do with Europe, past and present, and I recall having one particularly fascinating conversation with him when the Berlin Wall came down, for he seemed to think that he and his descendants needed to have a continued role in making Europe a better place.

The House of Commons had always been a great place to see the important personalities of the time, but the European Parliament was equally enjoyable in that regard too. Jacques Chirac, then Mayor of Paris and an ex-prime minster and of course eventually President of France, was a member of my group, though he was not a very regular attender. He spoke perfect English but chose not to speak it very often, though he spoke in English to me when we met. He was most interested in the Celts as a people and told me he had written a book about the origin of the Celts. I found his habit of putting an arm round my shoulders and leaning on me to be slightly strange and at first I thought it was a sign of affection until he explained to me that he had a painful leg, and often did it to ease the pain.

My closest friend in the group was Sean Flanagan. He was very well-versed in Irish culture and history of course, but he also had an excellent knowledge of Scottish matters. Indeed on one occasion he told me that he had been reading an account of the Battle of Culloden and that he had been so moved he had been unable to finish the story. He was a very proficient violinist and during his holidays he would spend much time attending concerts. At one of my parties Neil Fergusson managed to obtain a violin and Sean tuned it up in my bathroom before coming out and enchanting us with his playing. I arranged to have him made an honorary member of the Inverness Fiddlers when he visited Scotland on a group study tour and he was delighted.

Sean was a Lomé delegate too and when on overseas trips he always met up with Irish people living abroad. In Tanzania he visited his brother, who was a priest there, and as time went on I discovered that I too could and should meet up with Scots who were resident in the places Lomé met. Soon there grew up a habit of having a UK party in each place, usually given by the Ambassador or the Governor General, and I used to take Sean with me as my guest. He always enjoyed himself.

Another member of the group was M. Coste Flore, who had been France's chief civil servant before becoming an MEP. He seemed at first to be a bit pompous, but in fact he was merely dignified, and beneath the dignity had a very kindly heart. He told me a marvellous story about President Pompidou whom he accompanied to London for his first meeting with the then Prime Minister, Ted Heath. The two Frenchmen arrived wearing their best suits and found Heath wearing tweeds. They were shown to their state apartments and decided to change into less formal attire, as that seemed to be what was required. However when they returned they found that Heath had changed into full formal wear, whilst they had dressed down.

There was a rich variety of individuals who had become members of this first elected European Parliament, but what united them was a positive enthusiasm for Europe. However, this was not shared by some UK Labour MEPs, for the Labour group was split into pro- and anti-Europe factions. Even their leadership reflected this, and the annual elections for the European parliamentary leader could throw up either a 'for' or an 'against' candidate, and often did. Some on both sides of the UK political divide were very talented, but amongst the Tories in particular there seemed to be a lot of fresh-faced inexperienced youngsters who looked as if they had come straight from the playing fields of Eton. I once wondered aloud if some had been bought seats by their daddies.

The Tory leader was Jim Scott Hopkins, a former Westminster MP. He was hard-working, skilled and caring and he looked after these young men. His first task was to encourage them to make maiden speeches, but it was a sorry sight as each illustrated how little they knew. While this was going on one afternoon my German ex-general neighbour asked me, 'Winnie, wo haben Sie solche seltsame Menschen gefunden?' ('Winnie, where have you found such strange men?') I replied as a joke, 'Alle von Harrods.' ('All from Harrods') and explained that it was cheaper to get them off the peg by the half dozen. Then my German friend asked a more difficult questions, 'Und Elaine Kellet Bowman – ist Sie auch von Harrods?'

('Is Elaine Kellet Bowman also from Harrods?') I had to answer that this was not the case – it was more likely that the formidable Elaine had come direct from the Army and Navy Stores!

The Harrods remark caught on and was repeated and the next day the interpreters joined in with a joke, 'Why do the Harrods men resemble Devonshire cream? Because they're rich, thick and full of clots.' The remark spread like wildfire and soon everyone was calling them 'the clots' though occasionally they were called worse – for example by Sile De Valera, the granddaughter of President De Valera. She was tall, blond and very attractive and some of the younger Tories took a great fancy to her. She was not impressed, however, commenting to me one day after the Falklands War, 'Look, they even walk a different way from the rest of us!'

As the Conservative party changed its stance on Europe and became more and more sceptical, the Tories – even the able ones – began to have a harder and harder time of it. The problem was that the more they worked in Europe doing the job they were there for, the more they were criticised by the party at home. This is perhaps why a certain number of them moved from enthusiasm to hostility and started to subscribe to the ludicrous notion that the whole European dream is merely a conspiracy to sell out British interests and that MEPs are part of that conspiracy. They also came to believe that to have any influence at all they must be allied to the Christian Democratic European People's Party, the second largest in the Parliament. But this led to more schizophrenia for the Tories at home hated the thought of association with any type of European party, let alone one led by the Germans. So what started as positive engagement with Europe has eventually resulted in the Tories being the least enthusiastic Europeans and the most unhappy. I recall a journalist commenting on all this with the memorable words: 'The best way to torture a Tory is to make him an MEP!'

In contrast, my own position could not have been happier. Being in a group as opposed to being an independent meant that I could get motions lodged and amendments put, and in addition I had a wide-ranging circle of friends and could expect the inestimable benefits of a strong camaraderie in the Chamber.

The UK delegations often stayed in the same hotel and sometimes I dined with Jim Scott Hopkins. One evening he asked me what I thought was my greatest achievement and I replied that it was either winning

Hamilton or Moray and Nairn. 'No,' said Jim. 'Your greatest achievement is here, winning the Euro seat and putting your cause onto the international scene.' He meant by that not just in Europe but also out in the wider world, as a delegate to Lomé. He was right. I was beginning to make Scotland's case furth of Scotland's borders, and having it supported by the French and the Irish on all occasions.

I quickly decided that I must get a flat to rent in Strasbourg, so, being a lawyer, I wrote to the Strasbourg Bar enquiring if any of their members had property that would suit. A very successful court lawyer and her husband offered me a flat below theirs, intended eventually, I believe, for her mother. This made my life much easier for I could host parties, have friends to visit and stay and could leave clothes and other items between visits. The flat had a lovely balcony and day-room with a couch bed, a good bathroom and kitchen and another couch bed in the hall. It was ideal. The flat also allowed me to do some cooking and shopping locally and begin to find out about living in France. I adored the local shops: the grocer, the baker, the butcher and of course the hairdresser, and I noticed that almost everything for sale was French. The French had a pride in supporting their own country and a belief that their country was best at making the things they wanted. This extended beyond food and wine into radios, electrical goods, cosmetics and even cars. They were patriotic but not chauvinist and I understood why.

Of course I was only in Strasbourg for the Parliament sessions – much of the rest of the time I was in Brussels. There I also found somewhere lovely to stay – a top flat in the Square Ambiorix with a wide balcony that overlooked the city. I was very happy in both places.

As I was beginning to find my feet in Europe, it became clearer and clearer to me that I needed a member of staff to help with speeches, questions and research, and for the general back-up which was essential. I at first arranged to offer such a post to a beautiful blonde girl called Rosie who worked at SNP HQ, which was rapidly downsizing because of the disastrous election results and the great disappointment of the fiddled referendum. Rosie was captivating, clever and spoke French, and when I described her to my Irish colleagues they were desperate to meet her. An interview was arranged, which would have been a formality, but then Rosie announced that she was going to stay in Scotland and marry a violinist in the Scottish National Orchestra. Though pleased for her, we were all disappointed for ourselves.

I was then at something of a loss, and although I considered the issue very carefully, I couldn't think of anyone who might be suitable for the post. As it approached Christmas the problem was still unsolved until the evening I attended the annual Royal Findhorn Yacht Club Dinner Dance. I was an honorary member of the Yacht Club, having saved their moorings when I had been MP. A new law was about to allow the moorings to revert to the landlord and I was alerted to this by Lord Perth, the Crown Estates Commissioner. I asked for the committee of the club to meet in emergency session and they managed to apply to retain their moorings in the nick of time. The club was very grateful and offered me the position of an honorary member which, despite not being a sailor, I was delighted to accept.

My good friend Mary Fergusson was a person who had very early on in my time in Moray given me a warm welcome to Findhorn. She and her husband Iain owned the local Culbin Sands Hotel and Iain was commodore of the club. I had met their son Neil on one occasion when he had given me a trip in a small yacht and I knew that he had an honours degree in economics from Aberdeen University. At the Christmas dinner dance I got talking to Neil again and discovered more, and most excitingly the fact that he spoke fluent French, as he had taken time out from university to work in the French vineyards. An idea began to form in my mind and I asked him to call on me the next morning at my house in Lossiemouth. He did, and was very interested in working in Brussels; so I quickly arranged an interview with the group and he was deemed more than acceptable.

Neil literally changed my life. He became a friend and ally and in the end almost like another son. He was a natural when it came to adapting to work in the Parliament and to the whole culture of the place, and he was also a great touchstone for me when I needed to talk over Scottish attitudes and Scottish problems. He knew Moray well and had a feeling for the rest of the country. Equally importantly he had a feel for Europe and he immediately fitted in with the Irish and French staff and their lifestyle. Indeed he went on to marry an Irish girl, Allison, and to rise to high office in the Parliament.

Neil was also a great travelling companion, endlessly helpful and supportive. When my committees travelled, he accompanied me, and as each committee made two fact-finding trips a year, this was hugely helpful. In Rome, for example, he arranged for us to visit the Scots College as dinner guests. The visit had been urged on me for some time by George Thomson, the former MP for Galloway, who had studied there to become a priest but had left in his final year. The Scots College was most impressive and we dined well in a great hall, with the students dressed in black soutanes and red sashes. We retired to have coffee and brandy with the senior clerics, who were the college professors, after which they said, 'Now we will throw you to the boys.' We were shown into another magnificent room, fully expecting to be met with solemn Gregorian chant, but instead it was full of mostly young men who had changed into informal clothes and who belted out in greeting, 'Flower of Scotland'. It was wonderful to hear the varied accents of Scotland together in that room and their joie de vivre and curiousity were very stimulating. At one stage I was chatting to a more mature student and said to him, 'May I ask you a personal question?' 'Of course,' he replied, and I went on to enquire whether he ever had any doubts about his vocation and way of life. He smiled and said with huge humour but tremendous spirit, 'Just every day.'

With Neil in place it was possible for me to start to develop rapidly the work I needed to do for my huge constituency. There were piles of correspondence but also the need to speak as often as possible within the Chamber, and to raise questions of importance. Fishing was still at the centre of my concerns and at this stage the biggest worry was the threat of Spanish access to the North Sea after Spain became a member. Many assurances were given to Scottish fishermen, but in time all of them were broken. The UK members were quite hopeless on the matter – they would privately express their concerns but then vote as their parties told them, and their parties had always used Scottish fishing rights as a bargaining tool for concessions on other matters. I got no support at the times that it counted.

One of the major problems of these British parties is that they never (not even the Scottish members) went to Europe with Scotland at the centre of their concerns. They used to get particularly angry when another member from another country would refer to me as the 'member for Scotland' but it was obvious to all but the British that I was the only one that saw Scotland and Scotland's interests as my prime reason for being there. *Le Monde* once published a piece about me which called me 'Madame

Ecosse' and the name stuck, though the Scottish members were furious and would constantly refer to the epithet as 'self-styled'. It wasn't.

Another threat to the Scottish fishing industry and to our wider environment was posed by sub-standard tankers. In many areas, and particularly in the Minch, such tankers were disasters waiting to happen, and on this occasion I did get backing from some English Tory MEPs who were worried about the Channel and the West Country, as well as from Italian and French members, and later from the Spanish. In the end we did achieve a measure of regulation that drove sub-standard vessels and flag-of-convenience rust-bucket tankers out of European waters.

I was also concerned about unfair subsidies and European regulation which was inappropriate. There were subsidies, hidden or blatant, in other European countries that impacted greatly on our fishing industries, on the building of oil platforms, or shipbuilding, and on regional policy in general. The British Government always objected to these, but would do nothing to help those affected, as the Thatcher government was the most parsimonious on record. At the same time it would accede to regulations which were going to make the situation worse. For example, I was very concerned about the impact on island communities of new tachograph regulations for lorries. I asked for funding for the Highlands and Islands to overcome this burden and Roy Jenkins, then a Commissioner, in response said that he wanted to ensure that the EEC 'wore a human face', particularly in areas of deprivation. I seized on this phrase for later use, and was assiduous in quoting it when making demands for my area, which was in effect the periphery of a periphery.

Demands needed to be made. Road Equivalent Tariff would have been, and would still be, a tremendous boon, and as it works in Norway and Iceland, there is no reason that it would not work in Scotland. But the British Government has always resisted it. I had more success in ensuring there was support for agriculture in the Northern Isles, particularly when there were a succession of bad summers and winters, and with the support of a vigorous local campaign put paid to the prospect of uranium mining in Orkney. My agent in Orkney, Marjorie Linklater, was the driving force in that campaign and virtually every house and shop had a sticker in the window saying 'No uranium'. At the same time I took every opportunity to record my opposition to nuclear energy in general, and in particular my opposition to any prospect of nuclear waste-dumps in the Highlands and Islands. This was always a sensitive subject in my constituency, because of the presence of Dounreay, but it was one on which I could not compromise. I was polite but firm with those people who saw the employment that had been brought to a depressed area but I always felt that there were alternatives which needed to be pursued with vigour. At the same time I was wary of the malpractices I saw from other large employers – the multinationals – who got grants, used them up and then closed down their operations. The example of the pulp mill at Corpach was strongly in my mind.

On the wider scene I continued my work on human rights. I urged the European Parliament to appoint an Ombudsman for Human Rights and I had a particular concern for the situation of the Jews in Russia. An association had been formed across many parliaments in Europe whose aim was to help to free Jewish prisoners by adopting individuals and publicising their cases. My first adoptee was called Wulf Zalmanson, an engineer to trade, whose offence had been to teach Hebrew. I got schools in my constituency which had a department which taught Russian, or individuals who knew the language, to write letters to him. We believed that if he got enough outside attention then the authorities would conclude that keeping him in prison was simply counter-productive and in time he would be released to go to Israel.

I also arranged to go to Israel and meet members of the Israeli Government involved in the fight for the release of these prisoners. Happily Wulf was released and I met him at the Hilton in Tel Aviv. Though we had never met before we recognised each other as soon as he entered the hotel and we fell into each other's arms – it was a very emotional moment. When I had recovered my composure I asked him if anything we had done to help had ever endangered him, for this was a constant criticism of our actions. He replied by telling me the story of a fellow prisoner from the Ukraine who had no one working on his behalf. He never got any letters, until one day he received one from a Swiss MP. Wulf said, 'If you had seen the joy on his face at that moment, you would never ask such a question.'

Wulf had great spirit and humour. One occasion a Russian guard had mocked his continued study of Hebrew, saying, 'What's the point?' Wulf told him that when he went to heaven, he wanted to be able to speak to his ancestors, Jacob and Isaiah. The guard asked him what would happen if he went to hell instead. 'Well, I can already speak Russian,' replied Wulf.

The campaign for Russian Jews went on, using a variety of methods. My friend Leslie Wolfson fought the same battle as a lawyer, but his method was to instruct Russian lawyers and to take cases into Russian courts, which surprised the authorities and which had some success. All sorts of means were used but the aim was always the same – to help persecuted individuals and to insist that human rights were paramount. Of course the ordinary Russian people knew little about what was being done, supposedly in their name, and the boycott of the Moscow Olympics had surprised some of them. Stewart wanted to go and Terry wanted to go with him, but I refused as I felt that all methods needed to be used to show Russia the error of its ways. Stewart and Terry went, however, and Terry came back with a story that proved the point about ordinary people. On one occasion he had become separated from Stewart and got lost. A bus load of Russians found him, took him back to his hotel and then fed him up at their expense on lots of burgers. Terry said that he would never hear a word against ordinary Russians again!

That contrast between the views and desires of ordinary people and those of their governments is one that European politicians have to be constantly aware of. One Christmas, Stewart and I decided to go to East Germany, as it was obvious that the situation in that country was not stable and the current political situation would not last for ever. I wanted to see how East Germany was as a Communist regime, so close geographically and culturally to a European member state. Our first surprise was that everyone seemed so keen to speak to us. Stewart and I both spoke good German and that helped of course, but ordinary people wanted to converse and tell us about their lives.

Throughout East Germany there was a total 'go slow' atmosphere. There were some large stores but they had few goods of any kind in their windows. We travelled by bus in an organised group and all along the roadsides were huge hoardings with 'patriotic' slogans on them – propaganda with a capital 'P'. We saw the New Year in whilst standing in Karl-Marx-Stadt and there was much celebration. We were even invited to the home of a couple of people we met during the party. Despite high spirits at New Year, many Germans were unhappy about the division of their country.

An old couple in funeral black whom we spoke to later had been given permission to attend a family funeral and they had come from the west to do so. They were distraught at the division in their immediate family that the wall had created and their story was tragic, yet one which was mirrored all over the land.

I had arranged to meet two women government ministers and they took us out to dinner. One of them was a regular delegate to the Inter-parliamentary Union which was shortly due to meet in conference in London. I invited her and her husband to come and stay with us in Scotland after the meeting, but she declined, telling me very privately that she would not ask permission to do so, for it would be refused. So, despite appearances, things were far from open. Nonetheless one had a feeling that the situation was not one that could last for ever. People were too questioning and in time that, I was sure, would make the difference. And of course it did.

The basic question of human rights became more and more central to my concerns. In 1983 I made a very different trip to the Middle East with that issue at the heart of events. Madame Madelaine Fourcade, a member of my group, had been the leader of the French women's resistance during the war and one of her present causes was that of the Christians of Lebanon. When Madelaine told me about them I was struck by the fact that they spoke Aramaic, the language of Christ himself. They had lived in their communities for centuries, but now they were under threat and Madelaine repeatedly raised their plight in the European Parliament. Madelaine arranged an international association of parliamentarians who would show solidarity. This was to come together in Beirut and we were to be represented by Louise Weiss, the oldest woman MEP. However, she had to drop out and Madelaine asked me if I would go instead.

It was indeed a multi-national gathering – there were parliamentarians from Canada, Australia, Austria, Germany, Italy, Belgium, France, Norway, Poland, Mexico, Argentina, Brazil, Switzerland and the UK as well as myself from Europe and John Taylor from Northern Ireland. We were held up for hours by the Syrian police en route to the country but eventually we arrived at the Hotel Al Bustun in Damascus. While it appeared very grand it was quickly obvious that service was non-existent as the usual staff had been given leave of absence for security reasons. Students who were regarded as sympathetic by the Lebanese armed forces had been drafted in to look after us, though fortunately they did not have to cook; at least the hotel chefs had stayed at their posts.

The Lebanon, formerly a French mandate, had been declared a republic in 1941, but since then had been torn apart by disputes with Israel over Palestinian bases and by the civil war in 1975 and 1976. There was strong tension between the Muslim and Christian populations. The formal conference proceedings started off with the Lebanese national anthem and then an address of welcome by the Lebanese President Camille Chamoun, who went out of his way to praise the 5,000 young Lebanese who had died in the conflict and who also reminded us that 900,000 Arabs had come to live in Lebanon since the establishment of the State of Israel, of whom 610,000 were Palestinians. This whole situation had created a delicate balance which was easily upset.

Then we heard a speech from the real power in the land, Bashir Gemayel, the commander of the Lebanese Resistance Forces. The conference had opened on 1 April and M. Gemayel explained to us that the date had been chosen deliberately, for the 2nd of April was the anniversary of the Syrian invasion. He rejected any notion that the conflicts in Lebanon were 'civil' in origin and insisted that difficulties were caused by the actions of invading states. He told us that in his opinion the crisis in the Middle East was not restricted to the narrow field of Arab–Israeli hostility. That had now been overtaken by a wider conflict which had transcended its origins and spread to different countries. The crisis was a mobile one which moved in time and space and was in fact the contemporary expression of the long-standing problems of the area, with its two key issues of the protection of minorities from majorities and the rivalry between outside powers. Furthermore, he went on to argue, the two aspects were closely interwoven: tensions among the minorities served to fan the embers of rivalry between the great powers, and the rivalry among the superpowers very often provoked tensions among the minorities. It was an impressive performance and he concluded by urging all of us to use whatever influence we had to persuade Syria to withdraw and to allow

Lebanon to rebuild itself free from interference. In the afternoon we met various delegations and the Gemayel brothers hosted a reception. Madelaine and I spoke on the second day and there was a strong feeling of solidarity with a population that had seen and was still seeing very difficult times. The whole visit was an eye-opener as I had known little about the situation in Lebanon before.

One other trip I made, this time early on in my first elected term, was to Canada. I did this on behalf of the party as at one stage the SNP had branches in several places in Canada including Ottawa, Montreal, Vancouver and Thunder Bay. Those associated with the party also held an annual meeting to which an SNP speaker was invited. I actually went on two occasions and each time not only spoke but also appeared on Canadian TV and radio to put the case for Scottish independence.

The 1980 convention was held at Concordia University in Montreal and our Chairman in the Province of Quebec at that time was Donald Craig. I fell in love with Montreal immediately, meeting the Mayor and dining in a variety of wonderful places including a restaurant called 'Les Filles de Roy', which was named after the French girls who were officially sponsored to go and live in the province during the seventeenth century in order to provide wives for settlers and soldiers. The convention featured a number of distinguished speakers including three professors from Canadian universities who considered the demands of both Scotland and Quebec and made comparisons with devolved settlements elsewhere. In my speech I indicated the strong affection for Canada that existed amongst many Scots – something that some Quebecers did not like – and the view that was prevalent in Scotland was that whilst Quebec had the absolute right to decide on its future, many would be sad if it was forced out of Canada. However, I also recognised that Quebec, like Scotland, needed the right solutions for its problems and that Canada did not yet seem to be able to provide them.

I was conscious that this was a mixed message but it did accurately reflect what the party and much of Scotland was thinking at that time. Knowledge of Quebec and its enormous cultural and social differences from the rest of Canada was limited and even the PQ at that stage was looking for a new accommodation, rather than the full sovereignty that is now discussed.

In addition to attending the convention I went to Ottawa and visited the Canadian Parliament. My visit coincided with the first occasion on which Pierre Trudeau had answered Parliamentary Questions as Prime Minister and I got a round of applause from the Chamber before he got under way. He was most impressive and the format of question time, held each day at the start of the session, was much more challenging than anything I had seen in the House of Commons. Any question could be asked without notice and Trudeau actually engaged with the questioner and tried to give meaningful responses. I was taken to meet him after the session and I congratulated him on actually answering, something I said never happened at Westminster. Years later I met him again and he said to me, 'I'm still answering the questions.'

Later I went on to Thunder Bay before returning home, but whilst I was in Canada my seven cousins who lived there organised a magnificent party at which there were a hundred of my relatives, many of whom I had never seen before.

I have always felt that the SNP could gain great strength from the diaspora, particularly in Canada and America, and I do feel that as a party we have failed to capitalise on the support that we have in such places. These branches used to send people to Bannockburn, where the Quebecers were welcomed so warmly that it caused adverse publicity in Canada itself. Now there are no such delegations, though in recent years Michael Russell has visited Quebec twice on Parliamentary visits and has tried to re-establish links, and in 1998 he and Alex Salmond privately met the Prime Minister of Quebec and gave him dinner in Edinburgh.

In addition to parliamentary sessions, committee meetings and the inevitable travelling, the work of one's group is very important to a European member of Parliament, as is the work of so-called 'inter groups' – what we would now call 'cross-party groups'. I joined many such groups, including those whose concerns were Animal Welfare, Islands, Disabled, Minority Languages, Friends of Israel, Arab Friends and Unrepresented People (an intergroup that was founded some time in the late eighties by Alan Macartney, who was its chair). Some met very occasionally but, some, like the Animal Welfare Group (of which I ended up as Vice Chairman) got together every month. Others grew up and petered out; that was the fate of both the Israel and Arab groups.

The Animal Welfare Group had many battles to fight and one of our main aims was to improve conditions for animals in transit. Eventually we succeeded in getting Europe-wide legislation as to the maximum length of time animals were allowed to be without fresh water and food. We also fought to stop animal experimentation for cosmetic purposes and asked for all experimentation to be regulated to avoid any duplication and unnecessary suffering. In addition the group was constantly active in opposing cruelty to animals at certain festivals in Europe, as well as opposing fox hunting, but as these matters were usually seen as domestic issues we had great difficulty making headway.

My full Parliamentary group met regularly to discuss how to vote and what attitude to take on issues, but we also held at least two study days a year which actually took up the best part of a week, during which we would discuss papers written by ourselves or our staff, develop our collective positions and widen our knowledge. They were very important in building cohesion and broadening perspectives and they usually took place in the constituency of a group member.

I was very keen to get my group to the Highlands and Islands at the earliest opportunity. The Provost and city fathers of Inverness jumped at the chance and offered the group the use of the Town House for the formal meetings. The UK Cabinet had met for the first time outside London in that very place in 1921, when the subject of their meeting was Ireland, and in particular the negotiations for the Irish Free State. The relevant documents are hung in pride of place in the Council Chamber and it seemed an ideal place for my group to convene. The Irish members enthusiastically agreed, particularly Sile De Valera.

The Highlands and Islands Group study visit in the early summer of 1980 was a great success. We heard papers from a range of members and speakers, but we were also royally entertained. The City of Inverness hosted a dinner, as did the Highland Region. The group held a reception on the third evening of our visit and members had the chance to meet farmers, fishermen, oil men and many others. Their knowledge of Scotland and what Scotland wanted and needed from Europe was greatly increased. The Highland press, and some Scottish papers, saw that the visit was vital to a proper understanding of the Highlands and our needs in Europe and there was much attention paid to it.

On the Thursday of the group study visit I took the entire group to Skye, and although the mist was low over the hills, there were frequent cries of 'Dramatique!' and 'Romantique!' as the scenery unfolded. I had arranged for a friend from Forres who was a piper to be with us and wherever we stopped, at Eilean Donan for example, he would play as the members took coffee or wandered round. At Kyle the police ushered our bus first onto the ferry. M. De La Malene, our group president, was alarmed and said 'Winnie, this will lose you votes. This is not democratic.' However, I pointed out to him that all around us people were smiling and waving as the news of our visit had preceded us. As we drove onto Skye the sun broke through and there was the island in all its glory: the bus was almost silent as we sped down to Isle Oronsay to have lunch at Iain Noble's hotel. Earlier, at another stop, M. De La Malene, who was usually so very proper, came back onto the bus with a bottle of Talisker he had been presented with and proceeded to share it with those around him.

In addition to all our Highland and Island activities, I made sure that the SNP leader, Gordon Wilson, and some of our senior members had a chance to meet the group whilst they were in Scotland. These meetings were very valuable, cementing our place in the group and giving the Irish and French a clear perspective on who we were and what we wanted.

Later in the same year some of my group went to Athens, in preparation for the accession of Greece in 1981. We visited the Parliament and met the various parties, to see if any would be suitable partners for us. As a group we had been instrumental in getting passed the award of 15 per cent of available regional funding to Greece, and this made us very welcome indeed. As a former MP for Elgin and now as its European representative, I also had discussions with Melina Merkouri about the Elgin Marbles and promised to continue to raise the issue of their return, something I have gone on doing in the face of resolute opposition from the British Government.

I had a particular interest in courting the Greeks because their accession greatly increased the number of populated islands in the EC, and I wanted to make common cause with their island representatives. Of course their islands have virtually year-round tourism but they continue to suffer from depopulation and from considerable agricultural problems. The Greek Government was trying to establish small-scale industries along the lines attempted by the Highlands and Islands Development Board, but there were considerable difficulties in a land which was still experiencing much poverty. Although no promises were made, it was obvious that the fourteen new Greek MEPs, who would be nominated by their Parliament until the time of the next direct election, were going to be useful allies in a number of causes, and they would also be Europeans who looked to the Community to help them build a better future.

One of our 1982 study days was held in Madrid. I was early for our first group dinner and was waiting at the top of the grand staircase at the Ritz wearing a pink sparkly dress, when President Mitterrand arrived. He walked up the stairs and kissed me warmly on both cheeks, only to be pulled away by his anxious security guards. He must have mistaken me for the welcoming party. Some years later I met him again on a visit he made to the European Parliament and reminded him of the incident. He was gracious enough to laugh very heartily and then to say that it was not at all surprising that he had kissed me!

In Spain, which was then preparing for entry into the EC we met representatives of all the political parties. Amongst those we met during that visit was Señor De Fraga, who had been the Ambassador in London and who hosted the dinner at which I had discussed Catalonia with Spanish Embassy staff. Now of course there was a complete change, and Catalonia was governed, at least in its domestic affairs, by nationalist parties.

Spain had changed very much since I had visited it with Stewart in 1958. It was much more prosperous and there was a huge amount of new building going on. Freedom of expression had been firmly established and there was an anticipation about the future – one of the MPs from the Cortes that I spoke to said that Spain was 'living through exciting times'. He was right.

I went on from Madrid to Catalonia where the main concern of the parties was to preserve and entrench democracy. I was invited to speak to the Convergence, the alliance of nationalist parties that was in power, and I enjoyed my visit to the Catalan Parliament, which had 165 members and which could trace its origins back to the twelfth century.

We went to France on a number of occasions, most memorably touring Provence in a hired car and visiting the beautiful city of Avignon, the home of the medieval popes. Stewart, whilst hating driving in France, agreed to come along as I had long wanted to see that particular area of the country. I was not disappointed for I can still smell the cologne and the fields of lavender and the scent of tremendous cooking. The Mayor of Avignon was one of our group members and he arranged that M. De La Malene, myself and Paddy Lalor (as the representatives of our three countries) to receive the Freedom of the City during our visit, an honour that could only be awarded with the unanimous agreement of all fifty-three local councillors. I was delighted to get it but not sure what advantages it would bestow until the mayor assured me that if I wanted to come and live in the city I would not have to pay any local taxes.

Each of these visits brought home to all the members particular aspects of European life and local, national and sometimes international problems. In Ringkøbing in Denmark, for example, the group stayed right by the sea experiencing various aspects of the fishing industry as well as seeing at first hand the grave problems of coastal erosion. We met, as ever, the local officials and we visited not only a factory that made wind generators but also the tourist attraction of Legoland.

Stewart came with me again, as did my sister, on a study tour in the west of Ireland. On the way back by car we stopped in Derry for the night and dined at John Hume's house. The reality of the situation he lived in was brought home to me by overhearing one of his sons, then in his late teens, on his way out for the evening being reminded by John's wife Pat that he must phone her as soon as he arrived at his destination and again when he was leaving to return home. They lived with constant tension, but did so with great bravery and equanimity.

We then drove on to Belfast and as we arrived early at the ferry port I decided I wanted a drink in a real Belfast pub. Jean stayed in the car but Stewart and I went in and were enjoying ourselves until a man come forward and rattled a can under our nose. 'What are you collecting for?' I asked him. 'The Karate Club,' he replied. We made a swift exit.

Sometimes these visits were attacked in the press, particularly in Scotland, as 'junkets', but the knowledge that they gave group members was invaluable, and real action usually flowed from them. But even committee visits to parts of Europe were criticised in the press, including one in July 1983 by the Regional Committee to western Ireland. The

Stewart and Winnie with her father George and mother Chris Woodburn

The family, Queen's Drive, Glasgow, 1967

Street campaign, Hamilton by-election, 1967

Election newspaper, 1967

Handing over trial cases to John Boyle of the Glasgow
Bar Association after the Hamilton by-election,
November 1967

Aboard the Tartan Express, November 1967

Aboard the Tartan Express, November 1967

GEO Leslie Helen DAVINSON DAVID Rollo M Billy Wolfe ARTAH Donaldson DuJer Lees Provost BRAN

Oban SNP Conference 1968

SNP Conference, Oban, 1968. Left to right: George Leslie, Helen Davidson, David Rollo, Winnie Ewing, Billy Wolfe, unidentified, Arthur Donaldson, Douglas Lees, Provost Bain

Terry joins the Metropolitan Police, House of Commons, July 1968

Addressing protest in Hamilton against the compulsory registration of teachers
with the General Teaching Council, 1969

Meeting President De Valera, 1969

David Donaldson, Queen's limner, paints Winnie's portrait, 1969

Handing over the Scottish Covenant recovered from a builder's yard in Rutherglen, 1970

Crew of the *Goodwill*, Lossiemouth, 1973, with skipper Billy Campbell at the back

February 1974: 'The Magnificent Seven'. Left to right: Iain MacCormick, George Reid, Gordon Wilson, Winnie Ewing, Donnie Stewart, Hamish Watt, Douglas Henderson

With fish processors, Lossiemouth, July 1974

October 1974 : 'First Eleven' of SNP MPs: Andrew Welsh, Douglas Henderson,
Iain MacCormick, Hamish Watt, Winnie Ewing, Donnie Stewart, Gordon Wilson, Margaret Bain, George Reid,
George Thompson, Douglas Crawford

With Wendy Wood, Edinburgh, November 1975

Cartoon from the *Scottish Daily Express*, July 1978

A Bain cartoon concerning the Euro election, June 1979

Success in the election, Inverness, 1979

The Fianna Fáil members. Back, left to right: Niall Andrews, Gene Fitzgerald, Eileen Lemass, Mark Killilea, Jim Fitzsimons. Front, left to right: Sean Flanagan, Paddy Lalor, Winnie Ewing, Sylvester Barrett

With saltire and SNP Euro election candidates, 1984

Flying the Euro flag: election 1984

Alex Salmond, Kay Matheson and Winnie Ewing at the return of the Stone of Destiny, November 1991

SNP Conference 1992

Meeting with Gwynfor Evans when opening the Plaid Cymru office in Cardiff

Cartoon comment on the selection of Annabelle Ewing as by-election candidate in Hamilton South, 1999

With Otto von Habsburg

The Queen addresses the Scottish Parliament in Aberdeen, May 2002

Tartan Day in New York, April 2002, with Sean Connery and the Mayor of New York

committee had representatives from all eleven groups in the Parliament and in very atypical sweltering weather we visited Knock Airport, met tourist organisations, saw innovations in aquaculture, talked with members of the Galway Chamber of Commerce, were extensively lobbied about the need for a better transport infrastructure and learnt about the efforts to support the Irish language. Not only were these issues important for Ireland, they were important for Scotland too and I could gauge in the committee where sympathy lay, and how to pursue my own cases as well as those of other countries.

Sometimes the constant travelling did become irksome and even, on occasion, lonely, although company could sometimes be found in the strangest of circumstances. One evening in Luxembourg I was coming into my hotel to get ready for a grand French reception when I heard the hotel message boy call out, 'Message for Mr Lunney.' I went to the reception desk and asked if this Mr Lunney was a Scot. I was told he was, and as it is a very uncommon name I at once thought that it had to be my old Glasgow Bar colleague Frank Lunney, who often travelled to Europe, as he was very involved with the Catholic Church. I left a note at reception for him: 'Dear Frank, if you would like to accompany me to a grand French reception meet me in foyer at 7 p.m. Winnie.' At 7 p.m. a perfect stranger introduced himself to me. He had got my note and he was a Scots lawyer called Frank Lunney, but he was not *my* Frank Lunney. Until recently he had been working for the Hong Kong Bank, and as he was now about to take up a post in Luxembourg he was there looking for a home for his family. But he asked if he could still come with me to the reception, for he too was on his own. It was an ingenious way to find an escort and we had a pleasant evening.

The endless variety of life as a European MP was continually astonishing. Literally anything could happen, as I discovered one day in Strasbourg. The headquarters for the French Foreign Legion are in that city and early one morning a Glaswegian presented himself at the Parliament asking for me. Neil Fergusson went to meet the visitor who told him that he had 'shot the craw' from the legion – in other words that he had deserted. Members are given a new identity when they join and this one would not say who he was or why he had joined. But desertion is regarded as a crime by the Legion, and offenders are hunted down and returned to duties, or worse.

All Neil could do was give him £20 and send him on his way. We never heard from him again.

In Europe we all worked very hard – the European day is long and starts early – but we also played hard. Good company and good food were the norm and much valued and I found myself in my element. I also started to receive many visitors. At each July Strasbourg session, when the Scottish school holidays had started, Jo Docherty and Maire Whitehead would come to stay in my flat. Jo had been a European Parliamentary candidate and Maire a Westminster candidate and the two are the firmest of friends, great company but can be fiery. They both have strong Scottish accents and they became known as the 'girls with the rolling "R".' They were hugely popular with my Irish colleagues and made firm friends with many of them. They were even noticed by some of the English Tories and one, on being introduced and discovering that they were both candidates, asked me if we always chose our candidates because of their pulchritude. Invariably I would hold a party during their visit and encourage everyone present to sing or recite. On those evenings one could hear music and words from Ireland, France, Greece, Corsica, Italy, Flanders, Germany, England, Scotland, Portugal and Denmark. It was spellbinding and sometimes the evening took an unexpected turn, such as the one when John Hume did an Orange walk with Jo Docherty. John, who could have been a professional tenor, also used to sing, particularly that song about Derry – 'The Town I Loved So Well'.

The staff at the Parliament were also great company and very helpful. I was particularly friendly with Cliodhna Dempsey, a very senior official, and her partner Martin Joyce, who was a Scottish Nationalist and was in charge of the security of the whole Parliament. He had been a clerk in the House of Lords and was an ex-marine as well as a fencing expert. David Young, in charge of the Parliament's cash office, was also close to me as were some of the interpreters, including Leonora du Wahl.

My biggest delight, however, was in my own constituency, the largest in Europe, and also, I am sure, the most beautiful and full of the kindest people. Yet just getting round it to visit my constituents was a constant challenge. Difficult as it had been in Hamilton and in Moray, now I had an altogether different scale of challenge, and meeting it would be the determining factor in doing my job properly, and in retaining my seat when the next elections came around.

The Member for the Islands and Highlands:
Mostly At Home

T HE SHEER SIZE OF MY European constituency was daunting. From Moray to the Western Isles and from the island of Bute to all the islands of Shetland, it covered a substantial part of the entire country and was larger, much larger, than Luxembourg. Whilst I had visited almost every part of it at some point in my life, I could not claim to know all of it well, but I would have to get to know it very quickly indeed and to become a regular part of the lives of many communities.

My first thought was that I could best cover the constituency by learning to fly, like the councillor I knew from Westray in Orkney. But my family absolutely vetoed the idea for they had no confidence in my abilities to pilot a plane safely. Although not a great sailor, my attention then turned to boats. In the first summer after my election Stewart and I went on a cruise on a yacht to visit the islands of the west along with Lorna Blackie, Robert McIntyre and a friend of his who was a consultant and whose son, John, skippered the boat. The idea was that we would get round as many islands as possible and work out whether this was the best way to fit in a summer series of visits. However, after a number of island calls we were struck by the worst gales I have ever seen and sat stormbound in Mallaig. This was the same storm that caused devastation to the Fastnet Yacht Race, killing seventeen people.

Sitting in Mallaig, the fishing boats seemed huge alongside our little yacht, but the harbourmaster was deeply unsympathetic and wanted us out of there. We were saved by some Buckie fishermen who were also sheltering. 'Winnie is no takin' her boatie out there,' said one of them very firmly and menacingly, and that was that. But it also put paid to the sailing idea. Consequently I had to revert to using planes and boats operated by others, as well as travelling by car.

My touring was intensive from the beginning. Each year I tried to spend at least one whole week in Orkney and Shetland, one in the Western Isles and one in Argyll, which included the Argyll islands. I would also have to make more frequent and regular visits to Caithness and Sutherland, Ross and Cromarty, Skye and of course throughout Moray and Nairn. As I had always done as a Westminster MP I was determined to address any school who invited me or who allowed me to visit and would always be open to invitations to go to work-places and community organisations. I started off with the great advantage of having excellent relations with my own local authority and subsequently with all the others, once we had made contact. That was of huge importance in ensuring that we worked together to promote the cause of the Highlands and Islands and in particular to take forward the campaign for Objective One Status, a European definition which would free up resources for the area. Soon I was a regular visitor to council headquarters throughout the area, having lunch with officials and councillors, getting briefings and listening to concerns. Once again I was struck by how many people in senior positions had been Stewart's students, and that of course helped greatly.

My job, however, could not have been done without a network of agents throughout the area who were much more than simply campaign orga-nisers. They took care of my diary on visits, they were a valuable means of keeping me informed about key issues (though I took, and continue to take, all the local papers for the Highlands and Islands) and they made certain I was never left without the contacts to ensure that I could be effective. They were people of magnificent calibre – Willie Ross in Shetland, Marjorie Linklater and John Mowat in Orkney, Jennifer Mac-Donald in the Western Isles, Ken McColl in Argyll, Dr Kerr Yuill in Ross, Cromarty and Skye, John Bogle in Caithness and Sutherland, and of course Hugh Coulter in Moray. Each of them were outstanding indivi-duals and each commanded the respect of their communities, which was also essential. The bulk of the touring, which was done by car, was made much easier very quickly by the assistance of Kay Matheson, of Stone of

Destiny fame. She also acted as one of my agents and she drove me literally thousands of miles.

Kay's account of the recovery of the Stone was fascinating. The Stone was in two pieces when recovered from the Coronation Chair in Westminster Abbey and Kay took one piece away, whilst the other was carried off by Ian Hamilton, Gavin Vernon and Alan Stewart. Kay made her way north up through a cold and wintry night with her half in the car-boot and sought a bed from a fellow student at the 'Dough School' (the College of Domestic Science) whose father was the Chief Constable of the Manchester police force. He suspected nothing and was completely oblivious to the fact that the most sought-after piece of rock in Britain was sitting in his garage. When Kay reached the border there was a police check-point. She stopped and the policeman asked her if she had the Stone of Destiny. Using all her considerable charm she smiled and said, 'Of course, it's in the boot.' The policeman laughed and waved her on. However, later on they got on her trail and arrived at her home in Inverasdale, west of Gairloch. Fortunately she had established an alibi in the village, for she had helped dig the local bus out of the snow and the bus driver confirmed this, without saying that this had occurred not at the time the Stone was being removed from Westminster Abbey, but some time after.

Kay was very bitter when the Stone was returned and always regarded what she had done as a principled action and not as a crime. I used to love hearing the story because it was also one of my might-have-beens, for Ian Hamilton had sounded me out about taking part in the recovery, but I did not drive and that ruled me out. I would like to have been there for I too think it was the right, and a brave, thing to do.

Kay's house in Inverasdale became a sort of home from home for me as I toured the Highlands. Kay lived with her lively, genial and wise mother who was, as Kay was herself, a native Gaelic speaker and full of traditional Highland hospitality. No one ever passed the door without coming in, and those who came in never went away without tea and a *strupach*. I promised Kay that I would master Gaelic before I died but I began to despair as the years passed and my Gaelic did not greatly improve. However, as a result of Kay's patience and friendship I did manage to improve my reading and writing of the language, although my vocabulary remains poor. Nonetheless, whenever I visit the homes of old people who speak the language it is a fine thing at least to try to converse with them in their own. The subtlety of Gaelic lends itself both to joking and to the mildest of rebukes to learners. I once said to an old lady in Lewis, 'Tha an là brèagh an diugh' ('It is a lovely day today'). The lady startled me by saying 'Cha'n 'eil' ('Not at all'), but then added with a smile, 'Tha an là aluinn an diugh' ('It is a *splendid* day today'). Kay herself was known as 'Cailleach nan clach' ('Old Lady of the Stone') but I would always refuse to refer to her as such, saying that she was not a *cailleach* and that she should be called the 'Young Woman of the Stone' instead.

We used to have some fun together because she had a great natural sense of humour and would play up to any jokes or pranks. Kay remained single all her life, though not for the want of admirers, but on one occasion during my tours we went up to speak to some old men at a fank, where sheep were being dipped. As we got talking Kay told them that she was looking for a handsome old man because she had not got one, and there seemed to be lots there. One old crofter was eventually pushed forward for inspection, but Kay wittily said that he would not do as she needed a minimum of nine teeth in any suitor and that particular one clearly only had six! Kay knew virtually everyone in the Highlands and as my driver she not only covered the miles and got me from place to place safely, but also made the necessary introductions to the great and the good as well as lots of others. She accompanied me to other places as well and was particularly popular in Orkney.

Kay was one of the only people I have ever met who made her own whisky, and as her house was a long way off the Gairloch road, any Customs men would be seen coming from a considerable distance. Her mother didn't drink whisky herself but she offered it generously to all her visitors, and there were many. The whisky was put into empty bottles that had once contained legitimate brands of whisky, and if a Customs man called she would invite him to take his choice of the brands on display. The local customs officer must have known full well that it was all home-made, but he said nothing.

Kay worked as an itinerant teacher of Gaelic as well as undertaking work for the HIDB. However, she contracted severe rheumatism and this eventually stopped her driving, which put paid to her jobs and altered her entire life. Her mother also died and left her on her own, and fewer people called and stayed than had done so at one time, not least because it was hard for her to look after them and because she was unattached and that was still an issue in some parts of the Highlands. I owe Kay a huge debt of gratitude for all she did for me, and for her constant help with my Gaelic. But most of all I am most grateful for her friendship and I am so sad that she now has to live in a sheltered housing complex rather than in her own wonderful and welcoming home.

Willie MacRae, who had been SNP candidate in Ross and Cromarty, once asked me to speak on his behalf to Kay to ask her to marry him, but I was reluctant to play the part of go-between and I pointed out that she seemed devoted to her mother and would find it hard to leave her. Willie maintained, however, that he was devoted to Kay's mother as well and was quite prepared to look after both of them. In the end, nothing came of that incipient romance

Willie was a highly successful Glasgow lawyer, a partner in the firm of Levy and MacRae, having also had a distinguished career in the army during the war. He also had strong links with Israel. He was a magnificent orator with a big following in the party and was particularly inspiring and direct when talking of the 'obscenity' of Highland landlords, saying that we would put an end to landlordism by getting rid of 'the whole rick-ma-tick o' them'!

He was also a doughty campaigner and acted for the objectors during the inquiry into nuclear dumping at Mulwhacar in Galloway as well as being involved in some high-profile anti-drugs cases, earning the enmity of drug dealers.

In 1985 Willie was found dead some way off the main road north, on the stretch that rises up high between Invergarry and the road from Skye to Inverness. He was discovered, very strangely, by an SNP candidate and councillor from Dundee, David Coutts, who was travelling the road in the early hours with his girlfriend, a medical doctor. They called the police, thinking that Willie had been killed in a car accident, probably when his car left the road, but when he was taken to hospital in Inverness it was discovered that he had a bullet in his brain.

There were many strange circumstances surrounding Willie's death. The night he died he had been doing paperwork in bed in his Queen's Park flat in Glasgow and it had caught fire (he was, admittedly, a heavy smoker and had done this before.) The fire brigade had been called by a neighbour, but the fire was out by the time they arrived and Willie refused all help. He then set out for the largely ruined croft that he owned in the Highlands. The gun found at the scene of the 'accident' was not next to the body but some distance from it. The first police officer attending had failed to spot the bullet wound, and there were rumoured sightings of a man with a rifle in the vicinity just before Willie had supposedly crashed. No one knew why he was travelling north, though there were more rumours about some big story he was on to connected with nuclear dumping.

Many people admired and loved Willie and an annual commemoration of his death started to be held where his body had been found, and a cairn was erected by party members who brought stones from other parts of Scotland. His brother, who was a GP in Falkirk, was embarrassed by all the publicity, as was the party nationally, for there were an increasing number of articles about his death appearing each year in the press. The SNP NEC wanted to get to the bottom of the matter once and for all and asked me, as a lawyer as well as a senior member, to investigate in confidence. I undertook to do so, saying that I would report only whether I was satisfied or dissatisfied with the official version that he committed suicide.

I took precognitions from David Coutts, from Willie's neighbours, from some of his clients and his partners. I talked to the garage he regularly stopped at when travelling north, but when I asked to see the Procurator Fiscal in Inverness and to ask why there had been, remarkably, no Fatal Accident Inquiry (which should have been mandatory considering the circumstances), I was up against a brick wall. The Procurator Fiscal had just taken early retirement and would not talk to me, even in confidence. Then the Lord Advocate refused to see me too and would not respond to any questions. Given all this obstruction (which was clearly deliberate), I had to report to the NEC that I was not satisfied with the official account of suicide, and that remains my position today. I do not know what happened, but I think it is important that the truth emerges, despite the time that has passed. Why the State refuses to let the truth be known is a pertinent question.

I was now entering the stage of my life when I was facing the reality of the deaths of close friends and family. When I won Moray and Nairn in

1974 my sister-in-law Jessie told me that my brother John was seriously ill with motor neurone disease. This is a terrible disease for which there is neither a known cause or a cure, and he suffered greatly. Towards the end Stewart and I would visit him sometimes on a Friday and the sight of him nearly broke my heart. But then, before he died, Jessie was told that she had cancer, and although she fought bravely, she lost the battle. Between John's death and her own she often used to come to stay with me in Lossie and we became very close.

John always seemed to me to have been the perfect gentleman. He had joined up before the war started, had worked hard during the war and after and had been the perfect son, brother and husband. He smoked a pipe moderately, hardly took a drink and played active sports, and yet he had been struck down in his prime. It seemed very unfair and I took a deliberate decision to help those with motor neurone disease, as well as the charities trying to find out more about it, and did so in both the European and the Scottish Parliament.

My sister Jean was making a great success of her life at the Scots Bar and took up all sorts of challenges. Despite being widowed with children, at forty-seven, she had studied and been called to the bar at fifty-two and now sat on the Bench a lot as a judicial assessor, becoming the Scots Bar expert on social security. In addition she served as a community councillor in Garnethill in Glasgow. My brother David had also found himself a widower, for his wife Sarah contracted cancer and died. He started to come to visit me frequently in Lossiemouth and often accompanied me as my escort, for Stewart was still working in Glasgow.

Nonetheless Stewart was increasingly able to accompany me to events and one of the things he came to was the annual Up-Helly-Aa in Shetland. From the start of my European Parliamentary career I made an annual week's visit to Shetland at the end of January, and each year I took a different guest. I tried to explain the spectacle and excitement of Up-Helly-Aa to Stewart before he came and I had taken photographs and shown them to him, but when he actually came to see it he was mesmerised and said, infuriatingly, 'Why did you not tell me about this?'

The whole population of Lerwick is involved in the events. In the morning the longboat is viewed by the entire population, including the children, who have a school holiday. There are about a score of 'squads' who have spent many months beforehand preparing their costumes and working out not just what they will they appear as, but also their 'acts', which are performed in the various 'halls' that are open for the night. These squads (all men) embrace all occupations and provide a community solidarity during the winter, though there is a residency qualification – one has to have lived in Lerwick for five years to become a squad member. The chief figure in the celebrations, 'Guisar Yarl', is chosen annually from one of the squads and his becomes the lead squad in the procession (the Yarl Squad) who are always dressed as Vikings. There is a wonderful civic reception in the Town House on the evening of Up-Helly-Aa, to which I was always invited. It was customary at this reception to don a Viking helmet and get one's photo taken for the *Shetland Times*, and every guest did so if asked. I recall seeing Jim Wallace so attired, as well as many others, but when Michael Forsyth visited, as Secretary of State for Scotland, he refused to put the helmet on. A little boy, dressed as a Viking, must have overheard his refusal because he came up to him, pulled his trouser leg, and said, 'Hey, Mister, why won't you wear the helmet?' Forsyth had no answer.

As for places from which to watch the burning of the boat itself I was spoilt for choice, for not only was there a fine old lady with a Lossie connection whose flat had a prime view (and who once showed me a traditional Shetland knitted lace shawl which could literally pass through a wedding ring), but I also became friendly with the Norwegian Honorary Consul, Frank Garriock, whose windows overlooked the site of the longboat and from which one could see all the squads as they paraded past. The squads all parade through the town and past the Town House, which flies the Shetland Viking flag, the black raven.

The first time I visited Up-Helly-Aa I found myself in the Grand Hotel which was one of the halls visited by the squads, who have to remain sober throughout the night as they have to repeat their act in all of them. The halls are usually dry too, though there is plenty of drink taken in houses and elsewhere. I remember the Grand Hotel because, for some reason, I had to use the public phone and was waiting to do so while a poor commercial traveller from England was explaining to his wife why he had been delayed in Shetland. He had arrived on the Monday, not knowing that the Up-Helly-Aa celebrations were about to start. Tuesday would be a write-off, and Wednesday would be a day of recovery. He was clearly not, therefore, going to do his business and get home much before the end of the week. He was making heavy weather of the call, for, as he explained about the Viking longboat, the squads, the torches, the procession and the halls he had to constantly stop and say, 'No, I have not been drinking.' Eventually he finished his call, turned to me with a rueful smile, shrugged and said, 'Well, now that's done, I might as well enter in the spirit of things.'

These visits to Shetland were always a high point of the year and brought back memories of my visit in 1967 between winning Hamilton and taking my seat. I would often meet people who had heard me speak when I had been in Lerwick then and I made and kept many good friends on the islands. During the Up-Helly-Aa week I would usually go to some of the other islands as well – Unst, Yell, Whalsay, the Skerries and even Fair Isle, though travelling was often difficult and the weather cruel. I always enjoyed each of those islands with their tremendous diversity and the people were enormously kind and hospitable.

That was, of course, also true of the islands of Orkney to which I went at least once a year. Marjorie Linklater was not only my agent, but my closest friend on the islands. She lived in a very quaint house which had once been the island's fever hospital and had a fine library and many excellent Scottish paintings. I wanted Marjorie to write a book about her fascinating life – she had met everyone famous in the arts world – but she told me that her late husband, the novelist Eric Linklater, had made her promise that she would never write about her life, particularly with him. She felt that if she broke that promise he would haunt her.

Marjorie had been a very beautiful young woman and retained that beauty to the end of her life, keeping fit by riding round the island on a bicycle. She was respected throughout the islands, having been an elected councillor and a pillar of many of the local societies. She was also a formidable campaigner who always had a cause, whether it be the (successful) attempt to stop uranium mining on the islands or the sale of the TSB by Thatcher's Tory government. Marjorie died whilst I was still a European member and I missed her greatly, for my visits to Orkney were never the same again. Her funeral service in the magnificent St Magnus Cathedral was packed and was a fitting tribute to her standing in the islands, and the great many things she had done for the community.

Marjorie was a stalwart for the SNP in Orkney, which was not the most fertile territory for us. However, we did have as a member the oldest woman on the islands, a Mrs Clayton, who was 106. Until almost the end of her life she stayed alone in a small house with a long sitting-room that had a window at each end. She had a home help but otherwise looked after herself, and I used to enjoy calling on her. She used to pour out, for herself as well as for me, a large sherry in lovely crystal glasses. She was once interviewed by the BBC when I was there and was asked what the secret of her longevity was. She thought for a while and then said, 'I was brought up in a farm and we had to work very hard every day. But we played hard too, often dancing into the wee small hours.' Then she added, 'And I just had the one man!'

Stewart loved Orkney – even more than Shetland – and we took a holiday there together at one stage when I was a Euro MP. We went walking every day and Stewart found it remarkable that wherever one was, one could always see the sea. The islands are also wonderfully green, in contrast to Shetland or the Western Isles, and it is always said that whilst Shetlanders are fishermen who happen to have a croft, Orkney men are farmers who happen to have a boat. The islands are also rich in archaeology – in fact they boast some of the richest and best-preserved archaeological sites in Europe – and there was always much European interest in Orkney in that regard, as well as in others, for it is a prime site for developing the alternative energy sources of wind and wave power.

The third major island group in my constituency was the Western Isles. Once again I tried to spend a complete week there at least once a year, and to cover all of what they call 'the long island' from the Butt of Lewis to the island of Barra. As the years passed and as the Islands Council began to improve roads and ferries and build causeways, this trip became easier, though the final link in the chain – the causeway to Eriskay and the new vehicle ferry to Barra, was only put in place in 2002.

My agent in the Western Isles was Jennifer MacDonald, who always took a week's holiday to drive me round. Jennifer was a widow with four children and had been married to a Barra man who worked all over as an engineer. After his death Jennifer had to give up the croft on Barra and she moved to Stornoway, where she could work as a nurse and, as a single parent, give her children greater opportunities. Jennifer was an ideal travelling companion as she had friends and relatives throughout the islands. In addition the Island Council was always welcoming and hospitable and the Western Isles SNP members were a colourful bunch who had built branches in Lewis, Harris, Uist and on Barra. I had many firm friends amongst the members including Peter MacLeod, Alasdair Nicholson (who later became our candidate), Bert Frater and many others including the Johnsons in North Uist (who owned a guest-house at which I usually stayed) and a young Michael Russell, who was working on a film and TV project based in Uist and whom I first met at the bar of the Creagorry Hotel in Benbecula during the 1979 referendum campaign when I was touring with Donnie Stewart.

I worked closely again with Donnie Stewart from my election to the European Parliament in 1979 until he retired from the House of Commons at the 1987 General Election. The local constituency chose as his replacement Iain Smith, a native Gaelic speaker whose parents still lived in Lewis. Iain was a wealthy man who owned garages but who had also invented a photographic process which he had patented and which was used worldwide. There seemed to be some resentment at his success and he was mercilessly attacked by the vitriolically pro-Labour newspaper, the *West Highland Free Press*, which was piloted by Brian Wilson, a Labour MP by this time and a former Labour candidate in the Western Isles. The WHFP was founded to provide an independent voice in the West Highlands and in the Western Isles and in its early years it was a highly successful campaigning newspaper that spoke for all the people. But over time it became more and more a mouthpiece for Wilson and his prejudices and is now so silly and slavishly New Labour that is not taken seriously by most people.

Iain fought hard, but lost the seat to a friend of Brian Wilson's, Calum MacDonald. The constituency party then chose Frances McFarlane, the daughter of a long-standing member in Lewis, who taught in Castlebay in Barra. A naturally talented politician she did not, however, have the strength of support she needed, nor were the times right for her. It was also very hard to fight the seat from Barra, where transport links were poor. She was followed by Anne Lorne Gillies, famous as a Gaelic singer and broadcaster, but she too was traduced by the *WHFP*. She did not, however, make it easy on herself by getting married for the third time just at the start of the campaign, for the voters of the Western Isles are politically radical, but socially conservative.

Despite having these three excellent candidates the SNP proved unable to retake the seat, though the fourth candidate, Alasdair Nicholson, has come very close both at Westminster and Scottish Parliament elections and may yet do it. Perhaps one of the problems is that Donnie Stewart fought and held the seat in such a remarkable and unique way. He was popular across the political spectrum and attracted votes from people who were not natural SNP voters, many of whom have returned to their original allegiances.

The main issues in the Western Isles are always fishing, transport, land and population. The depopulation of the islands still continues and getting work to the islands is a huge difficulty. This was particularly true of the smaller islands, which have greatly benefited from the building of causeways which at least allow travel to and from the neighbouring larger islands.

I always used to love visiting the island of Berneray, just off North Uist. The local Church of Scotland Minister, the Revd Roddy MacLeod, was an SNP member and a councillor and had been strongly tipped to be one of the island's first representatives to the Scottish Parliament in 1979, had it been set up. He once took me round the island to meet the population – at that time not much more than a hundred people. We met on the way a little girl aged about five and Roddy addressed her in Gaelic. She replied, however, in English. I then tried my Gaelic on her and she did the same. Roddy explained that she was a very bright little girl but that she was an avid viewer of TV (which had just come to the islands in colour) and that as a result she preferred to speak English, as they did on television. He said to her, 'What has happened to your Gaelic?' and she responded very gravely, 'My Gaelic has gone all gone away to sea.' I still regard that response as one of the saddest I ever heard because the little girl was losing her culture as well as her tongue, and all because of the dominance of another culture and its easy accessibility.

The Reverend Roddy, as he was known, had been brought up on North Uist and during his university course had come back to preach on Berneray, which was without a minister. The congregation had liked what they had heard and had held the vacancy open for him so that when he qualified he could return and stay on the island.

One of the persistent problems of the Western Isles is the disposal of old cars, and this is particularly noticeable in places like Beneray, where cars are used until they die and then abandoned in a corner of the croft. Roddy was continually annoyed by the mess this created and devised his own Act of Parliament to create penalties for not disposing of cars properly. He even photocopied an Act from the House of Commons to mock up an official document which outlined, for example, where cars were to be removed to, and how far away they had to be from a house or a field boundary. He pinned a copy of his 'Act' to the public noticeboard at the ferry pier and it clearly had results, as islanders were now consulting him about its contents. However, he was worried that inventing an Act of Parliament might be an offence and asked me what I thought the legal penalty might be. I said that I doubted that even the law of Scotland had the ingenuity to provide a schedule of punishment for such original but beneficial mischief.

Having so many islands in my constituency (ninety-six in total, which was more than any other member except some of the Greeks, who had 220), I became something of a European expert on islands and my group usually passed island problems on to me. This was how I got to know Father Peicinn, who was referred to me by the Irish members. Father Peicinn had gone to Tory Island off the west coast of Ireland – an island large by Scottish outlier standards, with 350 people on it – in order to spend his last restful years. But when he got there he found that there was no regular public transport service and that the people lived with the perpetual threat of being unable to get to the mainland, and the likelihood that the island would be evacuated. The Irish Government had evacuated the Blasket Islands just after the war and had an even poorer record on helping island communities than the British Government.

Father Peicinn was determined that Tory would be saved and I agreed to take up the fight, greatly assisted by an Irish member of the group staff, Nora O'Brien. We arranged an exhibition of places with no public transport, including two Greek islands, in order to draw in wider support. We showed photographs and paintings from Tory, which had a good artistic community, and we started a petition to the European Parliament, encouraging members to sign. Father Peicinn took up residence in a nearby seminary and he sat in the Parliament's entrance hall offering glasses of wine, soft drinks, conversation and then a chance to support his cause. Many members did so as he had great charm and powers of persuasion. Even Ian Paisley stopped me one day to ask, 'Winnie, where is your wee priest today?' and he signed and was photographed supporting Tory. The campaign worked and public transport was provided, saving Tory and giving it a future.

Securing Objective One Status for the Highlands and Islands would, I knew, be crucial in allowing my island communities to survive, and that was a campaign that I continued to wage throughout the 1980s, as well as campaigns for Road Equivalent Tarriff and for other measures that would support such communities.

Of course I travelled all over my constituency regularly, but it was the intensive nature of my visits to the islands over many years that gave me the chance to really understand what was needed and how to get it. And I got used to a life that required me to get up at 5 a.m. to travel to Brussels or Strasbourg for a week and then rise at 5 again to be able to take the plane to Stornoway or Sumburgh, or to be driven to a hundred other places where there were meetings to be attended, cases to be heard and people to meet. I was almost fifty when first elected to the European Parliament, but I enjoyed the work so greatly that I did not feel the years passing, though my sixtieth birthday took place at the start of my third term in Europe, when I was still doing thousands of miles in the Highlands and Islands every year, and many more thousands throughout Europe and the world.

It might have been expected by that stage that I had seen the last of campaigning for election to Westminster, so many people were greatly surprised when I became candidate for Orkney and Shetland for the General Election in 1983. The SNP had lost its deposit in the constituency in 1979, gaining only 935 votes (less than 5 per cent), and the party nationally had gone through a very difficult time since then. But I believed it was the right thing to do. It was vital we had a candidate, and as there was no one available as the election approached I was not knocking anyone else out of the frame. In addition I felt it might help to increase my Euro vote in that area and the next European elections were due in only a year's time. I had no expectations of winning but I was right about the Euro vote, as I have taken the majority there in every direct Euro election since.

The 1983 election was held in June and the weather was by and large good. The beauty of the Orkney and Sheltand landscapes (and the sea-scapes) was unforgettable, and despite this being a strong Liberal constituency (Jo Grimond was just standing down) there was a lot of goodwill towards me. The family all came up to help and found the experience of campaigning in an island constituency very different.

I stayed on a number of islands as I toured, seeking votes, and one night I found myself on the island of Stronsay. The proprietor of the hotel I was staying in told me that he had a new boat and that he would take me on a short trip the following day if the weather was good. It was, and we set out to visit Papa Stronsay, an even smaller island which had been a fishing centre and where many fisher-girls had stayed when working the east coast. Indeed later in Lossiemouth I met two local women who had done just that. When we landed on Papa Stronsay we were met by a man accompanied by a number of children of different races. He and his wife were teachers and they had adopted a number of youngsters and lived on Papa Stronsay in the summer and in Egypt in the winter. It was a fascinating lifestyle and he was charming and interested, saying to me that I must be desperate for votes if I had come all the way to Papa Stronsay. He promised that, for that reason alone, I had just got two more.

As expected, the young Liberal candidate, one Jim Wallace, who had been the candidate in his home constituency of Dumfries in 1979 and a Euro candidate in the south of Scotland, won the seat easily, though with a reduced majority on 1979. However I took the SNP from fourth to third, notching up over 3,000 votes and taking 17 per cent of the vote (much higher than the national average in that election), so I not only saved our deposit but also greatly increased our standing. I had also enjoyed the experience and had shown that nowhere in Scotland was completely impossible territory for the SNP if people were prepared to work. In time we found a local candidate for the seat, a Moray loon called Willie Ross who lived in Shetland, and when the seat was split in two for the Scottish Parliament elections Willie stood in Shetland and John Mowat, an Orkney man, in Orkney.

The 1983 General Election was a good preparation for the 1984 European Election. As I stood once more I had the consolation of knowing that I had worked hard, travelled extensively within my vast constituency, visited many schools, homes, factories, Highland Games and fêtes, and that I had been preparing for re-election for some time. During 1983 Stewart had had an idea for a video that could be shown throughout my constituency and I got agreement that this could be financed by the information budget of the European Parliament, as it showed what a member did and how the European institutions worked. Runrig kindly agreed to let me use one of their songs on the video and Stewart arranged a network of video agents throughout the area who would assist by drawing up lists of local people to be invited to video evenings at which there would be cheese and wine, a chance to see the film, and an opportunity to ask questions. The video would also be available to any interested elector.

The video, which lasted only half an hour, was seen by thousands of people in many communities across the Highlands and Islands. My opponents objected, but the European Information Office had sanctioned the expenditure and it did build interest in the European Parliament and its relevance to my constituency. It also confirmed my view that my constituency was also the most beautiful in Europe, a fact that I used to reflect on when flying over the islands and the mainland and seeing the lochs and mountains and seashores. At those times I was very conscious of my immense good fortune in having been elected to represent such a place of infinite variety.

Stewart was, as ever, a power-house of ideas, slogans and campaigning techniques. The video was a master-stroke but there were lots of other imaginative innovations, including the intervention of a group of SNP students from outside the Highlands who travelled, and slept, in two vans. They were led, and led well by a young activist with long hair called John Swinney! They travelled alongside me, covering thousands of miles, though I insisted on sleeping in hotels. The result bore out their profes- sionalism and of course Stewart's. It was also testimony to the satisfaction that the voters seemed to have in what I had been doing. I increased my majority from 3,883 to 16,277, an almost five-fold rise, and I won in many areas in which I had lost in 1979. Once again Russell Johnston was gracious in defeat and made a pleasant speech of congratulations, though clearly he was very disappointed to be second once more.

The first event after my re-election was a study day in the Camargue in the south of France, which had been arranged for some time. When

Stewart and I arrived at the airport Tom Earlie, the group's Secretary General, met us and told me that M. De La Malene needed to see me urgently. De La Malene told me that the French Gaullists had increased their seats to twenty and that as a group needed twenty-one members, they wished to invite me to join as quickly as possible. The name of the group was to change from the European Progressive Democrats to the European Democratic Alliance. I had already sought and gained permission from the SNP National Executive to continue my group arrangement if it was feasible, so I was able to confirm my membership there and then. But I was surprised when De La Malene added that the group wished me to be First Vice President, in effect deputy leader. I told him that I was sure that the Irish, who would bring a number of members, would not be pleased to lose what was theirs by right, and it was then that De La Malene dropped the bombshell – the Irish were still dithering about which group to join and had even been talking to the Socialists. De La Malene was surprised too, and not a little annoyed, saying to me, 'Winnie, these Irish, are they men, or mice?' Fortunately good sense prevailed and the Irish decided that they would remain with us; the group was reformed and worked well. We had, alas, lost our Dane, Ky Nyborg, but we were joined by a Greek member, a Mr Butos.

I was now the First Vice President of a happy group of twenty Gaullists, eight Irish, one Greek and one Scot. But I was also appointed as Chair of the European Parliament's Committee for Youth, Education, Information and Culture and this was a great privilege and a great opportunity. When M. De La Malene wasn't present I chaired the meetings of the group, which never pleased some of the Fianna Fáil members. But the French used to like it because I was always brisker and faster than De La Malene and the meetings were conducted more easily and speedily.

I tried to be a similarly direct and efficient Chair of the Education, Sport and Culture Committee, which held a public hearing during my time as convener into the Heysel Disaster, which took place on 29 May 1985 and which led to the deaths of thirty-nine Italian and Belgian football fans and a five-year blanket ban on English clubs in European football. We appointed a Dutch Christian Democrat as rapporteur and she enquired into football safety and regulations at football grounds throughout the member states. In her report she highlighted the Scottish experience, for

Scotland had banned alcohol not only at matches, but prior to the game as well. She said, 'If Europe has a football violence disease and there is a case for change then we should all follow Scotland's example.'

My main accomplishment in the chair was the delivery of a programme which involved colleges and universities finding a partner in another member state and then exchanging students, which became known as the Erasmus Programme. The original plan was for students to undertake an exchange of one academic year, which would start with a three-month language immersion course and which would lead to a qualification which would be recognised throughout the European Union. The idea was entirely based on the historic experience of Scots law students who, before the Union, would go to Paris, Bologna or Rome to study. It seemed to me that if we were serious about building European under-standing and solidarity, this was a fine place to start and would inculcate in the young a knowledge of Europe and its importance. The UK and Germany were not initially supportive but eventually we got the plan through albeit one which involved a large degree of local autonomy regarding some elements of the programme, which meant that some students had a shorter time in the host country than was ideal, and some had no compulsory language training – a very important element of the original plan.

One of the advantages of the scheme was that we were determined from the beginning to cut down on European bureaucracy, and the adminis-tration of Erasmus was put in the hands of the academic institutions themselves, thus saving time and expense. I travelled widely to promote the scheme. Amongst the many thousands of students who have benefited from it over the years is my sister's grandson, Patrik, who went to Caen. The scheme is now recognised as being a ground-breaking innovation and I was very honoured to receive an honorary doctorate from the Open University in recognition of my role in establishing it.

Once I had been re-elected, my schedule of visits across the Highlands and Islands began again, as did the flow of people who came to visit me in Brussels and Strasbourg. On a very hot July day in 1985 I welcomed a bus-load of SNP supporters that included Vi Donaldson, widow of the former party leader Arthur Donaldson, and at well over eighty one of the oldest visitors to the Parliament. On that day there was an empty flagpole outside the Parliament, as Norway had voted against entry, leaving one pole too many. The sight of it was too much for some of the younger Nationalists who, led by Alasdair Allan, later a researcher in the Scottish Parliament and then National Secretary of the Party, produced a saltire and proceeded to raise it to fly alongside the flags of the other member states. Surprisingly, there it stayed for twenty-four hours for I and Scotland had good friends amongst the security staff and a blind eye was turned until some UK members objected strongly to the sight of it.

The new elected Parliament contained a large number of those who had been in the previous one, but a new member of my group was Eileen Lemass, the daughter-in-law of the former Taoiseach Sean Lemass and the sister-in-law of the then current Irish Prime Minister, Charlie Haughey. She herself had also been a member of the Dail, having fought her late husband's seat, but now she was in Europe and I greatly valued her presence and, very quickly, her friendship. It was sometimes not easy for a woman MEP on her own, but now I had found someone with whom I could go about and socialise and also work with in the group. Together we would often go for coffee or a drink and, as two women talking, we found it easier in that way also to make friends with other women across the groups.

One summer I went with her to Ireland and, along with a friend of Eileen's called Margaret Byrne, we toured the country, staying at wonderful bed-and-breakfast establishments and each evening finding a new musical pub to enjoy. We took a cool box with us and during the warm days we would find a lovely spot beside a loch or on a mountain side and cook lunch with two small gas stoves. It was an idyllic trip. During our holiday we got talking about Northern Ireland and attitudes to it in the south. Eileen had instant recognition wherever she went, and she agreed that I should conduct a small survey in each of the pubs we went into to find out roughly how many people in the south had actually been to the north, how many had any desire even to visit it, and how many wanted a united Ireland. Eighty per cent of those we asked had never been, didn't want to go, and had no great interest in seeing the north join the south. None of us were surprised at the results, though they are counter to popular political opinion.

Despite having Eileen's support and friendship, I did miss having an SNP colleague with me in Europe. I had hoped that in the European

Elections of 1984 we would win the North-east of Scotland, our best hope, but it was not to be. The party was still not clear of the difficulties it had experienced in 1979, and although it was recovering our vote rose substantially in the 1987 Westminster election when our share was 14 per cent and we won three more seats – we were still having some difficulties.

My daughter-in-law Margaret – who to my delight had married Fergus in 1983 – won Moray back that year, and that was a tremendous joy to me. Alex Salmond, who had been expelled during the 79 Group problems, won Banff and Buchan and Andrew Welsh came back for Angus. Nonetheless there were disappointments. Donnie's seat was lost and Gordon Wilson lost Dundee East, which he had held for thirteen years. All in all we seemed to take a couple of steps forward, and then always one step back. Emulating the great progress of the 1970s still seemed to elude us and the Thatcher government was deeply inimical to Scotland and to Scotland's views. Of course it had never been elected by Scotland, a fact which caused great tension and produced what was called the 'democratic deficit'.

But Labour seemed incapable of overcoming this deficit, for although they were still committed to Home Rule, the actions of their MPs in Scotland seemed lacklustre and produced few useful results. There was a joke going the rounds at that time which went 'How many Scottish Labour MPs does it take to change a light bulb?', the answer to which was, 'None, because Scottish Labour MPs don't change anything.'

For me the one bright hope was the interest that Europe showed in Scotland and the way in which it was possible to put Scotland's case – as well as the case for the Highlands and Islands – constantly before a European audience. Thatcher's hostility to Europe and her handbagging of any and all useful European initiatives had led to much criticism of her across the EU and many of my fellow MEPs understood how difficult it must be in Scotland, where she seemed to be doing enormous damage without any mandate.

During my second term I was constantly asked when Scotland was going to show that it had the mettle to throw off this type of rule and speak for itself. I could only reply that that was up to Scotland to decide, though my colleagues and I were working hard to bring it about. As the third direct elections approached I was desperately keen to show Europe and the world that we were once again making progress.

12

The Member for the Highlands and Islands: No Longer Alone

I HAD GREAT HOPES of the 1989 elections. The previous November the SNP had won the seat of Glasgow Govan, campaigning on the record of the 'Feeble Fifty' Labour MPs in Scotland, and that pressure had at last started to bring results, with the establishment of the Constitutional Convention. However, the Convention was rigged against the SNP from the beginning, with an absolute determination by Labour not to allow the option of independence to be put to the people no matter what emerged during the discussions. Like the majority of the members of the SNP National Executive I had favoured taking part in the Convention until I learned about this. From then on I supported the withdrawal that had taken place, for it seemed to me that the SNP would simply be used, as it was in the 1970s, to provide cover for Labour with no intention of taking things forward. We needed to be free to apply maximum pressure and constantly ratchet up the argument.

My own campaign in the Highlands and Islands went like a dream. It was clear from the beginning, with Russell Johnston not standing, that I was likely to win, and during the campaign itself I received a tremendous welcome wherever I went. The sobriquet 'Madame Ecosse' seemed to be applied everywhere; it had obviously caught on and my work for Scotland in Europe was greatly appreciated. The biggest tangible sign of that was the securing, at last, of Objective One Status for the Highlands and Islands, which opened up the prospect of considerable resources for much-needed infrastructure and employment projects. 'Objective

Won' was the headline in my Euro Election Campaign Paper for the 1989 elections.

The criterion for achieving Objective One status was that the GDP of the applicant region had to be no more than 75 per cent of EEC GDP. Objective One funding was designed to bring such places up in the league table of economic prosperity and to allow all areas of the EU to benefit from membership, including the poorest. Despite the figures, we failed in our first application, and though discussions in the Council of Ministers are held in secret, through my close Irish connections I was able to piece together what had happened. The truth was that the UK did not press the Highlands and Islands case with any vigour or determination at all – and indeed far from supporting the Highlands and Islands cause, Margaret Thatcher actually opposed it. Despite this stab in the back the Highlands and Islands Councils continued to lobby regularly in Brussels and Strasbourg.

During our second attempt, I was suddenly told that just at the period of decision, Argyll and Bute did not qualify and would have to be excluded. I was actively touring Argyll and Bute when I got this alarming news and I said publicly that I would never agree to such a change in our proposals. This resulted in the Secretary of State for Scotland, Ian Lang, warning me that if I pressed for Argyll and Bute I risked the total loss of funding. Nevertheless, I put my head above the parapet and continued to encourage the whole group, not just part of it, and happily for me my stance was successful, though it was a nerve-racking time.

At the negotiations, which lasted into the small hours, our UK Ambassador to the EU was Sir John Kerr (who later became UK Ambassador to Washington). Sir John was able and ready to press the case for Objective One for the Highlands and Islands and he succeeded in circumstances in which government ministers would probably have just stopped trying. Neil Fergusson, my assistant, was up all night waiting for news and I spent a sleepless night too at my home in Miltonduff. Nothing came through that night, but the next morning I was in the garden when Stewart called me in, saying, 'That's Number Ten on the phone for you.' I replied, 'That will be right,' thinking that it was just one of Stewart's jokes, but it actually was Number Ten, where Sir John had called in on his return from Brussels and from where he was ringing to tell me the good news.

Objective One Status meant that the Highlands and Islands was able to gain many millions of pounds of European money which was matched by millions more in UK resources. Many a harbour, road and many vital infrastructural projects were now able to go ahead in all parts of my vast Euro constituency, and that was a wonderful boost.

I must admit that given this background I expected to win, but even I was surprised at the extent of my victory. From a majority of just over 3,000 ten years earlier, I now had a majority of 44,695 and my nearest opponent, this time the Tory Albert MacQuarrie, was 34 per cent behind, gaining only 16 per cent of the vote to my 51 per cent. This was the first time I had ever gained an absolute majority of votes cast, and it was a tremendous feeling.

My delight was tempered, however, by our very narrow failure in the North-east of Scotland. Allan Macartney went into the election needing a 6.5 per cent swing, and he almost made it, coming only a mere 2,613 votes behind Labour, with the Tories, who had held the seat going into the election, pushed into third place. It was agonisingly close and I was bitterly disappointed for Allan, as well as for the party. Allan had not been helped by a spat that blew up during the election over redundancy notices issued to cleaners working for the SNP-controlled Tayside Council. Although this was strongly spun against us and the facts were never allowed to come out, it did show some political naivety on behalf of our group of councillors. I suspect it may have cost Allan that election, given the very small Labour majority, but another factor was the decision to hold the Glasgow Central by-election on the same day, splitting the SNP's resources and drawing much effort into that constituency that might have been applied elsewhere. As it was, we failed to win Central and also just failed to win the North-east.

The election finished with Labour holding seven of the eight Euro seats, and the Tories with none, although they had held two since 1979. The contest did however establish the SNP as the main challenger in Scotland at last, a position it had been moving into in the polls after Govan. Nationally we had taken a quarter of the votes, 5 per cent more than the Conservatives.

After the 1989 election the question again arose about which Parliamentary group I should join. This time the choice was not so clear as the

French Gaullists had moved more to the right – a reflection of French politics in general after the alarming emergence of the Front Nationale under Le Pen. Towards the end of the previous Parliament I had found that quite often my hand was going up to vote differently from the rest of my group, and although I did have a negotiated right to freedom of voting, I felt uncomfortable with some of the stances my colleagues were taking.

I was once more invited to join the Rainbow Group which had formerly been called the Technical Group, and which had sought my membership twice before. The use of the word 'rainbow' was significant, for the day's proceedings in the Parliament were printed with all speeches in the language in which they were actually given, and each language had a colour – orange, of course, for the Dutch, royal purple for English and so on. Our parliamentary record was not called 'Hansard' but 'The Rainbow' and the group's name reflected this diversity, which I found attractive. I also found the strongly nationalist base of the Rainbow Group to be appealing. Members included the President of Sardinia, the leader of the non-violent Corsican Nationalists, the first President of Catalonia, the first Prime Minister of the Spanish Basque Region (from a non-violent Basque nationalist party), the Mayor of Andalusia, the Flemish Nationalists, two Italians from the Lega Lombardi, four Danes from a new party, a German Green and a very famous Irish member, Neil Blainey, who styled himself as 'Independent Fianna Fáil' and who was also a member of the Dail.

My old group did invite me to rejoin, so a decision had to be made, and I took the issue, as I always had in the past, to the SNP National Executive Committee. The leader of the Flemish Nationalists, Jack Vandemeuleb-roucke, came over to meet NEC representatives and this time the SNP decided that the Rainbow Group was the best place for us, and for me.

Most of my new group had bucked the system in their own member states in order to be elected and were naturally independently minded. This give us a lot in common and in time I discovered that we were all strong characters – as we had to be – and good company. Stewart, who by now was a regular visitor to Europe, contrasted the new group very favourably to the old and that made me absolutely certain that I had done the right thing.

There were of course some differences which had to be borne and accepted. For example, in my old group so many of the French were mayors of cities that there was not a lot of competition to speak, as they were not good attenders. But in the Rainbow Group everyone wanted to speak on every topic as often as possible, for that was our nature. Speaking opportunities became harder to get, though the secretary general of the group, Herman, was a Flemish Nationalist and a great fixer, as well as being hugely supportive. He could usually iron out all the difficulties for the group members although he was regularly faced with extraordinary challenges. The oddest moment occurred when Mario Melis, the former President of Sardinia, forgot totally which hotel he was staying in. It took Herman about fifty calls to find it again. Herman could be forgetful too – on a study day in Copenhagen he alleged someone had stolen his pyjamas from his room, but they were found where they should have been – under his pillow!

The group was not short of characters. Ex-President Melis, for example, was used to red-carpet treatment and he used to snap his fingers for attention when sitting on the Rainbow bench in the Parliament. When nobody jumped to help him he would get enraged, so eventually it had to be explained to him that he needed to get a secretary or assistant. Once he found one, his manner became more acceptable, though I suspect the new assistant did not find so. However, his saving grace was his oratory, which was brilliant. Stewart was in awe of him every time he heard him and called him the 'Rolls Royce of orators', a description which stuck as he was particularly happy to be referred to as a 'Rolls Royce'.

The four Danes were individualists, each in total contrast with the other. One was a very serious man who had no sense of humour and who went to every available reception and ate voraciously at each. Another, a Mr Bonde, was a brilliant speaker and author but was profoundly against Denmark's membership of the EC and wrote endless articles and books on the topic. The two women were both very glamorous. One was an ordained Lutheran pastor and Stewart found it surprising that she smoked and drank. Her name was Ulla Sandbaek and inevitiably she got nick-named 'Oh la la'. The other woman member, Brigit Bjornvig, was very sophisticated and artistic and was married to Denmark's most famous living poet. Birgit was the co-chair of the group along with Jack Vande-meulebroucke, and Neil Blaney and I were on the bureau of the group with a number of others.

The Irish members of my old group did not hold it against me that I had moved elsewhere and understood my reasons. That group itself had changed greatly, for M. Chirac, Dr Bray and M. Mesmer were all gone and there were new members from France and Ireland. I was heartbroken that my dear friend and companion Eileen Lemass had lost her seat despite having the second highest vote in Ireland. Unfortunately the only higher vote in the Dublin constituency was for fellow Fianna Fáil member Niall Andrews, so she lost her chance to return to Europe. Whilst open lists are more democratic than closed lists in that voters can choose who to represent them, it does pit party members against each other and often the best and most hard-working members suffer. All list selections have that drawback, as the SNP was to discover in 2003.

The fact that the Rainbow Group consisted by and large of a wide variety of nationalists from Belgium, Italy, Spain, Ireland and Scotland, amongst other places, meant that we held very exciting and interesting study days, at which the various members were keen to explain their cause and show the virtues of their home regions. We visited Andalucia, Corsica, Italy, Catalonia, Flanders, Copenhagen, Inverness and elsewhere, and it was soon obvious that, roughly speaking, we all came from a left-of-centre perspective and were supportive of human rights, social justice, self determination, the Third World and the return of real power to the various cultures and minority peoples of the community. The group had also a wide range of languages represented in it, including Catalan, Basque, Corsican, Sardinian and, of course, some Gaelic.

But our group consisted of not just the elected members. Surrounding it was a larger group of seventeen parties, many of whom did not have an MEP but who came from the same political and philosophical stance as ourselves. This grouping was called the European Free Alliance and I ended up as President of the alliance for there was a great interest in, and affection for, Scotland in every part of Europe. The EFA included the Fresians, the Occitans, German speakers from Belgium and a host of others, including those who spoke dialects such as Strasburgois and Luxembourgish. It was an alliance and a cause without borders and Neil Blainey and I tried to make sure that Irish and Gaelic were always included in the languages that were fought for.

The group was also not a static one. We enrolled a Portuguese academic called Professor Canavero at one point. He was a very handsome man and was descended from a previous Portuguese prime minister. But there were also departures from the group. As time went on the utterances of the leader of the Northern League, Umberto Bossi, became more and more intemperate, much to the embarrassment of his own members as well as anyone else, and the final straw was the decision he forced on his party to go into government with the Italian fascists. Although we were almost at the time of the next election, we decided to ask Signor Morelli and Signor Speroni to leave the Rainbow Group.

Signor Morelli was very gracious about the expulsion and it was privately agreed that they would go but would sit as independents and remain friendly with us, as they were usually no trouble at all. However, they broke that agreement very quickly and were soon ensconced in the Liberal group, of all places. (The British Liberals at that time had no UK MEPs but they would have been members of that group had there been any Liberal MEPs, and were associated with the group.) Accordingly I was astonished to be attacked about the Northern League by Charles Kennedy, MP for Ross and Cromarty, who had always been very friendly towards me and who Donnie Stewart had hoped might one day join us, a hope we had about several Liberal MPs, who, alas, usually failed to have the courage of their convictions.

Charles accused me, my party and my group of consorting with fascists because we had had the two Northern League representatives with us, although they were no longer part of our group. This was an astonishing piece of cheek considering where Morelli and Speroni were now ensconced and I was very offended. A similar attack was made at the same time by George Robertson, then MP for Hamilton but later Defence Secretary and then Secretary General of NATO. I have always got on well with him and his wife (and of course he had been an SNP member in his early days), but his attack was unprincipled.

The years with the Rainbow Group were busy ones, like all my time in politics. Although I was perforce speaking less in the chamber, I was paid a very great compliment in 1990 when the interpreters in the Parliament started to use my speeches as test pieces. The majority of MEPs read their speeches but in the House of Commons this had always been frowned on, so my speeches were usually extempore and the interpreters said this made them more interesting and more colourful, and good to practise with!

The key issues of the time for me were very much those that had dominated the preceding ten years, and chief amongst them again was fishing. However the negotiating hand of the UK on this matter – indeed on all matters – had been greatly and grievously weakened by what was called 'le juste retour': Mrs Thatcher's obsession with getting money back from Europe.

The Tories were bad enough about getting money back, but they were worse when it came to taking advantage of matched funds. Scheme after scheme that would have helped Scotland was stillborn because the UK Treasury would not come up with its share of the payment. Speaking at this time of the difficulties that were being caused, I said:

> Mrs Thatcher uses up all her muscle in this sterile battle for monies to swell the coffers of the Treasury. I would rather all the muscle were used to protect our vital industries which she leaves defenceless and to secure funding for structural policies such as the IDP in the Western Isles or the ACP for the Highlands which Europe offered to fund and which she refused to match. By focusing her whole stance on her 'money' she loses out in every fight that matters, from steel to shipbuilding and from farming to fishing. We end up with the worst of all possible worlds. Now 'England go Home' is seen more and more among the graffiti of Strasbourg and Brussels.

The Thatcher years badly damaged the image of the UK in Europe and by extension damaged Scotland's prospects there too. It is little wonder that they used to tell a joke in Brussels that went like this: 'How can you tell the planes bringing the UK delegation? Because unlike the others, they carry on whining after the engines are switched off!'

The fishing industry was continuing to suffer greatly. It was being slowly strangled, caught between increased competition from other European boats (and with the dread prospect of the Spaniards catching more and more as derogations ran out) and demands from scientists for measures that would decimate the industry in the name of conservation. In a major speech on fisheries in 1990 I said this, which sums up many of the difficulties that were being experienced and which have simply got worse:

It is hard to do justice to the gravity of the crisis facing the fishing industry and the ancillary industries, processing, boat-building, and chandlers. Ordinary words seem too tame in the present circumstances. We have an uncaring government who appear to be writing off all the jobs involved and all the survival chances of the numerous dependent communities. Moreover our government does not fight for the industry at the European table. My dire warning is that if there are not total U-turns by the government we will see in the twenty-first century us eating fish caught by Spanish boats in Scottish waters.

The only good result from all this is that it has driven the processing and catching sectors of the industry to act in concert and to take a unified stand recognising their mutual interdependence. They demand reasonably that if the mesh size is increased then the rules must be the same for all member states. They demand de-commissioning and grant for processors to conform to the 1992 hygiene regulations. In other states there are grants of 50 per cent (not in the UK). Surely this is unfair competition. If we do not preserve and nurture our processing then the future will be for the Humber and not for Scotland. Twenty firms have closed with a job loss of a thousand. We cannot let the very infrastructure of our industry be wiped out.

The picture is not brighter on the aquaculture side, one of Europe's most rapidly growing industries. A major problem is salmon dumping by the Norwegians. For years in Europe I have demanded action against Norway for dumping cheap fish into the European Community and for a minimum price. For years the Commission has refused though they were quick to take action to protect Mediterranean interests against competition in the tuna sector.

The dumping has driven many small producers in Scotland and Ireland out of business who have been encouraged to invest their life savings and efforts into fish farming.

Another problem is the extraordinary way we have allowed Spanish and Dutch boats to register in our fleet and acquire bits of our precious quotas. Britain took no action for years and then when they did, the European Court took a look but did not stop it.

Nineteen ninety two is coming. The Spaniards argue that then there can be a free-for-all. The Spaniards are organised and aggressive and for some years I have been a lone voice warning the Parliament, quoting the black and white print of the agreement made and warning the UK government who do not appear to be interested.

The problem with the Spanish fleet lay in their belief that they would be able to get total access to Scottish waters in 1992, whereas the British Government believed that the agreement would last until 2002. By that time there was precious little to save, and, despite the existence of the Scottish Parliament, still no will in the UK to save it. The whole UK membership in the European Parliament – including the Scottish contingent – regularly voted with Spain against the interests of the UK fleet, two-thirds of which was based in Scotland, where there were and continue to be many dependent communities. The UK still does not permit Scottish ministers to lead at European Fishery Councils, even when matters of predominantly Scottish interest are being decided on. Incredibly the Scottish Executive meekly accepts this situation – Labour and Liberals together doing nothing to help! It is little wonder that Scottish fishermen look with envy at other countries – even at tiny places like the Faroe islands, where the exclusive fishing zone under local control is 200 miles. Local management is the only answer and it is a scandal that it is still not in place. No other nation in Europe has been so careless with one of its key industries.

I continued to be a member of the Fisheries Committee and tried to fight the good fight for Scotland, usually on my own. It was interesting to note that at the 1994 European elections all the other UK members of the Fisheries Committee, including Labour's Henry MacCubbin in the North-east of Scotland, lost their seats, perhaps because no one in the fishing communities would vote for them.

Working with the fishing industry representatives and those of the fish processing industry was not always easy. Nonetheless we did get a reasonable degree of consensus about what was required to put the industry back on its feet, and that plan – to phase out industrial fishing (much valued by the Danes whose quotas just seemed to go up at every negotiation); to increase gradually mesh size and at the same time increase minimum fish size; to stop dumping of fish at sea; to close areas where there is an abundance of immature fish and to close spawning grounds – got widespread support. However, the annual agony of the fishing negotiations within Europe continued and each time it seemed that Scotland lost out.

Scotland also was losing out – sometimes dramatically – in the area of manufacturing industry, the whole base of which was decimated during the Tory years. The destruction of our steel industry came to be seen as the heart of that process, and there was much European discussion of the matter. The European Community admitted that if Scotland were independent our steel industry would not have been shut down and moved to Wales at considerable expense. But the Tories and their apologists continued to claim the opposite. I fought tenaciously for the Scottish steel industry, but my appeals all fell on deaf ears.

Whilst fishing and steel were issues of paramount national importance, there were also many others, local and national. Stewart read twenty Highlands and Islands newspapers every week and had the cuttings ready for scrutiny when I returned home, along with the piles of mail and the lists of phone calls. Though he was somewhat impatient by nature, he was infinitely kind and enquiring when constituents phoned with a problem, and they often commented on this.

I rarely ever stayed in 'Europe' over a weekend, for I had to return to pick up the threads of life and get on with things that were waiting for me. Almost invariably I had constituency engagements to fulfil, often in widely diverse parts of the Highlands and Islands, so I usually tried to leave on a Thursday so that I could have a full Friday in my own area. I recall on one occasion being at the airport in Strasbourg late one Thursday afternoon and being greeted by a Scottish Labour MEP with the words, 'Skiving off, are you?' I pointed out to him that he was waiting for the same plane, and that soon shut him up.

Going home now meant going to Miltonduff, not Lossie or Queen's Park. Stewart eventually decided to take early retirement and we agreed that we should seek a family home in Moray. We went after several houses in Lossie, but were always outbid either by fishing skippers or by RAF officers. Stewart got fed up with this process and started to look around more widely and we soon found the house at Miltonduff, which was small to start with but which we have greatly extended.

Miltonduff nestles near a distillery – something difficult to avoid in

Moray, which has more distilleries in it than any other constituency in the UK – and is a totally rural village with a real sense of community, although it is only three miles from Elgin. The house is surrounded by fields and woods and there are lovely walks in every direction, although the house also has a sizeable garden – much larger than the little walled garden in Lossie which I always adored, and which we substantially improved. Of course we named the house 'Goodwill', just like my first little house in Lossie.

Miltonduff is near Pluscarden Abbey. When I moved there I discovered that each Christmas there was a service which was held jointly between the local Church of Scotland and the abbey and I started to attend.

I began to visit the abbey when I could and became very fond of the monks and their civilised way of life. On my first trip I nervously drove my new sports car, a particularly risky thing to do as I had hardly driven in ten years. The monks said to me, 'Leave it to us – we will look after you' and so far they have!

Now based in Miltonduff, Stewart was able to accompany me to lots of events and constituency meetings at which he was very helpful and usually extremely sociable. However, towards the end of his life he became more and more reluctant to move out of the house at all, a situation that was not helped by his increasingly poor health nor by his hip replacement which meant that he could only cover a very few miles although previously we had often walked for long distances across the Moray countryside.

Before his ill health dominated his life he took regular daily exercise and would often go into Elgin to visit the shops, the bank, the garage, the post office, and my secretary, Marion. When he died I was overcome by the many letters I had from local shopkeepers, all of whom had known him. We regularly teased him about his expeditions, calling him the 'mad shopper of Elgin', for he would always return home with something, briefcases, wallets, files, office equipment – the list was endless. Eventually he would be coming home exhausted and I asked Fergus if he felt that the time had come to discourage these trips. 'Not at all,' he replied, 'they are Dad's therapy!'

During our whole marriage we both had a great interest in painting. First of all Stewart commissioned Sandy Goudie to sculpt my head, and after that both of us could not resist buying paintings and sculpture, and we have ended up with a fine collection including an Armour, two Donaldsons, five Robertsons, two Cunninghams and many by other Scottish and local northern artists. We also collected many photographs from our years together of family, friends and events in my political career. When I was elected to the Scottish Parliament and got a small flat in the New Town in Edinburgh I suddenly had some more wall space to fill, but that was quickly covered.

The pleasure Stewart and I derived from our paintings cannot be measured. In the last decade I have taken to painting myself and although I am never satisfied with the results, time flies when I am at my easel. Stewart was also passionately keen on music of every description except country and western. Eventually we had players and radios in every room in Miltonduff which usually pumped out classical music although when Stewart heard a pop song he liked he would play it often.

My five years with the Rainbow Group were busy and active but I have to admit it was nice to come home to Miltonduff at weekends. It seemed surprising when the 1994 election came round, for it didn't seem like five years since the last one, although there had been a Westminster General Election in between, at which the party had greatly increased its vote but failed to pick up any more seats – a dismal record which the new party leader, Alex Salmond, was keen never to repeat.

Gordon Wilson decided to step down from the leadership in 1990, having served for over ten years, and when it happened Margaret consulted Stewart and me about standing. I counselled her against it, pointing out that if she had been courting the constituencies and branches assiduously in the year before, she would have established a momentum as Alex Salmond had undoubtedly done. But to start from scratch over a few weeks and months meant that it was going to be a well-nigh impossible task. Nonetheless she felt she had to stand and was encouraged to do so by Gordon Wilson himself as well as by Jim Sillars. I of course supported her decision to the hilt.

Alex Salmond was one of those who had been briefly expelled from the party during the fracas after the 1979 election which came to a head at the Ayr Conference at which Gordon lost his temper and precipitated a walk-out. It is fair to say that Alex and I had not been close and that I had no great sympathy for the group that emerged around Jim Sillars, of whom he was one. Nonetheless he had proved himself to be a formidable politician, taking Banff and Buchan back for the SNP in 1987 and establishing a strong parliamentary reputation. Alex had been positioning himself as leader for some time – he had become Deputy Leader in 1987 – but his relationship with Gordon and the existing leadership was poor. His strength lay in his telegenic abilities and his popularity with the members, but Margaret was also very popular and had more experience.

Margaret's greatest problem lay not in her own campaign, ably run by Fergus, but in a parallel campaign run for her by Jim Sillars and Alex Neil. They did not consult and were campaigning only to try and stop someone from winning whom they regarded as having broken away from the overwhelming Sillars influence. Margaret often didn't know what things were being done in her name. Some were strongly counterproductive, including silly and bitter personal attacks on Alex Salmond by Jim and his cronies.

The result, when it came, was almost inevitable. Alex won convincingly, with a slick campaign run by Michael Russell, which had sewn up vast areas of the country before the contest had even started. Margaret was brave and gracious in defeat and the party's affection for her grew even more.

Though we had seemed to make much progress between the leadership election in 1990 and the 1992 General Election, this progress did not convert into parliamentary seats. John Swinney and Alasdair Morgan should have won the seats for which they were candidates, but came second again, and the Tories, who were expected to be eliminated as a Scottish political force, managed to maintain a little credibility. Labour's inability to win an election which seemed to be theirs for the taking was also a blow to the prospect of constitutional change, and there was much discontent afterwards which led to some cross-party campaigning under the banner 'Scotland United' and which culminated in a huge demonstration in Edinburgh for the European Summit in December 1992 at which Margaret very cleverly described Scotland as being reduced to acting as the 'tartan waitress' at the European top table.

Labour began to get cold feet about such a mass movement and slowly disengaged itself. Neil Kinnock resigned and John Smith, who was well known to me, was elected Labour leader. The SNP's profile in Scotland continued to grow and Alex began to show himself as a fine leader of the party, always to the forefront and able to take on all comers.

This was the context for the 1994 European elections and again we hoped to make some progress. However, in May as I was campaigning on the streets of Granton-on-Spey in the run-up to the election word reached us that John Smith had suddenly died, and all campaigning was suspended by every party.

As a solicitor I had employed John as an advocate, but he had also been a client of Stewart's. I never divulged that fact but in company in the Commons John would often joke about it. Indeed one day, hearing him do so, I said to him, 'It is you that has told everyone, not me.' Eventually when John was elected Labour leader Stewart advised him strongly to employ another accountant, and when John demurred, Stewart simply said that he thought it was wrong for the relationship to continue.

Unlike so many Scottish Labour politicians John did not believe in backstabbing or the type of rudeness that typified their treatment of anyone with whom they disagreed. He was charming, witty, good company and kind, and he was also a brilliant advocate and a highly skilled politician. Labour could not afford to lose him. As a lawyer he had a subtle mind that was not above making alliances for the common good and on one occasion when I was in the Commons he, Nicholas Fairbairn and I put our heads together over a clause in a Bill that seemed wrong for Scots law, won the matter and went off for a celebratory drink.

John's death overshadowed the entire campaign and it was difficult to get a feel for what would happen, although I was sure that I would win again. When I arrived at the count on the banks of the River Ness with my stalwart agent Hugh Coulter, Fergus was there looking out for me. He greeted me with the words, 'Mum, it is merely a question of whether you have doubled or trebled your majority.' In fact I had increased it by 10,000 and had secured 58 per cent of the vote, leaving Labour trailing some 35 per cent and 55,000 votes behind me and the Tories another 4,000 votes behind that. The Liberals, who in 1979 had come within 4,000 votes of winning, were now reduced to a mere 13,000 votes, just over 10 per cent of the poll – this was also in a seven-candidate race, as opposed to a five-candidate one the time before.

I was elated at the result, but that was also due to the fact that during the count we heard that Allan Macartney had won the North-east as well. He had overtaken Labour's Henry MacCubbin, a fellow member of the Fisheries Committee with me, with ease, gaining a 31,000 vote majority and almost 43 per cent of the poll. I had not had a good relationship with MacCubbin for, although he had the biggest fishing interests in the whole of the UK, he kept voting again and again for the measures that would benefit the Spanish and damage his own constituents. I did warn him on several occasions about what was likely to happen but he clearly did not believe me and continued backing the position of the UK Labour Party against Scotland. He had now paid the price. Stewart later bought me a daft mechanical bird which could imitate sentences. One sentence we taught it and which we replayed often was, 'I will never have to meet Henry McCubbin again!'

Allan's victory was an enormous boost to us. To have an SNP colleague in the European Parliament was a long-held dream which had at last come true. Allan was a dedicated long-term Nationalist who had fought several seats and had gone on battling no matter the result. He richly deserved his victory.

Allan had strong Moray connections. His father had been the minister of St Giles in Elgin and Allan was brought up in the Old Manse, now the Mansfield Hotel. A man of overwhelming charm, Allan's father had also been minister at Pluscarden and his wife is buried in Pluscarden cemetery, which he visited regularly before coming on to have lunch with us in Miltonduff. He had started his career as a missionary in Africa, and Allan had been born there, but after a stint at the Scots Kirk in Vienna he finally ended up as minister of St Machar's in Aberdeen. Now his son was celebrating victory in that same city.

There was enormous delight throughout the whole SNP but particularly in the Highlands. We went straight from the count back to Miltonduff to drink champagne and eat bacon rolls – it was a hearty celebration!

Although I now had a colleague, my fellow members in the Rainbow Group had not fared nearly so well, and many had lost their seats. The group, in fact, no longer existed and the first thing Allan and I had to do was find a new home. A group did, however, emerge which contained some remnants of the old group, including the Flemish nationalists but which had at its heart the French radicals. It was obvious that this was the right place for us and we joined, and were accompanied by a Valencian and some Italian radicals. Neil Blainey was the co-chair, which helped us enormously, and the group leader was Catherine la Lumière. The French Radicals were a substantial and historic party and their members were often distinguished in their own fields. One was a doctor who had been heavily involved with the international aid group, Médecin sans Frontières. Nonetheless there were problems with so many individualists trying to work together, and Allan was a master diplomat, always working to keep the peace. We continued to be deeply involved in the European Free Alliance.

During the European elections both my Labour and Conservative opponents continually claimed that belonging to a large group was essential, as only a large group could deliver protection for Scotland. This was the same argument perpetually used by the Unionist parties to argue against independence within Europe for Scotland, contending that the UK votes helped Scotland to achieve results she could never achieve on her own. Over the years there was regular criticism of my choice of groups, with the suggestion that they were ineffective and unable to deliver. Nothing could have been further from the truth. The two largest groups in the Parliament – the Socialist group and the right-wing group – were actually locked in a perpetual and uneasy alliance, attempting to carve up all the positions and ensuring that there was a Socialist president for one part of the five-year term and a right-wing president for the next part. The result was that the smaller groups were able to achieve much more by being flexible and forming alliances on the basis of what they needed and wanted. The new European Radical Alliance Group intended to do just that, and challenge the dictatorship of the larger groups.

Once we had found a group Allan and I then had to divide the portfolios between us, but this was not a problem. He agreed to take over fishing, an issue which had worn me down and at times almost broken my heart. It was devastating to hear the EU blamed all the time when the real culprits were the UK MEPs and the UK government. Particularly culpable were Heath and Wilson, who could have done so much more. All the details came out when their parliamentary papers were eventually published, but I am sure there is more to come as more recent government papers become available.

Alan also took over my Third World committee, the Development Committee. He was particularly suited to this, having spent his early years in Africa. He was a gifted linguist and could speak Afrikaans, which meant that he could also more than get by in Dutch. He was soon very well respected on the Development Committee and enjoyed it hugely, as did his wife Anne, who came to Europe as his secretary and assistant.

Allan was in his element in Europe. He took the chair of a new inter-party group for the unrepresented peoples of the world – Native Americans and Canadians and many others. Soon, whenever one saw a person in colourful national dress looking lost in the corridors in Brussels, one would say: 'Allan Macartney's office is just down there,' for people were invariably looking for him.

I too was ready for some new challenges. I took membership of the Economic and Monetary Committee, which was going to be a key area for debate, although I knew I would have to do a great deal of homework.

One of the considerations regarding both group membership and portfolios was always the postion of our Scottish staff. Sam Barber had come to us from Party HQ where she had worked in the research department. She quickly settled in, having a superb grasp of languages and a good manner. Neil Ferguson, whom I had first employed in 1980, had done superbly well too. He had risen through the ranks of the European Parliament staff to become Co-Secretary General of the group and was admired by all, for he was unfailingly helpful, polite and usually very funny. I constantly urged Neil to think about standing himself and he did so in the European Elections in 1999. Unfortunately the party did not place him high enough up the list to get elected, and I believe by failing to do so they missed out on gaining an exceptional Euro MP with the experience that would have made him truly one of our great representatives. I personally was enormously blessed to have had him working so closely with me for so long.

Neil was a strong source of advice as Allan and I endeavoured to carve out our mark in a Europe which was tired of the UK. We were now at the fag end of a long period of Tory rule and Major and his government had a very low standing in Europe. The other member states believed that he blocked many European initiatives, not because he didn't believe in them but solely to appease his right-wing back benchers at Westminster. It was not very difficult, but I was always conscious that I had to disassociate myself from his stance and all that was perceived to be 'British'. My own party's open and inclusive vision of Europe was a huge contrast and Alan and I tried to personify it on every occasion.

That was one of the reasons why I was so exercised when my integrity and honesty were openly attacked by, once more, Labour MEPs and why I personally went to court for the only time in my life in order to defeat the slur.

It happened like this. On one occasion in 1995 in the European Parliament we had two debates covering various aspects of unemployment, the first on a Wednesday and the second the following day. I was always a very regular attender in the Chamber, as I usually worked there as well, and I was able to hear the debate on the Wednesday but chose not to speak until the Thursday.

The Wednesday vote was a formality as pre-meetings of all the main groups had made it clear that most people were going to vote in support of the motion. At the time of the vote I got a message that the Commissioner for Fisheries, Emma Bonino, was willing to see me to discuss a number of urgent matters. I had sought this meeting for some time, but before leaving the chamber to see the Commissioner I asked my own whip if my vote was needed. He explained that the vote was not contentious, so I went to see the Commissioner, who was a personal friend.

The following day I was called very early on to speak and my speech was clearly reported in the Rainbow. This was an unusual day, as, for the first time, all MEPs had a vote on the appointment of the Ombudsman. During the vote the actual session of the Parliament was closed and the vote had to be taken and retaken because the required percentage of each vote was not reached. The voting was also by secret ballot. One had to sign one's attendance each day in at the Parliament, which could be done in one corner during the voting period.

Owing to the voting confusion, I forgot to sign in. However, in such eventualities one could prove one's attendance by producing one's travel ticket to the cash office. I had also been recorded as having spoken that day (although owing to the delay in producing the Rainbow in various languages, it was not available until early the following week), so it was indisputable that I had been present. However, a number of Scottish

Labour MEPs including David Martin and Hugh MacMahon had noticed at one stage that I was not in my seat and had checked to discover that I had not signed in. They then appear to have drawn some unwarranted conclusions.

When I returned to Miltonduff on the Friday I got a phone call from Angus MacLeod, a journalist on the *Sunday Mail*, who asked me about my non-attendance at what he called 'a vital employment debate' the day before. I was genuinely puzzled for I had been there and although I had not voted on the Wednesday (which he knew), my speech on Thursday was on the record. Our conversation however, irritated me, as he did not have the facts and was most persistent. He clearly was being fed information from someone, and I resented his implication that I had been at fault and was not taking my responsibilities seriously.

On the Sunday I received a call from Murray Ritchie of *The Herald*, who told me that there was a piece in the *Sunday Mail* by Angus MacLeod attacking me for non-attendance and, by implication, of claiming my allowances but not bothering to turn up or vote. Murray let me see the Labour press release that had stirred this up. It had quotes from Martin and MacMahon and was headed 'Where Was Winnie?' Murray then asked me for my response, as he was planning to run the story himself.

I immediately decided I had to challenge this. It was bad enough personally to have such an accusation made, but as President of the SNP it was also a slur on the entire party. It was nothing less than an accusation of dishonesty and I was not prepared to be so accused. I told Murray that if his paper published the accusation again it would find itself defending an action, and I then wrote to Martin and MacMahon demanding an apology whilst instructing my solicitors to write to the *Mail* and make the same demand, though in this case the apology was to be public and they were to pay £3,000 to the Highland Hospice.

Once the evidence of my speech was produced, the paper realised it hadn't a leg to stand on, and although they were prepared to negotiate grudgingly on an apology they would not pay a penny to the hospice and I felt that the allegation was so grave that I must proceed with an action. I instructed Colin Sutherland, QC, who thought I had an unanswerable case.

Nonetheless the *Sunday Mail* continued to bluster and the case dragged on for over a year until it was set down for the first sitting day in 1997. Stewart had been a tower of strength and had told me not to worry about the costs invovled in fighting the case. Just when I thought we were going to have our day in court, however, a new difficulty arose: the original judge could not act as he was a close personal friend and his substitute refused to act because he had been a close friend of my late brother-in-law. It looked as if we were going to have to accept a further delay, until July, when Colin Sutherland was offered a settlement by the paper which gave me a goodly sum in recompense and also paid all my legal expenses, which were reaching about £50,000 at that stage. They were also prepared to make a written apology. Much as I would have liked to have had the whole matter aired in public, I was tired of the time and hassle this had taken, so I accepted the offer.

Despite such distractions I was still enjoying my work in the Parliament and particularly in the area of Human Rights, which was one of my biggest interests as well as one of Alan's. The Parliament frequently attempted to intervene to stop executions and persecution throughout the world and often it was successful. Some critics of the Parliament – often Tories – said that our eyes were too frequently on the far corners of the world and not often enough in our own backyard, but I have always felt that the unjust treatment of any human being is of equal importance wherever it happened. John Donne was right to say that 'no man is an island, entire of itself . . . any man's death diminishes me, because I am involved in mankind'.

The EU also had some bargaining power in many of the cases we discussed. For example, when we debated the situation in Chechnya and called for a cease-fire we were dealing with a Russia that looked to Europe for all kinds of aid and help with development. In Iraq and Kurdistan we took the same stance and constantly opposed the daily violation of human dignity and the endless suffering of the population under Saddam Hussein. We discussed the dreadful situation in Algeria where there were and are hundreds of executions every month, including those of children, and we urged the cessation of a European-financed programme in Tibet which would have encouraged more and more Chinese to live in that country, a deliberate tactic taken by the Chinese government in order to perpetuate its illegal occupation. Given the range of concerns the Parliament had I was keen that we formalised our activities and I called by resolution for human rights to be the portfolio of a single European commissioner and for the establishment of a standing group which would act as Human Rights observers throughout the world, monitoring and promoting such rights in every country. The thorny issue of the accession of Turkey arose on several occasions and whilst I was not unsympathetic to enlargement of this sort, Turkey's Human Rights record was very bad and did not seem to be improving.

If I labour the point about Human Rights it is only to show that the popular conception of the European Parliament as some sort of clearing house for bureaucratic trivia is very wide of the mark. In fact it is a myth, perpetrated by eurosceptics, both Labour and Tory, and re-iterated by newspapers whose owners are also anti-Europe. The European Parliament is an emerging institution, but it is one that does an enormous amount of good work on the ground in member states, as well as outside Europe. Donnie Stewart used to say that if everyone in Scotland got the chance to spend an hour watching the House of Commons at work, it would do more for Scottish independence than any amount of canvassing. I felt the opposite about the European Parliament: if Scottish voters could come and see it at work they would be enthusiastic about its potential and keen to see their country play a full part as an equal member in Europe.

The Parliament can find itself in the midst of difficult situations not of its own making and have to exercise sensitive judgements. In 1995 we almost found ourselves in the middle of a fishing war when the Canadians boarded a Spanish trawler just outside the Canadian 200-mile limit. The debate in the European Parliament was heated and sometimes stormy, with the Spanish calling for compensation, threatening to send warships and suggesting that they would impose visa restrictions on Canadians entering Spain. They also asked the Parliament to bar the visit of a Canadian parliamentary delegation which was due shortly. Allan Macartney and I were not unsympathetic to the Canadian stance for we knew the damage that Spanish trawlers could do. Nonetheless we recognised that the Spaniards had a case and we accepted the illegality of the Canadian action. However we urged the removal of the threats and bluster from the situation and we pointed out that talking is always better than fighting – a key European tenet. That middle line prevailed and the Canadian parliamentarians duly arrived. I was on the delegation that met them and it was obvious that they were nervous about their reception, although the only Spaniard due to be there absented himself in a form of silent protest.

By the time the delegation arrived certain facts had emerged. The catch on board the Spanish boat consisted of almost 90 per cent immature fish and in addition there was a secret hold containing 35 tonnes of plaice which was a banned species in those waters. The boat had cut its nets before being boarded but the Canadians recovered them and discovered that the mesh size was considerably below that which was legal. Nonetheless the boat and its skipper were released but, given the circumstances, it was hardly likely or just that the Canadians would pay compensation for the catch, as was being demanded. The Canadians were correct to say that whilst there is a right of free fishing on the high seas, such a right is subject to wider conservation interests. Little wonder that the Canadians were annoyed and little wonder, in solidarity with the Canadian position, that some North-east fishermen started to fly Canadian flags on their boats.

The year 1995 was also designated by the European Union as the 'Year of Lifelong Learning' and I spoke on the subject in the March session. Having been awarded an honorary degree by the Open University I chose to talk about the fantastic achievements of this university which had opened its doors to all and which helped those with no qualifications to achieve their potential. I described in my speech how it was thrilling to be capped at the same ceremony as an eighty-year-old man and two inmates of Scottish jails, and how good it was, when the usual graduation photographs were being taken to see so many graduate grannies surrounded by their admiring grandchildren! When I was Chair of the Education and Culture Committee I had done a report urging other member states to follow the British example and establish open universities of their own. Few however had done so, so the UK university was now taking students from France and Belgium as well and giving many more people a second chance, including those in remote areas who could never hope to be able to attend a conventional institution.

In my speech I also recalled Jennie Lee, the member of Harold Wilson's cabinet who was responsible for getting the idea of the Open University passed. I recalled an occasion when I was MP for Hamilton when Jennie had enthused to me about just gaining cabinet approval for the OU that very day and had asked me to be sure to back it in the Chamber. I paid tribute to Jennie for it was her commitment and determination that had ultimately opened doors for so many.

Some months later I got another honorary degree, this time from my own Alma Mater. The ceremony was held on 21 June 1995 and I topped a distinguished list of honorary doctors. I was immensely proud of having been chosen by Glasgow University for the honour and it gave me a great deal of happiness to accept it. After the ceremony we had a lovely party in the College Club. Bill McCue, the well-known Scottish singer, insisted not just on attending but also on singing in celebration and there was other musical entertainment as well. All three of my goddaughters attended and all of my family too, as well as many, many friends and colleagues.

With Allan in Europe as well, it was possible for me to spend a little more time in Scotland and I was able to travel even more in my constituency, opening fêtes, attending Highland Games, meeting with councillors and other local representatives and taking up local issues. I was proud of being the member for the Highlands and Islands and I always felt a tingle of romance when the term was used, particularly in Europe. Of course I was also working for the party in every part of Scotland and had become Party President after Donald Stewart, a position that entitled me to attend the National Executive and to make an annual address at conference. I also began to ensure that I spent a week at least at each of the Parliamentary by-elections, supporting the candidate and getting out on the street to secure votes for the party.

The SNP loves by-elections, and in the absence of a Parliament in Scotland they were always intense, high-profile affairs, subject to huge media scrutiny. In May 1995 Roseanna Cunningham won Perth after a massive struggle in which, for the first time in many years, we were seen as the front runner, with all the difficulties which that entails. I went to the by-election on the last Saturday and remained to campaign in a constituency that I was to get to know very well when my daughter Annabelle took over the Westminster seat from Roseanna in 2001.

There had been much coverage of a row prior to the by-election when Roseanna withdrew from the selection after not being placed on the final list by the election committee, only to be re-instated by the NEC and subsequently selected by the constituency, which she had fought pre-

viously in 1992. Whatever the rights and wrongs of what was a complicated situation, she and Margaret Ewing remained the best of friends and
worked well together in the House of Commons after the by-election. The
press seemed to want to blame a whole range of people for what had
happened, not least myself, but Roseanna and I have always got on well
and there was no animosity between us – quite the reverse in fact. In any
case such was the publicity Roseanna had that she became instantly
recognisable in the streets of Perth, a factor that worked greatly in her
favour and she scored a run-away victory.

My list of speaking engagements continued to grow and by now I must
have spoken on more SNP platforms with more SNP speakers than any
other person before or since! I spoke at conferences, to various trade and
other associations, at St Andrew's Nights and at Burns Suppers including
the Luxembourg Burns Supper, which was held on a June night in 1997,
complete with pipers and haggis.

The year before I had been given another honour – that of becoming the
Honorary Conservator of the Scottish Privileges in Veere. Veere is a town
in Zeeland in the Netherlands which for over 200 years was entirely
administered by Scots who had gained valuable trading privileges and
who guarded them jealously. Scots ran the civil and criminal courts and
monopolised trade in Veere right up until the Napoleonic invasion, at
which time the Scots fled for their lives. Diligent Scottish clerks had kept
impeccable written records for the entire period of their activity there.
Indeed the records were so perfect and so detailed that they were regarded
as a national treasure in the Netherlands and Veere had to fight to keep
these records there, rather than lose them to Amsterdam.

To this day there are Scottish houses in Veere and a Scottish museum,
as well as the Grote Kerk (Great Kirk). In the mid 1990s the people of
Veere and the local authority mayors of the area decided they would like to
revive the old Scottish title of 'conservator' as a means of renewing links
with Scotland. The committee formed to undertake the task approached
me in addition to representatives from the City of Edinburgh and St
Andrews University to discuss the issue. When they learned that I spoke
Dutch they asked me if I would accept the title, having got clearance first
from none other than the Queen of the Netherlands. I of course accepted
and duly attended a fantastic celebration in Veere, which is no longer a

port but which sits by a lake created by the brilliance of Dutch water engineers. The event on the 19 September 1996 was attended by Dutch and Scots traders, including some from Edinburgh and Fife, as well as by many others. I made a speech in Dutch in the ancient town hall and was accompanied by one of my SNP supporters from Findhorn who had been involved in the liberation of Veere at the end of the Second World War.

I have been back to Veere three times for other events and value my honorary title very strongly indeed. But I value all the honours that I have been given, such as the Honorary Membership of The Royal Faculty of Procurators in Glasgow which I received in June 1997.

I was as enthusiastic about representing my constituency as I had ever been, despite having reached sixty-five, the age at which many people are thinking about, and taking, retirement. But the constant support of my family and happy family events always kept me going. During this period there were a number of family weddings. My nephews Mark and Simon got married, and then Terry announced that he was going to get married too. On 12 April 1997 he tied the knot with his Irish fiancée, Jacqui Murphy, at the beautiful church in Luss by Loch Lomondside. It was a magical spring day with blue skies and a touch of snow on Ben Lomond, reflected in a calm vermillion-coloured loch. Jacqui's Irish relatives were great fun and very generous – the reception was held at Cameron House and had two bands, not one, and the champagne flowed all night. Terry's wedding to Jacqui gladdened my heart and they have continued to delight me by producing my first three grandchildren – Ciara, Jamie and Sophie – who I adore and I love to spend time with.

The spring of 1997 was busy. The General Election in May produced the expected Labour landslide and the removal of a discredited and at times disgraceful Tory government. Labour now had to decide if it would bring forward a devolution scheme and in what way, for it had been riven the year before by a dispute about a referendum, or rather two referenda.

Despite the Labour landslide, the SNP increased not only its share of the vote, but also its seats, taking at last Tayside North and Galloway again and holding Perth, the first time we had ever held a by-election win. Now we had six MPs, our largest number since the 1970s, and were in a good position as Scotland's second party, challenging for government in the new Scottish Parliament. The party decided to back a double 'Yes' vote in the referendum, despite some opposition from a few individuals, including Gordon Wilson. The campaign for the referendum of September 11 1997 learned from the lessons of the dreadful referendum in 1979, even though it was badly disrupted by the tragic death of Princess Diana.

There was a substantial degree of joint campaigning during the run-up to the referendum and the outstanding performer on television was Alex Salmond, who won over many wavering voters. The overwhelming decision of Scotland was to have a Parliament with tax-raising powers and the SNP very quickly started to prepare for the Scottish Parliament elections which would be held in 1999. By early 1998 the SNP was rising spectacularly in the polls, giving the prospect of real progress with a Scottish Parliament.

Much of the burden of preparing for the election fell to the party's deputy leader, Allan Macartney. Allan had become deputy to Alex Salmond and he fulfilled the role, as usual, with great commitment. Allan was always an enormously hard worker and all through that year and the following one he was deeply immersed not just in his party tasks but also in his European work and in his role as Rector of Aberdeen University. Allan masterminded the selection process for the Scottish Parliament and for the European Elections which were due in 1999 and which would be, for the first time, fought on a national list. He was constantly active in screening candidates, recommending selection methods and implementing decisions of the NEC and National Council. He was also overworking in Europe as well. Of an evening in Brussels he and I, along with his wife Anne, would usually meet for an hour in the bar with Neil, Allison and Samantha. Then when I went home to relax and have dinner Allan usually went back to his office and worked until midnight. To add to it all he still continued writing academic papers and showing an interest in academic matters. He just, I suspect, could not stop himself.

On the night of 24 August 1998 he was in Perth, overseeing a European selection meeting. Afterwards he went to the Salutation Hotel to talk to the SNP Chief Executive, Michael Russell, about some details of the Scottish Parliament selection process, and then he drove back to Aberdeen. The next morning he was dead, killed by a massive heart attack. The whole of Scotland, and the whole of the European Parliament, mourned his passing. The many obituaries in the newspapers all reflected on the fact that at fifty-seven, there was no more fulfilled, happy and hard-working politician in Scotland. They also noted what a gap he would leave in the ranks of the SNP. Anne was very dignified but obviously heart-broken, as were his family and his many friends, but she bravely came over to Europe just after the funeral (which was held in St Machar's Cathedral, his father's old charge) to hear the tributes paid on the Parliament floor.

I had had him as my only party colleague in Europe from June 1994 to August 1998 and I deeply missed his presence, advice and companion-ship. I found the European Parliament to be a much less congenial place without him. I had already announced that I would not be standing for the European parliament again as I intended to stand for the Scottish Parliament. Now there would be no one to continue in Europe with a degree of experience which we had been counting on and the party would also lack, at a crucial time, his sound counsel and sterling efforts.

One of the strangest and most difficult things about politics is the way in which it simply carries on no matter what the personal tragedies. We were all mourning Allan's passing but we also knew that there would have to be a by-election and we had to get someone into Europe who could provide continuity at the next European elections, which were due in much less than a year. After very brief discussion the ideal candidate was found – Ian Hudghton, who was the leader of Angus Council. He was a popular choice and the by-election, held in November 1998, was almost a formality. Ian won overwhelmingly, helped admittedly by the self-destruction of the Labour campaign whose candidate falsely claimed local roots in the North-east until this was exposed by a Sunday paper, at which stage she made things much worse for herself by claiming that she had, at least, been conceived in the constituency!

Ian quickly settled into the Parliament, ably assisted by his wife Lily and soon I was introducing him everywhere and making sure he was taking up the reins and providing a stable presence for us which would last through the next elections.

My decision to come home, so to speak, after almost twenty-five years in the European Parliament (both nominated and elected) had not been an easy one. I had been thinking of it for some time when, in early 1998 at Robert McIntyre's funeral in Stirling (how many good and dedicated Nationalists who had given everything to the struggle, I reflected on that day, had died before we had managed to get at least a little power back to Scotland), I raised the issue privately with Michael Russell and Alex Salmond. Both were enthusiastic about my wish to stand for the Scottish Parliament, seeing it, as I did, as a logical final step in my political career and as a strong affirmation of my belief that the Parliament (even this devolved Parliament) had to be made to work. They also believed that I would attract votes wherever I stood, thus boosting the party's performance.

There were hurdles to be overcome. Where was I to stand for example, as I did not want to choose a constituency and had already decided I would prefer to be only on a list. The announcement was made in May 1998 and received much coverage. *Scotland on Sunday*, for example, headlined my decision and quoted me as saying, 'I have campaigned for, argued for and longed for a Scottish Parliament and now I want to sit in it. I see the parliament on offer as important in its own right but also as a base camp on the journey to independence.'

I was very excited about the prospects of sitting in the first Scottish Parliament in 300 years, but I knew I would miss Europe. It is a place of great excitement and the most exciting thing is probably the ability to achieve a huge amount of consensus. I also knew that I would miss nothing in Europe so much as my work on Third World issues. That had been exemplified by my time as a member of the Lomé Assembly, which I believe ranks amongst the most important things I have been involved with. So before telling the story of my life in the Scottish Parliament – my third Parliament in thirty-six years of front-line politics – I want to tell something of Lomé and travelling the world in support of development and a wider vision of prosperity.

13

The Member for the Highlands
and Islands – Lomé

O NE OF THE MOST exciting and worthwhile trips of my life was that
which I made to the 'front-line' states in Africa (that is, those states
which bordered South Africa, then governed by a vicious apartheid regime
that was internationally shunned) in January and February 1982. The
delegation to which I had been appointed consisted of a range of MEPs
from various groups and some African, Carribean and Pacific (ACP)
delegates, including the Speakers of the Jamaican, Djibouti and Cameroon
Parliaments. There were also some observers, including an English Tory
MP. The delegation was to visit Angola, Zimbabwe and Zambia to consult
with governments, MPs and others, as well as to investigate South African
harassment and the actual needs of these countries. During the tour we
would also attend the Lomé Assembly, being held in Zimbabwe, and
afterwards I would go on with others to Malawi and Kenya.

It is necessary, I think, to give a little bit of the background to Lomé
before describing the events of the trip to Africa. The Lomé Convention is
a parliamentary assembly of delegates from EU member states and ACP
States. It is called 'Lomé' because the first Euro Convention on the subject
was signed in the city of Lomé, the capital of Togo. The Lomé Convention was created because most of the states in the European Union had
been colonial powers at one stage or another. It was clearly important that
the access to markets that had been part of the colonial system should not
be cut off simply because of the new European arrangements, and that
new systems would have to be put in place. Lomé was essentially the

infrastructure around which these new systems could be built, but it became much more. When Britain joined the EU in 1974, for example, the main exporting market for Jamaica was the UK, and in order for Jamaica to be able to continue to sell her rum, sugar, bananas and minerals access to the EU had to be maintained. At first the emphasis of Lomé had been on aid, but as time went on a much better motto emerged. 'Trade, not Aid' was the watchword, because trade ensured long-term growth and improvements in infrastructure and capability.

I was elected to Lomé when I was a member of the Development Committee. I was honoured to be chosen and it quickly became one of the central parts of my working life. During my time as a Lomé delegate I visited twenty-six ACP States and in each case met heads of states and ministers as well as many others, and I would not have missed these experiences for the world. I also managed to bring the full Lomé Assembly to Inverness, the only time that it has met in the UK.

The Front-line States Delegation undertook its trip at a time of great sensitivity. South Africa remained in turmoil, experiencing constant protests including a widespread trade boycott, though these were met with brutality and repression by the Government. Deaths in detention were frequent and the South African security services and others were actively trying to undermine the front-line states as well as the anti-apartheid movement in other countries.

The European Parliament had generally been strong and constant in its opposition to apartheid, though much more could have been done and some of the member countries were not as principled in their opposition as many of us would have liked. The decision to send a delegation to the front-line states arose out of that situation, and as I had been deeply involved in the issue for many years, I was very glad to have been chosen to be part of it.

We arrived in Angola on 23 January 1982. We met the president, Mr Dos Santos, and we saw their young parliament, with its 211 members, in action. The independence of Namibia was central to their concerns, and South African hostility to Angola was deep-rooted, particularly as Angola supported Namibian independence. South Africa's involvement had prolonged the vicious civil war.

The country's future was a matter of worry, particularly considering the strong presence in the country of Russians and Cubans, who had rendered considerable assistance, though at the price of deep suspicion from the West. The Cubans provided, amongst other things, doctors, who were paid very little but who were immensely valuable. Despite being rich in natural resources Angola had been impoverished for generations, and the situation was made even worse when the Portuguese departed, taking with them much of the valuable industrial infrastructure as well as most of the export potential and almost all the technical know-how. We saw many buses simply abandoned because there were so few mechanics to get them going again.

In order to understand something of the country we made a long excursion into the south, to the town of Lubango. It was a bumpy journey in two minibuses and when we arrived we found that we were scheduled to stay in what had been a brothel. Fortunately it had locks on the bedroom doors, for during the night would-be customers kept trying to get into the rooms. There was no running water, the toilets didn't work, and my bed seemed to contain a virulent nest of what in Scotland we would call 'wee beasties'. I could not sleep, so whilst I was waiting for the Red Cross official to come and try and get rid of my infestation I joined Mr Bersani, the Italian head of the delegation who seemed to be constantly on the phone. Next day we visited a refugee camp which held several thousand people. The government told us that there were over 60,000 refugees in the country in total. UNICEF was in charge and had established a make-shift hospital, once again staffed by Cuban doctors. Although there were UNITA slogans on the walls (UNITA was financed by South Africa as part of its policy of destabilising Angola) we heard many revolutionary songs being sung, complete with clenched fists.

Our next stop on this very wearing trip was Zambia. Once again we met the Prime Minister and were briefed by the Foreign Minister and his officials. They explained that the country was forced to rely on South Africa because it was an important source of raw materials. The Zambian people utterly and completely rejected apartheid, regarding it as a crime against humanity. Their economic dependency on South Africa was repugnant to them, but vital. Nonetheless the Zambian government were critical of the EEC, feeling that not enough was being done to pressure the South African regime and that too many links were being maintained.

They regarded, as all of us did, the occupation of Namibia by South Africa as illegal and were annoyed that not more was being done to end it. They were also very troubled by South Africa's use of land mines in the south of Zambia and the waging of a low-level type of guerrilla warfare which was creating many refugees. Despite their criticisms, the Zambian government was very welcoming and they often stressed how much they wanted to talk to people like us and how much they enjoyed it. They accepted that our fact-finding mission was also an indication of European solidarity against South Africa and they were grateful for that.

From Zambia we went on to Zimbabwe where we were not only to take further evidence, but also to attend the Lomé Convention. If anything Zimbabwe was suffering even more than its neighbours from South African interference and from the baleful influence of the apartheid system. South Africa deliberately kept Zimbabwe short of oil and supported political violence in the country. It had been behind the blowing-up of buildings, such as the ANC office, and had demolished vital infrastructure, such as bridges. Most land in Zimbabwe – and land was always a big issue there – remained in the hands of white farmers, some of whom were sympathetic to South Africa, and migrant workers who had returned to Zimbabwe found it hard to get employment.

We met Robert Mugabe himself on 1 February. He had been described to us by one of his ministers as 'The finest captain of them all' and he cut an impressive figure. He had become Prime Minister in 1980, leading his political party, ZANU (PF), to victory in the country's first democratic elections after first heading the Zimbabwe delegation to the Lancaster House Conference in 1979 which had resulted in a peaceful settlement of the Rhodesian question. For more than two decades before that he had been active in politics and had been the key figure in forging a united front against the Smith regime. He was, it was obvious, formidably clever. He had been a teacher for twenty years before entering politics and when in jail he had taken two more degrees as well as finding time to tutor his fellow prisoners. Mugabe spoke passionately to us of the end of division in his country and of the warring sides which had been enemies but which now had to work together. He wanted an end to race superiority and race inferiority and instead wished to see an egalitarian country in which all races could co-operate for the national good. He told us how difficult it had been to make one army out of three previous warring factions, but also told us how it had been done successfully. He then went on to roundly condemn South Africa for its aggression, its acts of sabotage and its continuing hostility to democracy and the rest of the continent.

I found Mugabe a charismatic figure and at that time he was, although he has now clearly and sadly changed from being a visionary leader to being a violent and oppressive despot. That is a great tragedy, for it seemed to me and to many of us who met him that the potential was there for the development of a leader of immense national and international standing who could bring so much good to Africa.

It was during this meeting that he asked me how my party was faring in Scotland, for he was obviously well briefed and very knowledgeable about world affairs. I had to tell him that it was not faring as well as I would like and he responded by saying, 'Ah well, the people of Scotland are not yet sufficiently oppressed!' I have never forgotten that conversation.

Our meetings took place in Salisbury which was very like an English country town, full of gardens and fountains. It appeared to be a relaxed and pleasant place, and there was obviously freedom of speech and a free press. Zimbabwe looked as if it was on the mend and moving forward, despite its difficulties, and it pains me greatly to read the press reports now, as so much potential has simply been wasted.

Spouses of MEPs often came to the Lomé Assemblies at their own expense but Stewart usually missed out, as he was teaching. On this occasion I had invited my sister, Jean, to come for a few days and she was due to arrive the afternoon of the day on which we met Mugabe with the rest of the partners. I managed to get an official car to meet her and I went to the airport to greet her and bring her back to Meikle's Hotel ahead of the other delegates, so that I could get her settled in.

The reception desk gave us the key to Jean's room but when we arrived in it we were bewildered (and slightly alarmed) to discover not the single room I had booked but a double suite with two bathrooms, filled with flowers and baskets of fruit. Naturally Jean thought that this was far too extravagant and indeed wondered if she would be able to pay for such luxury, so I went back down to the desk to ask why she had been allocated such accommodation. The staff were very obliging but would only say that this was indeed the room that Mrs Forsyth was to get and that the cost of it would be the same as a standard single room. I asked for, and got, written confirmation of that assurance but we remained very puzzled as to what was going on.

However I soon discovered the reason. The luxurious suite had just been vacated by none other than Barbara Castle, the former Labour cabinet minister, who had arrived in Zimbabwe some days before and who had spent her time attacking the country for spending money on hosting Lomé whilst also criticising MEPs for accepting Zimbabwe's hospitality. This, understandably, aroused much anger both from ACP delegates and from MEPs. Obviously Mrs Castle did not want to give any ground for a counter-attack, so she had quickly vacated the best suite in the hotel before the delegates arrived. The hotel management felt it could then only allocate the suite to someone who was representing neither the ACP states nor the European Parliament. Jean was the only person who did not appear on the register to be connected with either, and therefore she benefited as a result of Barbara Castle's unfortunate attitude!

More baskets of fruit and flowers kept arriving, and Jean just settled down to enjoy herself. In fact we held a small party in the suite, with everyone bringing the contents of their own mini-bar. The free liquor in the cabinet meant for Barbara was left untouched!

On our first evening in the hotel our Front-line States Delegation booked a table in the bar in order to celebrate the birthday of Arthur Williams, the Speaker of the Jamaican Parliament, and delegation leader. By this time – as happens with most such delegations – we had all become close and we were enjoying ourselves when some white youths started to object to our party. Their difficulty appeared to be that they did not like to see whites and blacks being so friendly and I was shocked by such naked racism. The hotel moved quickly to have them ejected but it left a nasty taste.

When the Lomé Convention got under way, Jean went off on various trips with the spouses including a visit to the ancient city of Zimbabwe which was hundreds of years old. Its walls had no plaster and were built just like Scottish dry-stane dykes. She also got to see the Victoria Falls, just as I had a few days before. Another interesting excursion was to visit a farm owned by one of the white farmers who was a Scot and the uncle of Moira Anderson, the singer. He had started a training school for Africans to teach them how to cultivate their own land and had built houses for those who were being trained. It all appeared, at that time, to be very encouraging and the farmer himself was full of praise for Mugabe.

The Convention itself opened with an address by the Revd Canaan Banana, President of Zimbabwe. He was delightful and reminded us that Zimbabwe had become the 153rd member of the UN and a member of Lomé in 1981 – two big steps forward after many years of difficulty. The focus of the convention was very much on the problems of Southern Africa, and the members of the Front-line States Delegation were much in demand, as the ACP states were keen to hear what conclusions we would draw. We tendered a report for the convention and I spoke on the third day. I quote some of the speech below, because it is a record of my feelings about the situation in South Africa and how Europe responded to it:

I was brought up in Scotland and I quote our national poet, Burns, 'Man's inhumanity to man makes countless thousands mourn.' Our mission to the front-line state saw sordid scenes of this inhumanity caused by the South African State bent on pursuing its obscene partnership of Racialism and Greed.

The suffering people we met wanted us to return and tell the world what we have seen. This report must not be allowed to gather dust. It must be circulated to all MEPs and MPs in our own states, all trade unions, chambers of commerce, universities, political parties and to the man in the street. We must all ensure this is done and I believe the Commission ought to help. This will cause a fresh wave of awareness that the world cannot permit apartheid to continue.

They expect us to mount a strong opposition to Apartheid and I must also condemn the hypocrisy of the EEC. The Code of Conduct remains voluntary. It must be enforceable. I must quote the Prime Minister of Zambia on these matters, for his words are wise and true: 'Lukewarm sanctions may prolong the agony. What is needed is severe sharp shock treatment. I refute the argument that black Africans will suffer. Africans are prepared to suffer. What after all is the better long-term investment? Investment in SA which has reached maximum development or in fifty-two African Countries with a great potential waiting to be developed? The quicker the fifty-two succeed the quicker the death knell is sounded for a racist South Africa.'

May I end by making a tribute to the peoples of the front-line states, especially Angola? They were short of everything, even water. They had so little and they gave us so much. I pay tribute to their indomitable spirit and their courageous solidarity with Namibia, whose people will ultimately prevail as do all peoples whose determination is fixed on the road to freedom and self-government.

The speech was well received by both MEPs and the ACP delegates and it was also much reported at home.

I found Zimbabwe a fascinating country and greatly enjoyed my visit. When I was there I became intrigued by the evidence all around of an ancient and developed civilisation and in particular by the stone birds which were much in the news at that time, as a priceless collection of five of these birds, removed by colonialists at the turn of the century, had just been returned. The birds had been in South Africa for almost ninety years but were exchanged for a rare collection of insects. Now the birds were in the Queen Victoria Museum in Salisbury, before being taken to what would be their permanent home at the Great Zimbabwe Ruins Museum near the Lowveld town of Fort Victoria.

We had, regrettably, very little time for sightseeing in Zimbabwe, for immediately after the convention I travelled to two more countries to see what the EEC was doing through Lomé and what more we could do.

Malawi is known as the 'warm heart of Africa' and we soon discovered a country of fantastic pride populated by a rich mixture of blacks, whites and Asians. We were met by the Speaker of the Malawi Parliament, Mr Khonje, who told us that the government boasted that there was no corruption, no muggings and little violent crime and that aid was guaranteed to reach its target. However, he was unable to admit there was a free press, for there clearly wasn't.

Our days were packed with meetings, although we did not meet the president, Dr Hastings Banda, who had trained in Edinburgh and who made frequent visits to Scotland, though as his grip on the country tightened and he stamped out any opposition, these visits were becoming less and less welcome. We got something of the flavour of this, however, in our discussions with the British High Commissioner and the EEC representative. The ruthlessness of his regime was a tragedy because Malawi, like so many countries in Africa, is a beautiful place with much potential. Lake Malawi, Africa's third largest lake, is vastly impressive with wonderful uncrowded beaches that would make a tourist paradise.

I was particularly fascinated by the city of Blantyre, which has a population of over 200,000 and is central Africa's oldest municipality (established in 1895), as well as being the country's main commercial, industrial and communications centre. I had, of course, been the member at Westminster for the Scottish Blantyre when I represented Hamilton, which caused much interest, and there were also many other places in Malawi with Scottish names. The whole country seemed to feel a tremendous bond to Scotland and the potential for Scottish aid and trade was great.

Because of the president's own professional interest in health the country's health programme was impressive, with nutritional rehabilitation for the poorest and training given to mothers on how to feed their children – projects which were funded by the EEC. We saw some efficient co-operative farms in the Bwanje Valley and we also visited a fishing project where almost 4,000 fishermen, working in canoes, managed to make a living. Fishermen who used traditional methods were licensed and the positive environmental benefits of their activity were officially encouraged.

We saw projects galore in Malawi – not just fishing but boat-building, hand carving and fish farming. Many only existed because of EEC aid and it was clear that our help was making a difference. Our days in Malawi were packed with visits and meetings, and at all of them we got broadly the same message we received elsewhere: it was time for the European states to become serious about their opposition to South Africa and to plug the loopholes in sanctions and contacts.

Our final visit was to Kenya. The country has white coral beaches, plains trodden by the hooves of thousands of animals, cool highlands, the Rift Valley, rain forests at the bases of snow-capped mountains, deserts, a colourful tribal life and a sophisticated capital city, Nairobi. Kenya also has a long coastline on the Indian Ocean, on which contact with the outside world was made, firstly with Arabs, then the Portuguese, and finally the British.

The Arab influence on the country is particularly strong in the port of Mombassa, where there is also a lively mix of ancient and modern. The old Arab town, with its twisting streets, historic mosques and medieval houses, dhow harbours and bazaars is contrasted by the up-to-date hotels and restaurants.

In Kenya we dined with the Belgian Ambassador and met the Heads of Mission from the EEC countries. We visited development programmes, attended the opening of a new secondary school and saw irrigation schemes, all funded by EEC money. I opted out of one of the visits in order to meet a very famous Kenyan woman MP. Phoebe Muga Asiyd was very active in setting up self-help and working groups and she had even gone to the length of wearing Arab dress when trying to work with Arab women near the Somali border. She was a most impressive person, full of energy and determination and she gave the lie to any suggestion that opposition in Kenya had been persecuted out of existence, though things were becoming difficult, and later got more so.

Once again the message about South Africa was clear, even from these states which were not on the front line. The EEC had much to do in addition to its greatly appreciated and beneficial aid schemes.

The Front-line States delegation continued to put pressure on the EEC and its member states with regard to action against South Africa and our stance was welcomed. We were a constant reminder that European countries must not weaken in their opposition, no matter how individual governments try to trim and twist according to circumstances and their own national interests. I went on asking questions about the issues and raising them in the European Parliament Chamber for many years.

In addition to my concerns about South Africa, I also remained very interested in the prospects for African nations as a whole. I was able to visit Tanzania, and two years after the Front-line States Delegation I attended the Lomé Convention in Brazzaville in the Congo after a period as a guest of the Somalian govement in connection with work I had started to do on Third World fisheries – an extension of my interest in fishing which had arisen from my constituency concerns.

In Tanzania I had met the President, Julius Nyerere who, as he had often been pictured, was sitting in his famous rocking-chair at his comfortable residence in Dar-es-Salaam. He had been educated in

Edinburgh and was keen to chat about the city and about Scotland, a country of which he was very fond. My delegation also had talks with the Foreign Minister, who had been a near contender for the Secretary General's post in the UN, and who had been his country's ambassador to that body. Inevitably we talked about the necessity that his, and other, African countries had of trading with South Africa, despite the economic war South Africa was waging to destabilise other African nations.

One of my clearest memories of my trip to Tanzania was the thrill of seeing the Masai people. The group that came to the hotel were immensely dignified – tall and thin and good-looking, wearing what struck me as kind of tartan cloth robes with yellow and red stripes. They danced in a most energetic fashion, leaping to great heights from a standing position and they appeared very strong and healthy. But they did not want to be photographed, believing that the camera would steal their spirits.

The Masai are not native to any one country but are nomadic, walking the mountain-tops and herding their animals wherever they choose. They particularly value a mixture of blood and milk to drink, drawing the blood off their animals in small amounts through wounds they seal with dung and from which the beasts recover quickly. I was very taken by this story, recalling the experience of Scots during famine years in the sixteenth and seventeenth centuries, when the same thing would be done, though the blood would be mixed with oatmeal – the origin of the black pudding.

As my interest in Lomé grew I began to make serious speeches in the Assembly and in the European Parliament about world fishing, as it seemed to me that the problems of fisheries worldwide needed a more systematic approach. This led to an invitation from the Somali Government for a small committee to spend ten days in their country, meeting the Fisheries Minister and others to look at the problems they had.

The Somalian delegates to Lomé had always been friends, and they often reminded me of Italians in appearance and animated style. On arriving in Mogadishu, the Somali capital on the southern coast, I was delighted by the architecture, which was a lovely mix of Arab and Italian. The people were mostly very slim and rather beautiful. Most spoke Italian and Arabic and many also spoke English.

On my first evening I was given a tour of the city and saw the old fort, the many tree-lined streets, the main school, the Ministry of Animal

Welfare and the Ministry of Finance, the Sports Complex, the technical college and the university.

The country is bounded to the north by Djibouti, to the west by Ethiopia and to the south by Kenya and has a coastline of almost 200 miles. Outside the cities, which were very westernised, the majority of Somalians lived a nomadic life. Many Somalis had emigrated in recent years but the place seemed happy at first sight (though there was much trouble ahead) and its 7.5 million people were served by a very diverse Parliament of 170 members. The country had secured a form of democracy at that time, and the vote was available to all those over 18.

My first meeting was with the Fisheries Minister and the Harbour master of Mogadishu. They told me that the huge waves and strong currents on the west coast created problems for fishermen, but on the Indian Ocean side there were more favourable conditions. The minister told me that Somalia never traded with Saudi Arabia despite its proximity and that most of its aid came from the Eastern bloc. However, there was a strong desire in the present government to change this situation and to actively seek trade and aid elsewhere, particularly from the EEC.

This changing policy was obvious as one noticed the influx of Western banks and hotels, and the country was attracting back assistance and investment from its former colonial powers – Italy in the north and Britain in the south. The north and south had finally joined together on 1 July 1960 and now the united nation was trying to make up for lost time and lost opportunities. The tension of the Ogaden, the disputed region of south-east Ethiopia which formed part of Italian East Africa and was populated mostly by Somali-speaking nomads, continued, although a peace treaty was eventually signed in 1988. However, by then there were even bigger problems for the country, with many warlords gathering to try to influence events and, of course, profit from the people's misery.

A woman government minister, Fodama Omai Hoshi (one of only nine women in the Parliament) was in charge of my programme and her particular concern was the eradication of female circumcision. The UN were assisting with a programme in which volunteers did not just visit villages, but went to live in them in order to educate older women about the obscenity of this practice. This was hard, as most such women not only believed in the tradition, but thought it had religious significance, although it is not mandatory under Islam and indeed is not justified in the Koran. Somalia has been a Muslim country since the twelfth century and such beliefs ran very deep, even if they were wrong. The minister herself had been circumcised but she was adamant that her daughter would never be put through the same suffering.

One day she took me to an orphanage called La Fole which housed 625 children and 152 staff. The place had been started by Italian nuns and some of these had stayed on and were very old, but they were still working there under the supervision of Somali nuns. I could not but notice immediately that almost all the children in the orphanage were female and when I asked about this I learned a strange fact. Very few of the children were actually orphans. Their mothers had taken them to the orphanage and put them under the care of the nuns before they were due to be circumcised and left them there until it was too late, according to their tradition, to do so. It was a practical and personal step to resist female circumcision and it was a very surprising example of the exercise of practical Christianity in the midst of a Muslim country.

I was taken to see various fishing projects including a factory for building simple fibreglass boats. These would not have been able to withstand the open sea, but were a possibility for inshore fishing and they had the great advantage of being easy to make and needing little maintenance. I also saw a project which involved the teaching of navigational skills. These and other projects were helped with aid from the Scandinavian countries, the world leaders in aid then as now, and their assistance was both practical and long-term.

On one of my trips along the coast the car allocated to me broke down in a small village. Soon I was surrounded by a huge crowd of people, but they were very friendly and there was no hint of menace or difficulty. Another car was eventually produced and we drove on to eat in a large hotel where I was to stay. After eating I was also shown to a tent-like structure with matting on the floor, and before I entered my guide took a flaming torch and swept around the edges of the matting. I asked why, and he said only one word: 'Scorpions!'

I was hardly reassured by this but I got ready for bed and, carrying a candle, visited the adjoining bathroom, where I could not but notice, there in the middle of the floor, illuminated by my candle, the largest scorpion I had ever seen. In panic I ran out of the door of my tent but there was total blackness all around and no sign of anyone, least of all my guide. There was, however, a bulky doormat, so I put on my heaviest shoes, grabbed the doormat, and rushed back to the bathroom where I threw the mat over the scorpion and jumped up and down vigorously for ages. Then I ran to the bed, with my shoes still on, and covered myself up totally.

Later I was taken to see a hospital where visiting Italian surgeons were carrying out operations. Each of them had volunteered a week each year, free of charge, to help, but although I was invited into the theatre to watch an eye operation, I quickly backed out when it started. The surgeons themselves were enthusiastic but very realistic; one laughingly explained to me that in these circumstances there was no way that any operating theatre could be kept sterile or free of germs, but that they just had to live with the situation.

My trip was a wonderful experience and I learnt a great deal, particularly about fishing and about the prospects for developing a sustainable fishing industry in countries such as Somalia, which had great potential. I had also visited the People's Assembly, been received by the Speaker, Mohammed Ibrahim, lunched at the British Embassy and met some Scots expatriates. I had particularly profited from discussions with the fishing expert at the British Embassy, Adrian Sandies, and after those discussions I spent some of my last few days in Somalia finalising my fishing report for the Lomé Assembly, which was about to meet in Brazzaville, to where I was to fly via Addis Ababa.

At the Lomé Assembly, and at meetings, we all sat in strict alphabetical order, Lomé MEPs by surname and representatives from the Lomé states by country. Ewing was always next to Ethiopia and that meant that I had come to know well the Ethiopian delegate, His Excellency Dr G. Berhan. He had remained in post for many years, despite the huge upheavals in his country, for although related to the Ethiopian royal family, who had been brutally deposed by a communist regime, his diplomatic skills were of such a high order that he was retained by the new government. He had always urged me to visit and when he knew that I was coming he arranged for me to be met by car and provided a programme for my overnight stay. This programme included discussions with representatives of the communist regime, followed by a dinner given by one of Colonel Mengistu's ministers, who had also invited diplomatic representatives from the UK, Germany, Italy, Belgium and Spain. The UK attaché spent the meal looking very worried and perplexed. He clearly could not work out what his proper response was to a sole Scottish Nationalist being given such red-carpet treatment, but he was too diplomatic to say anything directly to me.

The visit was far too short but I have never forgotten it. In my formal discussions we talked of the country's unused lake resources which might enable a fishery to be developed, and we considered possible agriculture projects. I was also taken to what was claimed to be Africa's largest market.

It is said that Ethiopia is the oldest country in Africa and one of the oldest in the world. Certainly it contains some of the oldest human remains ever found and has been inhabited longer than almost anywhere else. Tradition has it that the first emperor, Menelik I, was the son of the Queen of Sheba and King Solomon of Israel, but whatever the truth is the emperors reigned for 2,000 years until Mengistu's communist regime took over by force in 1974, killing Haile Selassie and many others.

Haile Selassie had been a moderniser and had caught the imagination of the world with his dignified but determined stance before, during and after the Italian invasion. He was restored to power with the help of the British in 1941 and continued his programme of road-building and progressive change, but the people were impatient and the Mengistu regime, although brutal, was supported by many who saw the old ways as being contrary to the benefit of the majority of the people. However, Mengistu's close relationship with the Soviet Union and his repressive methods alienated his support and eventually he was himself overthrown.

I wish I could have stayed for far longer, as a single day gave just a tantalising glimpse of the place, and in particular a glimpse of the elegant and beautiful Ethiopian women, who are famed throughout Africa. But I had to move on to the Congo to attend the Assembly.

Many years later, the memory of that one night in Addis Ababa was jogged by a chance encounter. I was often invited by the Presiding Officer of the Scottish Parliament, David Steel, to assist him with meeting and talking to the foreign consuls in Edinburgh. At one reception an elderly representative of the Spanish Consulate came up to me and asked me if I remembered where I had met him before. I did not, and he then told me that he had been present at the dinner in Addis Ababa given by the Mengistu Government in my honour. Both of us had travelled long and far since that night, but it was a great reminder of how the world can sometimes seem a small place.

Brazzaville was a very lively place – a humming city of over two million people in a French-speaking country which had become independent in 1960. It was and is very rich in minerals and capable of strong agriculture, and it has the benefit of a good port at Pointe-Noire. The Congo River is the fifth longest in the world and it was of course Stanley, who rescued Livingstone, who first traced the river from source to ocean, a journey of almost 3,000 miles.

The Assembly was productive. I was given the opportunity to report on my visit to Somalia and was also delighted to get the fisheries report through and approved unanimously. I was also able to formally thank my Ethiopian host, and neighbour.

Barbara Castle, however, was back on her crusade against Lomé and turned up for the Assembly. When we sallied forth to the first reception I walked into the room, only to see her wearing exactly the same red chiffon dress with a pattern of white marguerites as me! I had bought it from a very posh dress shop in Aberdeen; it had cost me £75 and I was more than prepared to laugh the matter off as a funny coincidence. Barbara, however, was not. When she saw me she charged across the room and said in a peremptory tone, 'You will have to go and change.' I simply replied, 'Barbara, let's just get two glasses of wine and a photographer, who can take a shot of us clinking our glasses and toasting our excellent taste.' But she would have none of it, and after giving me another dirty look she flounced out of the reception, returning some time later wearing a different dress!

I was somewhat distracted during the Assembly because I had accepted an invitation to go on from the Congo to Zaire (formerly the Belgian Congo) to see some EEC projects there. The delegation was to include a German Liberal, a Belgian Socialist, Maryiasa van Hemmeldonk, and another Belgian, the Major of Bruges, Mr Van der Viele, a Christian Democrat. However Van Hemmeldonk had been active in the Belgian press, criticising the Government of Zaire, and Van der Viele was unacceptable to the Zaire government for another reason, so I had to become leader of the delegation, something I had not done before. The Belgians had a poor reputation in Zaire and it was little wonder, given that they had been the most brutal of colonialists in that country.

While Zaire was interesting, and the projects clearly much needed, I did not enjoy the visit as much as my single night in Ethiopia nor my time amongst the immensely friendly people of Somalia. Nonetheless I was glad I had gone and seen even more of Africa.

During all these visits I was touched and impressed by the interest that was always shown in Scotland and in our cause, even though by comparison we had so much more than many of those we met. In a sense what I was doing was not simply working for the citizens of Europe in extending the hand of friendship and co-operation with the ACP nations. I was also trying to ensure that when Scotland was further on in the process of becoming independent and when our case was before the United Nations, then there would be enough hands going up for us in support, and that those hands would come from countries which had heard personally about our situation and who knew us to be fair-minded people, keen to play a part in the wider world and take our place round the UN table between Saudi Arabia and Senegal.

On 2 November 1967 at Hamilton, I had said, 'Stop the world, Scotland wants to get on,' and throughout the years I was involved with Lomé I remained very determined that on the day when the people of Scotland finally stood up for themselves at home it could not be said that the international community of nations had been left unprepared for our arrival. I could not hope to visit every state nor meet every government, but, through Lomé, I was able to put our case forward wherever I could go and be heard.

To begin with the Lomé Assembly and all other meetings were held in Luxembourg but other states also wanted to host such events, so we started to go to Rome and Berlin. Another impetus for this change of venue was the institutional racism that was still present in parts of an otherwise very civilised Europe. During my first Lomé Assembly in Luxembourg I noticed an example of this in the members' bar of the new Parliament building when I went up to order drinks for three friends one evening. There were two black men in front of me, but the barman was ignoring them and quickly turned to me. I insisted he served them first, which he did with bad grace. Later I spoke to other ACP delegates and they, reluctantly at first, began to tell me of incidents of discrimination which they had suffered in Luxembourg. Clearly this was absolutely unacceptable and the best way we could show this was by moving the venue of our meetings.

Once the Assembly had started to meet elsewhere I decided I would try to get it to come to Scotland, in particular to my own constituency. This idea was I met with huge enthusiasm and total cooperation from everyone I approached – the Highland Council, Inverness District Council, the Highlands and Islands Development Board, the local Tourist Board, the Inverness Chamber of Commerce, the craft associations and even An Comunn Gaidhealach. So, after deliberating on our plans, we got together to send a formal invitation for the Assembly to meet in Inverness. The invitation was enthusiastically welcomed by many, including the Tory Group, but not by Labour. Janey Buchan said that there were not enough hotels in Inverness, whilst others argued behind the scenes that there were not enough brothels! I knew that I was quite unable to deal with the second point, but that the first was simply not true.

The invitation was first made in the Congo at the Brazzaville Assembly in February 1984 and I then confirmed it at the Lomé meeting in Berlin in September 1984, when I submitted a formal letter of invitation from the Provost of Inverness. The British Tory Government gave the proposal its full blessing and Lord Gray – formerly Hamish Gray, who had been a member of Parliament for part of Inverness until 1982 – wrote a strongly supportive letter which was backed up by a telex from Malcolm Rifkind, then a minister in the Foreign Office.

As the time for decision came closer Inverness District Council put in a power of work, providing the Lomé staff with full details of hotels and their costs as well as negotiating special deals and arranging cut-price air fares on Dan Air flights from London. The proposals for hospitality were lavish and included lunches, receptions and a cruise on Loch Ness. The Eden Court Theatre, one of the best conference venues in Scotland, was offered free of charge and a detailed programme for spouses and guests was put forward.

The decision was set to be made at the Burundi meeting. On the first morning of the meeting Inverness and Luxembourg were the only two venues which had delivered formal invitations, but then at the very last minute a telex arrived from the Greek government offering to host the Assembly in Athens in September 1985, although they gave no details of hotels or hospitality and only the sketchiest information about the proposed venue or, indeed, anything else.

On the Thursday of the Burundi meeting I put my case for Inverness, Colette Flesch did the same for Luxembourg and a new member put forward the Greek case. The initial voting was Inverness 16, Luxembourg 6 and Athens 20. Luxembourg was then eliminated and on the final vote Inverness had 19 and Athens 20. I smelt a very large rat. No warning had been given that the final vote was about to take place and consequently many members who would have voted for Inverness were missing. These included the Scottish Labour MEP David Martin and my own group leader M. de la Malene. Their votes certainly would have been enough to have swung the vote but I was also assured by the Commonwealth ACP members that they wished to see the meeting in Scotland as did the Francophile group.

Then it emerged that the Greek MEP who had made the proposal was offering as the venue a conference centre outside Athens which her husband managed. In addition it became open knowledge that the Socialist group had favoured Athens solely because many of their members wished to assist in the forthcoming Greek Parliamentary elections. The ACP representatives to Lomé were not enamoured of the Greeks in any case. Greece had shown very little interest in Lomé and since Greece became an EEC member its delegates had virtually never attended any ACP meetings.

I returned to the fray. I told delegates that the District Council in Inverness had already booked the Conference Centre and had block-booked four large hotels. These bookings could not be held open indefinitely and I appealed to the bureau of the Assembly to overrule what had been an advisory vote, very narrowly carried in suspicious circumstances. My argument won the day, and Inverness was confirmed by the bureau as the location for the September 1985 meeting.

Now it was full speed ahead to finalise the arrangements. Lady Ellis, the Vice President of the Tory Group, gave me some very good advice when she suggested I ask Princess Anne to open the Assembly. I wrote to the princess and her office asked me to send a full note on Lomé, which I did. She quickly accepted the invitation and this did a great deal to enhance the interest in the convention from Europe and from the ACP delegates. Her aides explained to me that the princess always wrote her own speeches and she duly did so for Lomé, making an address that was much commented on and very favourably received. After the opening ceremony she asked me, 'Have I steered myself through the mountain of difficulties?' and I was able to assure her that she had.

I was determined that the Assembly would be well covered in the press, so I made an appointment to see Robert Maxwell, whom I had known in the House of Commons. I put to him the absolute necessity of getting appropriate publicity for this great international occasion which would bring half the world to Scotland and which was the only occasion that Lomé had ever been invited to meet in the UK (a situation that remains). He was very sympathetic and promised me good coverage in the *Daily Record*. He was as good as his word and the paper allocated a top reporter and a top photographer and made sure that we had front-page coverage on each day of the Assembly. Although many other journalists were annoyed by this special treatment, it provoked a certain competitiveness which enhanced the event!

Donnie Stewart and Gordon Wilson lodged a Commons Early Day Motion welcoming the convention to Inverness and I arranged for a video about Lomé to be sent to all secondary schools in the area, which resulted in not only much educational activity but also in the presence of hoards of young autograph hunters outside the conference itself. When I later was in Malawi a government minister told me a wee boy had asked him, autograph book clutched in hand, 'Where are you from mister?' When he replied, 'I'm from Malawi,' the boy said, 'Sorry, got you already!'

The opening of the convention was magnificent. Eden Court by the river looked at its very best, with the flags of half the world flying and a piper to welcome all the delegates. The top table was sparkling with dignitaries, including the Secretary of State for Scotland and Highland chiefs. On the first evening there was a reception in the beautiful and historic Town House of Inverness. Princess Anne asked if I could get some delegates in a circle, one from each state, so that she could speak to all of them. She did so and stayed very late. We were then piped across the road and on to the Caledonian Hotel, where the first course at the convention dinner was haggis. I explained that those present should each pour a small whisky, as supplied, over the haggis and they took my advice with delight.

Of course many of the ACP delegates had had happy associations with Scotland through the Scottish teachers, engineers, ministers and missionaries whom they had met in their own countries. Now they were seeing the land from which these people had sprung and appreciating the hospitality and traditions of the place. They were usually enchanted.

The hospitality was indeed lavish during the entire convention. George Younger, the Tory Secretary of State, had said to me long before the event that whilst he welcomed the Convention coming to Scotland, he was not prepared to spend a penny on it, and that included money on hospitality. 'Not a penny,' he emphasised and I replied to him, with some resentment, 'Don't worry, Highland hospitality doesn't need your penny.' However, by the time the plans were being finalised he decided that after all he wanted to host a reception, so we had to find a slot. At his event the whisky ran out before all the delegates had arrived and the always witty interpreters started to refer to it as the 'bring your own crisp party'!

On the second day the EEC states entertained all the delegates and on the Wednesday night the Highland Council hosted a dinner at Cawdor Castle. I had rarely seen our African delegates so excited and so inspired by anything, for they had all read Shakespeare's *Macbeth* at school and that evening they were given the run of the castle by Lord Cawdor himself. Of course my European colleagues had been just the same when they visited the place. The Highland Council laid on a pipe band, dancers and the Inverness Fiddlers, and my dear friend Sean Flanagan played amongst them again. That night I was very proud to be the member for the Highlands and Islands and to have been able to bring so many people to see our rich culture.

On the Thursday evening the Sheriff Principal invited all the attending lawyers to a reception in the Castle. He met the Lomé state's lawyers and that was also a popular and worthwhile occasion. Afterwards there was a ceilidh hosted by one of the European Commissioners which featured a choir and singers. After they had performed, the delegates were invited to sing and a lovely Kenyan woman stepped forward. Her country's ambassador to Lomé was married to a Scot, and she knew – and, to our delight, sang for us – 'The Skye Boat Song'. A French delegate – later the Speaker of Djibouti – said in rapture, 'C'est une culture a part.'

After a hard week of discussions as well as much partying, the Friday was given over to a cruise on Loch Ness. But I did not go, for just as the Lomé preparations were coming to fruition Donald Barr's lovely young wife died of cancer. It had been diagnosed whilst she was pregnant and the baby had been born early – three months early in fact – and she died on the very day she was due to give birth. It was a terrible tragedy and the funeral was exceptionally moving. Donald, as a musician, had arranged for French, Gaelic and Scots songs to be sung. Donald said to me as we left the funeral, 'You shouldn't be here,' for he was always very thoughtful and kind and he was constantly in touch with what was happening. But I said immediately to him, 'Yes, today this is exactly where I should be.'

For many years afterwards the Inverness Assembly was talked of as the best Assembly ever. It was also a historic event for we managed to get through both houses of the Assembly (the ACP and EEC delegates) the final and firm end of any equivocation about the matter of South Africa and apartheid. This quickly became known as the Declaration of Inverness.

I think the Inverness convention was one of the best things that I was able to achieve both for Lomé and for the Highlands and Islands. It brought not only much revenue to the city, but also an international recognition, and it allowed delegates to learn something of Scotland and appreciate our position. In the struggle to get Objective One funding it undoubtedly helped with MEPs. It also did a great deal for the cause of Scotland and her freedom and it helped the SNP to look outwards.

During my years as a Lomé delegate I visited many other places as well. In 1981 I was in Sierra Leone, and of course I visited other African states as well. I remember particularly fondly, though, my visit in 1983 to the West Indies and Jamaica, perhaps because it also led to a family connection with that island.

The 1983 trip started with a visit to Barbados. The EEC representative on the island was John Broadhurst, and I became very friendly with him and his wife, a friendship that continued for many years. We were taken to meet many people with Scottish and European connections, not least the British High Commissioner, who was Viscount Dunrossil, the Chief of the

Clan Morrison, and who, because he had a house in North Uist, was technically a constituent of mine. Scottish connections also extended to place names – there was a district called St Andrew – and of course to the history of the island.

We called on the Governor General on the first day of our visit and then went into a long series of meetings with ministers and officials, culminating in lunch with the Deputy Prime Minister at the aptly named Paradise Beach Hotel. The Speaker of the Parliament hosted a reception at the official residence of the Prime Minister. We were all very impressed with the vigorous nature of democracy on the island, which had a completely free press with two competing newspapers.

Barbados is one of earth's paradises – indeed sometimes it seems too good to be true. It is peaceful, non-racial, reasonably prosperous and enormously beautiful. The islanders are religious but not extreme and they drink rum in moderation. Educational standards are high, though those that are educated tend to leave for at least part of their career, and there was some resentment about the fact that an island originally of slaves was becoming an island where one had to leave in order to succeed.

Barbados had a high economic dependence on the sugar industry, particularly since the collapse of the cotton industry, and there was also some commercial fishing, though at that time not enough to can and export. Water was scarcer than one would want and with limited underground supplies this matter caused some concern for the future, particularly with regard to the plans for developing tourism. It was also building a successful place in the world as an offshore financial centre.

We had only two days on the island before we had to depart for Dominica, but we did manage to visit a sugar factory and to see something of the countryside as well as some EEC-aided projects. Our time in Dominica was even shorter, but again we saw a couple of projects and we were entertained by the Prime Minister, Eugenia Charles, who was famous for cutting a dash at international events. Fascinating and engaging as Eugenia Charles was, it was her brother, Basil, that I mostly remember from the visit, for I had one of the most enlightening conversations of my life with him. He was a doctor (trained at Edinburgh University) and the then head of the UN leprosy programme, and he was home on holiday when we visited.

In my travels I have always been particularly interested in the medical and social issue of leprosy – perhaps because I remember reading about it in the Bible as a child – and I have visited a number of leper colonies. The people working in them have always struck me as being extraordinarily dedicated, and one of the teachers I saw in such a colony was a Scotsman who had devoted his life to helping lepers.

Dr Basil Charles however, opened my eyes to the issue. He assured me that leprosy was totally curable if drugs were available at the outset and that those who were in leper colonies were those whom the system had failed to help in time. Indeed, he said that the disease was so curable that he would rather catch a dose of leprosy than a dose of the flu! The thing both he and the world community had to achieve was to make drugs and advice available everywhere. He singled out the Indian Government for praise. They had a fine programme, but one of the problems that was hardest to overcome in India was the tradition of begging and the deliberate policy of some either to allow their relatives to become de-formed by the disease and earn money that way, or to accept the disease themselves with a sense of fatality and do the same.

It was a very happy and yet very sad conversation. It was wonderful that so much could be done so easily, yet it was tragic that we did not yet live in a world where enough was being done.

Dominica had been a victim of a disastrous earthquake and many thousands of its people had been forced to leave. The government knew they needed to promote the island's economic and infrastructure as well as obtain competitive advantages, although they had received help from the US Peace Corps, which had done an excellent job.

Given the volatile nature of the landmass, the opportunities for devel-oping geo-thermal energy were considerable, but the biggest potential seemed to lie, once again, in fisheries, and there was an EEC-supported scheme to breed prawns as a commercial fish farming venture, which we saw during our visit.

We went on for a brief visit to Antigua, but we were soon on our way to Jamaica, which was to be the main focus of our tour.

Jamaica seemed a happy island, though there were underlying social tensions. Its economy was reasonably healthy and it had a good trade in bauxite, from which aluminium is made. The coffee industry was dependent upon cyclical world prices and although the island used to export 180,000 tonnes of bananas a year, there was considerable worry that the quantity had now dropped to 30,000 tonnes. There was now some diversification into other forms of agriculture, such as winter vegetables, but the sugar cane plantations were not flourishing and the Jamaican government was annoyed that in the vital rum trade it appeared as if French Guadeloupe was being favoured by the EEC in quota allocation.

The Jamaican government and those we met had some strong views on Lomé. They were supportive on the whole but they felt that they had specific product arguments that were not being heard, particularly those surrounding sugar and rum. They were backed up in these views by many of the commercial representatives we met, including a Scotsman from the old sugar company of Tate and Lyle, which had started in Greenock and which, at that time, still employed about 250,000 people world-wide. The general quota system operated by the EEC came in for much criticism. We noted what was said and agreed that it should be discussed within Lomé and within Europe.

We visited a banana plantation, met Foreign office representatives, representatives of the National Planning Authority and the Sugar Industry Authority and saw at first hand the difficulties they had. These visits backed up the overall message very effectively.

The delegation and guests spent a morning at the University of the West Indies in Kingston. We were met and guided round by the Pro Vice Chancellor, Professor Lalor, and taken to lunch with the Vice Chancellor, Professor Preston. The campus was a wonderful space for learning, beautifully landscaped and staffed by lecturers from many parts of the world. As I walked around an idea came to me, and towards the end of the visit I told Professor Lalor about my son Terry and the fact that he had so far failed in his applications to study at Scottish universities. I wondered if they took paying students for a year or so in preparation for elsewhere and he was very warm about the prospect as they encouraged overseas students.

Thus it was that Terry came to study in Kingston for a year. He found the prospect exciting and Stewart and I made arrangements to transfer enough money for fees and maintenance to a bank in Kingston which he could draw on. However, when he went to register on the first day he was told that he would only have to pay one third of the advertised fees, as he was an overseas student! This was at the same time as Margaret Thatcher was tripling the cost of studying at British universities for overseas students, freezing out thousands who wanted to come here and vastly reducing the subsequent influence in the world that such students provide.

Terry studied hard and passed his first-year examinations set by the University of London and when he returned to Scotland the presence of Kingston and the University of the West Indies on his CV eased his way into the Scottish university system. The venture was a great success and he enjoyed it enormously. However, it was not without some difficulties. During the year there were outbreaks of violent trouble in Kingston and Terry and his companions (many from families of US businessmen on the island) were advised by the principal not to go into the city. After a while he said he began to feel like a prisoner, no matter how lovely his surroundings. His perspective on the world changed, for in reading the local press and listening and watching the local media he claimed later that he began to realise that the very self-important UK was not the centre of everyone's attention and not even of much interest to many.

My experiences as a member of Lomé could fill a whole book and it has been hard to know what to include and what to leave out. For a number of years I was not only commuting virtually every week between the Highlands and Islands and Europe, but I was also travelling frequently all over the world and being received as an honoured guest, meeting those who took on the awesome responsibility of ruling and improving their own nations. It give me an entirely new perspective and a much deeper understanding of the many problems and possibilities that exist in every nation which need to be met with energy, enthusiasm, vision and determination. I saw nothing that failed to convince me that Scotland was more than capable of applying the same if its people were allowed to become not just nationalist, but truly internationalist in their politics. And I saw nothing that did not make me think that we could play a very full part in the world again if we were permitted to do so – moreover a part which would be welcomed by the vast majority of other states.

Even when I ceased to be a Lomé member I would often met the ACP and other delegates and hear what was happening in their countries. I also continued to take up international issues in the Parliament chamber.

One of the things I continue to miss about the European Parliament is the wider perspective and that immensely diverse group of people from all continents whom I met frequently. But the challenge of returning home to Scotland's first democratically elected parliament was one that I could not resist. I was eager to contest the first election and get on with what I knew would be my last political job.

14

'The Scottish Parliament is Hereby Reconvened'

M Y DECISION TO stand for election to the Scottish Parliament had been welcomed in Scotland and by the party in principle, but now I had to find a seat to fight, or list to get on to.

The party had originally decided that individuals could not stand only on a list; they would have to contest a constituency as well. I was quickly offered the constituency of Argyll and Bute, and also that of Caithness and Sutherland. I loved both areas and had travelled them extensively in the twenty years I had represented them in the European Parliament, but therein lay the problem: I did not wish to have to choose between them.

My position was sympathetically understood by most, but Gerry Fisher, a great prop and comfort to me in my days as the Hamilton MP, when he lived in London, was now the self-appointed guardian of the SNP constitution and all its procedures, and he spoke against the proposal at our National Council. I responded by arguing that I was not opening the floodgates to a whole new category of candidate, but that I was simply in a unique position which would not be replicated in the future as the European constituencies were being abolished in favour of a national list.

The party sided with me and it was made permissible to stand on the list alone, a situation that benefited two other of our first thirty-five MSPs – Bruce Crawford and Fiona Hyslop. However, no SNP candidate in the second election in 2003 won in the same way.

Standing for a Scottish Parliament was the culmination of all I had worked for over the years. The run-up to the election was hectic. During 1998 we had led the opinion polls but as the year turned our lead was being chipped away. Some key issues still had to be dealt with, not least that of taxation, and the party's brave decision at its Special Election Conference in Aberdeen to reject tax cuts in favour of public services was mercilessly misrepresented by Labour and its many sycophantic allies in the press.

Then came the Kosovo war. Alex Salmond's broadcast – in fact a reply to the Prime Minister's statement, the first time that the party had ever been granted such an opportunity – was spoken from the heart. Many, many Scots and others furth of Scotland agreed with him but Alex's choice of language (no doubt because of his strong feelings) alienated some. Again this was viciously spun against the party by the usual Labour suspects, with George Robertson and Robin Cook in particular taking a stance that was hypocritical and which they knew was dishonest. At least Robin Cook came to his senses when the Iraq war loomed and put principle before position.

I was particularly angry at the way in which Alex was treated, and Stewart and I put together a leaflet called 'What Alex actually said', which I paid to have printed. However, when I offered it to the party, they refused to allow it to be used widely, instead decreeing that it could only be handed to people who raised the topic first. I disagreed on this and still do.

By the time the formal campaign opened the SNP was behind in the polls and Labour was flinging everything it could. 'Divorce is an expensive business' was Labour's theme and it was presented in stark and dishonest terms. I think I have never fought an election in which the governing party lied so much and tried to spread so much fear in an electorate which should have been encouraged to be positive and hopeful about the future.

As usual in an election campaign I undertook a mammoth amount of travelling, particularly in the Highlands and Islands. I visited all of Moray to campaign not just for myself and the party but also for Margaret, who was seeking the dual mandate, at least for a while, as all our sitting MPs were. I helped Fergus in Inverness, and he confided in me that if he did not win, he thought that he would no longer attempt to gain a seat either at Holyrood or at Westminster and instead devote himself to his legal practice: a sentiment I recognised from my own feelings after Hamilton. This was Fergus' third attempt to take Inverness and I am strongly of the opinion that three attempts are the most a candidate should make in any one place.

I took part in a major rally in Edinburgh along with Sean Connery at a time when the party seemed to be falling even further behind in the polls, and when it was vital to retain confidence and to carry on putting out a message of hope to counteract the very negative propaganda that was coming from Labour and from the Tories. Sensibly the party's campaign was flexible enough to recognise that some unconventional tactics were required, and in the last ten days there was a new energy in it which swung votes back towards us. I was most heartened during this time to see the roadsides in the Highlands covered in SNP posters.

The election count was nail-biting. As the candidate at the top of the Highlands and Island List I was reasonably sure of being elected, but the big questions for me were whether Fergus would win at last and how many others would join me on the list. Fergus did win – and he richly deserved to. Margaret, of course, retained Moray and Duncan Hamilton, the candidate in Argyll, who was second on the list, was also returned. Alasdair Nicholson in the Western Isles did very well too, and all in all our vote in the Highlands and Islands reflected our increasing strength. Jim Mather was unlucky not to make it as the third list member, but I was sure that he would be in at the next election.

Nationally we also secured some important gains now that proportional representation was in place. Our thirty-five members included all six of our Westminster MPs along with George Reid – back in a Parliament after twenty years – Margo MacDonald in Lothian (she who had last been elected in November 1973), Michael Russell, the party's Chief Executive, the very able young star, Nicola Sturgeon, who won in Glasgow, and a range of others. We had both the youngest member (Duncan Hamilton) and the oldest (myself). We had secured the election of more SNP women than ever before to a Parliament which would have the second highest proportion of women members in the world.

Although we had not won we were the second largest party and would be the official opposition – which was a huge step forward from the early 1960s when we had had no MPs at Westminster at all. Once again it looked as if we were on our way forward for in one night we had elected more SNP members to a Parliament than we had in our entire previous history.

I had been preparing to go to Edinburgh for some time. Due to Stewart's skill and perseverance with his stock market investments I was able to purchase a flat and some months before the election I signed a piece of paper for a property in the Dublin Street Colonies, although it was not even built at that stage and I was the first purchaser in the scheme. Eventually it took shape, along with its small garden and tiny parking place and I was able to move in in the autumn. It was wonderful to have somewhere to go home to after a day of parliamentary engagements and also to have somewhere to entertain and to invite my friends to share my experience of the new Scottish Parliament.

Before the Parliament formally met, the SNP group got together and elected its officers. Margaret was unanimously elected as Group Chair, with Alex of course as Leader and John Swinney as Deputy Leader. Bruce Crawford was nominated by Alex as Chief Whip, a post that has to be confirmed by the group, but he was agreed to. Alex then started to form his Shadow Cabinet, selecting Michael Russell to take on the vital negotiating post of Parliamentary Business Manager, which would be crucial in the early days. Fergus was given responsibility for rural affairs.

All the new members met to take the oath on 12 May 1999, some six days after the election. The clerks of the Parliament had been very keen to find out the date of birth of each member so that the oldest (in accordance with the Scotland Act) could be asked to take the chair at the first meeting before members had signed up and elected their own Presiding Officer. By very good fortune I was three months older than John Young, a former Glasgow Bailie who had been on Glasgow Council with Stewart.

It was a wonderful thing for me to have the opportunity to open our new Parliament. I was the first member to take the oath, which I took in Gaelic, and then I took the Chair while all the other members were sworn in. Alex Salmond spoke for all the SNP members when he formally objected to the wording of the oath, imposed by Westminster, and indicated that the SNP recognised the sovereignty of the people, not the sovereignty of the crown, a position that is clearly backed by Scottish constitutional law.

All the SNP members were wearing the white rose of Scotland, which brought to mind the poem by Hugh MacDiarmid:

> The rose of all the world is not for me
> I want for my part
> Only the little white rose of Scotland
> That's sharp and sweet and breaks the heart.

Indeed the sight of our Parliament reconvening was so sharp and sweet that it did touch the heart. The galleries were full with friends, relatives and onlookers. Fergus discovered, unsung and unnoticed amongst them, William McDougall, the last of the Seven Men of Knoydart, whom he took to be introduced to most of the other MSPs.

There were also moments of pure joy, such as when Susan Deacon's little girl Clare, aged twenty-one months, shouted out from the gallery at the sight of her mother below. I must admit that I had tears in my eyes then, and when Margaret, now MSP for Moray, came down the left corridor into the well of the chamber to take the oath and Fergus, now MSP for Inverness East, Nairn and Lochaber, simultaneously came down the right one. They took their oaths together and I was very proud and very happy to watch them from the chair of the Parliament and to know that we were all being watched by Stewart, Terry and Annabelle in the public gallery.

My whole family was therefore present when – all members having been sworn in – I made my speech. I had promised Robert McIntyre years earlier that if I ever got the chance to be in a Scottish Parliament I would draw attention to the fact that it was never abolished, but only adjourned, and now I had the chance to honour that commitment.

I shall quote my speech on that May morning in Edinburgh almost in full, because I think it is probably the most important and historic speech I have ever made:

> I have the opportunity now to make a short speech and I want to begin with the words that I have always wanted either to say or to hear someone else to say: the Scottish Parliament, which adjourned on 25 March 1707, is hereby reconvened.
>
> I could not say those words until all members had been sworn and the Parliament really had been convened.
>
> This is an historic day and, after a long time in politics, I am aware that we owe a debt to many who are not here and who did not live to see the promised land. I would like to mention a few people from across the parties: Arthur Donaldson, Robert McIntyre, Alick Buchanan-Smith, Johnny Bannerman, Emrys Hughes, John Mackintosh and John Smith – today is the fifth anniversary of his death. I would also like to mention my colleague Allan

Macartney, who so nearly lived to see the day. There are many others, but I have been able to mention only the people who have been my friends. Many people are named in the history books; many are not, but all of them have made this moment in history possible. I give my thanks to every one of them.

As everyone knows, I have been a member of two Parliaments. I spent eight years in the House of Commons and I have spent twenty-three in the European Parliament – which does not sound so long if it is said quickly. Until July, I will be the mother of the European Parliament. I hasten to add that I am not the oldest member of that Parliament, although I am the oldest one here, which is very disconcerting – I think they must have made a mistake on my birth certificate!

I have several practical and sincere hopes for the Parliament. The first is that we try to follow the more consensual style of the European Parliament and say goodbye to the badgering and backbiting that one associates with Westminster.

Secondly, in the House of Commons, I found there was a Speaker's tradition of being fair to minorities. I am an expert in being a minority – I was alone in the House of Commons for three years and alone in the European Parliament for nineteen – but we are all minorities now, and I hope that the Presiding Officer, whoever that may be, will be fair to each and every one of us.

My next hope is that this Parliament, by its mere existence, will create better relations with England, Wales and Northern Ireland, and I believe that wish to be in the hearts of the peoples of all of those countries.

My last hope is that everyone who was born in Scotland, some of whom, like me, could not help it, and everyone who chose Scotland as their country, will live in harmony together, enjoying our cultures but remaining loyal to their own.

The speech got tremendous applause throughout, particularly when I formally reconvened our gathering after 292 years, and although commentator Iain MacWhirter described me afterwards as one of 'the greatest ham actors of Scottish politics', I have been called worse. Ruth Wishart put it better, perhaps, when she wrote of my speech: 'If she never says another word she has said enough.'

The Scotsman used my opening words as their banner headline the day afterwards, for they seemed to strike a chord everywhere and the press coverage was enormous with pictures and quotes sent round the world. Kirsty Scott of *The Herald* put the atmosphere of that day very well when she wrote: 'This was the day for buttonholes and broad smiles and first-day nerves and proud relations. No crowds no pomp no fuss – that can wait for July. But there was a great sense of purpose, existence even. This was a day the capital and the country could lay a hand on its political heart and find it beating.'

After the ceremony Duncan Hamilton presented me with a bouquet of white Scottish roses on behalf of the SNP group and then I went to lunch with my family along with Fergus' agent, Norman Will, and his wife. Then it was back to the chamber for the election of the Presiding Officer, at which point I demitted the Chair. George Reid was nominated but Labour were determined not to have a Nationalist, so they gathered behind David Steel, who had been Liberal leader and was now a peer. He was duly elected but George became one of the Deputy Presiding Officers, along with Labour's Patricia Ferguson. At the end of a long and highly significant day in Scottish history we finished by having our photograph taken by the talented Scottish photographer Robin Gillanders, who in homage to the great early photographic image of the General Assembly mimicked the same type of composition to show the 129 new members setting off on an equally vital journey in service of their native land.

The period between our oath-taking and the formal opening of the Parliament was a busy one, but it was also somewhat messy. The euphoria stayed with us for a few weeks, though, as we took up our new positions. Apart from the Leader, Deputy Leader, Whip and Business Manager, who had seats they nearly always occupied, the rest of us could sit where we pleased within our own allocated area. My step was light and my spirits were high and I encouraged our members to start vigorously on the task of proving that we had the talent to be a Government. That would mean speaking and asking questions as well as working out in the country.

As Party President I was allocated my own office, and Margaret, as Group Chair had one to herself too, as did the leader. But apart from these most members had to share not just with their staff, but also with other MSPs and their staff. As members began to recruit their assistants there developed some serious overcrowding and the noise on the second floor of PHQ, as the office building on George IV Bridge quickly became known, was sometimes overwhelming.

Labour, however, was not prepared to allow the Parliament to settle in by ensuring that those administrative matters which could have been agreed amicably were done in that way. Jack McConnell, as Finance Minister, for example, was obstructive and unhelpful about members' allowances. There was also devious double-dealing about the allocation of the so-called 'Short money' (named after Labour's Ted Short who had introduced funding to assist opposition parties at Westminster when he was Leader of the House), which resulted in the Liberals being allocated funds though they were in government, and the amount promised to the SNP and Tories was halved without consultation. There was also a refusal to offer special support and assistance to the Leader of the Opposition, though such assistance was normal in every other Parliament in the Commonwealth and in Europe.

Other issues soon soured the public mood and were taken up by the press, who were keen to damage the very thing they had just celebrated in case it got above itself! I now wonder whether Labour took this obstructive tack very deliberately, not wanting the Parliament to become well respected, because a well respected devolved Parliament might also be supported if it wished to move on to independence!

Of course one of the main difficulties was that the Parliament had met very quickly after the most bitter election campaign I can remember, and there was still a hangover from that battle in the minds of everyone involved. In addition, the European elections were fought almost as soon as the Parliament had met for the first time. These were also closely contested and although we retained two seats and brought in Professor Neil MacCormick to join Ian Hudghton I was very disappointed that we only just missed getting a third member elected under the new all Scotland list system. Anne Lorne Gillies, who had fought the Western Isles in 1997, was within a few thousand votes of securing a third elected place for the SNP, which would have been tremendous.

Although the Parliament convened in early May it was not formally opened and vested with its powers until 1 July. Labour wanted us all to go away for the summer immediately after, leaving no opportunity to scrutinise or question ministers, but we fought hard for the right to start asking Parliamentary Questions straight away and to have at least one day of formal business, including the first Question Time for the First Minister, before breaking up for the recess. Eventually we got our way.

The first of July dawned showery and somewhat overcast but nothing could dampen the mood of the people of Scotland or their MSPs. It seemed as if half of Scotland was crowding the Royal Mile that morning as we processed from Parliament House down the Mound and into the Church of Scotland Assembly Hall, which was our temporary home. The Queen, the Duke of Edinburgh and Prince Charles were all there and the crown of Scotland, the most precious one in Europe, was taken from Edinburgh Castle and carried in by the Duke of Hamilton.

There were fanfares, specially composed music and readings, including one by my favourite actor, Tom Fleming, who recited a poem by Iain Crichton Smith celebrating the three languages of Scotland. The highlight, however, was Sheena Wellington's singing of 'A Man's a Man', during which she encouraged the MSPs to stand and join in the final verse. It was a sensational moment of unity and plain Scottish speaking which typified the best things of our country. I have to say that the Duke of Edinburgh looked most uncomfortable, particularly at the verse which goes 'A King can mak a belted knight / A marquis, duke, and a' that / But an honest man's aboon his might / Guid faith he mauna fa'that'.

The Queen's speech, which she wrote herself, was gracious, non-patronising and even enthusiastic in parts. The First Minister, Donald Dewar, also rose to the occasion with the best speech I ever heard him deliver and it was non-partisan for a change. Prince Charles, however, somewhat let the side down when he remarked to an SNP MSP about the white rose of Scotland which we were all wearing again, 'How fine to see you support the white rose of York!'

Outside there was a procession by school children from all the different parts of Scotland, carrying brightly coloured banners. I stood with Sean Connery and his wife, Alex and Moira Salmond, Andrew Wilson, Cathleen Russell and many others to watch them all go past and I went out and spoke to the children from the Highlands who led the parade. I then walked up the Mound with Sean to the reception and lunch in the Signet Library. There were huge cheers from the people on the pavements and those who were 'window hinging' in the old Edinburgh tradition. As we made our way up Sean said to me, 'This is the happiest day of my life,' and I must admit that I felt the same way. We had a Parliament again! There was something in the air that day – a sense of optimism and hope which was virtually tangible.

In the evening there was a reception hosted by the Queen at Holyrood Palace. George Reid was taking her round and when they got to me she asked first if I was the doyenne of the Parliament, a question which I was not sure how to answer. She had a glass of wine in both hands, for some reason, and this gave her no doubt a welcome respite from hand-shaking. In our chat she enquired if it was really true that three of my family were in the Parliament, and I confirmed it. She thought this was remarkable, but then thought it was even more remarkable that we almost had four, as my daughter Annabelle had fought the Stirling seat and done well.

Life was sweet as we moved into that first summer recess. Stewart was in good health and we had planned a real holiday, the first we had had for some time. In addition I was surrounded by my clever and happy family and I had a grandchild. I saw my sister and her warm and affectionate family regularly and I was also firmly settled not just in my superb home in Miltonduff but also looking forward to moving in to the New Town and my little flat. To cap it all I was confident that our long-awaited Parliament would come into its own, earn success and dignity and lead Scotland forward.

Alas, there was a cloud on the horizon. Stewart and I had planned to go to Shetland in early August to see the tall ships, which were calling at Lerwick as part of the Tall Ships Race but we had to cancel when my brother David died. He had been ailing for some time and had been in a nursing home in Elgin, but his death was still a shock. He had always been very close to me and had called his first child Winifred after me. He taught me to walk as an infant, and much else besides, after he returned from his appalling experiences in the Japanese POW camp. Neither Jean nor I felt able to speak at his funeral as it would have been too hard. The funeral was very well arranged by David's second wife, Sila, and his step-son delivered the oration in which he recalled David's experiences as a POW, his first marriage and the untimely death of Sarah, his move to Lossiemouth and his second marriage, at which time he became secretary of Moray Golf

Club. He was, as his step-son called him, a gentle man who had done so much good in his life. Despite the torture he had endured as a prisoner of war of the Japanese he had no animosity in him.

Each death of someone close is traumatic. I have lost two brothers and two sisters-in-law who were more like real sisters and, of course, my parents. I suppose that as we grow older we are always likely to experience loss, but it never gets easier, and worse was to happen, though fortunately I did not know so at the time.

I have also lost many dear friends. Janette Jones – a councillor in Kilsyth, a candidate for Westminster and Europe and an SNP Vice Convener – was one of the most loved activists the party has ever had. She had a wise head and a warm heart and she always gave good counsel.

I also felt the loss of my dear, long-standing friend, Ewen Bain. He was a cartoonist of genius and created Angus Og, the Highland Beatnik (as he was originally called) whose adventures gained a huge following. By happy coincidence Ewen was in the same class at school as Stewart and he married my oldest friend, Sheila, whom I had known since my first day at school.

The same month that David died, King Hussein of Jordan also died. I had met him when I was the First Vice President of my Group in Europe and I warmed to him and what he was trying to do in the Middle East. I wrote to his widow telling her of my admiration for him, and had an unexpected and very personal reply.

When the Parliament resumed in September 1999 – with the Edinburgh Festival safely out of the way, for such was the pressure on us in our temporary building that it was deemed impossible for us to sit until the Festival was over – we quickly settled down into the routine of Chamber and Committee work, correspondence and questions, and, of course, activity in our regions and constituencies.

I had asked to be a member of the European Committee and the Whips and Business Manager had agreed and I was very pleased to get the chance to tackle the issues with which I was deeply familiar. However I soon found that the committee, as run by Labour in the person of Hugh Henry, the former leader of the very biased Labour administration on Renfrew Council, was a waste of time. The committee frequently considered legislation as passed by the EU in which we had had no input and which we could not change. Our discussion was largely pointless for what we should have been doing was looking ahead, not backwards. I argued that when a rapporteur was appointed in Europe to draft a proposal that would lead to legislation, we should contact that person and meet them at an early stage to acertain if any report was likely to affect Scotland. In that way we would be contributing positively, not just commenting after the event. I got support in my view from my SNP colleagues, from the Independent MSP Dennis Canavan and from the Tories, but Hugh Henry continued to insist on doing it his way.

I stuck with the committee for a while but I became very disillusioned by it and I eventually asked for a transfer to the Petitions Committee, which, under the convenership of the independently minded Labour MSP John McAllion, was very much more to my taste. The committee was, in great part, the most important survival from the pre-Union Parliament of 1707 in which any individual could approach the legislature with either ideas or complaints. In our modern guise, this meant that groups, associations and electors were able to petition Parliament and they were guaranteed a courteous and reasonably speedy hearing. This approach is common in other European countries but of course it was entirely alien to Westminster, for the so-called 'Mother of Parliaments' is thirled to a notion of sovereignty which is very anti-democratic.

The petitions we received were many and varied and, unfortunately, there was no guarantee of action when we passed them on to the other Parliamentary committees, though some we pushed very hard. By and large the committees of the Parliament did act on them, though, for example in helping to stop three primary schools in Argyll closing, and in deciding upon the proper colour for the saltire.

The committee system of the Parliament is the jewel in its crown. Members of committees usually work across the party divides and listen to ideas. When they were established the Conveners were appointed by the d'Hondt system, so each party got a proportionate share of such positions. Membership was also proportionate and no one party had a majority on any committee, though the Liberals were still far too inclined to prop up Labour when it was in any difficulty. The combination of roles that the committees undertook – standing and select – and their flexibility meant that the Parliament could undertake a heavy programme of legislation almost immediately, which was necessary because Westminster had never been able to give the time to bring Scots law up to date on important matters (such as the long overdue abolition of feudal land tenure) and was far too given to bulky 'Miscellaneous Provisions' Bills which were hard to scrutinise and even harder to change.

Scottish Parliament Committees were much more like European Committees than Westminster ones, but, alas, the format chosen for Ministerial and First Ministerial Questions was so restrictive that it resembled the bad old ways of Westminster rather than the sharper and more challenging Question Times I had seen in Canada and other places. The very rigid formula that was imposed meant that one was hardly ever allowed a second supplementary, and it is only when one gets to this stage that one begins to get answers. Ministers were also permitted to go on far too long, and the period of notice required to question ministers removed any spontaneity and much relevance. The sight of such a dull procedure certainly turned many people off the Scots Parliament in the early days and although the press used to turn up for First Minister's Questions, they were absent for much of the rest of the proceedings and they failed to cover many important debates.

Nonetheless the opening of the Parliament created a great deal of continuing interest as bodies all over Scotland – and furth of it – began to realise that they could now contact their representatives much more easily, have their concerns discussed and make their points. For the first two years this meant that we were faced with invitations almost nightly as group after group and company after company sought to meet MSPs. Our Whip rightly insisted that there was an SNP presence at every event, particularly after word began to spread that most Labour members seemed to shun meeting anyone. We were lobbied in the most open and accountable way and it was good to meet so many people who wanted the Parliament to work.

There were also foreign delegations and visitors galore, and indeed so many came that Alex Salmond (and after him John Swinney) could not cope with the demands and I was often asked to assist. It was a great delight to dine in Edinburgh Castle with Prince William of Orange and with a group of American Senators, to lunch with Indian MPs and to meet on many occasions our vastly increased number of consuls, often accompanied on special tours by their Ambassadors or High Commissioners from London or distinguished politicians from their countries.

Another task I readily performed on behalf of the party was to make sure that congratulations were sent world-wide when they were due. It was a particular pleasure to be able to write to my old friend John Hume when he and David Trimble received the Nobel Peace Prize. I kept in close touch with all my Irish former colleagues – in Fianna Fáil and the SDLP – as well as with my friends in the European Free Alliance and I received many congratulations from them when I was elected. They continued to show a warm interest in Scotland and its future.

There were sadder occasions to attend as well and we all had to take part in them. One example was the tribute that Fergus made to the last man of Knoydart, who had been present at the first day of the Parliament but who died in the autumn of 1999. Just over a year later I lost a very dear friend when Jimmy Logan died. He had openly supported my candidature in Hamilton, as did his father Jack Short. He was a regular visitor to the Commons between 1974 and 1979.

Towards the end of that first year a Parliamentary delegation paid its first visit to Brussels to mark the opening of a Scottish presence there. I had been the Mother of the European Parliament and was a member of the European Committee, but I did not get invited, which brought back memories of how Labour had treated me in Hamilton. I remarked on the matter and got a letter from Jack McConnell, who was responsible for the invitations, but it was as usual far from satisfactory.

Labour did not have an easy time in these first months of the Parliament. Our opposition was effective and prominent and our front bench team soon began to prove that they were more than a match for the members that Labour had chosen through their very restrictive selection process. Some of our new and unknown members were also very talented, such as Irene McGugan, who was appointed depute spokesperson on culture and eventually became depute for children and education, where her strong professional knowledge of children's issues and social work made her a well respected authority on the subjects and one whom Labour and the Liberals tackled at their peril.

Another difficulty which came to bedevil the whole Parliament, quite unfairly, was the saga of the Holyrood building. It is now obvious that the whole mess was the result of a very irregular process of selection, in which Donald Dewar was determined to have his own way, no matter the cost, and in which some civil servants displayed their old pre-devolution arrogance and unaccountability. We opposed the site at Holyrood (the Calton Hill site was much better and would have provided a fine ambience as well as a visible presence), and we argued that the project should stop at an early stage whilst the Parliament decided what was best for the future. We came very close to winning a Parliamentary vote on that matter, but it was the Liberals who sided with Labour and allowed them to scrape by. I believe that if an accurate cost of the building had been given at the beginning, the people of Scotland might have accepted that it would take £400 million to produce a world-class home for its new Parliament. After all, much more was spent on the Dome and even a set of new offices at Westminster cost almost as much. But Dewar insisted that the cost would be £40 million, was determined to have his own way and not to go to Calton Hill (which he wrongly thought was a 'nationalist shibboleth') and then, as the cost grew, kept on insisting that everything was fine. Once it was obvious that it was not, the whole project was dumped on the Parliament and Labour tried to run away as fast as it could. All this turned the public off and made the Parliament look tarnished.

Labour had also experienced a severe electoral fright within months of having settled in on the Mound. They say that lightning never strikes twice in the same place, but it is strange how Scottish by-elections defy that widely-held belief. The town of Paisley has seen three by-elections in recent years, and Hamilton has also had three. The first was mine in 1967 and the second was fought well by Margo MacDonald in 1978. Then, in the summer of 1999, George Robertson, Labour's Defence Secretary, was appointed General Secretary of NATO (taking a peerage into the bargain) and a by-election was called for the seat he had won from Margo.

My practice was now to ensure that I spent a week at any by-election, using the loudspeakers, calling on shops, working the streets and making sure that there was energy and visibility. On this occasion I was even gladder to do so, and to spend more time, for my daughter Annabelle was chosen as the candidate. The press of course had a field day with the connection, with one particular cartoon showing me as an old crone, and there was much talk of political 'dynasties' and such like. But Annabelle had done very well in the May 1999 election as the candidate for Stirling and the local constituency was keen to have her as the by-election candidate.

I had of course refused to stand again in the constituency after my defeat in 1970 and I was slightly worried what the local reaction would be to that fact. I need not have been concerned for I received the warmest of welcomes which at times almost moved me to tears. In the streets of Hamilton and Blantyre women who had been my constituents came up to embrace me and to introduce me to their children and grandchildren. It was the same with the party activists, some of whom were still working away for the party, thirty-two years on.

I was soon convinced that the by-election could be won. The Labour candidate was another of those 'buggins turn' individuals who lacked any distinction, and there was some local feeling that George Robertson should have stayed and worked for his constituents. However the party did not seem to share my view. Our activists did not turn up in their usual numbers and Labour deliberately made it harder for the SNP by choosing to hold the by-election on the Thursday of our annual conference. It had long been a tradition that by-elections were not held during party conferences, but of course Labour would resort to any tricks it could find to ensure that it won.

I was right and the party was wrong. Annabelle came within 600 votes of winning and indeed on the night of the count Labour were initially very worried as the boxes were opened and the SNP votes piled up. At one stage Annabelle saw John Reid, a neighbouring MP and Labour Minister, wandering about looking extremely concerned. Despite the disappointment – for we could have brought off another sensation at Hamilton and repeated the surprise of 1967 – Annabelle lived to fight another day and went on to win Perth at the 2001 Westminster General Election.

As the year reached its end I agreed to take part in a novel form of fundraising for the party, when Pete Wishart, a former member of Runrig and now a committed SNP member who would go on to win the Tayside North seat at the Westminster election, produced a CD for sale which not only included me singing but also Alex Salmond in a duet with Anne Lorne Gillies. Stewart insisted that I sent copies far and wide to all sorts of unlikely people as a sort of publicity stunt and I did so, getting charming if bemused replies from Ted Heath, Lord McCluskey, Michael Forsyth, and my old friend Gwyneth Dunwoody. All were kinder than the press comments. I was surprised to be asked for interviews at this time that were nothing to do with the CD and in which I was treated more kindly than I was used to, particularly by the *Daily Record*. Clearly people were taking the party seriously again.

The first challenge of 2000 was the Ayr by-election. This was set for March, but it took place within the context of another major row that was damaging the Parliament, that over the repeal of Section 28 of the Local Government Act, which was a Thatcherite measure which sought to prevent the 'promotion' of homosexuality in schools. The issue of repeal was a difficult one and one which I thought should be a matter of conscience. In any case the whole topic was very badly handled by Labour from the start, with the announcement of repeal being given by Wendy Alexander in an off-the-cuff remark during a speech in Glasgow, which led many to believe that it was merely a gesture to some sections of Labour support who were becoming disillusioned with the new Scottish Executive. Moreover it was a gesture that was seen to cost nothing.

Very quickly that was proved untrue. The entrepreneur Brian Souter waged a private campaign against abolition, complete with a postal referendum, and whilst Labour wriggled on the hook, with much opposition within its own ranks, the SNP took a principled position which, whilst I respected it, I still thought was wrong. We should have said very clearly that it was a matter of conscience for each member and each voter and allowed our members to give their opinions on this basis.

Our candidate in Ayr was the formidable Jim Mather, who had nearly won in 1999 as the third placed person on the Highland List. He nobly and firmly stuck to the party line on Section 28 but the Tories had a field day and it soon became obvious that the fight was between us and them. I kept meeting Phil Gallie, the Tory list MSP in the street, and in informal chats he forecast events so exactly that it seemed the Tories knew exactly where each and every Tory supporter was. Phil of course had been the Tory MP for Ayr from 1992 to 1997, succeeding George Younger, and although he had lost the seat, he was still very much in touch with it.

I booked in to a hotel in Ayr for the last week of the by-election along with my friend's Yvonne Murgatroyd and Lila McIntyre, Robert's widow.

The party provided us with a car and a volunteer driver, and the car, of course, had a full set of loudspeakers mounted on top!

Ayr has the largest open-air market in Scotland and we spoke to the hundreds who were attending, whilst standing beside Labour activists such as Jackie Baillie, a very clever and pleasant Scottish Executive Minister who was doing her best in a hopeless situation, made worse for Labour by the obscenity of the recent 50p a week pension rise which was seen by most old people as an insult. The local Labour controlled council then added injury to that insult by proposing to close a much-used local social and welfare facility for the elderly.

Yvonne and I left the market to tour the surrounding villages which are part of the constituency, but Lila would not be prised away and remained on duty and campaigning until well after every Labour volunteer had given up. Then she followed Brian Wilson MP and Henry McLeish MSP round the streets until they resorted to sheltering in a café. She promptly followed them in and after a while they accepted defeat and went back to the Labour rooms. McLeish later asked me, 'Who was that strange woman?' and I was able to tell him that she was the widow of the SNP's first-ever MP, and that she was still working tirelessly for the cause.

The Tories duly won the by-election and their candidate, a farmer called John Scott who had done a great job in founding the Farmers' Market movement in Scotland, went to Holyrood. More surprisingly he was returned again in 2003, fighting off a renewed Labour challenge.

In the early part of 2000 the new members of Parliament had got down to work on an ever increasing legislative programme when I discovered – through my interest in lodging a private members bill on the need for local consultation before any growing of GM crops – that many Parliamentary procedures were still being evolved. In particular there was a great shortage of assistance in drafting and proposing members' legislation, something that was always hard at Westminster and should have been easier at Holyrood.

I had a number of other causes in which I was active, including that particular interest of mine, the deaf. Each MSP can apply to have a members' debate, which takes place after voting at 5 o'clock, and I was successful in tabling one of these on the issue of sign language. Scotland had only thirty-five sign language interpreters, compared to 350 in

Finland, for example. During the debate the whole gallery was packed with deaf people and signers stood facing each group. My concern for the deaf led to several further invitations including being principal guest at Donaldson's College. Many of the children attend as boarders from the age of three and my heart was very touched by their keenness to learn and by the work of the staff. I carried on with this issue throughout the Parliament and had the privilege of asking the last question to the First Minister at the final question time in March 2003 on this topic.

I had many visitors, just as I had during my first years at Westminster, and some of them, like John Cairney, had been my guests then too. I introduced John to David Steel amongst others and most of my callers, like Sheriff David Smith, also knew other MSPs and we spent time with them. A high point was the visit of Fr George Thompson, formerly our MP for Galloway and now a priest in Dalbeattie, who was invited to take the weekly 'Time for Reflection'. It was wonderful to see him again, and in such a context.

Although there were many political issues that were raising their heads – fishing, the loss of objective one status for the Highlands and Islands, Section 28, the start of the long fox-hunting dispute and the move of the Parliament to Glasgow for three weeks in May, – it was two other events that dominated the summer and autumn of 2000.

The first was the totally unexpected decision of Alex Salmond to resign the leadership of the SNP. Alex had done ten years, which is about the usual length for an SNP leader, but no one dreamt that he was thinking of going until he made the announcement in June. He, of course, notified me in advance but I was shocked too, for although I had strongly supported Margaret against him during the leadership election I had grown to think very highly of him and his abilities. He was quite unique in the way he could argue a case on television and command a presence wherever he went. I did realise that the burdens of office were very great but it had seemed to me that he was just getting into his stride in the Scottish Parliament and his subsequent decision to stay at Westminster and give up his seat in the Scottish Parliament after just two years was difficult to comprehend, although the party was very fortunate in having someone of his ability who could lead in London, particularly as all the other MPs were standing down and there would be an entirely new group.

The result of the leadership race was never really in doubt. A number of individuals were canvassed to stand, or thought about putting their names forward, but it was obvious that John Swinney was the front-runner from the start and soon he emerged as the only serious contender, not just because he had been Deputy Leader but because he was well known and well respected throughout the party, and indeed well liked too.

No sooner had we elected our new leader than Labour also suffered the loss of theirs – though in much more tragic circumstances. Donald Dewar had been ill for much of 2000 and had required a major operation, but he seemed to be on the mend and indeed had come back and taken over his post again, which had been occupied in the interim by Jim Wallace. At the start of the October recess he fell outside Bute House, and this seems to have precipitated a clot which proved fatal within twenty-four hours. His funeral in Glasgow Cathedral was a massive affair and there was a genuine public sadness at his passing, for he had been seen as the father of devolution, even though I think it would not have come about had it not been for the relentless threat of the SNP.

Henry McLeish was elected by Labour as his successor in a very rushed process, although he was challenged by Jack McConnell. However, of greater interest than the internal Labour machinations was the prospect of two by-elections in Glasgow Anniesland, where Donald had been both MP and MSP.

Despite all these events I had managed to get a holiday on Gigha in July 2000 and to visit Canada in October. My sister Jean came with me to Gigha and I drove to Argyll to pick her up. Soon we were on the ferry and transported to what I have always thought of as a very magical island. When we got there the island was abuzz with the prospect of a community buy-out and some people thought I had come deliberately to lend my support. That was not true, and we settled in to a small cottage adjacent to the hotel and enjoyed beautiful weather during which we could both paint as well as visit the fish and food factories and call on a sculptress friend of Lila McIntyre.

Nonetheless I was not able to ignore the buy-out and over the seven days we were there I think every local worthy called to sound out my opinion. A committee had been formed to steer the purchase through and the island had a number of assets including the stately home, occupied by the laird, as well as some self-catering cottages and a nine-hole golf course. No one on the island had ever enjoyed complete security of tenure and there had been silly rules that stopped farmers competing with the laird for bed-and-breakfast guests. Farming was not working to its full potential on what is a very fertile little place.

I kept asking those who called on me, 'What do you have to lose?' I pointed out that Gigha was highly accessible, with a good ferry service and reasonable access to Campbeltown, which has an air strip. There was plenty of opportunity to reoccupy the farms that had been abandoned and to expand tourism and there was already a major draw in the National Trust Garden.

The local MSP George Lyon had got involved, quite rightly, but he had attended a public meeting at which he had called for a vote. That, in my view, was a big mistake because people were being asked to decide on a very important and possibly financially burdensome step without having all the facts and without thinking the idea through. The vote was not unanimous, as was inevitable, and that allowed the press to take up the theme of 'a divided island' which sowed further doubts in some minds.

I hope that my calmer questions helped to change a few minds and persuaded some who were teetering on the brink to take the plunge. In any case the buy-out went ahead and the islanders at last reclaimed their home – something I have supported wherever it has become possible.

In October Stewart and I went to Canada and fulfilled our long-standing desire to see the Rockies. We went to Vancouver where we were entertained very handsomely by a friend who was in the SNP and whose ancestors had come from Plockton. We went to Banff Springs and we saw what an enormous undertaking the building of the Pan Canadian Railway had been. It was completed at a place called Craigallachie, which of course is the war cry of the MacKenzies, and was named by the Prime Minister of Canada, a MacKenzie himself, who had ensured that the railway was built.

Canada is truly multicultural society. It is a country in which one is always aware of the human desire to lead a better, freer life even if this means, as it did for my father's sister Meg, a permanent exile from the place still thought of as home.

The need for Scotland to encourage its people to build a better, freer life was much in evidence when I returned from Canada, because I was plunged straight into the Anniesland by-elections. Our candidates were Tom Chalmers and Grant Thoms, and although it was pretty certain from the start that Labour would win, the final outcome was more disappointing for us than I had expected.

The reason for public apathy about the by-election was not difficult to see. I spent a week on the by-election campaign, as usual, and on the streets of the constituency I saw a level of deprivation that was truly shocking. People had virtually given up on politics and politicians and those that voted simply endorsed the status quo out of a sense of duty, not with any enthusiasm. The centre of the place appeared to be the Drumchapel Shopping Centre in which was situated Donald Dewar's constituency office. This shopping centre bore the marks of some sort of grand architectural plan, for it had a paved courtyard, a fountain and offices and shops all around. But the fountain didn't work; shops, bar two, were boarded up and the place was covered in graffiti. I began to feel a violent anger that the man who had been the most powerful politician in Scotland at one time had allowed such a situation in his own constituency.

But the Drumchapel Centre was only the tip of the iceberg. There were streets which were deserted, with houses shuttered and vandalised. There was rubbish everywhere and I reflected, as I was driven about, that I would not have tolerated such run-down estates anywhere in Moray when I was the member. I would have demanded action, shouting from the rooftops if necessary.

I recalled how easy it had been for successive Westminster Governments to write off the debt of the English housing corporations, the English water boards and even that of London Transport, but they would not write off Glasgow's housing debt nor that of Glasgow's transport body. Nor would they put the money into improving localities such as Drumchapel, where unemployment was the norm. But I could never recall the member for Anniesland getting publicly angry about this situation, nor agitating vigorously for the type of change that was essential. There were lots of good people working locally to help – holding classes, encouraging youth groups, teaching or doing social work – but their actions were constantly hampered by shortage of resources or lack of political backing. In these massive housing schemes, created by Labour, there was now a sense of hopelessness which only rewarded Labour at each election out of habit. It was the worst type of example of an inefficient and crumbling one-party state.

I was even angrier when Donald Dewar's will was published and it turned out that he held substantial numbers of shares in privatised companies. He had always opposed privatisation and spoken against it, and his electors had a right to believe that he had taken a principled stance. Now it was obvious that he hadn't done even that.

Our failure to do well in Anniesland was deeply disappointing, but within a matter of weeks we recorded a much better result in the Falkirk West by-election. Dennis Canavan held the dual mandate for this seat as an independent, having left the Labour party when he failed to be approved as a candidate for the Scottish Parliament, being too independent of mind and speech to suit modern New Labour. Labour decided to hold the election on 21 December, which was closer to Christmas than any by-election had ever been held. Once more it was a ploy to drive down turnout (whilst paying lip service to the need to increase participation) and to wrong-foot the SNP who were seen as the main challengers.

We had an excellent candidate in David Kerr, who worked for the BBC. He was personable, good looking, and an excellent communicator. I had an escort provided each day I was in the constituency, usually one of the list MSPs for Central Scotland – either Andrew Wilson (who was always very amusing) or Michael Matheson. We visited factories and old folks' homes as well as campaigning on the streets and once more I had a feeling that this by-election was not going to be the easy Labour victory they were expecting. People had been made suspicious of New Labour by the Canavan experience, and the Labour candidate, Major Eric Joyce, was virtually a New Labour clone, prepared to say anything and do anything instructed by the spin doctors.

Labour activists were thin on the ground and eventually they were bussed into the constituency from south of the Border in order to make up the numbers. One lunchtime Michael Matheson and I were in a café when some of the English Labour supporters came in and greeted us with enthusiasm. 'Together we will beat the Tories,' they said, showing their vast ignorance of Scottish politics.

I was right about the closeness of the result. On the last day Labour put in a frantic effort to knock up their vote but by tea-time we were hearing that they were getting worried as their voters didn't want to turn out. The count produced a much narrower result than was predicted, but again we lost by around 500 votes – a margin that could have been eroded with a campaign that was confident and determined. It seemed to me that we were losing our appetite for by-election success and that we would need to regain it if we were to start pulling off surprises – and we needed to do that to keep our momentum going.

During the autumn, between the Anniesland and Falkirk by-elections, I had been considering my future again and I became more and more certain that I was not going to run for a further term. As a result I wanted to start thinking about what I was going to do in my retirement. I asked Michael Russell, whom I knew had written books, about the prospects for my being able to write and have published my autobiography and he very kindly agreed to help me write a synopsis of what I wanted to say. Then he introduced me to Hugh Andrew of Birlinn, who was keen to publish the book. Slowly the idea took shape in my head, and I opened a number of files in which I started to put stories and thoughts as they came to me.

After the hectic travelling of Europe and the world I settled into a routine in Edinburgh. I would usually travel down from Moray on a Tuesday, and would stay until Friday, when I would fly back up. The weekends and Mondays were spent on regional work and on party activities, but it was good to have more time in Miltonduff with Stewart, who was still acting as my unpaid assistant, reading all the Highland newspapers and producing mountains of cuttings. These I would often work through, along with my correspondence, whilst sitting in the Chamber because my years in different parliaments had made me good at what was called 'bench duty'. I always tried to be present to encourage less experienced speakers or to make contributions myself, particularly on fishing, on Gaelic and on Highland issues.

Fishing remained a strong interest and as the crisis in Scottish fishing deepened, the Scottish Executive seemed quite unable to come up with appropriate solutions. There was strong backing for a tie-up scheme, rather than for wholesale decommissioning, but after the CFP round in December 2000 there was yet another attempt to reduce the capacity of the industry in such a way. This led to the most significant defeat of the Executive during the entire first term of the Scottish Parliament. On a Thursday evening in March 2001, when Labour members were already drifting off to their Scottish conference, the Parliament considered at the five o'clock decision time – brought forward a little because of the early conclusion of other business – whether or not to support such a scheme. The original motion that had been debated that morning had been from the Tories, proposed by their colourful fisheries spokesman, my fellow Highlands and Islands list member Jamie McGrigor. There had been the usual rant from the very unsympathetic fisheries minister, Rhona Brankin, who has a pathological hatred of Nationalists or indeed of any opposition, and strong contributions from a number of SNP members including our own fisheries spokesman, Richard Lochhead and his mentor, Alex Salmond, who was just coming to the end of his time in the Scottish Parliament.

When the vote was taken on Rhona Brankin's amendment, which stated Government policy, no one expected any upset. But a combination of a small number of Liberal Democrat rebels allied with a poor Labour turnout meant that the Executive lost the vote. The next vote was on Richard Lochhead's amendment, which the Tories agreed to, and although Labour tried hard to get more members into the Chamber, the amendment was passed. Then the amended motion, which backed a tie-up scheme, was put and it was a dead heat – 55 votes on each side. As the business of the day had been the Tory motion, it was the status quo, so the Presiding Officer had, by convention, to use his casting vote in favour of it. Thus Labour's policy was rejected by the Chamber.

Labour were furious. They made no statement that day but within twenty-four hours a junior Liberal Minister, Tavish Scott, who represented the strongly fishing constituency of Shetland but who had voted with the government, had resigned and the press were savage about the competence of this new Scottish Government. However to the charge of incompetence the Executive then added that of insufferable arrogance. They reintroduced their policy the following week and forced it through by a three-line whip on their own members, including the Liberals. The will of the Parliament was completely ignored and the fishing communities were justifiably incensed.

I had been thrilled by our victory on such an issue, but was devastated to discover on looking at the voting lists that although I had been present, my vote had not been recorded. It would have been inconceivable for me not have voted and I had pressed the right button so I immediately raised a point of order, but the Presiding Officer said he could do nothing. It was not the first time that the electronic voting system had let the Parliament down.

The year 2001 was always likely to be the Westminster General Election year, as terms there had a habit of lasting just four years and Tony Blair was known to be keen to find the right time to secure a second large majority. Despite the fishing vote, most of the Tory opposition was lacklustre, although in Edinburgh the Tory leader, David McLetchie, was proving to be a doughty opponent with a nice turn of phrase.

All our MPs had decided before the Scottish Parliament elections that they wished to return home, but it was agreed that they would hold a dual mandate until the first Westminster General Election. A series of by-elections would have been in nobody's interest. However, this meant that the six of them had an impossible time of it and I watched as my weary daughter-in-law caught sleepers up and down the country. We should never have permitted such a situation, not least because when they were in Edinburgh they had huge demands upon them, in Margaret's case chairing the group in addition to servicing her Moray constituency.

When Alex resigned as leader he indicated to a number of us that he was prepared to stay at Westminster beyond 2001 in order to lead the new and inexperienced group. Consequently at the election Alex demitted his Holyrood seat, which was fought and won by Stewart Stevenson, who had been a tremendous supporter of Alex for a long time. Alex was returned easily as the Westminster member. I took to the road for much of the General Election, travelling in areas as far apart as Ross and Cromarty and Galloway, and taking in many places in between.

The new candidate in Moray was Angus Robertson. Margaret and I were absolutely convinced from early on that he was the best choice for Moray and he fought a fine campaign. As an MP he has also proved to be exceptional.

In Galloway the election took place against the backdrop of a disastrous outbreak of foot-and-mouth disease which had resulted in the gruesome slaughter and burning of many thousands of animals. The Easter holiday, traditionally the start of the season, came and went without any tourists. When I stayed later on the only other guests in my hotel were soldiers who were there to take part in the widespread cull. Throughout the area the air was acrid with the smoke and smell of the pyres.

During my time in Galloway I became worried that we were going to find it hard to keep the seat and I badgered Alasdair Morgan to take more help from HQ. The state of the local organisation seemed poorer than it should have been in a seat that we held but Alasdair seemed supremely confident although the bad vibes I felt were echoed by others who visited, including Alex Salmond and Michael Russell. Alasdair continued to dismiss such views right up until the end of polling but then discovered that we had indeed lost the seat, by the smallest of margins. It was very frustrating to do so, and to allow the Tories a foothold again in Scotland.

Perth was a much more vigorous contest and it was exciting to be there to support Annabelle, who had been chosen to defend the seat held by Roseanna Cunningham since the by-election in 1995. Annabelle was a strong candidate who led from the front, and on her days in the pedestrian precinct she would never leave the street until all the opposition had folded up their stands and removed their workers. We were always much amused by the blue-rosetted Tories who would march up and down saying mildly, 'Save the pound', an obsession of their campaign nationwide which was never raised on the doorsteps as an issue by any voter.

In Perth I learned the hard way that telephone canvassing – now much used by all parties – is often inaccurate and that many people appear to give encouraging replies just in order to end the call. The impression it gave was that we were well ahead in Perth but in the end Annabelle had only a very narrow victory. I remain filled with admiration at Annabelle's bracing courage and calm in the face of all the difficulties of that campaign and I was delighted with the Perth activists who rallied round and worked their socks off.

Annabelle made her maiden speech in the House of Commons on Friday 13 July 2001. In a good contribution she said that thirteen was often regarded as unlucky but her own lucky number happened to be forty-eight, which was also her majority. In the customary tribute to previous MPs for the area she pointed out that Nicholas Fairbairn's first majority was only forty-eight and that he was in the Commons for over twenty years!

The results of the 2001 Westminster Election, whilst not disastrous, indicated that fighting for Westminster seats was going to be even harder than it had been before devolution. It also indicated that we still had much to do to build strong organisations, even in some of our key areas, though Labour's majorities were now smaller than they had ever been and change might still come suddenly.

One slightly sad downside of Annabelle's election, however, was the end of Ewing and Company, the legal firm I had started in 1957 when I was ousted from my lecturing job due to my pregnancy. In time Fergus and Annabelle both qualified as solicitors. Fergus became my partner and Annabelle then became Fergus' partner, when she left her legal firm in Brussels. But when both of them were elected it was obvious that politics was going to take precedence over law and the time had come for a final change. In 2001 Fergus finally negotiated the sale of the practice to Leslie Wolfson & Co., bringing to an end forty-four years of my family firm.

Politics, of course, was far from dull. The Holyrood building continued to escalate in cost and the SNP continued to force discussion on it in the Chamber. Once more we were promised a cap on the expenditure and were told that the current cost estimate was 'an absolute maximum'. Once more, no sooner had we received that assurance than the costs went up again.

One rare happy event in the saga was the visit of my old friend the Prime Minister of Catalonia, Jordi Pujol. He came to lay the foundation stone, and although he was much fêted by Labour as a 'good devolutionist' he was quite happy to say that Scotland needed further powers to at least match those he had in Catalonia. I wrote to congratulate him on those remarks.

Another visitor was Bertie Ahern, the Taoiseach. This visit was overshadowed by a Labour-inspired row regarding the plan for him to dedicate a Scottish national monument to the famine victims in Ireland when he was in Scotland, and indeed the visit had to be postponed from its original scheduled date.

When Bertie finally visited he was the third Head of Government or Head of State to address Parliamentarians. In the preious two instances there were two flags beside the Presiding Officer's chair, the saltire and the flag of our visitor's county. I stood at the head of the stairs in our building on the Mound to greet Bertie, for he was well known to me from my days working with Fianna Fáil. He was accompanied by Wally Kirwan, also a good friend of mine, who had frequently been in Europe. The Scottish Executive officials seemed surprised that Bertie embraced me so warmly but they had a bigger surprise coming because I had just noticed that there had suddenly appeared by the Presiding Officer's chair a third flag – the Union Jack. There was no precedent for this and I demanded that Paul Grice, the Parliament's Chief Clerk, remove it, for in Ireland the Union Jack is often seen as a symbol of repression. Grice told me that the Irish Consul had been consulted, though the Consul was present and immediately denied this. I pressed the point but when I pointed out that on previous visits there had been no Union Jack, Grice responded with the ludicrous excuse that this was because we previously had only two poles, but now we had three! My objections were noted but of course ignored. However, they were widely reported by the press and there was much comment on the matter, some favourable but some critical.

I suspect the sudden appearance of the Union Jack was due to the presence of Helen Liddell, the Secretary of State for Scotland, in the VIP Gallery. No doubt the Labour Executive had something to do with it, but our Parliamentary authorities should have resisted it and it was disgraceful that they did not.

Bertie didn't notice the flag when entering and during the course of his speech, but he did on the way out. When asked to comment he was, of course, the perfect politician and claimed he was not concerned. However, I doubted if that was the case and suspected only politeness prevented him from saying more. As it was, I subsequently found out I was right.

Bertie later unveiled the Scottish monument to the Irish famine victims. Such monuments were being built in many countries and this one was situated in the National Pilgrimage Centre at Carfin in Lanarkshire. I was invited to accompany John Swinney as his escort and we were seated in the front row along with Helen Liddell and Henry McLeish. The proceedings were conducted by Brian Dempsey, the son of the former member for Coatbridge and Airdrie, who was a complete gentleman and much loved in his constituency.

Brian introduced each of the guests, including John Swinney, but he made such a warm and special reference to me that many of the Labour guests were most surprised. A Scots piper performed a variety of music, including that wonderful Irish song that I knew so well 'The West's Awake', and then an Irish piper played a tune specially composed for the occasion. At the end we were all frozen, although it was meant to be summer, and we were ushered into a reception room where, much to my surprise, I was welcomed and kissed by John Reid, Henry McLeish and many other prominent Labour members. Chatting to them I said how pleased I was to hear 'The West's Awake', and I sang it with a Labour activist, greatly to the shock of all the others.

From the reception we were taken off for a splendid buffet at the Motherwell Civic Centre. Many of the guests were local Roman Catholic members and a lot of them were SNP supporters, who were delighted to see John and me. There were also quite a number of SNP councillors present, who mysteriously (of course) were not named in the official programme!

When I stood for the Scottish Parliament I had always made it clear that I did not expect to contest any more than one election and I had understood that my intention to retire from the Parliament in 2003 was common knowledge. However, this did not seem to be the case, and when I formally notified the constituency in July 2001 of my decision to conclude my political career the story got enormous coverage. So great was the interest, I could only think that there was a dearth of summer news, but I was gratified that it was almost all positive coverage with some kind things to say. Many people also wrote to me about my decision but I had no regrets or second thoughts – I had been a member of one Parliament or another for thirty years and it was thirty-four years since I had fought my first election. I was keen to spend more time with Stewart and my family and to enjoy my house in Miltonduff. And I wanted to travel and to learn new things without constant Parliamentary and public pressure.

Politics can give great pleasures and satisfactions, but of course it is also an unforgiving trade. When Henry McLeish became First Minister he had the goodwill of most of the chamber and he was usually very pleasant to deal with. Consequently everyone was shocked as what at first appeared to be a minor slip in his declaration of interests developed over months into a full-blown scandal and eventually led to his resignation. I am still unclear as to exactly what happened and why, but I suspect there was more of the human in the whole business than we were ever to know.

Henry's resignation was followed, once more, by a hasty Labour selection process which was beginning to make the whole Parliament look far less dignified and effective than it should have been. Wendy Alexander decided, at the last minute and much to the fury of her friends in the Parliament, that she would not run and Jack McConnell got what he had been seeking for so long. But no sooner had Jack been elected than he turned on most of the real talent on the Labour benches and installed his own cronies in the Cabinet. Then he announced that the Scottish Executive and Parliament should 'do less better', which was hardly the ringing endorsement of our new democracy that most people expected. I was more and more disappointed with the way in which Labour was deliberately dumbing down the Parliament and the expectations of the Scottish people, just as they had done for generations from south of the border.

Press criticism of the Parliament was becoming more and more strident and the decision by MSPs to award themselves a pay increase did not help the situation, even though it had been recommended by an independent arbiter. The root of that problem lay in Westminster's decision at the very start not to have equality of pay between MPs and MSPs, which was unfair, particularly as MSPs had taken much of the MPs' workload. But of course the Westminster members squealed like mad when it looked as if their numbers would be cut down, as envisaged in the Scotland Act, and the MSPs' numbers would stay the same – as indeed they should, given the workload and the need to sustain the committee system.

Some weeks before, the Parliament sat for a few days in Aberdeen (because the General Assembly Hall was needed by the Church of Scotland). I had been in America for the first time in ages. The occasion was the annual 'Tartan Day' celebrations, and although the Executive spent £300,000 on sending their representatives, the SNP contingent went at their own expense.

The American supporters of the SNP were our hosts and they were tremendous. The centrepiece of the celebrations was a massive parade in New York, where it seemed that millions were on the street to cheer. Sean

Connery and his wife and granddaughter led the parade with the Mayor of New York. Sean had met with the SNP contingent before the event and we had travelled to it in his limousine, but Jack McConnell was determined to try and push his way in so that he could be photographed by the *Daily Record*. However our strong kilted boys, Andrew Wilson, Duncan Hamilton and Colin Pyle, used their elbows to ensure that it was the SNP that was seen to be in front and alongside our long-standing supporter.

The whole crowd was waving bits of tartan and cheering and some New York fire-fighters said to me that it was the first time that the city had smiled since the Twin Towers, some seven months before. There were 10,000 pipers in the procession – a world record – and they included members of the Nairn Pipe Band, with whom I managed to meet up. After New York we flew on to Washington, where we were showered with hospitality by Allison Duncan, the SNP's legal representative in the United States, a graduate of Aberdeen University and now a senior partner in one of Washington's biggest legal firms. She put us up at her home and she arranged many things, including a meeting in the boardroom of her firm which was attended by the President's economic adviser and his team.

Having seen the suffering occasional by the Banana War (caused by the objection by politically influential American-owned companies to the preference given by the EU to Lomé banana exporters), I was keen to raise the issue of trade sanctions. Spurred on by an American complaint, the World Trade Organisation had imposed sanctions on Europe in retaliation and these had targeted Scottish companies, particularly those producing cashmere and biscuits. The effect had badly damaged the Borders mills and had been particularly savage in my own area, as in Moray both Johnston's Mill in Elgin and Walker's Shortbread had been affected.

The French had suffered with penalties against perfumes and handbags, but the Irish, always the Americans' favourite, had escaped, no doubt due to the huge influence of the Irish lobby in the States. The whole thing had demonstrated Scotland's impotence in the world and Westminster's indifference. The much vaunted 'clout' that Scotland was meant to get from being represented in the EU by the UK was once again shown to be a myth.

But I was also angry at America and the WTO. Indeed, the American-inspired action seemed to flaunt the democratic will of half the nations of the world as expressed in the Lomé treaties. It was outrageous that a few political donors with financial interests in banana production could have such an effect, and it showed that the USA had a tendency – even more pronounced now – to bully to get its own way. I played the bad cop in the meeting, constantly returning to this subject, but I did in the end get some degree of assurance about future policies.

We all had a tremendous time, and whilst Allison looked after us some of the time, we also fended for ourselves. However, my trip came to an end in a very upsetting and worrying way for Fergus phoned one day out of the blue. I was terrified that he had bad news of Stewart, but instead he had rung to tell me that Margaret had been diagnosed with breast cancer. She had only gone to the radiographer as part of a routine screening pro-gramme to give a good example to her constituents, but they had found a lump which required urgent treatment. I wanted to return immediately and Andrew Wilson very gallantly and kindly changed his plans in order to travel back with me.

Margaret was duly operated on and spent over eight hours in theatre as the surgeons reconstructed her breast. She was brave and cheerful throughout, though very ill, but when I went to see her she was still able to crack a joke, saying to me, 'Give up champagne, morphine is much better!' She had a bad spell of post-operative illness and it took a very long time for her even to partially recover. For a time everyone was dreadfully worried, Fergus most of all, but as ever he showed great courage and gave Margaret and us all strong support.

Margaret was clearly going to be off for some time but the rest of us went back after the Easter break to yet another government resignation. There had been great speculation at the start of the year that Wendy Alexander was disenchanted with Jack McConnell and with the way that government was being run, but she had been categorical that she had no intention of resigning. But unexpectedly a few months later she did just that, and then jetted off abroad leaving behind much consternation. Of the fifty-five Labour MSPs all but eight had now held some sort of office, and that after only three years. This did not seem to be a brave new way of running a country – it just seemed a jobs-for-the-boys-and-girls type of mess, the sort of mess that bedevilled the Labour-run councils in Scotland.

The Parliament had spent some time in Glasgow during the General Assembly in 2000. In 2001 the Kirk had agreed to use other premises, but it was keen to get back in to its own place in 2002, particularly as we should have been in the new building at Holyrood by then. Glasgow had been interesting, but the three-week sitting had been too long, so it was resolved in 2002 to spend a single week meeting in Aberdeen and to use the other two weeks for committee work. The Queen, as part of her Jubilee year, was to address the Parliament at this time, so that was also scheduled for Aberdeen.

Prior to the visit I had written to the Queen about a matter which had concerned me for a long time. The Queen was now universally referred to as Queen Elizabeth II, but she was *not* the second Elizabeth for Scotland; she was the first. The previous Elizabeth had only been Queen of England. This issue had been raised when she acceded to the throne and John MacCormick had taken a legal case all the way through the Court of Session, which, although he lost, had resulted in a very important judgment by Lord Cooper on the question of the nature of sovereignty in Scotland in which he had ruled that popular rather than parliamentary sovereignty was paramount here.

I thought that the Jubilee year might be an appropriate time for the Queen and the Royal Family to acknowledge the fact her the title should be different in Scotland, and had written politely to the palace about the matter. Of course the palace was not about to shift, particularly as – in the words of one MP – 'to all intents and purposes Scotland is England now!' Nonetheless there was much press interest in the issue and I found myself supported by, of all papers, the Scottish *Sun*!

When the Queen came to speak to the Parliament I sat beside John Swinney and resolved to keep an interested look on my face. However, the press must have been determined to present a different view, for when the pictures were published the next day, several of them had the whole SNP group looking very sullen, including myself. The Queen made a very civil speech, but it was obvious in the streets that there was no great outpouring of interest in her. She did not attract crowds, and those children who were bussed in by their schools, at the instruction of the local authority, had to be given Union Jacks before she arrived. Even so there were not many takers. The Parliament, on the other hand, was very well received in Aberdeen and very hospitably entertained. By and large I enjoyed the visit, particularly as there was better news about Margaret.

The main business of our Aberdeen sitting was consideration of Jack McConnell's legislative programme for the last year of the first session. It was an unambitous set of ideas, obsessed with issues such as dog-fouling, graffiti and vandalism and even managing to drag in celebrations of the Union of the Crowns for 2003, something with which he obviously hoped to discomfit the SNP during an election year and which the Queen was also dragged into announcing during her visit. Scotland needed a much more visionary government, keen to get our economy moving again, our industries flourishing, our fisheries protected and developed and our education and health services brought back to world-standard. Although these things were paid lip-service, the reality of the government's actions was quite different. As for the promised 'bonfire of the quangoes', designed to increase the democratisation of Scotland, not even a match had been lit.

There had been much criticism of the First Minister for his tendency towards cronyism, particularly when he appointed his closest associates to ministerial office, sidelining some real talents. There was a persistent suspicion, too, that Labour always appointed its own to public posts whilst keeping Nationalists in particular out in the cold. This was borne out by the fact that out of the twenty-one quango appointments made between January and September 2000 (those twenty-one being only those who admitted to party affiliation) sixteen were Labour, two were Conservative, two were Liberal Democrats and only one was SNP. Between October 2000 and March 2001 five out of seven new quango appointments had political links with Labour.

The Executive constantly claimed that it was rooting out cronyism and it trumpeted new rules which were supposed to identify which public appointees came from which party. But in reality the regulations were so loose and contained so many loopholes that it was possible for long-standing members of the Labour Party, who had not only stood as candidates but who had actually represented the party at public occasions, to be classified as 'non political'. To cap it all, it was then discovered that when Labour appointed some new individuals to oversee the whole process and clean it up, half of those selected to maintain impartiality were actually Labour Party members.

Of course the Tories had been past masters at this game as well and the solution was not just to have a strict system of regulation, but also to diminish the role of unelected bodies in Scottish public life. Quangoes had come to dominate every sector of Scottish activity, from the health service to justice and water supply and were responsible for spending a staggering £12 billion each year. Yet despite promises to dismantle the quango state, Labour in office had actually increased the number of such bodies.

The legislative programme annoyed more than the SNP, however. Missing from it was a commitment to introduce proportional representation for local government, a key Liberal demand. Though there was much huffing and puffing from the Liberals, once again they just meekly bore the insult, mollified by yet another promise from Jack that it would be 'in the next Parliament'. Many Labour members were, of course, root and branch opposed to PR as it would undermine their power base. Self interest and self perpetuation continued to be the order of the day for Labour.

Labour's inability to raise its game in order to serve Scotland was also seen in the continued petty sniping at Nationalists and Nationalism which occupied so much of their time. A typical example, from the Aberdeen session, was the following assertion by Alasdair Morrison, MSP for the Western Isles, who had been the Gaelic Minister and briefly the deputy to Wendy Alexander, but who was now on the back benches. Here is the offending part of his offensive speech:

> *Mr Alasdair Morrison (Western Isles) (Lab)*: I reinforce and associate myself with the comments that my fellow island MSP Tavish Scott made in his speech. I noted with interest Fergus Ewing's passing interest in matters that relate to the Highlands and Islands. I say to Mr Ewing and the *other nationalists* who continue to denigrate committed public servants that if they lived in the Highlands and Islands they might be better placed to comment on issues that relate to the area.
>
> The Highlands is a dynamic region. I instruct those who may not be as familiar with the Highlands as I am to pay attention to those of us who

choose to represent the Highlands in a positive way. They should not listen to the girning and carping of members who have been elected to represent the region but choose not to live there. That important distinction should be pointed out.

His whole manner in the Chamber indicated that he was including me in his attack, and I immediately wrote to him and asked for an apology, pointing out that I had lived in the Highlands, my constituency, for many years, indeed since before I became the Member of Moray and Nairn. In fact this was a period of time almost as long as he had been alive, and he should have the courage to correct the statement and issue an apology. He did not, of course, but I also raised the issue with the Presiding Officer.

After the Aberdeen session I was convinced that despite some adverse publicity for John Swinney we as a party were in a good position to build a strong campaign for the next Scottish Parliament elections which were just over a year away. However, as soon as we were back in Edinburgh there was an intensive period of lobbying and jockeying for position for the list selections, which were to be held throughout the country on the middle weekend of June.

The results, when they were announced, were very disappointing and very damaging to the party. Small numbers of people, often largely unrepresentative of true party opinion or just maliciously misinformed, were successful in demoting from winnable places some of the brightest stars and hard-working talents, in particular two of the leading Shadow Cabinet members and two of the outstanding Parliamentarians of the first session, Michael Russell and Andrew Wilson. Other good members with strong track records and impressive achievements as party spokespeople in the Parliament, such as Kenny Gibson, Irene McGugan and Fiona MacLeod were also relegated to places where their survival was virtually impossible. Colin Campbell, the only defence spokesperson we had ever had who commanded respect amongst the military and who had produced a superb defence policy for the party, was also unceremoniously dumped by his constituency in a vicious and hurtful manner.

It almost seemed to me that all these talented people were being made to suffer a grotesque punishment for working long hours for the party and building its profile whilst those who beat them were reaping rewards for merely conspiring behind the scenes for themselves. Whatever the reason I was heart-broken at this self-inflicted wound and very angry at those who had engineered it. Margo MacDonald also suffered a humiliation, and whilst she had been semi-detached from the group for the past couple of years, it was now obvious that she would consider standing as an independent, which would also damage the party. Knowing Margo she would also drag out the speculation so that she was never out of the newspapers.

I had always said that the SNP's primary aim in the first session of the Scottish Parliament must be to prove that it had the talent to be an alternative government. After much success in so doing, the party had suddenly committed democratic hari-kari in removing many of the people who carried most public confidence, who were the best recognised and who would make the best future ministers. Our task of winning in 2003 had, over a single weekend, been made much more difficult if not impossible. It was madness.

I was pleased, however, that at least the party in the Highlands had not gone down that road. Margaret, still convalescing, and Fergus retained their places on the list and, with their determined work, would surely retain their first-past-the-post seats. Duncan Hamilton had decided some months before not to seek a second term, wishing to take up a legal career before possibly considering coming back to politics. Whilst the decision was widely regretted and indicated a further loss of star quality from the Parliament, I think it was the right thing for him. One can have success and a high public profile too early in life and it can be a difficult burden to carry. Getting other experiences would only enrich his great abilities. The two most likely winning list places in the Highlands went to Jim Mather, now the candidate in Argyll, and Rob Gibson, a long-standing activist. Alasdair Nicholson in the Western Isles was unlucky not to be slightly higher on the list but had real prospects of defeating Alasdair Morrison.

The summer of 2002 was a depressing time as a result of this situation, although I was personally happy that Margaret was on the mend. I was still active on lots of issues but I did have one eye on the future and on the things I wanted to do. My set of folders into which I was to put the beginnings of my autobiography remained, however, largely unfilled, though I did make an effort from time to time to dictate a story or two or jot down a memory.

As the year progressed some of the annual issues re-asserted themselves. The regular CFP negotiatons had become a key point and this year it was suggested that the nine SNP MSPs with fishing interests should meet the Liberal Minister, Ross Finnie, to outline to him what we thought was needed. The CFP settlement was, however, more disastrous than ever, and once more it was the UK Minister who led the delegation, with Ross Finnie taking up the rear but having to take the flak in the Parliament and in Scotland. The situation with cod was particularly severe, and because of the issue of by-catching, this had a knock-on effect on other matters. Meanwhile Danish industrial fishing continued to flourish. Once more Scotland was paying a very heavy price for the long-term neglect of its interests by those who were meant to speak for it. After thirty years of involvement in the fisheries issue, it was almost more than I could take. Nothing had got better, and indeed most things were much worse.

Of course the Liberals had seen so much of their programme just ignored by Labour. The Skye Bridge tolls, another important Highland issue, had been a cause of much discontent since the bridge was opened and the Liberals had promised to get rid of them. But a whole Parliament passed and nothing was done, whilst individuals who did protest were dragged through the courts. The principle of public roads and the economic benefit of good communications were set at nought, but the Liberals continued to do nothing.

In the Highlands infrastructure is all, and a toll bridge is a disincentive to transportation. But the scheme that had done most for our infrastructure had been Objective One, and when this finished as a result of UK government indifference the prospects for continued improvement were much diminished. It was therefore extremely galling to discover, as I did, that the UK statistics which were used to allow the loss of Objective One were simply wrong. Towards the end of 2002 the Office of Government Statistics admitted that the Highlands and Islands should have qualified again and that they had miscounted by £100 billion! Instead of losing out by a whisker because our GDP was 76 per cent of the EU average, it was actually only 73 per cent!

Fergus called it 'the biggest blunder in the history of regional funding and one which will have massive consequences', and he was right. I had, at my last Highland convention as an MEP, got the support of all of the councils as well as the civil servants to continue to pursue Objective One funding for the next round but the UK did not put up any significant fight in the negotiations and settled instead for a transitional funding package which all Objective One regions got after they had lost their special funding status. The UK Government claimed that they had pulled off a huge coup in securing the transitional package, but in fact it only confirmed that Objective One status had been lost by that Government. Government ministers had just accepted the unacceptable without questioning the basis of the information they had received. In other words, once again they did not try hard enough. And now we knew that if they had tried, and had used the right figures, they would have won.

Nonetheless Highland representatives of the SNP have kept trying. In December 2003 Margaret Ewing raised the issue with the First Minister and asked once more if he would rectify the situation. No other self-respecting European state would ever have got into this situation, and certainly Scotland would never have been in it had it been able to present its own case in Europe rather than having to rely on representation by those who couldn't care less. Had it been able to present its own case in Europe. It would still be possible for the Highlands to lodge a backdated claim for Objective One money from 2000 to 2006 and then claim transition money of up to £250 million from 2006 to 2012.

In November 2002 I received a much appreciated honour at the Scottish Parliamentarian of the Year Awards in Edinburgh when I was given a life-time achievement award. The Scottish Parliamentarian of the Year event is hosted by *The Herald* and Zurich Finance at Prestonfield House, and that night, with Annabelle at my side, we were lobbied as we went in by angry fire-fighters in the middle of their dispute with a government which had behaved abominably towards them. I pledged my party's total support and was proud of our members who joined firemen on the picket line.

In my speech accepting the award I started by saying that Stewart believed he should have a lifetime achievement presentation for putting up with me for forty-six years!

I had a tremendous night at the awards ceremony. Much kindness was shown to me and for just a moment I almost regretted having decided to leave politics behind. These nostalgic sensations continued with me as the festive season approached but my resolve to retire returned stronger than ever and I had no second thoughts about it. As Stewart's general health failed he grew ever more exhausted and I felt the sooner that I could be there to look after him the better. In my retirement I could be with him without the weekly gap between Tuesday and Friday.

The usual Christmas preparations of gifts and cards were somehow even sweeter at that time as I began to think of the future at home. The first big occasion of the festive season was the annual joint dinner of the Ewings and the Cowans, and this year it was Annabelle's turn to host it in her lovely house in Comrie. We booked into an excellent hotel in the town and Annabelle did us proud. It was a very happy day and Stewart spent much of his time holding his grandchildren on his knee and teasing them. Bruce Cowan had his two lovely little daughters with him and we were all full of festive spirit. Our drive to and from Comrie reminded us how beautiful Perthshire can be.

On Christmas day Stewart and I were invited to Christmas dinner at our next-door neighbours, Angela and Jeff Hyland, and we had a magnificent time. Then came the 29th and a party in our house. Stewart again was in fine form and was the heart and soul of the event. On Hogmanay we were on our own and we brought in the New Year together. He was very loving and I asked him how he thought we would get on together when I was around all the time. He put his arm around me and said, 'We will do just fine.'

On Ne'erday itself I always go to the Moray Golf Club and then Stewart and I went on to first-foot Joyce Flett and Isobel Nelson. For the next few days we had a quiet time, talking about our plans. On Monday 6 January Stewart was discussing possible home improvements with a visitor just as I was about to serve omelette and chips for lunch. I turned off the cooker and the conversation went on and on. Eventually the visitor got up to leave and, as I was reheating the food, I stepped out of the kitchen to say goodbye. When I stepped back in the fat was on fire and I could not get the fire blanket to work. I called to Stewart to go outside. Jeff from next-door quickly arrived with his fire blanket and the fire brigade arrived within minutes. By then the fire was out, though they sprayed the walls to dampen things down. But Stewart suddenly collapsed and within seconds had lost consciousness. We called an ambulance which took him to Dr

Gray's hospital in Elgin and I followed it with the Hylands in their car. However he was dead on arrival at hospital.

Stewart had often spoken about leaving his affairs in good order and had said that when it came he wanted what he called 'the Rolls Royce of deaths' – a sudden heart attack. He had got his wish, for he must have died very quickly indeed. But I was numb with the shock, horror and speed of it all. Just moments before we had been preparing for lunch. Now my whole life had changed.

I returned to Miltonduff with the Hylands and went into their house to avoid the press, which somehow had already found out. When the family arrived I returned home. Jean and Deirdre made their way as quickly as they could and Terry and Jacqui brought wee Sophie, who was an angel of delight amidst the grieving. Margaret and Fergus took charge of the arrangements for the funeral which was set for Saturday 11 January. I wanted a truly great funeral for the Lossie folk who had taken Stewart to their hearts, as he had taken them. It was agreed that Fergus would do the oration and that it would take place in St Gerardine's, from which Stewart would be taken to be buried in Lossie Cemetery.

The days between Stewart's death and the funeral passed very slowly. I felt guilt-ridden but I had to make my way onwards without him. Fergus and the family dutifully got on with the planning, ensuring that there would be suitable refreshment and food at the Stotfield Hotel after the service and the graveside prayers. When the day came I was stunned by the turnout. There were local people, politicians both local and parliamentary, and some from other parties, friends, Stewart's former clients and a huge number of SNP members from all over the country. I was enormously touched by such affection for Stewart and such appreciation of what he had done. Fergus gave a tremendous oration, in which he rose to the occasion very eloquently. Towards the end of it he paid this tribute:

It was my father who persuaded my mother to stand as candidate in Hamilton. He then and for the rest of his life, played a part unique in the SNP. He produced and sometime designed for innumerable campaigns all kinds of material. These included badges using the Malky McCormick font with the word 'Scotland' and high-profile shopping bags emblazoned with slogans such as 'Winnie Again'. Sometimes he would wind up my mother with an ironic inflection and mock painful expression to the word 'Again!' He produced cassette tapes of various popular – or not so popular – tunes which would be interspersed with voice-over messages from the candidate, and leading lights of the party.

These techniques gave the party a high visual profile, and often conveyed a sense of excitement and momentum into a campaign. Patience was not a virtue he would have claimed for himself, and he did all of these things, from conception of the idea to instruction of the manufacturer – and incidentally signing the cheque for the bill – himself, whether or not the candidate was keen. Not for him, the endless round of committees, or meetings.

The Westminster years saw Stewart taking on the role of consort, supporter as well as father, accountant and lecturer. In the days before Parliamentary allowances, there was a deal of financial pressure, but he would always shield and protect all of us from that. In the seventies he stood as Parliamentary candidate to make up the numbers, and was then prevailed upon to stand for the District Council Election in 1977 for Glasgow. He did so on the basis that he stood in an unwinnable seat, against the then leader of Glasgow Corporation. I recall he commissioned a jumbo poster for the fascia board above the campaign rooms on Maryhill Road, which read, 'VOTE SNP ON 3RD MAY'. But when we put it up, we found that is was too long to fit. Eventually we cut down the message so that it fitted the space. It then read, 'VOTE SNP 3 MAY'. Well, more than three did, and he became the councillor for Summerston, and every other Sunday the three of us would deliver his newsletter to his constituents. John Young, MSP, and a Tory councillor, in a letter of condolence reminded us of the time when my father refused to leave the meeting of a committee of which he was not a member when it went into private session. My father was led out of the Chamber by a policewoman who later told John, 'What a charming man Councillor Ewing is.'

In the European years, my father's role as consort if anything increased in its scope and he frequently would send, in my mother's name, letters to the papers, local and national. Not for him the cliché-ridden banal prose so favoured by some of our Ministers. His style was incisive, coruscating, proactive. His political instincts were, to paraphrase a former leader of the party present here today, 'Attack, Attack, Attack!' But always with humour and style. His was also a rare intellect allied with a shrewd understanding that politics is more about power than policies. He could not fathom why Scotland allows powers to be exercised over us from Westminster, nor why we do not take the future of our country into our own hands.

Had he in his lifetime seen the dawning of the day, he would not have expected a diplomatic posting (I see nods of agreement from the party leaders past and present), but whilst he was, as *The Times* said 'an intensely private person', his contribution to public life in Scotland was immense.

It is rarer now perhaps for people to live their lives not for achievement of their own personal ambitions, but in the devotion to the service of another. That is a form of nobility without title. 'The rank is but the guinea-stamp the man's the gowd for a' that.' His generosity was spontaneous and unlimited, his integrity absolute and his company was often hilarious. He was a patriot, a stalwart, a Nationalist.

He was a rock in our lives. He was proud of his family and his family are proud of him.

After the reception in the hotel my closest pals returned to Miltonduff with me. Dear Kevin McInnes, who worked as my gardener and general handyman, played the pipes and his mother was also there for, out of kindness, she had come to sit in the house whilst we were all at the funeral because, as she put it, 'the whole world would know that there would be no-one at home'. Jacqui's parents came all the way from Cork and my dear friend Lorna was there along with many others. It was some comfort but I was still overwhelmed by what had happened.

At first I thought that I should return to Parliament as soon as possible, not least because I had a pre-election tour of Scotland planned. However, after a week or so I realised that I simply could not go back as quickly as I expected. Things were too painful and too difficult. Kay Ullrich, as Chief Whip, was very understanding and supportive and I was put under no pressure to return until I felt I was ready.

As one who had written letters of condolence all my life I confess I never had any comprehension as to how consoling such letters are. However there were so many that Margaret helped by getting some cards printed, and I tried to answer everyone in time. Many came from Moray shop-keepers as Stewart loved shopping and was known all around for teasing the ladies, and the letters brought back his humour and his joie de vivre as well as his kindness. I even heard from friends of decades ago.

It was these letters which made it possible for me to carry on, for I felt sadder and sadder and the days seemed to have lost their flavour. When I used to get back on a Thursday night or Friday afternoon, Stewart, who would have watched every political programme and read every newspaper whilst I was away, would very quickly start to point out to me all the SNP mistakes of the past few days. We would always argue about them, yet how I longed even for those arguments again.

As I sometimes do when I have strong feelings, I wrote a poem which, although I am not very proud of it, I reproduce here because it came from the heart and it says what I felt and still feel.

> Stewart has died but the sun shines on
> And I have dreary days to fill
> And dreamful nights of guilt to spill
> Of wee small hours we did not share
> And lack of loving talk and care
> Where do the dead go?
> What do the dead know?
>
> Why did you go and leave me here
> To face vast solitudes of fear
> As flavourless the days go by
> As countless memories make me cry
> Dear spirit hover round my head
> For in my heart you are not dead.

Eventually, of course, I had to go back to work. I summoned up the courage but the experience was traumatic for not only were tributes paid in the Chamber, but in every corridor politicians of all parties, staff, police and security guards wanted to say something. There was a huge amount of kindness also in the streets, where people would stop me, and down in the Dublin colonies, where I had my flat, all the neighbours expressed their sympathy.

The last period of this first session was busy with finishing legislation. I remained keen on Land Reform and spoke in the Land Reform debates, welcoming some of the measures but drawing attention to the need to continue to eliminate the obscenity of so much of our precious national asset being owned by so few.

I was very disappointed too at Labour's appalling behaviour over a Bill to give the Gaelic language secure status. This had promised by Labour, the Liberals and ourselves in our manifestos in 1999, but Labour kept making excuses and setting up 'task forces'. Eventually Michael Russell introduced his own bill to force the Executive to honour its commitment. This was only the second Gaelic Language Bill ever introduced, the first having been put forward at Westminster by Donnie Stewart. I was a signatory of Michael's bill and spoke in the debates on it. I had also spoken, in Gaelic, in the Parliament's first-ever Gaelic-language debate in March 2000.

The Parliament's Education, Culture and Sport Committee held extensive hearings on the bill and recommended it to go forward, against the Executive's wishes. Despite an offensive speech made by Alasdair Morrison (who had been Minister for Gaelic but had done nothing to bring a secure status bill to the Parliament), it was passed unanimously on a free vote. Then, in order to get it through, Michael met with civil servants, with the agreement of ministers, and accepted some changes to ease its passage. He was assured in these discussions that Labour was seriously considering allowing the bill to go through as long as it was changed in accordance with their wishes.

However, the bill was within about an hour of being passed, needing only one short committee session and a short chamber debate, when Labour pulled the plug on it, refusing to include it in the business programme by means of a procedural device. It was shameful and it was doubly so because days later at the very start of the election campaign Jack McConnell went to Stornoway and promised that he would introduce such a measure if re-elected. But he, along with Andy Kerr, the Finance Minister and a crony of Jack's, had just prevented its passage for purely party political reasons.

Our pre-election preparations culminated in a special conference at the new Drumkinnon Tower at Loch Lomond, which was a very powerful event. In tribute to my retirement I was given a beautiful decanter and a video message from Sean Connery and John Hume. It felt strange to be not contesting this election, but I had lots of things to do which I hoped would help.

There were also other occasions to mark my imminent retirement. The parliamentary group also presented each retiring SNP member with a lovely decanter, and the Presiding Officer gave a dinner for all such members. The First Minister invited me to an evening reception in Bute House at which his wife, Bridget, played the piano. The small party included musicians and others and it was good to see the official residence of the First Minister being put to such a use, though I still long to see a Nationalist in residence preparing Scotland for independence.

But then the session came to an end and we all went our separate ways to contest seats or to fight campaigns. I had resuscitated my plan to tour Scotland and I made it clear that I would go wherever I was asked to, if that would assist our cause. I didn't make it to Orkney, Shetland or Caithness but I did get to the Western Isles, and I was driven thousands of miles around the country by my stalwart friend Gwen Ross Williams. We worked hard on the streets of Dundee, Aberdeen, Moray, Inverness, Banff, Edinburgh, Glasgow, Irvine and lots of other places, and in general the reaction was good. But the election was being fought once more against the backdrop of war.

The SNP had ensured that the whole issue of Iraq and weapons of mass destruction was debated in Edinburgh long before the war, despite opposition to any discussion by Labour and the Tories. The ostensible 'victory' in Iraq in the midst of the campaign gave a brief boost to Labour and made many people think that the issue was over and settled. The fact that it was not, and that the public had been deceived, did not emerge until after 1 May, so Labour once more – as in 1999 – had found war very convenient in their effort to ensure continuing power in the Scottish Parliament, whilst the SNP had found once more that having a Scottish election on Scottish issues was as hard for this Parliament as it had always been for Westminster.

Another difficulty was a general negative attitude to all those involved in the Parliament because of things like the ever-rising cost of Holyrood, Section 28, smacking, MSPs' salaries and the like. It was quite unfair for voters to associate the SNP with most of these issues, where blame usually lay fairly and squarely with the Executive, but as we were seen as key movers in the Parliament, we were forced to take some of the opprobrium, deserved or not.

The SNP also had its own specific problems. Margo MacDonald had finally decided, after a long dance of supposed indecision in front of the press, to resign from the party and stand as an independent on the Lothian list. It was a typical gesture from someone who had once been so dedicated, hard-working and inspirational but who had come to see herself as more important than the cause, and it attracted much damaging publicity, although others who had been badly treated in the list selections gamely soldiered on to try to make sure that the party did well.

I think there are many reasons why the SNP did less well in 2003 than in 1999. Some I have given above, and there are probably many others, including the curious 'sameness' of all the manifestos, in which distinctive vision was sadly absent. But the main reason was probably the image of disunity which we had given as a result of our list selection debacle and the subsequent departure of Margo. Of course the maverick Dorothy-Grace Elder had resigned from the group sometime before, and the cumulative effect was to show us as a party not fully focused on our primary aim. The public does not like parties which are unable to come together for the common good, and I suspect that we were being given a warning about such behaviour. Nonetheless all the polls showed that we remained the principal challengers to Labour and it is from that position that we must move forward in unity of purpose and strong determination. The year 2003 may have been a salutary lesson, but when the electoral smoke cleared we had at least retained our position as the second largest party and there was still much to work for.

I was, of course, delighted and relieved that both Margaret and Fergus retained their seats, and retained them well. They had both been hard-working constituency MSPs. I was also pleased that we kept our two places on the Highland list, that Jim Mather was at last in the Parliament where he could contribute on the economic and financial issues in particular and that Alasdair Nicholson again reduced Labour's majority in the Western Isles. I was glad that we had taken three more first-past-the-post seats than last time, with victories in Aberdeen North, Dundee East (back in the fold at last) and Ochil, where George Reid scraped in largely as a result of good organisation and also the dreadful behaviour of his Labour predecessor during the firemen's strike. The final electoral arithmetic made George's election as Presiding Officer of the Parliament much more likely and I was very pleased for him when he won the post. However, I was bitterly sorry that Andrew Wilson and Michael Russell had found themselves too far down their lists to be elected again, and the Parliament and the party were going to sorely miss their contributions.

It was strange to be watching the Parliament reassemble in early May and not to be part of it. For over thirty years I had known the sensation of turning up for a new session, full of optimism and determination. I knew I would miss the cut and thrust of the work and my retirement, which I had looked forward to, was now going to be much emptier and more difficult than I had thought, having lost so tragically my partner of forty-seven years just at the moment when we could have had time together. Nonetheless I had my children and grandchildren, many many friends, a beautiful house, the means to travel and enjoy life, and I was determined to make a start on my autobiography, which I had been putting off for the last two years. I had a story to tell and I wanted to tell it. I was not intending to be idle and there were also subjects I wanted to study, places I wanted to visit and people I wanted to see. In addition I was still being asked to go to events and even to speak at them. So I was prepared for the future and for further adventures after a long life of many such adventures.

15

Looking Forwards, Looking Backwards

AFTER SO MANY YEARS when the weekly and daily routine was travelling, meetings, correspondence and events of all types, it was very strange to be suddenly at leisure, and even stranger to be in the house at Miltonduff without Stewart.

At the end of April, as the election loomed, many of the newspapers carried items about the conclusion of my long parliamentary career, and they were complimentary and pleasant. But I had no intention of sitting back and doing nothing, for I was ever mindful of a poem that Wendy Wood had given to me, many years ago, which said:

> I thocht whan I wis saxty
> I wad be quait and douce
> I thocht that steel-bricht energy
> An time wad mak a truce
> I thocht I wad be sittin
> Just knittin
>
> But my een see faur mair colour
> Than whan my hairt wis young
> Ma lugs hear faur mair music
> Than aa my youth has sung
> Ma thochts is strong and unco gay
> Aa the day
>
> I niver wis sae thrang afore
> I niver wis sae free

> I cud nearly caa the starn doun
> An hing them on a tree
> Whit? Sit doun an count the years?
> Nae fears!

The SNP in Moray had decided some time before my retirement to hold an event – which they called 'Winnie's Highland Fling' – which would be a sort of 'send-off' after twenty-nine years representing them in one Parliament or another. Although I knew about the event I did not know that they had also arranged a remarkable presentation – a hand-sewn quilt setting out my life's history. The quilters, who each contributed a panel, included many unlikely embroiderers, amongst whom was my daughter-in-law Margaret. The event itself, held on 30 May, was full of my old friends from far and near and I felt very honoured by the huge turnout which included party leaders and former leaders, MPs, MSPs and MEPs (from home and abroad), councillors and party activists and stalwarts.

Despite the fact that it was my evening, I was determined to do something for someone else as well, and I managed to turn the tables on Tom Howe, my predecessor as candidate, by making a presentation to him. I explained to the company that I had won the seat on Tom Howe's back and it was time that I showed the proper gratitude!

The whole evening was magnificent and it brought back a huge number of memories. It is a wonderful thing to have been made so welcome in this community in Moray, and particularly so in the little town of Lossie-mouth, which I still think of as home. How often in a lovely morning did I stroll down from the Square to the harbour and rejoice at the boats and their wonderful names. I was becoming more and more conscious of the traditions and strengths of the place as I was spending longer and longer in it – a great change from my very mobile lifestyle of so many years.

However, I was back in Holyrood even in the first month after retirement. But the Holyrood I was visiting was the Palace, not the Parliament, for I was an overnight guest of the Lord High Commissioner to the General Assembly, who in 2003 was David Steel. He and Judy were very good hosts and the other guests included Neil MacCormick and his wife Flora, Menzies Campbell and his wife, and Tom Fleming.

I was given the Duke of Hamilton's Suite and it was a novel experience.

Each guest was allocated a formal aide from one of the services and the Air Force aide was a young woman of great ability and charm. One funny moment was when the splendid representative of the Scots Guards said he knew me because we had been fellow students at Sabhal Mor Ostaig, the Gaelic college on Skye, doing Grade 3 Gaelic – a course I had taken a couple of years previously. It was, I found, always good to have a friend at court as he was very attentive, as were the Palace staff. They enjoy having guests in residence, for when the Queen comes she brings her own staff and they are sidelined.

My favourite item in the Palace is not any of the grand treasures but the large-scale picture of the Queen receiving the Honours of Scotland in 1953, with the handbag painted out and with the little page boy behind her. That page boy grew up to be an advocate whom I instructed, an MP and a Government minister who is now an MSP for the Lothians; for it was James Douglas Hamilton, who always points out the picture to friends when visiting the palace.

After this visit I said to a few friends that I was worried that I might be joining the Establishment, an impression borne out by my award of honorary membership of the Law Society of Scotland and which was followed only three days later by another ceremony at which I was the guest of honour of the Chancellor of the Open University at their graduation ceremony! I had also started the real work on this book, beginning to write up the many notes and thoughts that I had begun to put into my chapter files. I was determined to get on and finish the book during 2003 if I could. I also continued to have engagements to fulfil, and in early June I travelled to the Plaid Cymru conference in Cardiff, where I had been asked to speak.

In my speech I recalled the time I had spent with Gwynfor Evans, first in his generous campaigning in Scotland in 1966 and then in the House of Commons, where he was such a huge support and comfort. I told many of the stories about our times together, and about my visits to Wales, including the one about my father who had seen the picture of me at another Plaid conference presenting a bowl of white heather, and who had died before I returned to Scotland. To illustrate the importance of sticking to our principles as national parties and believing in our ultimate success, I told the Plaid conference about Gwynfor and a young Welsh Labour

MP, Elystan Morgan. Elystan had been a Plaid member but had deserted to get elected. When Gwynfor won in 1966 Elystan came up to him in the Commons in great agitation. 'What shall I do?' he asked him, for he still believed in the things that Plaid believed in. Gwynfor replied, 'Vote as I do.' 'And you know,' Gwynor said, 'he never did, not even once. Not even a single time!'

Gwynfor did not attend the conference, as he had now gone into almost complete retirement. However I went to see him at his home, and we had a tearful and emotional reunion. He said to me, 'I am ninety-one now, and only have one tenth of my life left!' It was clear that despite his age, his spirit was still indomitable.

I had another pleasant engagement to fulfil in June – the prize-giving at St Columba's School in Kilmacolm. I have always liked speaking at prize-givings and in schools but I approached this one with a little trepidation because my grandchildren were due to go to the school and Terry and Jacqui live in the local community. I worked hard on the speech, as I think it is important that there should be a clear, easily understood message in such things, and one which does not bore the children – I remember prize-givings from my childhood. My 'Ten commandments' went down very well with teachers, parents and pupils alike and a number of people asked me for a copy. In a sense they sum up much of my philosophy of life, and it is worth repeating them here, just as I gave them to the children on that June day.

> Firstly, even if you have achievements and abilities beyond those of your companions avoid developing airs and graces. Politicians dare not have airs and graces because if they do, they are at once cut down to size by the Press and the Public. This happened to me at the recent election in Oban, where I was standing campaigning on a street corner. A lady from the *Oban Times* said to her teenage daughter, 'That's Winnie Ewing.' Her daughter said, 'Yes, we got her at school.' Her mother gently inquired, 'Modern studies?' – 'No, history.'
>
> Secondly, I urge you to fulfil your talents. Many of you have talents yet undiscovered. Remember that line from Gray's 'Elegy in a Country Churchyard': 'Some mute inglorious Milton here may rest'. Seek new activities, new interests, new subjects to read and study, new cultural

activities and sports. Never think of things you cannot do. I represented
Orkney as part of my vast Highlands and Islands constituency. In many
islands a travelling library delivered a box to each household and each
family member could choose several books for a week. There was a lot of
cross fertilisation of lending as each delved into the books chosen by the
others.

Thirdly, never be bored, as boredom is an insult to your education and a
sign of intellectual laziness.

Fourthly, cherish the friends of your youth, but seek friends of all ages.
Old people often tell me that often in company they feel invisible, yet they
have interesting stories to tell and rich experiences to pass on.

Fifthly – and now I am halfway through – remember that parents and
teachers are people. Never underestimate their capacity for sympathy and
understanding.

Sixthly, always keep up with current affairs at home and abroad. Glance
at – even better, read – more than one newspaper and observe how
accounts of events vary. And the seventh point is related to that one.
Be curious and always ask questions.

My eighth request to you is for you to make sure you know your own
history. You must make a future for your past. We cannot understand
today without the knowledge of yesterday. I was not taught history
seriously at school. I never read of the Scottish Enlightenment when it
was said that at any moment in Edinburgh twenty men of genius would
pass by in the Royal Mile. My father used to boast about all the inventions
of the Scots from the telephone to tarmac to television. Recently an
American author wrote a bestseller called *How the Scots Invented the
Modern World*. But the writer was not referring to the telephone or the
television, but to the kingdom of thought, and of a time when packed
audiences in Scotland eagerly embraced all sorts of knowledge at lectures
and events. In Dr Johnston's tour of the Highlands, he said 'Even the
Meanest Cotter here can read, write and argue.' This was ahead of Europe
as we were one of the first nations to insist on compulsory education and
this was due to the Church. Even before then, when Europe was in the
Dark Ages, Celts in Dublin and Iona were writing learned books.

Ninthly, remember that there is a fascinating world out there. Take any
chance you can get to visit and to learn from other people and other

countries. In my twenty-four years in the European Parliament, I was privileged to serve on the Third World Committee and to visit twenty-eight countries. I saw how ill divided is our own world. For example, one water pump can transform a whole area, for women no longer have to carry huge pitchers of water on their heads. I once tried to lift a full one and could not get it off the ground! Then vegetables can be grown, because there is water to hand, and the whole diet is revitalised. I remember in Ethiopia seeing a man ploughing a rock-hard field. I asked, 'What on earth is he doing?' I was told there had been no rain at all for a year but in case it might rain he was tilling his soil to receive it. Such small changes, and such small help from others like the provision of a water pump also frees people to be themselves. In Uganda their President (not Idi Amin) said to me, 'In Africa we do not want to be recipients of western culture. We want to develop our own' He gave a light-hearted illustration: 'When you Europeans go to a funeral you wear black. In Africa we wear white. In Europe, your brides wear white. In India they wear red.'

And, finally, respect other religions and faces, other occupations and other income groups. Winston Churchill said, 'We judge a civilisation by the way we treat minorities.' I am an expert on being a minority. I was alone for three years in the House of Commons and also a party of one for twenty of my twenty-four years in the European Parliament. In treating minorities such as me, Europe came out on top.

There endeth the lesson. I wish you all well and those leaving full and happy lives. But on a personal note I will add a final commandment – when seeking your life's partner choose someone who will make you laugh!

In reviewing these commandments as I write this, it seems to me that I have tried to follow all of them during my life, and it has made my life all the richer. And I continue to do so, even in my retirement.

During the summer of 2003, in a break from working on my book, I decided to take a trip back to my beloved Ireland. I went to the Ring of Beare, south of the Ring of Kerry, where Jacqui's parents, Jim and Maureen Murphy, have a magical cottage on the coast, with palm trees and with mountains on both sides – on one the mountains of Beare, and on the other the famous Macgillycuddy's Reeks. The sunsets were spectacular and the company of my pals Jo Docherty and Fiona McInnes made the holiday. As I walked the Irish lanes, and visited small towns with my friends, I began for the first time since January to feel that I might be able to find a future without my Stewart. Later in the summer Jean and I went to Islay again, where we painted and where the same feeling of a possible future arose. No doubt it was a sign that I was slowly healing, though the pain would never fully go.

Despite having retired as a full-time politician, I remained Party President and although I thought of retiring from that post too, my family and friends advised me to continue for at least another year so that I could remain involved in what was happening and so that I could give what help I could. I was glad that I had decided well before the nomination date to stand again, for, whilst I was not opposed, there was a challenge to John Swinney.

It seemed to me an absolutely unnecessary and damaging challenge and I said so both publicly and to the press in August. I believed that John Swinney had the total support of all the sensible people in the party and, furthermore, I was very concerned that the challenger, Dr Bill Wilson, had little of the experience necessary for the job.

Anyone who aspires to political leadership should know not just the small corps of activists in his or her part of the country, but should know the party and the people from all over. Dr McIntyre was right to say that public confidence depends on private trust, and private trust can only be earned by much effort and time spent with people in many different places. All the SNP leaders had been people with that breadth of knowledge and I found it incredible that someone should aspire to lead who had not acquired it, and who in a real sense had not yet served even an apprenticeship. Such a challenge was a distraction and, moreover, one that would occupy lots of attention in the media, who liked a spat and who were by and large always keen to damage the SNP.

That such a challenge was possible with the support of so few branches also concerned me, and taken with the fiasco of list rankings it did seem that those who were arguing for root and branch reform in the party, now had the weight of argument on their side. I therefore also indicated publicly that I would be backing major internal reform.

The campaign was, as I predicted, bruising, with much adverse publicity. Nevertheless those who wanted the party to move forward were strong in their advocacy not just of John but also of the ideas we needed to carry us on. These included the primacy of a referendum, in which the people of Scotland had the opportunity to actively choose independence.

Devolution had changed many arguments, and this was one of them. For the first time the SNP had a clear route which would allow it to take government in Scotland and then move the Parliament and country on to independence. But those around the leadership challenger – and the usual suspects who are always against any leadership of the party – wanted to argue differently and essentially to turn their backs on devolution. Such an ostrich-like attitude would have been absurd and counter-productive.

There was a particularly notable exchange of letters in the press between Jim Sillars – still carping from the sidelines – and Alex Salmond on this matter in which Alex undoubtedly had the better argument. I liked all his contributions, but particularly this one:

Jim Sillars (Letters, 9 September) asks how an SNP government could secure a vote for an independence referendum without an absolute majority in the Scottish Parliament. The answer is that there may well be MSPs who support independence but not the SNP, and others who do not agree with independence but favour the issue being settled by the people. I know some of those in the latter category and I think he knows some in the former.

He repeats the canard that I put independence tenth in my priorities in the 1999 election. The reality is that the independence referendum was presented as a vital step to a new Scotland, and the manifesto related every single substantive issue within it to the importance of moving on to independence.

I have spent my entire adult life arguing for independence. He spent the first half of his political career arguing against it, and the past ten years attacking those who argue for it on the basis that we don't believe in it as much as he does.

I recognise the zeal of the convert, but the sad fact is that his contribution for many years had been entirely negative. His talent could have been really important for Scotland's cause. What a pity that he wasted it.

I always agonise over my conference speech as President and not having to make it anymore will be one of the great advantages of laying down a post I have held for many years. This year it was more difficult than ever, because I wanted to say something about the present situation in the party, and to indicate that disunity was only likely to lead to electoral defeat. I consulted my family and a few friends when I was developing ideas for the speech, as I always did. The final draft, though, was mine and I continued to work on it during conference itself, being helped with the typing by a member of the Headquarters staff. I knew that I would be delivering the speech after the result of the leadership contest was announced, and that also influenced what I would say. As it was, John won by an overwhelming majority, having been greatly helped by a rousing speech he made the day before which vanquished his critics. He then went on to win, again overwhelmingly, the debate on internal reform.

I usually speak towards the end of the last day of conference, so when I rose to speak in Inverness the hall was full. I made some remarks about the current political situation, in particular Labour's many failures and their dishonesty in going to war on false pretences. But as far as the internal situation in the party was concerned, I confined myself to a short but direct section in the middle of my speech, saying:

> I see an obstacle to SNP progress in the present internal party wrangling. Our strategy was to prove by our elected talent that we could form a government. Our strategy was not to select out the proven talent.
>
> When lack of trust is needlessly paraded in the press, the SNP loses public support. I say needlessly because we have three democratic bodies – conference, council and assembly. Any branch can propose and alter policy in all three. Some critics now were silent when the policies they are criticising were passed.
>
> But here a few facts. The SNP lost six seats, not eight. Labour too lost six seats, three to the SNP. John is not the first SNP leader to lose seats. Alex Salmond lost a quarter of his Parliamentary team in 1992 and led the SNP upwards and onwards to the establishment of a Scottish Parliament seven years later. Gordon Wilson in the 1980s lost a third of the party's votes but also continued to lead the party for another seven years.
>
> The SNP is a broad party and encourages debate. Even this week Gerry Fisher moved that we should revisit the settled referendum policy of the party, but Conference showed it had no appetite for such a debate. And let

me remind members, on that settled policy, of the Westminster dirty tricks department, which has no peers in ruthlessness, nor in unconstitutional behaviour. We must remain true to the UN Charter, which is clear: 'If a nation votes for self determination, the UN members must give support.' Referenda are used across many EU nations to establish particular policies clearly. Voters in a general election cast their ballots for parties on many issues. Such votes are motivated by many different factors. The argument for a single question referendum on independence put by, amongst others, one of Europe's leading constitutionalists – our own Professor Neil MacCormick – was passed not just by our duly constituted bodies. It was passed also on the basis of sheer logic and good sense.

I also drew attention to the utterly false description in the press of certain attitudes as being 'fundamentalist' and the practice of referring to the holders of such views as 'fundamentalists'. I told Conference that I – and Gwynfor Evans – were fundamentalists, as was everyone in the SNP, because 'the restoration of national sovereignty is our fundamental belief,' and I upbraided those who tried to divide the party by claiming that they believed in independence more than others.

Later on in my speech I quoted Margaret Ewing, who had told the conference the year before that 'the longest mile is the last mile home', and I enjoined my fellow members to show patience and to realise the wisdom of what Gwynfor Evans had told me years ago – to be prepared for a long haul. He always thought that I, and all the SNP, were too optimistic about the pace of change, but he knew that in time that change would come.

I have remained optimistic throughout the years, and am optimistic now. I believe that Scotland will be an independent country within Europe, an equal part of the wider world at last, and I believe that I shall see it in my lifetime. It is obvious to me how much my country has changed even in my lifetime, and that much progress has been made, though it is sometimes hard for the SNP to stand back and realise how much has been done.

For example, when I was a solicitor in Glasgow and then first elected to Hamilton I had a standing order with Smith's – the St Vincent Street bookshop – to supply me with all the new Scottish titles that came out. At that time there were probably one or two a month: now I could not possibly afford to buy even a tenth of them, so great is the flow of writing and thinking in this country and about this country. There is a new confidence in all things Scottish, which expresses itself in many different ways. I read the *Press and Journal* every day, and over 90 per cent of the wedding photographs have the groom in a kilt, or in trews. I suspect that fifty years ago, the number so attired for their nuptials would have been minuscule.

As I come to the end of my life's story – or at least that part of it up until now, for I like Gwynor's view of life, and by that reckoning I am still only three-quarters of my way through – I see Scotland as a nation emerging from a long period of colonial rule and slowly beginning to find its own voice and its own way forward. This is a difficult thing to do. It was Hegel who wrote: 'to be the object of contempt or patronising tolerance on the part of a proud neighbour is one of the most traumatic experiences that a society can suffer', and the Scots have suffered it for so long that we seem to have developed some sort of flaw in our psyche which makes us not only accept the situation but also be apologetic about our country, when we should of course be very proud of it.

There are many such forces acting against us as we begin to reassert ourselves. One of them is that the Government south of the border needs Scotland financially, emotionally and psychologically. That government – of whatever hue – has never understood Scotland or the Scots, but is very reluctant to let us go, for to do so would reflect on their ability to govern and would leave them having to confront the real problems of a small nation on the edge of the European continent. By holding on to Scotland they can continue to pretend to be important, to assume that they can punch above their weight. We are an essential part of maintaining such a false image. It would, in reality, be kindness to England to step away and let England be itself. In that memorable phrase from Douglas Crawford's maiden speech in the House of Commons we would 'cease being a surly lodger, and become a good neighbour'.

The rest of the world sees us differently. In the former British colonies Scots are remembered (usually) with affection, for they were teachers and ministers and engineers and they left things of value behind. We can make that contribution again, in the equality of nations, but we need to be free to do so. In Europe we are seen as a people of ability and generosity, with a positive outlook. We are frequently contrasted with the English, whose attitude in Europe has been to tell other nations what to do, rather than seek to find ways of doing things together. Much of Europe would welcome us with open arms as soon as we have the confidence to demand equality rather than subservience.

Westminster democracy fools itself when it regards its practices as the best in the world. The old-fashioned English system, with its unwritten constitution, has allowed prime ministers to become virtual dictators and has held Scotland in thrall against our best interests and against all logic. Harold Wilson was perhaps the most sympathetic to Scotland and, together with Richard Crossman, I think genuinely believed that change was needed in the relationship between the two countries – a belief held by the more thoughtful at Westminster for many years. Keir Hardie, in his election address for Mid Lanark in 1888 wrote that he was 'strongly in favour of Home Rule', being convinced that 'until we have a Parliament of our own, we cannot obtain the many and great reforms on which I believe the people of Scotland have set their hearts'. And even Winston Churchill believed it as early as 1911, when, speaking as the Liberal Candidate for Dundee, he said, 'We have to secure for Scotland a much more and direct method of bringing influence to bear on her domestic affairs. There is nothing which conflicts with the integrity of the UK in the setting up of the Scottish Parliament.'

That of course is the key issue for many Unionists – the slippery slope argument to which Tam Dalyell has been so devoted. Yet it is a profoundly undemocratic argument for it really says that the governance of Scotland must not be changed in case it makes us keen to extend our democratic right to choose how we live. If the Union is so good, those who fear a break-up should have no fears, but for my part I believe that the experience of self-government will lead to a demand for more and better self-government. Yet – and this is the only stance a true democrat can take – at the end of the day it must always be for the people themselves to decide. For Tony Blair, I believe, devolution was mere expediency – a promise that could no longer be denied. But having been forced into it, he is also determined to hamstring it and to limit the right of a free people to move forward. That shows how little he trusts democracy and how little he understands the democratic imperative on which our whole society must be based.

The puzzle for me is not in the English – their self-interest demands that they continue as they are until they are forced to change. The real puzzle lies in the Scots themselves – Scots like Willie Ross, who made a great profession of his Scottish feeling and who was a passionate admirer of Burns, the archetypal Scot. Yet Willie lacked the spark of ambition and vision to see the true potential of his country, and instead doggedly persuaded himself that our best interests would always lie in accepting meekly the diktat from south of the Border. No wonder he always seemed so unhappy and was always so curmudgeonly. Willie has his many successors in people like Brian Wilson, George Foulkes, Helen Liddell and countless others – Scots of potential who are prepared to sacrifice their nation because they cannot see clearly enough the truth of the present situation, or if they see it are afraid of its consequences, not least for their careers.

One glance along the Scottish Labour benches at Westminster shows how intellectually impoverished such an attitude is, and what dearth of talent it produces. In Labour the cult of the 'third man' still rules. They used to say that it was always the third man that was chosen for any Labour seat in Scotland, as the first would be dismissed as too clever and a threat to the quiet life of the Labour establishment or rotten borough, the second would be allied too closely with one faction or another, so it was the third that was chosen, and little was expected of him except to turn up and do as he was told. There are lots of those left at Westminster but they are there in the Scottish Parliament too.

Jack McConnell is, of course, the third first minister. Since he succeeded Henry McLeish, who had ability and vision but who lacked confidence, the old Scottish problem, little has happened and little has changed. A quiescent devolved Scotland is being delivered to his Labour bosses in London in exchange for his right to rule and exercise patronage. It is not what was meant to happen and it is little wonder that people are disappointed. There is a terrible dumbing down being practised by government in Scotland, a deliberate dampening of expectation.

The public sense of disappointment with the Parliament hurts me deeply. In part it is to do with the way in which Labour and the Liberals have governed – without vision and ambition and without listening to the people. But it is also a product of the grievous mistakes made by Donald

Dewar and others with regard to the new Parliament building. It is right to expose vigorously what has been happening, and Fergus has been in the forefront of such activity. But once that has been done, the cost of the building is not the biggest issue that confronts Scotland. The Scottish tendency to dwell on the negative, not the positive, is one of the problems. So is the hostile press, determined to knock down those whom it has built up and keen to belittle Scotland at every opportunity.

I find it astonishing that there is not a greater concern about the power of the press. I remember an Irish colleague from Fianna Fáil saying to me, apropos of the power of the British media and their slavish adherence to the status quo, that if the BBC had existed in 1919, Ireland would not have become independent. Often the Scots seem almost brainwashed by the media messages which constantly tell us that we cannot afford to be independent and that we are a poor wee backward country, quite unfit to make our way in the world. It is a democratic outrage that not a single newspaper in Scotland supports, or is even moderately neutral about, independence and the SNP. Almost a third of Scots choose a non-Unionist party yet the press and media are entirely Unionist. This situation is made even more problematic because of the Scots' fondness for reading and consuming news. We take more papers than any other country in Europe, yet our media diet is politically biased and sometimes even poisonous.

Much of this is do to with media ownership and control, which inevitably lies outside Scotland. But it is also to do with the cosy culture of cronyism, in which Labour in Scotland often gets an easy ride in return for easy stories supplied to willing journalists in which easy assumptions about the status quo are always made. Of course not all journalists are like that, nor all newspaper editors, but there are sufficient to make sure that very little changes and that there is a pressure against change.

What can the SNP do in such a situation? There is only one answer and that is vigorous, direct campaigning which takes the message to people's towns, streets and doors. It was how we won Hamilton and it is how any seat is won and held. Razzmatazz, a high visual profile, loudspeakers, leaflets and lots of door knocking. That is the way that the party has built its success in the past and that is the foundation on which its future success must be based.

Nowadays there sometimes seems to be an element of defeatism in some of our candidates and campaigners. They believe that some constituencies can never be won and that the effort they need to put in will not be rewarded by success. So they put in little effort. It is vital that such an attitude changes, for I believe that every seat – every seat – is winnable.

I showed again and again how votes could be won even in the most unpromising places – for example in Orkney, where I stood in the 1983 General Election and which subsequently voted for me in every European ballot. There must be no no-go areas, and no candidates who believe in no-go areas. The SNP must start with a strong self belief and let that self belief be seen everywhere. A shining example is that of Andrew Wilson, who in 2003 very nearly won Cumbernauld as a result of sheer campaigning effort, despite being dumped down the list by those who should have known better.

The SNP can only build its future and the future of Scotland on confidence – the confidence of success. Our message, internally and externally, needs to be one which emphasises the good things and emphasises our abilities. We live in one of the wealthiest countries in the world, yet a third of our children grow up in poverty. We are oil rich – the 'Scotland's Oil' campaign was one of the great achievements of the SNP and one for which the SNP owes Gordon Wilson a great debt of gratitude – yet we seem hardly ever to talk about oil these days. We need more of the French attitude, that attitude that is proud of producing the best and having the best, and is not ashamed to say so. We have lots of the best – the best scenery, the best beef, the best export record – and we should be shouting those from the rooftops. Such confidence will breed more confidence. It is no accident that there are some constituencies in Scotland, such as Angus, where the SNP succeeds generation after generation. It is because it expects success and it has worked for that success constantly.

I believe that the present angst about failing to make a breakthrough in the Central Belt of Scotland is deeply misplaced. The SNP is strong in many areas, like the North-east and the Highlands, and once we are strong throughout the other parts of Scotland the Central Belt will collapse for Labour like a pack of cards. We should be devoting our time to strengthening our organisation and performance in places all around Glasgow and

Edinburgh, surrounding them and then invading them, so to speak. Edinburgh will, of course, be the last to go, but go it will, for the whole of Scotland is susceptible to a message of confidence and optimism delivered on the doorstep by hard-working political campaigners. And they must be hard-working, *united*, political campaigners, because the party needs unity as much as anything else. We must trust each other before the people of Scotland will trust us.

But of course we must also watch what others are doing. Labour is in a historic decline, though its sheer dominance tends to mask that fact. Its lack of talent and vision is palpable, even though there are some able people still in the party who want to see change. I was very struck in particular with Wendy Alexander's open-minded approach to SNP economic policy, as expressed in her letter to Jim Sillars which was leaked to the media, even if she tried to redeem herself later in the eyes of the lumpen Labour members by constant attacks on us. She and some others know that there are good ideas across the political spectrum and that Labour as it is presently led in Scotland is going nowhere, and taking Scotland nowhere.

If and when proportional representation for local government is delivered, that will further erode Labour's Stalinist contest of local councils, and it will further decline. Its dead hand will be loosened and the Parliament and Scotland will begin to be able to move forward again.

The Liberals should be on the side of change, for they are a party with a strong Scottish radical history. Indeed at one time they could have claimed to be 'Scotland's party' but they have abandoned that aspiration in exchange for the crumbs from the government table. Without any expectation of being able to take power and use it – either north or south of the border – they have become the perpetual power brokers. Experience elsewhere in Europe shows that the public eventually tire of such parties.

The Tories remain a deeply anti-Scottish party, for their whole raison d'être runs counter to Scottish opinion and feeling. They are elitist and believe in the overwhelming power of money and rank: Scotland is egalitarian and wants equality to be the guiding principle. Nonetheless, they could change and if they were to adopt a more 'Scottish' position – perhaps of Scottish-based right-wing radicalism – then they might begin to come back from the margins.

The Greens will always now be around in ones or twos but their inherent extremism – for example their blanket objection to car ownership and road building – will keep them on the fringes, perhaps pricking the conscience of Scotland about matters such as GM crops, which was handled very badly by the Scottish Executive and by a Liberal minister who has gone against every Liberal belief.

The SSP are more of a threat to the SNP but I do not believe that they have a long-term future. They have picked up SNP votes by articulating a radical vision more energetically and effectively on the doorsteps and in the media than we have in recent years but that vision is so tainted by wild-eyed dogmatism (for example the nationalisation of the supermarkets) that the public will become wary of them. Indeed had it not been for the skills of my old colleague in Europe, Hugh Kerr, who runs their national operation so effectively, I believe that they would have collapsed by now. Tommy Sheridan, much regarded as a charismatic leader, is certainly an orator but I have always found him lacking in personal conversation or charm.

The PR system for electing the Scottish Parliament has allowed the SSP, the Greens and the Independents to flourish, but I doubt whether this will continue much beyond the second Parliament. Their inability to deliver anything will become a problem, and the party system, for all its faults, does ensure that there is a degree of accountability and discipline quite unknown to the mavericks. Nonetheless, the parties will have to become more responsive to the public again, as will politicians as a breed.

One of the SNP's present difficulties lies in that sameness of politicians. Thirty years ago it would have been impossible to have had a 'career' in SNP politics – indeed being in the SNP, as many of us knew to our cost, was positively bad for any career and it still often is. Now there is a career-structure developing, with individuals working as Parliamentary or constituency assistants and then moving onto lists or into candidacies. This has caused tensions and also produced a blandness which needs to be banished. SNP candidates should be judged not on who they know, or who they have worked for, but on their ability to lead constituencies, work hard, and believe that anything can be won if the right amount of effort is put in. They must also be in the forefront of recruiting new members and bringing in fresh talent so that the SNP becomes a party that people want to join and which expresses the whole country's aspirations. Internal reform is vital for that, but so is a new sense of excitement about the future and a new campaigning edge which refreshes our position in Scottish politics and builds on it. The SNP should always remember Compton Mackenzie's words in his rectorial address to Glasgow University: 'We, now alive in Scotland, are offered the grace of sharing in the rebirth of our nation.' It is a grace – an extraordinary privilege – and we should embrace it with both hands and our whole heart.

The SNP should be – and is – in a good position. The Parliament is our strong base camp on the climb to independence. Our job is to prove that we can govern, that we have the talent in our ranks to govern, and that we can, in government, build on the magnificent strengths of our nation. We must show that Britain is not good for us, and is not great any longer, but that working in partnership with England and with Europe we can achieve new things from a firm foundation of ability and wealth. We have to demonstrate our confidence and lead people forward in confidence. We have to be a truly national and international party, not just a 'nationalist' party.

We must push the Parliament to campaign for more powers and we must campaign for those powers out in the country. The concept of fiscal autonomy is one that is easy to understand and one which attracts widespread support already. The control of our own resources is essential for we are the only country to have discovered oil and still have become no better off. We also have vast supplies of the key resource of the twenty-first century – water – whilst there is a scarcity of it elsewhere, including England, and we have a huge ability to generate power by wind and other methods. Far from coming to the end of our riches, we are just coming into them.

Our education system must reflect our national hopes. There is still far too little taught about Scotland in schools and far too much official forelock-tugging and political correctness. In my own profession – the law – there are huge challenges ahead, including that of a Supreme Court which will weaken Scots law. We must be eternally vigilant that Scotland's short- medium- and long-term potential to govern itself and to be an independent nation is not being deliberately eroded by Westminster, whose actions on things such as the theft of our fishing waters (which took place by stealth as we were preparing to elect the first Parliament) and imposition of inappropriate ways of doing things can only weaken our institutions and our potential.

Sometimes when I look at the pressures upon Scotland and the SNP I am surprised that we have achieved so much. Without press support, with constant deceit and trickery from successive Westminster governments and with collusion in such practices from some of Scotland's own representatives, it is indeed remarkable that we have moved from being part of one of the most centralised states in Europe to a measure of self-government. Alex Salmond always maintained that it was that first significant move – the move to the Parliament – that was the most difficult. Once the Rubicon had been crossed, then it was possible to see more clearly how we could progress. Despite the difficulties the party has experienced in the last few years, I am sure that we can again march onwards and achieve our aims. The Scottish genie is well and truly out of the bottle.

As President of the SNP I have tried to be an active and dynamic force, showing an example and being prepared to campaign anywhere and everywhere. Even when I am not President I shall still want to go to by-elections and to take part in national and local campaigns, for it is by taking part that any member can contribute to the overall prospects of success.

But now that I have retired, at least from day-to-day work, I want also to enjoy this country of mine. I want to travel to Tiree and to Ireland, rather than to Tanzania and India as I did in the past, but I shall still travel. I shall be active in the European Election campaign of 2004 and the General Election that will follow it, most probably in 2005, when I will be working as hard as ever to ensure that Perth continues to return my daughter Annabelle. And then in 2007 I shall no doubt be on the streets of Inverness and Moray for Fergus and Margaret as well as elsewhere for others.

I have retained my little flat in Edinburgh and am planning to undertake a course of study on the history of the Bible to keep my mind active and to explore areas of interest which I have always had. I shall try and see my old friends more often than I have been able in recent years, to stay with them and have them stay with me in the lovely house in Miltonduff that Stewart worked so hard to perfect. And I shall paint and even perhaps write a bit more, though writing this has been hard enough!

Most of all I shall continue to support, argue for and seek independence for my country. From that day when I heard 'The Road to the Isles' being played on a steamer going 'doon the watter' I have known that independence for Scotland – normality for my nation – was the thing that needed to happen to allow us to be the people we can be. I have never doubted that it would come and although the road has been winding, it is coming ever closer. It is now within our grasp. I am proud to have been part of the struggle for it.

Some months ago a journalist asked me if I thought that I had been 'lucky' in my career, pointing to the seats I had won and my long tenure in Europe. I don't think I have been particularly lucky – I think I have worked hard, with the wonderful support of many people, but perhaps I have been lucky, for luck may be just that: the ability to take advantage of circumstance and commit one's all to a task without looking back. Yet now, in looking back, I realise that the act of writing one's autobiography is a bit like opening Pandora's Box. Some things I would rather not have remembered have come out as well as all the pleasant memories. It has therefore been a true reflection of life, even down to the fact that when Pandora's Box was finally emptied into the world, it still contained one item – hope. For I go on hoping and working for the future, confident of success in time.

There is one final memory that comes to me that seems to sum things up. One of the German members of the European Parliament whom I admired had been in a Nazi prison for the whole of the war, under constant threat of execution. One day he told me that while he was there he had with him a waistcoat. He bribed and cajoled his guards to bring him little bits of thread whenever they could and he used these tiny scraps to sew flowers on the waistcoat, eventually covering it completely. I was fascinated by the story and asked him what became of the waistcoat when he was finally released. 'Ah,' he said, 'I left it behind in my cell. I left it there along with my animosity.' I too have tried in this book to celebrate the kisses rather than remember the kicks, and as I finally put my pen down I hope I have succeeded, at least in part.

I began this book with the story of that very emotional moment as I watched the Tartan Express leaving me alone in London after my victory in Hamilton. Let me end with another Hamilton memory: the victory dance in Larkhall, booked and arranged before the vote with admirable impudence and admirable confidence by the Larkhall branch. If I close my eyes I can still see and hear everyone in that crowded hall singing, with total conviction, 'Deep in my heart, I do believe, that Scotland shall be free some day.' I shall always be able to hear those voices and those words, for that belief remains as strong as ever in my own heart. We *shall* be free some day.

Editor's Note

I first heard of Winnie Ewing's desire to write her autobiography in a pub in Edinburgh. From time to time I fell into conversation with Winnie as we both left the Parliament Chamber after voting in the early evening, or after one of the members' business debates which took place between 5 p.m. and 6 p.m. and which she regularly attended. As we walked down the High Street she would say, 'Buy me a drink', and, taking my arm, she would turn into the little close that leads to the pub in that area which she liked the most – The Jolly Judge.

Sometimes we were joined by Margaret and Fergus or any one of half a dozen other SNP MSPs or journalists who frequented that particular place. Winnie would inevitably tell a story or two about her time in Europe or at Westminster, normally in illustration of some current political point that was being made. Although many of us had heard some of the stories already, there were always new ones too and someone, at some stage, must have said that she should write them down, so entertaining were they and so salutary for those of us who were only in our first term as Parliamentarians.

One evening, when we were sitting on our own, she asked me if I thought she would be able to write a book about her life. She knew that I had written several books but, like most non-authors, she was terrified of the prospect of taking on something that she thought would be lengthy, difficult and perhaps impossible to achieve. I told her that of course she could do it, but that she would need to plan it out before she started, and she asked me to help her. I also warned her that, in Thomas Hardy's double-edged words, 'There is no pleasure in writing, only in having written.' She knew what I and Hardy meant but she was keen to have a go and accordingly, some months later, we finished a synopsis which laid out the details of eleven chapters. I then introduced her to Hugh Andrew of

Birlinn who quickly agreed to publish the book, preferably in the spring of 2003, just in time for the next Scottish Parliament election.

I advised Winnie to open eleven folders and to begin to dictate stories and anecdotes as she remembered them, putting the finished pages into chapter order as she went along. It would then be much easier to take each folder and make a finished chapter from it. She started to do so, but as the months went past she would often say to me that she was making less progress than she wanted, but intended to do more when she had retired. The spring of 2003 was clearly a target that would not be met, but after her retirement there would be plenty of time for writing.

It was obvious to Hugh and me from the beginning that she would need a good editor to collaborate on the book. It was my wife who suggested Daphne Reid, but although she was very interested and had the ideal qualifications of being an experienced editor, someone who was very knowledgeable about politics and a friend of Winnie's, whom Winnie trusted, she was reluctant to agree until after the 2003 elections when it would be clearer what George, her husband, was going to be doing. Winnie had already raised with me the possibility of my editing the book, but I found it hard enough to allocate time within my political and personal lives for my own writing, and was very reluctant to take on such a large-scale project.

But circumstance has a habit of changing plans and ideas. I knew almost as soon as I had lost my seat that it was likely Winnie would come back to me and ask me again, and indeed that happened within days of the election. I also knew that Daphne Reid would not now be available, as George had become Presiding Officer.

I was still not certain that it was a job I was ready to do, but Winnie can be very persistent and after discussion with Hugh it seemed an opportunity too good to refuse. A financial package was agreed to allow me to devote much of my time for at least six months and I drafted letters of agreement with Winnie which she quickly acceded to. One of those letters laid out the means by which we would proceed.

Winnie undertook to provide me with chapters in draft form on disk, which she would write in longhand and have typed by her secretary. Winnie's writing is, she admits herself, hard to decipher and I felt that I would be unable to make significant progress with the book within the anticipated time frame unless I had electronic text to work with. Winnie herself does not use a word processor or computer, so someone would have to key in what she had written. Winnie quickly found a temporary secretary who was willing to have a go.

Once I had edited each chapter she would see it – ideally by means of my going through it with her in Miltonduff. She would suggest changes and then agree the final text which would be provided to the publishers. When we had a complete book we would review the whole thing to see if any additions were required before formally submitting it for publication.

During the last few months of her time in Parliament – and particularly after Stewart had died – she had started to place more and more things in the folders and these gave her the opportunity to start drafting. She wrote at speed, with the first chapter coming to me before the end of June, though we had reached our final agreement only in the middle of that month. More followed at shorter and shorter intervals, for she devoted much time and effort to drafting, and in addition she started to give extra material to her son Terry and daughter-in-law Jacqui for them to type up and send to me. Soon a flurry of e-mails was arriving with lots of attachments! Winnie was also finding things amongst her papers that she thought would be helpful, so these would also arrive by mail, sometimes without explanation.

Editing the material was a long process. First Winnie's draft chapter would be printed out and read several times. Then I would start moving material about to provide a better flow as well as checking names and dates – where they could be checked – and adding in material about missing issues, which she or I would identify. Usually these were discussed on the phone and I would then summarise the discussion and insert the material. However, sometimes I would ask her for a new section to be written by herself – for example, the births of both Terry and Annabelle which were originally missing, and also the details of how she obtained Objective One Funding for the Highlands and Islands.

There were also on occasion repetitions in the text which had to be removed, bridges between stories and incidents to be constructed and a general flow inserted, but slowly the final chapter would emerge. Two chapters became overlong and had to be split, whilst the process also threw up the need to use more space on her experiences as an MEP, doubling the number of European chapters. The envisaged eleven chapters eventually became fifteen, and the final wordage which I estimated at just below 100,000 words when we started began to rise to the 190,000 plus that made up the final manuscript as submitted to the publishers.

The first ten chapters were discussed with her face to face in Miltonduff, where I would go for a night to read them through to her and to add material or correct inaccuracies that had crept in. The remaining five were sent to her for her to read first, and she returned them marked up with changes. This difference in approach was necessitated by the sheer volume of material. Once the chapters were agreed their drafts were supplied to the publisher for information and copies – punched for her growing ring binder that contained the almost final text – would be sent to Miltonduff. This resulted in some further small changes, often by return of post, including those of punctuation and spelling.

Winnie allowed one or two other people to see the final chapters once they were in her binder and they made the occasional suggestion or correction. Margaret and Fergus Ewing in particular took a keen interest and Margaret made valuable suggestions for the final chapter, which was originated differently. It was constructed firstly from material that had been intended for Chapter 14 but which related to the period after Winnie had retired, and then from the detail of a long discussion I had with Winnie just before Christmas 2003, during which we explored her political views.

The final complete text for submission to the publishers was eventually prepared (over the course of a single weekend) from the draft chapters already agreed, with the addition of a small number of additional 'fragments' that she had dictated during the process and which had not yet been incorporated into the text.

The technical issues were sometimes daunting but the pleasure of undertaking the task did not wane as I learnt more and more about a remarkable life and began to understand its significance in terms of Scottish politics and Scottish history in the last part of the twentieth century. Winnie Ewing is a truly unique politician, for working with very few others she put the idea of an independent Scotland on the international political map, whilst also building the national movement that we know as today's SNP. She is without doubt Scotland's most remarkable woman politician of her generation but also one of the very few internationally significant Scottish politicians of the modern age. Her story is therefore one of importance not just in personal terms, but also in terms of understanding the Scotland we live in today.

Her sheer longevity as an active politician is the first remarkable part of her achievement. In a party which – as I know to my cost – tends to change its favours with some rapidity she has retained the support and affection of the vast majority of members in her own constituencies and in the party across the country for the best part of forty years. From her election in Hamilton in November 1967 to her retiral from the Scottish Parliament, a period of thirty five and a half years, she was only out of elected office for just over four years. At the same time she remained a member – in one guise or another – of the SNP's National Executive Committee for all of that period and still does, in the role of Party President which she has occupied for almost fifteen years, being challenged for it only once, and that as an ill-conceived joke by a malcontent with no hope of election. It is a record that is unlikely ever to be surpassed, and certainly not by a nationalist politician.

Her record of electoral success is equally impressive when considered in terms of elections won. She has contested eleven Parliamentary elections as a candidate, and won eight of them, being returned – as a result of those contests – by two different Westminster constituencies, the largest constituency in the European Parliament and the largest region in the Scottish Parliament.

Having campaigned with her on many occasions and in many different places – from the Western Isles in 1979, through Larkhall in 1987 to Irvine in 2003 – I know that she has instant recognition from the vast majority of Scots voters and a manner on the streets which inspires confidence. Her unique technique of 'campaigning by shopping' – going into small shops to talk to customers and staff alike whenever she gets the chance – is remarkably successful, as is her devotion to high-profile activity using loudspeakers and as much razzmatazz as possible. Her energy on the stump is prodigious and she is always the last one to agree to stop at the end of a long and tiring day.

But it is not just as a long active political phenomenon that Winnie should be known. She has achieved the remarkable distinction within the Scottish National Party of being largely above the factionalism which has so pervaded that movement over many years. Although she was involved in attempting to reject the influence of the 79 Group and in taking action against its leading members, that involvement was more tangential than central, and was as a result of her long-standing friendship with individuals such as Gordon Wilson, rather than because of ideological concerns. Normally Winnie has stood above and apart from the internecine warfare that erupts from time to time, and indeed has counselled against it whenever it has taken place.

I think the reason for that stance is that Winnie Ewing is a simple nationalist. I use that term as a compliment, for what I mean is that her belief in independence is not ideologically bound to any part of the political spectrum. Whilst not a left-wing radical, she nonetheless espouses some left-wing and radical views on matters such as land ownership, human rights and immigration. Whilst not a right-wing conservative, she holds fairly conservative opinions on some matters of personal morality and social inclusion. I suspect that the type of Scotland she wishes to see as an independent nation is not that far different from the type of Scotland that we have now, enhanced by the ability to make its decisions and to play a full part in the world. But equally – and these are not terms she likes – she is neither a fundamentalist nor a gradualist in the nationalist spectrum. Or rather, she is both, for she fundamentally believes in independence, but she is politically mature enough to be absolutely certain that independence can only be gained by ensuring a growth in confidence in the powers of our existing Parliament and an extension of those powers.

She is, in other words, a pragmatist both in policy and political terms. She is also a pragmatist in personal terms, working with what is, rather than always desiring something better. She is prepared to compromise for individual and national good, but she always does so with her original aims in mind. She never abandons them.

Most of the splits and tensions in the SNP have come both from personal differences between individuals and from ideological disputes about the type of Scotland which the SNP should seek to achieve. Because the SNP has become more than a national movement which only wishes to achieve freedom, before dissolving itself, these tensions are perhaps inevitable. However, they are fuelled by a constant wish to control the levers of power in the party. Winnie has never felt the need to lead the SNP or to control it: she has been far more interested in ensuring that the party itself does well and that its overall aims are progressed. She has also been far more interested in making sure that she won and held seats herself, rather than watching what others were doing. That is another pragmatic stance.

These somewhat unique traits in the SNP explain both her popularity amongst members and her popularity amongst the voting public. Those she has helped and served know that she is more interested in people than in the abstract of policies: those that she has worked amongst within the party know that she will take her own line as she sees fit, and whilst never blate in expressing her point of view, they also know that she will not attempt to use the press or the party machine to enforce it. She is, above all, completely loyal to those with whom she works on a common cause.

Her larger-than-life personality, her great sociability (for there are few people I would rather spend an evening talking with and listening to than Winnie) and her kindness are aspects of her character that have made her much sought company wherever she has worked. They ideally suited her for a life in various Parliaments, for life in Parliament can often produce occasions where companionship and relaxation are essential and only to be found amongst other Parliamentarians and their staff. Such institutions take those with forceful but civilised characters to their hearts and such individuals become more influential than they might otherwise be. They are often distinguished and natural back-benchers, holding the conscience of the Parliament in their hands and Winnie – despite her prominent role in the party over many decades – is by nature that type of politician.

She is also that type of person. By no means an inveterate gossip – for she has too much charity and concern about others to be such – she nonetheless is a master raconteur who can hold and entertain a company with innumerable stories and anecdotes. But she can also respect confidences and give wise advice in private, and those skills are immensely valuable in politics too. They add to the respect in which people hold her, particularly those who know her well.

Nonetheless her sheer experience has given her an ability to influence matters much beyond that normally given to those who never achieve ministerial office. Reading much about Winnie's speeches, questions and interventions in the various Parliaments of which she has been a member, I was struck by how little of her considerable knowledge on a range of subjects had been properly used by either the SNP or Scottish public life in recent years. One of the downsides of a lengthy political life is the likelihood that new generations of politicians and journalists will invent the wheel again, rather than seek advice and guidance from those who have seen it all before. Inventing the wheel, after all, gets headlines, whereas caution and attention to useful precedent do not. Her adjournment debate in 1969 on economic statistics – a debate quoted in Chapter 5 – provides an uncanny precursor of the type of argument which was being made thirty years later by the SNP and in which Winnie was not involved at all at that time. Similarly much of the concern about Europe which presently occupies politicians was presaged by the arguments of the mid 1970s, in which Winnie was one of the most prominent Scottish participants.

The lessons that Winnie has to teach the modern SNP – and the Scottish Parliament as it struggles to re-gain popular support – are legion. For the SNP the example of doughty, determined and inspired campaigning needs to be learned (they are not old fashioned concepts but ones much needed in a cynical age of spin) as does Winnie's constant articulation of a positive and confident vision for the future, a vision shared by many in the 1970s and which is largely absent from Scottish politics today. Her ability to work by consensus in the European Parliament is something that all members of the Scottish Parliament should seek to emulate, whilst also seeking to recapture that sense of ambition and purpose with which she entered every institution of which she was a member.

Winnie Ewing's life shows that one can be inspiring, interesting and at times infuriating (in the best sense of the word) whilst also being keen to work with others in instilling leadership and vision for a whole society. It also shows that one can be personable, good company, entertaining, popular and successful without losing touch with one's humanity and one's beliefs. It is testimony to the power of self-belief and also to the power of hard work and determination to win despite the odds. Certainly it shows that some sacrifices are necessary and that sometimes personal sacrifice and personal loss are inevitable by-products of the decision to pursue a political career. But it also shows that it is vital to keep 'faring forward' in the words of Walt Whitman, rather than nervously looking backwards. And also inspiring others to fare forward too.

When I became SNP Chief Executive in December 1994 the office I was allocated as SNP Headquarters in Edinburgh's North Charlotte Street contained a large portrait – not a terribly good one it has to be said – of an individual whom I had never seen before. It turned out to be one of strongest financial benefactors of the party, Roland Muirhead, who had owned a tannery in Glasgow and who had spent much of his fortune trying to achieve self-government for Scotland.

The picture awoke a nascent desire in me to know more of the history of the SNP and the individuals within it. The SNP has always been poor at celebrating its own past, but slowly I acquired a range of artefacts, pictures, posters and other material which said something about the party's achievements and the individuals who had contributed to them. Key amongst those who had collected such things was Winnie and I persuaded her not only to lend the party one of the portraits of her that had been painted in the late 1960s and one of her famous posters from the Hamilton by-election, which was used for the cover of this book, but also to guide me in my search for other things. This she did.

Now the party headquarters has a range of materials on view that speaks of the past and shows that whatever is happening now, those who are working for independence are part of an older movement and the successors of individuals who, despite their prodigious efforts, received much less attention and experienced much less success. Modern-day members are truly, in the words of Sir Isaac Newton, 'standing on the shoulders of giants', but I was not completely aware of how true that was until I started to work with Winnie on her book.

This book shows what effort has gone in, over the past forty years, to change our country and to change it for the better and for ever. Previous autobiographies and biographies of nationalist figures have tended to be sketchy and sometimes rushed. This one I hope is different. It is very much a personal view, bound up in the life of a strong personality. But it also illustrates not only the passion for freedom that existed in some individuals at a time when such ideas were far from being widespread, but also how some of those individuals worked to achieve their dream.

This book appears at a time when that dream is less prominent in the public mind than it has been for some time. Perhaps it will help reawaken a vision for Scotland that is inclusive, ambitious but above all realisable. Perhaps it will also show the SNP and those outside the party that Scotland has been fortunate to have individuals such as Winnie Ewing pursuing their dream, and that more such individuals are needed now than never before.

Michael Russell
Feorlean
Glendaruel
April 2004

Index